Minorities in History

Historical Studies XII
Papers read before the Thirteenth Irish Conference of Historians at the
New University of Ulster, 1977

Minorities in History

D
3
I7I72
v. 12

Edited by A. C. Hepburn

Edward Arnold

© Edward Arnold (Publishers) Ltd 1978

First published 1978 by
Edward Arnold (Publishers) Ltd
41 Bedford Square
London WC1B 3DQ

British Library Cataloguing in Publication Data

Historical studies.
   12: Minorities in history.
   1. History – Congresses
   I. Hepburn, A. C. II. Irish Conference of Historians,
   13th, New University of Ulster, 1977

   904   D3

   ISBN 0-7131-6137-X

Printed in Great Britain by
Butler & Tanner Ltd, Frome and London

Contents

Contributors

A. C. HEPBURN is a Lecturer in History at the New University of Ulster, and Visiting Associate Professor at the University of Tennessee, Knoxville, 1978–9.

DAVID PARKER is a Lecturer in History at the University of Leeds, and Visiting Professor at Vanderbilt University, Tennessee, 1978–9.

THOMAS KLEIN is a Professor of History at the Phillips-Universität, Marburg, Federal Republic of Germany.

NICHOLAS CANNY is a Statutory Lecturer in History at University College, Galway.

IAN D'ALTON is an officer in the Department of Economic Planning and Development, Dublin.

DUNCAN J. MACLEOD is a Fellow of St Catherine's College, Oxford, and a University Lecturer in American History.

CHRISTINE BOLT is a Reader in History at the University of Kent at Canterbury.

DONALD R. MCCOY is a Professor of History at the University of Kansas, and was Mary Ball Washington Professor of American History at University College, Dublin, during 1976–7.

RICHARD T. RUETTEN is a Professor of History at San Diego State University, California.

T. G. FRASER is a Lecturer in History at the New University of Ulster.

ALAN SHARP is a Lecturer in History at the New University of Ulster.

A. E. ALCOCK is a Senior Lecturer in West European Studies at the New University of Ulster.

Preface

This volume of essays has its origin in the Thirteenth Irish Conference of Historians, held at the New University of Ulster, Coleraine, under a near-tropical sun, on 25–28 May 1977. Ten of the essays which follow are revised versions of papers delivered at the conference, while chapters 1, 8, and 12 have been written especially for this book. One conference paper, which dealt with another theme, is not included here.

The Irish Conference of Historians is held biennially at each university in Ireland, by rotation, and is sponsored by the Irish Committee of Historical Sciences in conjunction with the host university. I am indebted to the Chairman of the Committee, Professor K. B. Nowlan, the Secretary, Professor J. J. Lee, and their colleagues for their advice and encouragement in the preparation of the programme, although the essays which appear here are entirely the responsibility of the editor and contributors. Valuable comments were made during the conference, and at other times by those who acted as session chairmen – David Doyle, R. J. Hunter, and Professors R. Dudley Edwards, D. W. Harkness, J. A. Murphy, K. B. Nowlan, and W. V. Wallace. Helpful suggestions were also made by W. T. M. Riches and Helga Robinson-Hammerstein, and by several colleagues at the New University of Ulster, especially S. J. S. Ickringill, D. J. Sturdy, and Professor J. L. McCracken, who, as a member of the ICHS, also undertook the crucial task of 'go-between'. All the contributors read and commented on chapter 1, though I remain responsible for it. The graphs on pp. 91–2 were prepared by Gillian Coward of the New University of Ulster History Film and Sound Archive.

The conference was able to extend its horizons beyond Ireland and Britain, thanks to the Goethe Institute, which kindly sponsored Professor Klein's visit, while Professor McCoy was in Ireland as holder of the Mary Ball Washington Chair of American History at University College, Dublin. The smooth running of the proceedings owed much to the kind hospitality of Dr W. H. Cockcroft, Vice-Chancellor of the New University of Ulster. Particular thanks must go to Helen Agnew who, as departmental secretary, took on an administrative burden far beyond the call of duty, and to Peter Roebuck, the joint conference organizer, who threw himself wholeheartedly into the work even though his own academic interest, as an historian of the landed estate, is in 'minorities' of a rather different kind.

A. C. HEPBURN

The New University of Ulster
Coleraine, Northern Ireland

1

Minorities in history

A. C. Hepburn

I

This collection of essays claims no monopoly on the definition of the term minority. It accepts the everyday usage of that term and seeks to examine the extent to which common features and problems underlie that usage. It selects three broad and, at times, overlapping categories of what seem to have been the most important types of minority in modern history – religious, racial, and a looser group labelled at different times cultural, ethnic, linguistic or national – and endeavours to explore the nature and aspirations of some of those minorities, and the way in which societies have responded to them.

A typology based on the nature of the minority is cut across by another scheme of classification based on the objectives of the minority. Does it seek unqualified assimilation into the majority but is in some way resisted? Or is it a minority that wishes to preserve its separate status from attack or erosion by the majority community? A more complex typology might be constructed, but this dichotomy is a very basic one.[1] The former type is reflected in the definition put forward by the American sociologist Louis Wirth. A minority, he wrote, is:

> A group of people who, because of their physical or cultural characteristics, are singled out from the others in the society in which they live for differential and unequal treatment, and who therefore regard themselves as objects of collective discrimination. The existence of such a minority implies the existence of a corresponding dominant group with higher social status and greater privileges.[2]

We shall refer to this as an 'American-type' definition, in as much as it is concerned primarily with the problem of assimilation of migrant groups that have chosen (or in the case of slaves, been forced) to forsake their traditional allegiances. On the other side is the type of minority that finds itself overtaken by historical development, by changes in religious practice, by the movement of a frontier, or by a change in political control. The objectives of such groups are summarized in the United Nations definition of minorities of 1950, which we may label for convenience a 'European-type' definition:

> those non-dominant groups in a population which possess and wish to preserve ethnic, religious or linguistic traditions or characteristics markedly different from those of the rest of the population.[3]

'American' and 'European' in such a context represent not geographical categories as such, but simply the location of the original stimulus for the definitions. The Quebecois, for example, are a 'European-type', whereas the new Commonwealth immigrants to Britain constitute 'American-type' minorities.

We may note here that one feature common to both the Wirth and UN definitions is the emphasis on dominant status rather than numerical superiority as the converse of minority. A minority group may, therefore, outnumber a dominant or majority group. This is of course a semantic absurdity, but no more than that. The term 'dominant minority' is used occasionally in the chapters that follow to identify dominant groups that lack numerical superiority. The numerical factor is but one variable among the many that determine the character of inter-group relations. The subject matter of these chapters is the whole range of relationships in societies characterized by conflict arising out of the intermixture of religion, race, language, ethnic or national affiliation, or culture.

Minority problems, so defined, may be said to have existed at almost all stages of history. There is no reason to exclude the Israelites in ancient Egypt for example, or the Britons under Roman rule, from this classification. But after the rapid absorption of a succession of barbarian invaders, medieval Latin Christendom had relatively little in the way of minority problems. It was effectively monolithic in its religion and high culture, with a low level of socio-economic diversity and population movement. The travellers and the literate had in Latin a common tongue. The concept of linguistic minorities had little meaning, and racial or ethnic intermixing was on a small scale: Jews in many towns and the Moriscoes in Spain were among the few groups that retained their visibility. In such circumstances the only minority problems likely to emerge on any scale were those where the minority could be produced from within a society, that is through religious deviation. What social or other basis there may have been for the Albigensians, the Hussites or the Lollards cannot concern us here, but their placing of themselves outside the monolithic structure of Latin Christendom ensured that they would be isolated as minorities and, when possible, driven out of existence.

The growth of towns in the high medieval period marked the reopening of opportunities for cultural and ethnic intermixing. Further changes in the sixteenth century – the rise of bureaucratic state power, the Protestant Reformation, and the continued economic diversification – greatly accelerated this trend. Reaction to the challenge of religious dissent, which came no longer from a monolithic Christendom but from equally monolithic nation states (or more local consolidating powers) became a central feature of public life, because of the large numbers involved. The same political changes that permitted the religious fragmentation of western Europe required religious uniformity within those fragments. It was this situation that produced the religious minority problems typical of the early modern period.

At the same time more general changes in society and economy produced other sorts of minority. Improvements in trading communications and sea power, and associated security considerations, brought about developments in colonization that, while not entirely new in character (Crusader and Arab settlements posed similar problems), now occurred on an increased scale. Thus Ireland and Virginia became contexts of struggles for political control in which numerical minorities were in fact the dominant groups and subjugated groups were very much larger. Failure to incorporate the native Indians into colonial society in a manner useful to whites led to the implementation of African slavery in the American colonies, which in turn created a new species of inter-group relations.

If the Enlightenment and the ideals of the American Revolution first posed a challenge to the slave system, it was the growth of an industrial and democratic society in the north that brought it to an end. Informal social constraints none the less acted to maintain much of the system, which has only been effectively undermined by the twin impacts of urban migration and federal intervention in the twentieth century. It should be noted, however, that in some minority contexts, Ulster perhaps most conspicuously, thoroughgoing urbanization and industrialization have made remarkably little difference to the character of inter-group relations. Elsewhere democracy and literacy, interacting with changes in the international balance of power, were at the root of important new minority developments in Europe. If it had not been for the increasing inability of two multi-national empires – first the Ottoman and then the Austrian – to maintain stability in eastern Europe, then the successful drive of their component parts for 'national self-determination' would not have been possible. On the other hand it was the very inability of the old multinational states to find effective ways of coming to terms with the challenge of resurgent Slavonic linguistic groups in a democratic age that contributed towards their general weakness. In particular the growth of the public sector of employment, especially the bureaucracy and the teaching profession, placed a premium on control of this apparatus.

II

How have minorities in modern history responded to their circumstances, and what factors have affected their development and treatment? Numerical size, both in absolute terms and relative to the size of the majority, is clearly an important determinant of behaviour. A dominant minority which is very small is especially vulnerable – to a reversal of roles or expulsion in the case of military defeat or withdrawal of support by an outside power, as those who directed the early plantations in Ireland and Virginia were aware, or as the white Rhodesians have now come to realize; to assimilation into the host community (perhaps on favourable terms) as happened with the Anglo-Normans in medieval Ireland; or simply to loss of political leadership, without further penalty, as happened in southern Ireland in the late nineteenth century. Size may also, conversely, affect the position of a non-dominant minority: Belfast Protestantism was far better disposed towards the small number of Catholics in the city around 1800 than it was to the large and rapidly expanding community of fifty years later;[4] urban blacks were considerably less segregated in North American cities before the great migration of the First World War than they have ever been since.[5] The Canadian Sikhs were also a very small group, but in relation to the overall population of British Columbia, and more especially in the context of an area which was clearly in the early stages of rapid development, their sudden arrival seemed to threaten a white supremacy that was already uneasy over immigration from elsewhere in Asia.

Intermarriage is one of the ultimate measures of the assimilation of a minority into the larger society. Unless the minority is a very large one, it is likely to be absorbed completely within a few generations. But in fact inter-group marriage has been very effectively contained in modern history by forces wishing to prevent alterations in the existing population structures. For religious minorities there have always been barriers of various kinds. In early modern Europe, where local communities tended to be virtually exclusive, the problem did not often arise. Where it did occasionally occur, as in France, the government's increasing isolation of the Huguenots meant that it withered away by 1650. In view of the increasingly wide gap between the Catholic and Protestant churches in the first four centuries after the Reformation, there was clearly no middle ground of doctrinal compromise on which mixed religious matches could be based – they did occur, but the offspring had to revert to one side or the other. Religious segregation in education has been another potent force against mixing. In contemporary America, where intermarriage between groups of different national origin now takes place on a large scale, there has been considerably less erosion of religious barriers.[6]

When differences between groups have been very marked, in terms of physical or cultural characteristics, or socio-economic differences, then pressures against intermarriage have been especially great. In modern South Africa, where the maintenance of racial distinctions has become central to the philosophy of the state, and where white numbers are uncomfortably small, legislation has forbidden inter-racial sex altogether. But in early American society, where the nature of chattel slavery facilitated casual sexual relationships between master and female slave, the line was drawn differently. Once it was established that offspring of mixed blood were deemed to be of negro race, that no intermediate caste would develop, and that all children of slave mothers would themselves have slave status, then white society had found an effective way of controlling its problem. It seems fairly certain that after the ending of slavery black–white sexual liaisons decreased quite considerably, but meanwhile the increase in white contact with native Indians drew attention to the question of miscegenation in that quarter also. Resistance to overt relationships was fairly strong in white settlements where contact with Indians was uneasy; such support, theoretical and practical, as there was for red–white mixing was to be found among missionaries and others who were, by and large, assimilated into the minority Indian community rather than vice versa.

Control of education, especially higher education, has been a key feature of inter-group conflicts throughout modern history. From Bishop Fenouillet's victory over the Huguenots at the University of Montpellier in 1613[7] to Governor Wallace's defeat 'in the schoolhouse door' at the University of Alabama in 1963, from the Victorian resistance to the admission of non-Anglicans to Oxford and Cambridge and the Irish struggle for a 'national university' that was 'Catholic in atmosphere' to contemporary demands for an entirely Welsh-speaking staff at the University College of North Wales, it has been acknowledged that control of university education means controlling both the character and the membership of the next generation's elite. The fellow of Trinity College, Dublin who opposed subsidized higher education for Catholics on the grounds that 'a stupid or even mediocre youth turned by charitable assistance into a profession ... might become a discontented and possibly dangerous member of society, instead of remaining a useful agriculturalist',[8] was at one in this with the foreign office official who thought that 'any special language of the peasantry' in eastern Europe might be used for instruction in elementary schools, but not in universities, which were so often centres of political agitation. The English-speaking government of Ontario took a similar attitude towards French.[9]

Elementary education, no less a feature of minority disputes in the later modern period, must be considered in the wider context of the minority 'homeland'.[10] If a minority occupies a cohesive homeland – a bloc of territory within the larger state which it dominates numerically – then although it is defined more clearly as a target for hostile centralizing forces, it gains a certain strength, both organizational and psychological, from its cohesion (among minorities without homelands, witness the success of Zionism, the persistence over a century of the American 'back to Africa' movement and the recent half-hearted call for 'six southern states', and the curious South Moluccan independence movement in the Netherlands). For just as the size of a minority affects its behaviour and its treatment, so does its distribution within a state. A small minority, like the seventeenth-century Huguenots, at between five and ten per cent of the French population, and still more the South Tyrolese, at less than one per cent of the population of Italy, could have made little impact if dispersed widely among the majority population. In terms of protection of a minority's language, religion, and general cultural features, both in elementary schools and in everyday life, the homeland plays a crucial role. But it does not necessarily have to be 'historic' or entirely delineated from majority-inhabited territory, or entirely in one lump, to have some effect. Quite small clusters of areas – isolated Huguenot communities in the Cévennes, the Falls area of Belfast, the Harlem which so exhilarated Langston Hughes and other black writers in the 1920s[11] – all of them maintained, whether they liked it or not, distinctive features associated with the race, religion or ethnic background of their inhabitants. In such areas very precise separation of communities can be achieved in very small areas by legislative means or, far more frequently, by residential choice, economic pressures or social constraints. It has facilitated the provision of *de facto* segregation in local schools for many religious and linguistic minorities, who did want it, and equally for blacks in North American cities, who have not wanted it. It has, in modern democratic societies, given voting power to consolidated minorities which they would not have possessed as dispersed particles. On the other hand, it has made such minorities more 'visible', resulting frequently in greater majority resistance.

The role of socio-economic circumstances in determining the character and development of minority problems has been considerable. We can see below that inter-group relations in the seventeenth-century English colonies in Ireland and Virginia shared a number of common features. What caused their development to diverge was less the relative numbers of the subjugated populations, for the native Irish population was small in the seventeenth century, than the economic growth and consequent large-scale migration of a dominant white population to America. The root cause of the failure of French Protestantism lay in its inability to harness the power of dynamic social forces in the way that Puritanism had done in England. It was the force of economic demand, mainly, which determined the direction and volume of slave labour into the eighteenth-century American colonies and created the gulf that was to develop between the slave-holding south and the free north after the Revolution. It is difficult to think that the sectarian rivalries which advanced *pari passu* with the economic growth of Victorian Belfast would have been so intense had there been a greater and steadier demand for skilled labour and a smaller reservoir of surplus rural labour. The circumstances here contrast sharply with the situation in the United States during the Second World War, where Roosevelt could simply issue an order directing that there be fair employment opportunities for blacks in public employment and anywhere else that public contracts were involved. Only in a highly dynamic economic situation could such a policy be expected to make a significant impact within a reasonable amount of time. War, in this case, was the stimulus for rapid social change. It has also, by intensifying the centralizing tendencies of the state, become a hothouse test for the ultimate loyalty of many minority groups, producing on the one hand the 'double victory' outlook of American blacks during the Second World War (against aggression abroad and racism at home), and on the other hand the 'England's difficulty is Ireland's opportunity' attitude of Dublin in 1916, shadowed in Austria-Hungary by the wartime responses of the Czechs and Serbs.

III

How have dominant groups, international agencies and other forces attempted to resolve minority problems? In early modern Europe regimes of all kinds permitted diversity of religious belief and practice only with the greatest reluctance. Such ideological independence challenged the assumptions both of the small almost proprietorial states of the Holy Roman Empire, where *cuius regio eius religio* was the guiding principle for at least a century, and of the larger centralizing states of western Europe. Where compromise was sought, almost always arising out of military necessity or war-weariness – as at Nantes in 1598 or Westphalia in 1648 – it was most often regarded by states as an act of weakness, to be rescinded whenever possible. Expulsion (for leaders and irreconcilables) and obligatory reconversion (for such of the rank and file as would accept it) were the minority policies of European governments in the age of Reformation and Counter-Reformation.

For racial and national subject populations the policies were similar – in seventeenth-century America the early policy of 'civilizing' the native Indians (sometimes by winning over their chiefs, sometimes by throwing them over) was replaced after early massacres by the preferred London policy of thoroughgoing separation, which implied expulsion. In Ireland the English government also advocated separation, and the second half of the century saw a move towards it. But the less favourable balance of populations, and the much narrower differences in economic development between settler and native, meant that 'civilization' or 'conversion' remained in practice the basis of policy in Ireland. It was an increasingly half-hearted policy, however, inclining later on towards pluralism, so that by the end of the nineteenth century the dominant group was hard-pressed in three quarters of the island to resist a reversed assimilation process.

The American failure to assimilate the native population led to the importation of African labour from the mid-seventeenth-century onwards. The slave system, with its source of supply lying outside the region, meant that many of the minority difficulties which might otherwise have concerned a dominant regime did not in fact apply. Instead there were different problems – maintaining the system against erosion by intermarriage, manumission and, as north and south grew economically more disparate, the ending of northern slavery. The rhetoric of the American Revolution, which threatened to pose a serious challenge to the system, was in fact circumvented by the virtual dehumanization of slaves to chattel status in the social philosophy of the age.

During the course of the nineteenth century many states came to accept a reasonable degree of pluralism for religious minorities. But fundamental changes in western economy and society, bringing population migration on a much larger scale, the growth of popular literacy and urban employment, and demands for democratic political participation, brought new problems as far as other types of minorities were concerned. The policies of British governments, which are considered in a number of chapters in this volume, did not incline towards ethnic or racial pluralism in the nineteenth or early twentieth centuries. Subconsciously perhaps, the guiding principles of power politics were transposed from the international arena to the internal structure of states. British policy was not to institutionalize minority protection but to 'back a horse' – to choose the force which seemed most likely to be able to maintain stable power in an area and support it unreservedly. The implication was that soundly based states were by nature unitary states, that existing minorities should be absorbed wherever possible (as in eastern Europe after 1919 or in Ulster after partition) or otherwise isolated for separate development (as in southern or eastern Africa), and that the growth of new minorities (as in British Columbia) should be firmly discouraged. 'Minority protection' was seldom necessary, and in cases where it was, the purpose was not to sustain the minority but to facilitate its peaceful absorption.

The experience of the past fifty years, in the western world and elsewhere, has tended to shatter this confidence. The new 'national' states of eastern Europe proved singly unable to absorb their minorities in the inter-war period; the Catholic minority in Northern Ireland remained quiescent longer, but has more recently emerged alongside a new generation of 'national' minorities whose activities are challenging the old-established view of western Europe as a bloc of unitary national states. British Columbia was effectively reserved for white development, but elsewhere fluctuations in the supply and demand for labour have brought large movements of population in recent years. In Britain a permanent multi-racial society seems inevitable, unless there are bizarre political developments, and while the residential status of immigrant workers in continental European states is more circumscribed, many of the related social problems are none the less present. In the United States the migration of blacks from the rural south to the urban north has been part of the same pattern, revealing in its course that assimilation requires more than the dismantling of the slave code and of the less formal 'Jim Crow' structure which followed it.

The final chapter in this volume explores in more detail how the legal protection of minority languages and cultures and of the civil rights of individual minority members has provided insufficient guarantees for the future development of those minorities that wish to continue their collective existence; how in a changing world 'equal treatment' with the majority in law may not prove to be equal treatment in fact. The problems outlined in that context similarly apply to those minorities that seek no more than assimilation into the majority society. Where the South Tyrolese, the Quebecois or, until 1974, the Turkish Cypriots sought to defend their existence in their homelands by means of a degree of preferential treatment in the areas of jobs and housing, so too have blacks and other depressed minorities in America, followed more recently by some immigrant spokesmen in Britain, sought 'affirmative discrimination' in these areas. In effect, this means preferential treatment for the future in order to even out some of the imbalance in the social structure brought about by hostile discrimination in the past. (In Northern Ireland, where residential segregation in depressed districts is very tight, such demands have been limited to pressure for aid to be directed to certain precisely defined districts, not to categories of people as such). Paradoxically, assisting minority groups in such a way implies the registration of all minority individuals in order to establish eligibility – at best an institutionalization of discrimination, at worst the creation of a bureaucratic structure which may do no harm to 'European-type' minorities that wish to continue a visible existence, but which may prove a double-edged weapon for the 'American-type' minority that wishes to assimilate. Conversely a rapidly expanding economic environment, which may create opportunities for helping 'American-type' minorities effectively without resort to affirmative discrimination, may pose a dangerous threat to many of the more static 'European-type' minorities.

All the minorities discussed in this book have a history of sustained visibility, whether their problems remain in the present or were terminated long ago. There is no space here to consider those groups whose past is more shadowy or remote, or to reflect at length on the contagious nature of minority demands in the contemporary world. For now that many western countries are taking a more tolerant view of minority aspirations, the organization of political activity on an 'ethnic' basis is increasingly commonplace. Glazer and Moynihan have identified this phenomenon as possibly the most important new basis for political organization since the emergence of 'class' in the last century.[12] If their prognosis is correct, then in cases where the ethnic group occupies a physical homeland the political effects may be devastating. Furthermore, the success of ethnic politics encourages others to follow suit. Just as homosexuals and women's rights campaigners are finding it advantageous to present their demands in a 'minority' framework, so an increasing number of cultural and ethnic groups are appearing to take up the politics of minority rights. How are *bona fide* candidates for cultural protection to be distinguished from crypto-secessionist humbugs? When is 'cultural protection' or 'devolution' the appropriate governmental response to nascent demands for political independence, and when is it simply the precursor of such demands? Is a policy of *laissez faire* towards 'European-type' minorities the only means of avoiding the perpetuation of anachronisms? When is pluralism a permanent arrangement, and when is it only a half-way house on the road to further change? Is the unitary state the only type of political system with a long-term future in the modern world?

The historical essays that follow can seldom offer direct answers to such questions. The contributors hold a wide range of views on present-day minority problems. But it is hoped that these studies of some of the more important minority problems in modern history may provide a framework, an historical perspective, against which these general questions can be considered.

Notes

I have benefited in the preparation of this chapter not only from the written work of my fellow contributors, which will be apparent, but also from their comments on an earlier draft.

1 G. E. Simpson and J. M. Yinger identify four types of minority objective (pluralism, assimilation, secession and reversal of status) and seven types of majority policy (forced and peaceful assimilation, pluralism, legal protection, population transfer, continued subjugation and extermination). *Racial and Cultural Minorities* (3rd edn, New York, 1965), pp. 16–25.

2 L. Wirth, 'The Problem of Minority Groups' in R. Linton (ed.), *The Science of Man in the World Crisis* (New York, 1945), p. 347.

3 United Nations Economic and Social Council, Sub-Commission on the Prevention of Discrimination and the Protection of Minorities, *Definition of Minorities for the Purposes of Protection by the United Nations*, Doc. E/CN.4/Sub 2/85 of 27 December 1949. I am indebted to Dr A. E. Alcock for this reference.

4 I. Budge and C. O'Leary, *Belfast: Approach to Crisis* (London, 1973), p. 10.

5 See for example A. Spear, *Black Chicago* (Chicago, 1967), pp. 14–15.

6 Simpson and Yinger, p. 371.

7 See below, p. 15.

8 Cited in A. C. Hepburn (ed.), *The Conflict of Nationality in Modern Ireland* (London, forthcoming), document 34.

9 See below, pp. 215, 224.

10 For discussion of this concept see below, p. 234.

11 See S. E. Morrison, H. S. Commager and W. E. Leuchtenburg, *A Concise History of the American Republic* (New York, 1977), pp. 570–72.

12 N. Glazer and D. P. Moynihan (eds), *Ethnicity: Theory and Experience* (Cambridge, Mass., 1975), p. 2.

2

The Huguenots in seventeenth-century France

David Parker

In the period between the passing of the Edict of Nantes in 1598 and its revocation in 1685 French Protestantism displayed two contrasting features. One was the capacity to survive decades of pressure and intimidation. The other was the inability to turn defence into offence and make any progress towards achieving a dominant position. What follows is essentially a commentary on this contrast.

Protestantism never claimed the allegiance of more than one Frenchman in ten and the most recent systematic survey suggests that there may have been as few as 856,000, a mere four or five per cent of the population.[1] Some authorities have detected a marginal growth in Huguenot numbers in the middle years of the century but this was certainly insufficient to offset the decline in their organized strength.[2] Three decisive military campaigns mounted by Louis XIII in the years 1620–22 deprived them of most of their strongholds, leaving them powerless to prevent the suppression of their political assemblies, which the crown had long desired.[3] The dramatic siege and capture of La Rochelle in 1628 put paid to any hopes of recovery and the Huguenots were reduced to holding infrequent national and provincial synods. Carefully watched over by royal agents, these bodies were firmly forbidden to meddle in affairs of state and were unable to resist further measures designed to hinder communication between the individual churches and to break their contacts with the European Protestant movement.[4] Grievances were not to be addressed to the king by the synods but were to be referred to the *chambres mi-parties* established by the Edict of Nantes for this purpose. Despite their bi-partisan composition the effectiveness of these courts had always been questionable, and it was further circumscribed by a decree of 1629 which incorporated the two situated in the Protestant south in the hostile *parlements* of Bordeaux and Toulouse. They were finally abolished in 1679 without ever having offered more than a limited method of obtaining justice, or of combating the growing harassment of the Huguenots.[5] Officers were prised out of public and judicial bodies, merchants were obliged to open shop on Sundays, and artisans were excluded from the guilds; pastors were molested in the course of their duties while their congregations suffered increasing pressure from Catholic missionaries and preachers.[6] After 1659 no national synods were permitted and the Huguenots found

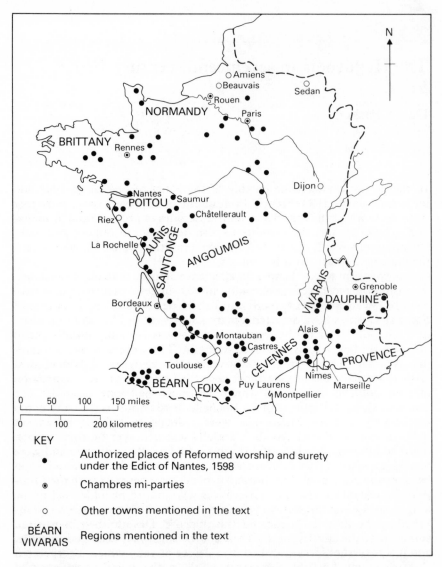

The distribution of Huguenots in seventeenth-century France (based on a map in J. H. M. Salmon, Society in Crisis: France in the Sixteenth Century, Ernest Benn, p. 298).

themselves almost defenceless in face of the violence to their churches and persons, which culminated in the forcible mass conversion of the 1680s.

Yet force was required. Despite the long years of intimidation, government plans for a 'peaceful' reunion of the two faiths had to be abandoned.[7] The principal urban strongholds of Protestantism displayed an amazing resilience. Montauban, having successfully withstood a siege of three months in 1621, emerged after the Peace of Alais in 1629 with its predominantly Huguenot population largely unaffected and its municipal autonomy intact. Immediately steps were taken to undermine both: the Jesuits returned, recovering control of the college, while the Huguenots were obliged to surrender half the places on the municipal council. In order to attract Catholics of substance to the town, first new venal offices were created in the *présidial*, then a treasury office was established and finally a Cour Des Aides; but the results were disappointing and in the 1660s and 1670s a drastic reduction in the size of the various municipal corps was effected in the hope that the small number of Catholic notables might fare better in the elections. This tactic proved little more successful than the first; when the troops arrived in August 1685 they made an estimated 17,000 converts in the region, of whom perhaps 9,500 inhabited the city, nearly three quarters of its population.[8]

Even at La Rochelle, which had been punished for its disobedience by the destruction of its municipal autonomy and where the Catholics were in complete command, the surviving Protestants showed remarkable tenacity. Excluded from public office, submerged under an influx of Catholic religious orders, in the home of a new bishopric established there in 1648, the Huguenots nevertheless remained the most wealthy and comfortable section of the populace, dominating the merchant community.[9] They also constituted a third of seafaring men and a half of their officers.[10] Although by 1676 the numerical position of the two religions was exactly the reverse of the situation in 1610, this was the result not of conversions but of immigration combined with the prohibition forbidding Protestants, not formerly inhabitants of La Rochelle, to settle there.[11] Conversions to Catholicism did not exceed thirty a year between 1676 and 1679 and even the repressive measures that followed – annulment of noble titles, discrimination against artisans – seem to have made a limited impact on the Huguenot faithful. Between 1679 and 1685 there were only 181 abjurations recorded in the town;[12] as at Montauban, it took the violence of the soldiers to achieve what church and magistracy could not.

Although French Protestantism was not predominantly a rural phenomenon, there were some areas of the countryside where it proved equally difficult to eradicate. The lesser nobility of Saintonge and Aunis clung tenaciously to the reformed faith as did the mass of the population of the Vivarais and the Cévennes – the last great centre of resistance.[13] Strung out too across the south of France were numerous lesser communities, with about 3,000 inhabitants or less, which remained enclaves of Protestant dominance – le Mas D'Azil in the Pays de Foix, Puylaurens in Haut-Languedoc, Mens-en-Trièves in Dauphiné.[14]

The explanation for both the persistence of the Protestant faith and its failure to progress is bound up with its highly provincial character. Its base lay in the west, south and southwest of the country. At Paris there were only ten or twelve thousand Protestants in a population of 400,000.[15] Important Huguenot minorities had existed in the principal towns of Normandy but they appear to have suffered irreparable losses in the 1570s and a further decline has been observed after 1650, while in the urban centres of Brittany the Protestants were a negligible force.[16] In the rural areas of northern France the Huguenots constituted an insignificant and very dispersed minority, with their churches often dependent on the protection of one or two seigneurs. However firmly entrenched the Huguenots were in their provincial outposts, not one major centre was won north of the Loire, and the heart of the realm remained solidly Catholic. Nothing illustrates better the provincial character of French Protestantism than the contrast with the situation in England: there the Reformation had been a unifying force radiating outwards from the centre bringing light into the 'darkest corners of the land';[17] in France it took root precisely in those regions where opposition to the centralizing policies of the crown, the attachment to traditional liberties, was strongest. It became an impediment rather than an aid to royal consolidation of the realm.

Unlike their English counterparts the Huguenots never successfully penetrated the state apparatus. From the outset in England, in Professor Dickens's apt phrase, 'the coherence of Anglicanism depended on the state'.[18] Crucial sections of the political classes represented in parliament and the legal profession were won for a reforming policy making possible first the destruction of the legislative independence of the Catholic church and then the imposition of reformed doctrine. The government, 'captured by the reformers after the death of Henry VIII', decided what should be read in church and played an instrumental role in the production of the prayer books of 1552 and the Forty-two Articles of the following year. As Mary quickly discovered in the next five years, it was not possible to prise the reformers out of their key positions nor to persuade the gentry, however conservative they might be, to relinquish their hold on church lands.[19] Henry IV of France, on the other hand, ascended the throne a Protestant and discovered that his realm was ungovernable unless he abjured. With the sole exception of the Duc de Sully, the highest offices remained in Catholic hands.[20] Totally isolated at court after the assassination of the king in 1610, the resignation of the great minister soon followed. Nor were the Huguenots any more successful in penetrating the *parlements*, where their numbers were never sufficient to overcome the hostility they encountered. This was true even of the *parlements* at Toulouse and Bordeaux in the Protestant heartland. Both remained militantly Catholic and played a significant role in combating Protestant influence. Partly as a result the population of these cities and their immediate hinterlands was largely Catholic, despite the strength of Protestantism in the neighbouring provinces. Thus while the Huguenots were unable to develop roots in the heart of the realm, the attachment of the upper echelons of the magistracy to Catholicism endured in the Protestant south.[21]

Likewise the establishment of Protestant hegemony among the intellectual elite also proved impossible. The early interplay of humanism and reforming ideas as represented by that remarkable woman Marguerite d'Angoulême was hopeful, especially as it offered prospects of royal protection.[22] In Agrippa d'Aubigne the French Reformation could claim the most renowned humanist warrior;[23] in Ramus, perhaps the most brilliant French philosopher of the sixteenth century.[24] Significant sections of Parisian society – architects, doctors, painters, writers, economists – remained Protestant until the opening decades of the seventeenth. Yet the early promise faded way. After the outburst of iconoclasm and sacramentarianism of the 1520s, royal protection of the new learning was lost and the violence and bitterness generated by decades of warfare did not create the best atmosphere for the acceptance of new ideas.[25] Ramus, whose influence was probably greater in England and certainly in the Netherlands, was murdered in the Massacre of St Bartholomew in 1572, without having made a dent in the scholasticism and obscurantism of the Sorbonne. Despite the ground gained in some of the established institutions of learning, notably the universities of Montpellier and Bourges, the French Huguenots found it necessary to establish their own academies and colleges – a separatist tendency that reflected and confirmed the minority status of the Huguenot party.[26] As the monarchy and the church recovered the initiative, the freedom of the Protestant colleges was increasingly circumscribed. At Montpellier the way for the Catholic restoration was paved in 1613 when Bishop Fenouillet secured appointment as head of the university.[27] After 1629 the Jesuits, who had made steady progress since their return to France in 1603, were able to penetrate the great Huguenot centres.[28] At Montauban, as we have seen, they quickly gained control of the college and in 1659 its Protestant section was transferred to the lesser town of Puylaurens.[29] Nîmes was suppressed in 1664, Sedan in 1681 and the remainder of the colleges in the next four years.[30] But these were only the final blows dealt after the Huguenots had been displaced as leaders in the educational field: Moliere, Bossuet, Descartes, Corneille and Louis II de Condé (the most famous descendant of the Huguenot princes of the blood) all passed through Jesuit hands. The Oratorians also played a vital role in the education of the nobility.

At Paris the Huguenot intellectuals tended to be assimilated by the establishment: Saloman de Brosse built the Luxembourg palace for Marie de Medicis[31] while Antoine de Montchrétien, in dedicating his seminal treatise on political economy to the regent, formally presented to the government the most completely argued case for state regulation of the economy.[32] The imaginative entrepreneur and doctor, Théophraste Renaudot, who combined the organization of public and very open scientific conferences with the free dispensation of medical advice to the poor and an employment exchange, survived the hostility of the faculty of medicine only with the protection of Richelieu who made him editor of the *Gazette de France*; but this post appears to have been bought with his abjuration which, however, failed to appease his enemies. When the cardinal died his establishment was closed down.[33] The failure of the Huguenots to penetrate the state apparatus or to secure a dominant position in intellectual life highlights their dependence on military strength.

From the outset of the religious wars the Huguenots had claimed the allegiance of an impressive proportion of the French nobility, including some of the most illustrious families in the land and many of the most renowned military commanders. This feature of French Protestantism has long been recognized but it has been strangely underestimated in explaining how the Edict of Nantes was obtained. For it was essentially the refusal of the Huguenot leaders to bring their forces to the relief of Amiens, taken by the Spanish in March 1597, that wrung the Edict out of a begrudging king. Only the recapture of Amiens in September enabled Henry to limit the concessions made to the Huguenot assembly, which had retreated to the safety of Châtellerault beyond the Loire; and only when he passed by Châtellerault with his army in March 1598 was the hassling terminated.[34] Thus by virtue of their armed strength the Huguenots were able to wrest from the crown liberty of conscience, a degree of freedom of worship, access to public office and even royal subsidies for the upkeep of the towns and forts in their possession.

Yet the Edict of Nantes, far from providing a basis for renewed advance, turned out to be the high water mark of Huguenot success; it was followed by a slow but unmistakable retreat. Part cause and part consequence of the retreat was the Protestants' own attachment to ideas of passive obedience and their growing royalism. For a period, in the aftermath of the Massacre of St Bartholomew, Huguenot writers had espoused arguments justifying resistance to tyrannical rulers and Hotman had even attempted to demonstrate the popular elective character of the monarchy.[35] But such views made little permanent impact on Protestant thinking. Indeed with the accession of Henry IV to the throne it was the ultramontane Catholics who developed justifications of resistance and even tyrannicide, while the Huguenots became the most devoted supporters of royal authority. The assassination of the king in 1610, carried out by a man who, albeit demented, was clearly afflicted by the idea that Henry IV was an ungodly tyrant, served only to confirm the royalism of the Huguenots.[36] Nothing reveals this more dramatically than the curious sequence of events following the closure of the Estates-General in March 1615, when the Huguenots in momentary alliance with Prince de Condé raised the standard of revolt.[37] Ostensibly the immediate objective of the rebels was to prevent the imminent celebration of the marriage alliance that had been sealed between the royal houses of France and Spain; but the first demand of the Huguenots was that the crown should accept the article that had headed the *cahier* of the third estate and about which the regent had refused to countenance any discussion. This had declared in unequivocal terms that the king had no temporal or spiritual superior on earth and that no one could absolve his subjects from the allegiance they owed. So the Huguenots found themselves defending the traditional gallican viewpoint.[38]

Moreover, in responding to the challenge of ultramontane ideas, the Huguenots went farther and farther along the absolutist road. Jesuit writers, basing their arguments on St Thomas Aquinas, tried to distinguish between political and religious institutions in order to ascribe to princely power a specifically human, and therefore limited, authority. On the contrary, insisted Pierre du Moulin in his widely disseminated *Bouclier du Foi*, 'obedience due to kings and magistrates proceedeth from the divine law and is grounded upon the ordinance of God ... there is no power but of God, the powers that be are ordained of God; whosoever therefore resisteth the power resisteth the ordinance of God'.[39] The depth of Huguenot convictions came out clearly in their reaction to the execution of Charles I: the provincial synod of Angoumois, Saintonge and Aunis – previously a centre of resistance – advised its pastors to 'diligently exhort those in their care and particularly well qualified people not to depart under any pretext whatsoever from the complete fidelity and obedience which are due to the King'.[40]

As this reference to 'well qualified people' might suggest, the leaders of the Huguenot church were not simply royalist but conservative in a wider sense. Although there had been an influential congregationalist movement inside the church in the 1560s many of its supporters were wiped out in the Massacre of St Bartholomew. Subsequently the less democratic concepts of church government propounded by Beza came to dominate and the individual churches were subject to the discipline imposed by a hierarchy of provincial and national synods.[41] By the early seventeenth century there was even a tendency to suggest that in principle an episcopal system was entirely reasonable and that only circumstances explained its absence from the French reformed church.[42] Not everyone would have agreed, but the attitudes that gave rise to such views received further impetus from events across the Channel. In 1644 the synod of Charenton, learning that in certain maritime provinces 'there do arrive ... some persons going by the name of Independents and so called for that they teach every particular church should be governed by its own laws, without any dependency or subordination unto any person whatsoever in the authority of colloquies or synods in matters of discipline and order ... fearing lest the contagion of the poison should diffuse itself insensibly, and judging the said sect of Independents not only prejudicial to the word of God but also very dangerous to the civil state', declared that 'nothing may be innovated or changed amongst us, which may in any wise derogate from the duty and service we owe unto God and the king'.[43] The same view was elaborated upon in Amyraut's *Gouvernement de l'Eglise*, specifically produced to combat the views of the English Independents. He recoiled in horror at the diverse fashions in which 'each administered the sacraments or did not administer them, blessed marriages or did not bless them, led or did not lead the assemblies in the temples'.[44] Clearly, he concluded, the destruction of the presbyterian or episcopal systems meant republicanism, and loss of liberty.[45] There could be no better illustration of the fact that the Huguenot church was led by men who had simply not broken free from conventional notions about the need for hierarchy and order.

Consciously, almost desperately, the Huguenots sought to remove from their faith any radical social or political implications. Quickly passing over their role in the religious wars they insisted on their claim to be considered good Frenchmen and good Christians.[46] What separated them from the Catholics were certain doctrinal issues relating to the nature of the euchar- ist, the sacraments, the authority of the papacy, the invocation of the saints, relics and, above all, the part played by good works in procuring salva- tion.[47] 'There is nothing more fundamental to our religion', declared Amyraut 'than the teachings which concern the means of obtaining remis- sion of sins and eternal life.'[48] On this issue there could be no compromise; but the Huguenots certainly had no intention of raising relatively insignifi- cant questions of discipline and the ecclesiastical hierarchy in unnecessary and mischievous fashion.[49] What was important was man's relationship with God. Through the influence of Amyraut and the academy of Saumur which he dominated for nearly thirty years, the doctrine of justification by faith was restored to a central position in Huguenot thought, as Pro- fessor Armstrong has persuasively argued.[50] Faith became the condition of man's covenant with God; thus not only good works but also the theory of predestination assumed a subordinate role. Orthodox speculation about the order of God's decrees – whether he had initially decided to save a few from the sinful mass of mankind or whether he had first sent Christ to save all – seemed to Amyraut and his followers a largely fruitless exer- cise. For, so complete was man's dependence on God that it was not poss- ible to penetrate the mystery of why some believed and some did not, why some were saved and others were not.[51]

Amyraut's theology, although immensely contentious, corresponded to the tendency for French Protestantism to become a highly personal, almost introverted religion, preoccupied with the means by which the individual could achieve eternal life. 'We have too long run after the imaginary dreams and imaginary things of this world. . . . We are born to see beyond the sun and the moon; the earth is too lowly to be our goal; it is necessary to have a higher and richer objective.'[52] These lines written by Isaac Arnauld in 1599 reflected a retreat from reality which became increasingly widespread as time passed. 'God who holds empires in his hand,' declared Du Plessis Mornay, 'will dispose of them to his glory.'[53] To the travails of this life man had to discipline himself in preparation for the next, utterly dependent as he did so on the mercy of God. Jacques Fontaine, pastor and refugee, imprisoned after many hardships in 1684, was accused of pre- venting the abjuration of his fellow prisoners. 'I consider', he retorted, 'that the conversion of a soul is exclusively the work of the spirit of God; therefore the perseverance of these men in our faith cannot be the result of any human influence, but solely of the action of Him who plumbs the depth of our being.'[54] Thus French Protestantism developed into 'a sort of stoicism sanctified by piety', which as Vinet observed over a century ago had nothing in common with Puritanism.[55]

Indeed there could be no greater contrast than that between the con- servative, introspective, defensive Huguenots and the active, radical, combative Puritans. In some ways the comparison is also valid in relation to the Dutch and Scottish Calvinists as well. For it was they who most boldly developed and used Calvin's cautious remarks about the right of the inferior magistrate to resist ungodly tyrants. In the Netherlands this notion fused with the traditional idea that it was the king's duty to preserve the liberties of his subjects and that of the Estates to limit the arbitrary exercise of monarchical power. Philip II was deposed in 1580 on the grounds that kings were appointed to serve the people and not the other way round.[56] Although, as has sometimes been suggested, the Puritans did not produce such precisely formulated theories of revolt, courage was eventually found to execute Charles I for treason against the people. This could hardly have been done without the impact made by Puritan ideology. As Professor Walzer has shown, the Puritans took up with vigour Calvin's identification of the saint and the good citizen, making no distinction between private and public morality.[57] Indeed they emphasized that political office was a religious vocation and expected parliament to act against sin.[58] Preachers also saw nothing amiss in intervening in matters of state for in 'a universe of irreconcilable forces only the saints could impose some minimal order on earth.'[59] Their imagery became ever more subversive in its implications: the monarch was likened to the captain of the ship of state who would be guided by the crew rather than the head of the body politic which controlled its members.[60] Some preachers came very near to saying that God did not need princes.[61] Religious conviction overflowed into a comprehensive and urgent demand for change, spelt out by Thomas Case to the Commons in 1641:

> Reformation must be universal.... Reform all places and callings, reform the benches of judgement, the inferior magistrates.... Reform the universities, reform the cities, reform the countries, reform inferior schools of learning, reform the sabbath, reform the ordinances, the worship of God.... You have more work to do than I can speak.... Every plant which my heavenly father hath not planted shall be rooted up.[62]

Much of the explanation for the radical character of English Puritanism lies in its interaction with the most dynamic social forces. This is not just to suggest that nascent capitalism and Protestant individualism had something in common, or that Calvinist emphasis on the dignity of labour appealed to the industrious yeomen. What was really striking, as Professor Hill has long argued, was the way in which nearly every Puritan concept was filled with social implications. For instance there was the marked tendency in Puritan thought to exclude from the church the idle *rentier* at one end of the scale and those without vocation at the other.[63] In other words, the true elect would be drawn from those middling sort of people – independent producers, lesser gentry, small traders – who were coming violently into conflict with the establishment on a whole range of issues. The same point is illustrated by the battle over Sabbatarianism, which acquired social and political dimensions never paralleled in France. As Hill has shown, the idea of six days' labour and one of rest corresponded to the demands of an increasingly urbanized, commercialized society. It got rid of wasteful saints' days; it offered independent producers increased income, servants a day of rest, masters an opportunity to advance the education and edification of their household. When Archbishop Laud, fearful of the subversive character of the Puritan Sunday, introduced *The Book of Sports* in order to encourage the traditional pastimes of the rural world, opposition was immense: here was a collision, not just of two faiths, but of two ways of life.[64]

To see in Puritanism the ideology of a clearly defined capitalist class would, however, be misleading. The interests of the small independent producers did not coincide with those of the gentry and merchants represented in parliament; their separatist religious tendencies, and the social egalitarianism which often flowed from them, frightened many of the well-to-do and pushed them back into a defence of the established order. None the less, their shared opposition to popery, to episcopacy, to interference with property rights and other aspects of government policy, ensured sufficient common ground for long enough to carry through the assault on the hierarchy. Of course many of the gentry were pushed along faster and farther than they might have gone of their own volition; but, then, if they were at all prepared to pursue the struggle they needed the people.[65] They needed them in the unprecedentedly hard-fought elections for the two parliaments of 1640,[66] and above all they needed them to build the New Model Army, an army fired with religious enthusiasm and able 'to link up the hitherto obscure radical groups scattered up and down the kingdom'.[67] Without going as far as Mr Manning, who accords to the people the decisive role in the events of the 1640s, it is difficult to object to Hill's view that 'without the backing of large numbers of humble men Puritanism could never have challenged the crown and the bishop: the civil war could never have been fought and won'.[68]

This summary of the ideological and social characteristics of Puritanism, although no doubt a grave disservice to both Walzer and Hill, will assist in throwing the defensive posture of the Huguenots into sharp relief. In part, of course, their stoical resignation flowed from failure, and it grew more marked as the prospects grew more gloomy. Yet lack of ideological conviction was a cause as well as a consequence of defeat. The royalism and conservatism of the Huguenots left them prey to government propaganda, which skilfully juxtaposed statements of its determination to crush rebels with reassuring words about liberty of conscience.[69] Confused, divided and hesitant, the Huguenots were unable to meet the crusading fervour of their opponents. Major military setbacks, such as the destruction of the Huguenot army at Riez in Poitou in 1622, or the decisive defeat of the Rochelais fleet in September 1625, which left the town totally isolated, can be attributed as much to loss of nerve as to lack of resources.[70]

One major problem for the Huguenots was that they were never able to present themselves as a leading patriotic force. Both their Dutch and Scottish brethren had been able to advance in struggles against the domination of alien rulers.[71] Similarly the Puritans attracted much sympathy as the most militant anti-papists in a situation where the papacy, tyranny, and antipathy to France and Spain were constantly associated in people's minds, and in which the foreign policy of the early Stuarts was open to attack. By contrast, except during the regency of Marie de Medicis, the anti-Habsburg foreign policy of the French crown, and its general independence vis-à-vis the papacy, allowed the Huguenots no opportunity to emerge as the principal, or even the most distinct, champions of the national interest. Indeed after the defeat of La Rochelle, its last mayor and the great Huguenot warrior the duc de Rohan found it entirely reasonable to come together with their former enemies in the armed service of a king whose foreign policy to them seemed wholly admirable.[72]

A second reason for the defensiveness of the Huguenots lay in the nature of the Edict of Nantes. Bitterly opposed by them where they were dominant, because it restored lost rights and possessions to the Catholics,[73] the Edict imposed limited and legal objectives on their struggle wherever they were in a minority. Interpreted strictly, the act granted freedom of worship in those places where it had been permitted by an earlier act of 1577, in those where it had been practised in 1596–7, and in one or two *faubourgs* of each town, *baillage*, or *sénéchaussée*. Services were also permitted in the domiciles of those seigneurs possessing rights of high justice.[74] Certain major towns – Toulouse, Dijon, Beauvais, and Nantes – were excluded.[75] The towns and fortified places that were ceded, together with the royal subsidies, were granted for eight years only and there was no obligation on the king to renew this provision.[76] While those that had already abjured Catholicism were not to be molested, the Edict gave no assurances about future converts.[77] Scope for Protestant expansion was further limited by the stipulations that they could establish schools, and print and sell books freely, only in those places where public worship was permitted. Books printed elsewhere needed authorization in each case.[78]

The *parlement* of Rouen refused to ratify the Edict for ten years.[79] Everywhere the Huguenots were involved for decades in an unending series of battles to ensure its proper implementation; to secure freedom of residence and exemption from the *tailles* for their pastors, free access to public office, payment of the royal subsidies, the unhindered operation of their schools, to combat government prevarication over the appointment of Huguenot commanders to their forts and strongholds, and so on. Periodically the government promised that commissioners would be dispatched to the provinces to ensure the application of the Edict, but complaints about their non-arrival persisted for years.[80] After 1629 legislation was gradually introduced which further limited its value, and from the late 1650s it was smothered with restrictions. The one and only way in which the Huguenots broke through the Edict of Nantes was in securing the *de facto* right to hold political assemblies, which had been specifically prohibited. This was wrung out of Henry by 1608 and lasted until 1622. Huguenot organization was further improved in 1611 with a decision of the National Assembly to allow adjacent provinces to convene small councils in the event of any danger to their churches. Although this enraged the government, which saw them as seditious and republican, such councils were in fact summoned only three times, and on each occasion in response to a real threat. The elaborate financial military and judicial constitution produced by the last National Assembly in 1621 was also drawn up only after the crown had effectively declared war on the Huguenots by its forcible restoration of Catholicism in the autonomous principality of Béarn.[81]

Catholic accusations that the Huguenots wished to set up a republic therefore had little foundation. Compelled to resort to arms to maintain their position, they never escaped from their defensive posture or mentality. Precisely at the same moment as conflict became unavoidable the great Huguenot nobility, fearful of being branded republican, subject to royal intimidation and bribery, began to defect *en masse*, so that by 1622 the Huguenot party was deprived of virtually all its leaders of rank. At the moment of crisis the greatest strength of the Huguenot church became an irremediable weakness : the naturally conservative, hierarchical inclinations of the noble warriors either took them back into the royal camp or left them in a state of indecision.[82] Effectively the leadership of the Huguenots now passed into the hands of the oligarchs of their principal towns; and in general they were no less conservative, no less ambivalent in their attitudes than the nobility. Their prime interests lay in defending their privileged position in the social hierarchy, advancing themselves as hereditary officeholders or important landowners, and preserving the ancient fiscal, military, and judicial privileges of their particular municipalities. They looked to the king as their immediate superior to protect their liberties and their royalism was deep.

Protestantism did, of course, appeal to other sections of the population apart from the nobility and the urban patricians; but even where the largest single element in a Huguenot community was made up of small merchants and artisans, they were usually outnumbered by their superiors in both consistory and town council. At Montpellier by 1670 there was not a single artisan on the consistory;[83] at La Rochelle no one practising a mechanical art could be elected.[84] The consistory at Paris was dominated by the legal profession and the merchants.[85] Even in a small, highly compact, overwhelmingly Huguenot community like that of Mens-en-Trièves in Provence, where metal, leather and textile workers accounted for two thirds of the population, they occupied only a third of the places on the consistory.[86]

In some places antagonism between the population and the oligarchs probably contributed to a decline in the popular base of French Protestantism. At Rouen where the Huguenots steadily declined in numbers from mid-century it has been observed that class conflict appeared to be synonymous with conflict between Huguenot masters and Catholic artisans.[87] Much earlier the print workers of Lyon, having been won for the reformed faith, were rapidly lost again as a result of the way in which the consistory interfered in both their strikes and pleasures.[88] Even where there was a basis for common ground between the lower orders and the notables the latter did not exploit it. Perhaps alarmed by the widespread resistance of the peasantry of the Midi to paying the tithe, a resistance which appeared to threaten seigneurial rights in general the first national synod in 1559 included in the discipline of the church a canon which declared that although priests were not entitled to tithes they were nevertheless to be paid 'because of the king's command and for the avoidance of scandal and sedition'.[89] Put this sentiment together with the sort of tribute paid by Amyraut to the 'lofty and generous virtues of the nobility'[90] (so different from Puritan utterances) and it can be seen how little the Huguenot church offered the people in the way of reflecting, or developing, their own values and interests. Professor Walzer has rightly observed that the Huguenots were never able to match the democratic radicalism of the Catholic League which, if it failed to block Henry IV's accession to the throne, certainly 'served to reinforce the hold of Catholicism on the major cities' in the last two decades of the sixteenth century.[91]

In other words French Protestantism proved unable to establish for itself the sort of broad popular base which Puritanism found in the 'middling sort' of people. But notwithstanding the emphasis on Huguenot attitudes described above, it should be made quite clear that this weakness in French Protestantism was not just an ideological one. Huguenot values fairly accurately mirrored the nature of French society, the actual dominance of the nobility and the entrenched urban oligarchs: the 'middling' groups did not occupy anything like the important position they had in England. The artisan population, although not insignificant, was largely confined to the towns and these remained enclaves in a rural, traditional world.[92] Here there was no equivalent of the class of independent small farmers of England;[93] here Protestantism made little impact. The huge mass of the population barely eked out a living in a world dominated by the rhythms of the seasons and the ecclesiastical calendar – a world of saints and images, of religious rites and festivities; and they had absolutely no intention of giving these up for the Huguenots.[94] As in England two worlds confronted each other and two cultures. But in France the urbanized, commercialized world was not in the ascendant; and in their immediate hinterlands the domination of the larger towns had profoundly negative effects. Merchant oligarchs and magistrates saw in the countryside only a ready source of agricultural produce, of domestic labour in the textile regions, and the possibility of acquiring some land which they invariably exploited in the same way, albeit more ruthlessly, as the nobility they displaced.[95] Battening on to the rural world without transforming it, the urban patriciate certainly did nothing to offset – and may have contributed to – the diminished vitality of the French economy which, apparent by mid-century, further reduced the always inadequate openings for Protestantism in the countryside.

There is, as Professor Le Roy Ladurie has graphically illustrated, one highly significant exception to this picture and it is one which arguably proves the rule. For in the Vivarais, and most clearly in the Cévennes, Protestantism by the seventeenth century had dug roots that refused to be torn from their mountain soil and left an enduring imprint on its culture. This was a region where the divide between town and countryside had been eroded by the social and numerical dominance of an artisan population. Scattered throughout the Cévennes in their small communities, the leather, textile, and iron workers provided the means by which the reformed faith passed into the patriarchal family structures of the peasant farmers and from them to their servants who, according to Le Roy Ladurie, suffered from as harsh a puritan discipline as was to be found anywhere in England. It was, he says, a joyless world where profit and asceticism went hand in hand.[96] It was also one in which the will to resist remained unbroken and once again in 1702 the inhabitants of the Cévennes took up their arms in one last, hopeless, apocalyptic burst of defiance.

Nowhere else did the weight of the 'middling' people provide French Protestantism with such a broad, comparatively homogeneous social base. True, the lesser bourgeois and artisans of La Rochelle, irritated by their exclusion from the councils of the town and the timorous resistance of the patriciate to government intimidation, revolted and for over a decade – from 1614 to 1626 – imposed a more democratic constitution on the municipality.[97] But given the geographical and economic isolation of La Rochelle, this movement was unable to link up with popular movements elsewhere: Protestantism was precluded not only by its own conservatism but also by the unintegrated nature of French society from furbishing the ideological armoury for popular discontent. Nor did urban oligarchs constitute a suitable medium through which Protestantism could have developed a unified opposition with the possibility of achieving ideological hegemony. The French bourgeoisie was riddled by corporate and inter-urban sectional rivalries. For some, Protestantism was a useful weapon with which to defend their privileges, but radical Catholicism might serve just as well. Marseilles, once described as the 'new Rochelle' by virtue of the vast array of privileges that it preserved long after the Huguenots had been defeated,[98] lived for a time under the sway of a militant Catholic dictatorship; its merchant élite had little time for Protestantism.[99] Ironically the success of the Huguenots in capturing some important urban centres, and dividing towns into Protestant and Catholic, probably hindered rather than assisted the transformation of the bourgeoisie into an integrated class. In this, as in so many ways, French Protestantism fulfilled a social function which was the complete antithesis of that fulfilled by its English counterpart. Moreover the French bourgeoisie lacked anything resembling the English parliament which would have brought their representatives together. Only the nobility came near to offering a national leadership and their conservatism was in the end fatal to the Huguenot cause.

Protestantism was unable to transcend the unintegrated nature of French society or to overcome the sectarian nature of opposition. For a period the common faith and organization of the Huguenots obscured the social antagonisms within its ranks, although the nobility certainly found the restraints placed upon them irksome, while the bourgeoisie, with some justification, regarded their noble brethren as reckless adventurers likely to drain the towns of their resources and endanger their privileges.[100] With the political and military collapse of the Huguenots, any hopes of creating a united resistance to the crown evaporated. After 1630 France entered a period of massive unrest, involving all sections of the population, and culminating in the Fronde, which temporarily forced the court into exile. Had the opposition been united in aim and organization it would have been overwhelming. But great nobles revolted for their own ends, lesser ones against the privileges of a few, officeholders opposed the creation of new offices, and the lower orders attacked the fiscal agents of the crown. Uneasy cooperation all too often broke down as each group, each town, each corporate body strove to survive in the maelstrom. A postscript from that once proud Protestant citadel of La Rochelle makes the point. During the Fronde it sent a delegation to court to make known its loyalty; but the two delegates returned not with some token of the king's gratitude to the whole municipality but with titles of nobility for themselves and for six friends. Anger was immense, for henceforth they would be exempt from taxation.[101]

In a society so divided, sapped by economic depression, torn by social and political unrest, where the only point of stability was his Most Christian Majesty, Protestantism might endure; indeed it showed a remarkable capacity to adapt to the miseries and uncertainties of this world, transforming itself into a highly personal religion equipping the faithful to accept their lot on earth with dignity and offering hope of eternal life in heaven. Almost consciously the Huguenots abandoned attitudes which carried subversive implications, leaving only their theology between them and their fellow countrymen. Nothing could illustrate better the fact that a religious minority, which was no more than that and failed to link up with wider social forces, stood little chance of achieving a dominant position. But then, Protestantism in France could never have become the instrument of revolutionary social and political forces. Such forces simply did not exist. French Protestantism reflected the society which moulded it – provincial, stubborn, royalist, conservative, hierarchical, divided and, ultimately, despairing of the human condition. Unlike the English Puritans who sensed their strength and confidently envisaged their rule of the elect on this earth, the Huguenots waited, with increasing stoicism, for their deliverance from it.[102]

Notes

1 S. Mours, *Le Protestantisme en France au dix-septième siècle* (Paris, 1967), Chapter 3.

2 W. C. Scoville, *The Persecution of Huguenots and French Economic Development 1680–1720* (Berkeley, 1960), p. 7.

3 'Articles de la paix de Montpellier le 19 octobre 1622' in L. Cimber et F. Danjou, eds., *Archives curieuses de l'histoire de France depuis Louis XI jusqu'à Louis XVIII* (Paris, 1834–40) series 2, II, p. 318.

4 J. Quick, *Synodicon in Gallia Reformata or the Acts, Decisions and Canons of those famous National Councils of the Reformed Church in France* (London, 1692) II, pp. 430 ff.

5 C. Benoist, *La condition juridique des Protestants sous le régime de l'Edit de Nantes* (Paris, 1900), p. 218. *Chambres de l'Edit* were established by the Edict at Paris, Castres, Bordeaux (or Nérac) and Grenoble. See Articles 30–53 of the Edict of Nantes, most readily available in R. Mousnier, *L'assassinat d'Henri IV* (Paris, 1964). Until 1629 the *chambres* in Languedoc and Guienne were autonomous but provision was made in the Edict to end this when it became necessary, Article 30; see P. Gachon, *Quelques préliminaires de la Révolution de l'Edit de Nantes en Languedoc* (Toulouse, 1899), pp. 136–7.

6 The evidence for the harassment of the Huguenots comes from a wide variety of local sources, much of it collated by E. Benoist, *Histoire de l'Edit de Nantes* (5 vols, Delft, 1693–6), which although partisan has stood the test of time.

Mours emphasizes the calm of the years 1630–60 and compared to the decades both before and after the violence was certainly less. But despite a certain caution imposed by its alliances with Protestant powers pressure from both the government and the Catholic Orders was incessant. See A. Rebelliau, 'La Compagnie du Saint-Sacrement et les Protestants' *Revue des Deux Mondes*, series 5, XVII (1903), pp. 103–35. R. Kleinman, 'The Unquiet Truce: an Exploration of Catholic Feeling against the Huguenots in France 1646–64', *French Historical Studies* IV (1966), pp. 170–88.

7 P. Blet, 'Le plan de Richelieu pour la réunion des Protestants', *Gregorianum* XLVIII (1967), pp. 100–129.

8 H. Lebret, *Histoire de la ville de Montauban (s.l., 1668)*, pp. 364–6; R. Garrisson, *Essai sur l'histoire du Protestantisme dans la généralité de Montauban* (Mialet, 1935), pp. 46–129, 239.

9 L. Perouas, *Le diocèse de La Rochelle 1648–1727: sociologie et pastorale* (Paris, 1964), pp. 136–7.

10 Scoville, pp. 56, 136, 152.

11 Perouas, pp. 305, 1137.

12 *ibid*, p. 318.

13 *ibid*, p. 129.

14 Mours, pp. 73 ff.

15 *ibid*, p. 62.

16 *ibid*. pp. 63–5; Scoville, pp. 11–12; P. Benedict, 'Catholics and Huguenots in Rouen: The Demographic Effects of the Religious Wars', *French Historical Studies* IX (1975), p. 226.

17 C. Hill, 'Puritans and "The Dark Corners of the Land"', *Transactions of the Royal Historical Society* XIII (1963), pp. 78–102.

18 A. G. Dickens, *The English Reformation* (London, 1964), p. 180.

19 *ibid*. pp. 109–279.

20 There were a few Protestants in the highest administrative posts including two of the three *intendants des finances*; one of them, Isaac d'Arnauld, had two brothers who were *trésoriers de France* and *conseillers d'état*. But their influence on government policy could only have been marginal and Sully was used by the King largely to reassure the Huguenots. The desire of Henry IV to have a Catholic household is revealed by the enormous pressure he put on his sister to abjure. See J. Pannier, *L'église réformée de Paris sous Henri IV* (Paris, 1911), pp. 76 ff.

21 D. Buisseret, *Sully* (London, 1968), p. 70, suggests that a large proportion of the *parlement* of Paris was Protestant but the evidence for this is weak. See J. H. Salmon, *Society in Crisis: France in the Sixteenth Century* (London, 1975), p. 133, for a summary of the position in the *parlements*.

22 Marguerite d'Angoulême, the sister of Francis I, married Henri d'Albret, king of Navarre and was mother of Jeanne d'Albret, and thus grandmother of Henry IV; she was but the most eminent of a galaxy of aristocratic women who offered protection to the early reformers. Salmon, pp. 120–21.

23 Théodore d'Agrippa d'Aubigné (1551–1630); perhaps best remembered for his epic poem of the Protestant cause, *Les Tragiques*.

24 Ramus or Pierre de la Ramée (1515–72); the most formidable opponent of scholastic philosophy and the grip of Aristotle on the universities who in 1551, with the protection of Henri II became the first professor of mathematics at the *collège royal*. He did not espouse the Protestant faith until 1561.

25 R. Knecht, 'The Early Reformation in England and France', *History* CLXXXIX (1972), pp. 1–16.

26 The contrast here is with England where the Protestants were able to penetrate

the established institutions of higher education and whence came a large proportion of their converts and preachers. Both the early English reformers and later
the Puritans made a vital contribution to the national development of secondary
education.

27 P. Corbière, *Histoire de l'église réformée de Montpellier* (Montpellier, 1861), pp.
173–4.

28 The Jesuits had been expelled from France in 1594 because of their suspected
complicity in an assassination attempt on Henry IV. Salmon, p. 292.

29 M. l'Abbé Chalumeau, 'Le collège de Montauban sous la direction des Jésuites
1634–1762', *Bulletin archéologique, historique et artistique de la société archéologique du Tarn et Garonne* LII (1944), pp. 41 ff.

30 Mours, p. 157.

31 De Brosse, probably born before 1571, became Architecte général des bâtiments
du roi et de la reine in 1614. Before he died in 1626 he 'ended up with total
emoluments worth 2,700 [livres]', enough to live comfortably. D. Maland,
Culture and Society in Seventeenth Century France (London, 1970). See also
E. et E. Haag, *La France Protestante* (2nd edn, Paris, 1881) III, pp. 194 ff.

32 A. de Montchrétien, *L'économie politique patronale. Traité de l'économie politique*
ed. T. Funck-Bretano (Paris, 1889). Montchrétien himself only secured a minor
post at Paris and, although his ideas taken up later by Richelieu were to provide
a rationale for bringing Protestant enclaves under government control, he died
fighting in Normandy in 1620.

33 H. Brown, *Scientific Organisations in Seventeenth Century France 1620–68* (New
York, 1967), pp. 17–30; E. et E. Haag, *La France Protestante* (1st edn, Paris,
1858) VIII, pp. 409–10.

34 Salmon, pp. 295–6; Mousnier, pp. 126–7; J. Faurey, *La monarchie française
et le protestantisme français* (Paris, 1923), pp. 81–6. L. Anquez, *Histoire des assem-
blées politiques des réformées de France* (Paris, 1859), pp. 156–8.

35 F. Hotman, *Francogallia* (1573). Like Philippe de Duplessis-Mornay, the prob-
able author of the famous *Vindiciae Contra Tyrannos* (1579), Hotman subsequently became strongly royalist in his views.

36 Mousnier, pp. 7–19.

37 L. F. H. Bouchitté, *Négociations, lettres et pièces relatives à la conférence de Lou-
dun 1616* (Paris, 1862), p. 114. The Huguenot assembly meeting at Grenoble
finally agreed to join with Condé on 15 October. He concluded a separate agreement with La Rochelle in December. 'Diaire de Jacques Merlin' ed. A. Crottet,
Archives historiques de la Saintonge et l'Aunis (La Rochelle, 1878) V, p. 227 (hereafter Merlin). But early in January 1616 Condé opened negotiations with the
court. See Bouchitté, p. 256.

38 For the Estates-General see Mousnier, pp. 242–6, 250–64; and pp. 348–9 for
a text of the article of the Third Estate. For the grievances of the Huguenots
drawn up by the Assembly, see E. Benoist, II, p. 174. For the agreement
between the Assembly and Condé see Bouchitté, pp. 149 ff.

39 P. Du Moulin, *Bouclier du Foi*, originally published in 1630. The citation is
from the English edition of 1636, p. 556. Du Moulin was pastor at Paris from
1599 to 1620, whence he went to become professor of theology at Sedan, where
he died in 1658.

40 N. A. F. Puaux, 'L'évolution des théories politiques du protestantisme français
pendant le règne de Louis XIV', *Bulletin de la Société de l'histoire du Protestantisme français* LXII (1913), p. 388.

41 R. M. Kingdon, 'Calvinism and Democracy: some Political Implications of
Debates on French Reformed Church Government', *American Historical
Review* LXXIX (1964), pp. 393–401.

42 See Pannier, p. 280, and the companion volume *Histoire de l'église réformée de Paris sous Louis XIII* (Paris, 1922), p. 223, for Du Moulin's increasingly 'episcopalian' stance.

43 Quick, p. 467.

44 M. Amyraut, *Du gouvernement de l'Eglise contre ceux qui veulent abolir l'usage et l'autorité des synodes* (1653), p. 302.

45 *ibid.* pp. 394–5, 416.

46 See notably Amyraut, *Apologie pour ceux de la Religion sur les sujets d'aversion que plusiers pensent avoir contre leurs personnes et leur créance* (Saumur, 1647). This is an apology in every sense of the word; for a refreshingly perceptive view of Huguenot attitudes to their past see E. Labrousse 'The Wars of Religion in Seventeenth-Century Huguenot Thought', in A. Soman, ed., *The Massacre of St Bartholomew* (The Hague, 1974), pp. 243–51.

47 Itemized most carefully by P. Du Moulin, *A Short View of the Chief Points in Controversy between the Reformed Churches and the Church of Rome* (London, 1683), p. 6. This was originally written in 1636.

48 Amyraut, *Du mérite des oeuvres contre les opinions de La Milletière* (1638), p. 217.

49 P. Du Moulin the younger, *Défence de la Religion réformée contre l'impiété et tyrannie de la ligue rebelle d'Angleterre* (1650). In this the Puritans are accused of deliberately raising questions of discipline and the ecclesiastical hierarchy in order to avoid doctrinal matters on which there was general agreement. Although Du Moulin the younger had settled in England such sentiments reveal exactly where French Protestants stood.

50 B. G. Armstrong, *Calvinism and the Amyraut Heresy* (London, 1967), *passim.*

51 *ibid.* pp. 60, 84–5, 162–9.

52 Pannier, *L'église réformée de Paris sous Louis XIII*, p. 306.

53 P. de Duplessis-Mornay, *Mémoires et correspondance* (Amsterdam, 1624–52) IV, p. 191.

54 J. Fontaine, *Mémoires d'une famille huguenotte* (Toulouse, 1877), p. 113.

55 Père Vinet, *Histoire de la prédication parmi les réformées de France au XVII siècle* (Paris, 1860), p. 20.

56 Ch. Mercier 'Les théories politiques des Calvinistes dans les Pays-Bas à la fin du XVI et au début du XVII siècle', *Revue d'Histoire Ecclesiastique* (1933), p. 50.

57 M. Walzer, *The Revolution of the Saints: A study in the Origins of Radical Politics* (London, 1966), p. 55 and *passim.*

58 C. Hill, 'The Political Sermons of John Preston', in *Puritanism and Revolution* (London, 1962), p. 258.

59 Walzer, p. 161.

60 *ibid.* p. 180.

61 Hill, 'The Political Sermons of John Preston', p. 267.

62 Cited by Walzer, pp. 10–11.

63 Hill, 'William Perkins and the Poor', in *Puritanism and Revolution*, p. 236; Hill, *Society and Puritanism in Pre-Revolutionary England* (London, 1964), pp. 142–3.

64 Hill, *Society and Puritanism*, pp. 145–218.

65 This theme is most recently developed in B. Manning, *The English People and the English Revolution* (London, 1976).

66 C. Hill, *The World Turned Upside Down* (London, 1972), pp. 18–19.

67 *ibid.* p. 69.

68 Hill, *Society and Puritanism*, p. 135.

69 President Jeannin urged the Government not to give the impression that it was conducting a religious war but to follow the policy of Henry III 'who having

ruthlessly made war against them [the Huguenots] with seemingly invincible forces ... decided to maintain the Edict in their favour sincerely and in good faith.' *Mémoires et négociations* ed. Michaud and Poujalat (Paris, 1836), p. 693. Whether by design or miscalculation Marie de Medicis did follow a policy which entailed alternately provoking the Protestants and confirming the Edict of Nantes. Richelieu developed this art to a fine level. E. Benoist, II, p. 14; C. Drion, *Histoire chronologique de l'église protestante de France jusqu'à la Révocation* (Paris, 1855) I, pp. 306, 316–17.

70 D. Parker, 'The Social Foundations of French Absolutism 1610–30', *Past and Present* LIII (1971), pp. 72, 87.

71 On the death of James v of Scotland in 1542 Marie de Lorraine became regent. A struggle ensued for control which the French won and the young Mary Stuart was betrothed to Francis II. John Knox was exiled. Marie de Lorraine died in 1560 and Mary Stuart was subsequently deposed. It was in this turbulent situation that Knox wrote his *Appellation* (1558), justifying rebellion against ungodly tyrants before returning to lead the struggle himself.

72 Parker, p. 87. For a penetrating discussion of Rohan's apparently contradictory attitudes see F. Meinecke, *Machiavellism: the Doctrine of Raison d'Etat and its Place in Modern History* (New Haven, 1957).

73 Merlin, pp. 85–100, gives a good account of the arduous negotiations which were necessary before the Rochelais would accept the Edict. For Montpellier see L. Guiraud, 'La Réforme à Montpellier', *Mémoires de la Société Archéologique de Montpellier*, 2nd series, VI and VII, (1918), II, pp. 561 ff.

74 Edict of Nantes, Articles 7–11; *Article particulier* 6.

75 *Articles particuliers* 20, 24, 25, 31. Further restrictions can be found in 29 and 30.

76 Brevet of 30 April 1598, in Mousnier, p. 331.

77 Edict of Nantes, Article 19.

78 Edict of Nantes Article 21; *Article particulier* 38.

79 Mousnier, p. 135.

80 The *cahiers* of the Assembly of 1611 are in E. Benoist, II, pp. 14 ff. Huguenot reaction to the royal replies can be found in Henri de Rohan, *Véritables discours de ce qui s'est passé en l'assemblée politique des églises réformées de France, tenue à Saumur par permission du Roi* (1646). For the assembly of 1615 see 'Articles accordés par les deputés du Roi à M. le Prince' and 'Réponse aux cahiers présentés au Roi par ceux la Region' in Bouchitté, pp. 745 ff., 757 ff. The demands of the last Assembly of La Rochelle are in A. de Barthélemy, 'Actes de l'assemblée générale des églises réformées de France 1620–22', *Archives historiques de Poitou V* (1876), p. xxi.

81 Parker, p. 71.

82 *ibid.* pp. 73–8.

83 Corbière, p. 191.

84 E. G. Léonard, *Problèmes et expériences du Protestantism français* (Paris, 1940), p. 30.

85 Pannier, *L'église réformée de Paris sous Henri IV*, pp. 447–8.

86 M. P. Bolle, 'Structure sociale d'une paroisse réformée en Dauphiné au XVII siècle', *LXXXV Congrès Nationale des Sociétés Savantes 1960* (Comité des Travaux Historiques et Scientifiques, Section d'histoire moderne et contemporaine), pp. 425–6.

87 Léonard, p. 28.

88 N. Z. Davis, 'Strikes and Salvation at Lyons' in *Society and Culture in Early Modern France* (London, 1975), pp. 1–16.

89 Quick, p. lvi.

90 Amyraut, *Apologie*, p. 3.

91 Walzer, p. 115; Salmon, pp. 257 ff.

92 In some areas significant sections of the rural population had, of necessity, to seek some form of by-employment in cloth production but this was not usually their prime source of income, and far from laying the basis for a class of independent rural artisans, their activities made them increasingly dependent on the merchants who bought their cloth and provided them with both raw material and financial assistance.

93 Most regional studies suggest that only 10 per cent of the peasantry were economically independent, and these were likely to be *fermiers* or agents of the large lay and ecclesiastical landlords.

94 'We will dance despite the Huguenots' said the *laboureurs* of Montpellier. Le Roy Ladurie, *Paysans de Languedoc* (1969), p. 181.

95 Of course in the long run the subordination of the rural outworkers to the merchants of the towns contributed to the development of capitalism and the depression of the second half of the century probably assisted the concentration of capital in the hands of the larger merchant-entrepreneurs. Also the consolidation of large landed estates around some cities by the urban bourgeoisie prepared the way for the Revolution. But these developments were very drawn out and only came to fruition in the transformed economic and social conditions of the eighteenth century.

96 Le Roy Ladurie, pp. 186–93. My former colleague Dr D. Nicholls has pointed out that a socially similar Protestant population can be found in the sixteenth century in the immediate hinterland of Dieppe. Here the explanation for the retreat of Protestantism must presumably be sought in other factors – the effects of the wars of religion, proximity to Paris, geography and so on.

97 Parker, p. 86.

98 A. Crémieux, *Marseilles et la Royauté sous la minorité de Louis XIV* (Paris, 1971), p. 21.

99 M. Zarb, *Les privilèges de la ville de Marseilles* (Paris, 1961), pp. 206, 213, 228–30. Salmon, pp. 262–4.

100 For instance the 'constitution' drawn up by the Assembly of La Rochelle in 1621 gave very little freedom to the generals and nobility appointed to command the military forces. Financial, political and judicial sovereignty lay with the assembly and there were a number of acrimonious disputes with nobles who distrained goods, or refused to pay debts.

101 *Factum de l'opposition formée par les habitans de la Rochelle à l'enthérinement des lettres de Noblesse obtenues par leur deputies* (s. 1., 1653).

102 There was one notable movement of passive resistance organized from Toulouse in 1683 by the churches of the Cévennes and Bas Languedoc. But as was appreciated by one of its principal organizers, the 'mere handful of people' who were prepared to participate 'only served to throw into high relief the resignation and obedience of our body.' Cited by E. G. Léonard, *A History of Protestantism* (London, 1967) II, p. 423.

3

Minorities in central Europe in the sixteenth and early seventeenth centuries

Thomas Klein

The term minority within the context of the political structure known as the 'Holy Roman Empire of the German Nation' is extremely difficult to define for the sixteenth century. Of necessity minority or majority must be related to a specific political structure and its population. The problem of minority increases in direct proportion to the degree of actual governmental control over the territory concerned. Personal unions between states which remained otherwise independent of each other could hardly produce genuine minorities; but minorities could arise within individual member states of such a personal union. Real unions could generate genuine minority problems either through their privileges of representation in the constitutional and administrative institutions or through the operation of common rights and institutions. The uniformly organized modern state, which in the area of the former Holy Roman Empire came into existence only in the nineteenth and twentieth centuries, has – by comparison with earlier periods – minority problems of quite a different nature, or can produce them as a result of its more elaborate and effective structure. All this is of course well known to historians, but it seems worthwhile to recall here that the state structure of the Holy Roman Empire, from the beginning to its end around 1800, existed largely without any centralized power that could penetrate to the grass roots. For this reason minority problems manifested themselves only in specific instances and on a limited scale.[1]

Linguistic–cultural minorities as such play a relatively insignificant role in the grave problems and conflicts of the sixteenth century. Such minorities existed of course[2] – the Czechs, Slovaks and Sorbs within the kingdom of Bohemia and in the areas of Moravia, Silesia and the two Lusatias, fiefs of the Bohemian crown,[3] and the French-speaking population along the western borders of the Empire,[4] to name only a few. It should also be mentioned that minorities which were German in language and culture lived under the Polish crown (in West and East Prussia)[5] and in Hungary (western Hungary).[6] To a considerable extent, though not exclusively, these were typical minorities created by an empire of the more antiquated type. Effective power diminished towards the borders, which were consequently ill-defined, thus permitting minorities to retain a degree of autonomy. (Omitted from this survey are the Swiss Confederation with

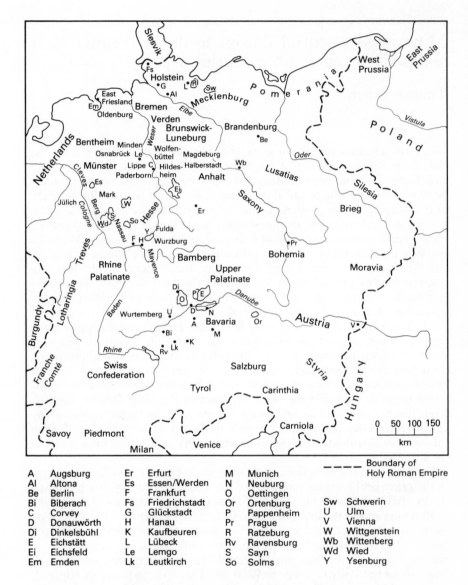

A	Augsburg	Er	Erfurt	M	Munich	
Al	Altona	Es	Essen/Werden	N	Neuburg	
Be	Berlin	F	Frankfurt	O	Oettingen	
Bi	Biberach	Fs	Friedrichstadt	Or	Ortenburg	
C	Corvey	G	Glückstadt	P	Pappenheim	
D	Donauwörth	H	Hanau	Pr	Prague	
Di	Dinkelsbühl	K	Kaufbeuren	R	Ratzeburg	Sw Schwerin
E	Eichstätt	L	Lübeck	Rv	Ravensburg	U Ulm
Ei	Eichsfeld	Le	Lemgo	S	Sayn	V Vienna
Em	Emden	Lk	Leutkirch	So	Solms	W Wittgenstein
						Wb Wittenberg
						Wd Wied
						Y Ysenburg

- - - - Boundary of
Holy Roman Empire

The Holy Roman Empire in the sixteenth and early seventeenth centuries (only places mentioned in the text are shown).

its linguistic varieties, northern Italy which can no longer realistically be considered part of the Holy Roman Empire in the sixteenth century,[7] and the northern Netherlands which seceded completely from the Empire in the course of the sixteenth century.)

The problems of cultural or national minorities within the Holy Roman Empire would have been acute, if the Empire had indeed constituted an effective state structure in the modern sense. But precisely the opposite was the case. The significance of the feudal constitution – which rested on the personal obligation between liegelords and vassals, emperor and territorial overlords – for the internal order of the territorial states varied considerably, but on the whole it can be reasonably argued that its importance declined in many regions. The expansion of the power of the state, which distinguishes the middle ages from the modern period, occurred not in the Empire but rather within the individual territorial states. The intensification of state power is marked by the transition from the '*Pax et iustitia* state' (*Friedenssicherungsstaat*) of the middle ages to the 'bureaucratic state' (*Policeystaat*) of early modern times, which regulated not only peace and justice but also social and economic relations. This development reduced the significance of the Empire.

Viewed against this background, the minority problem within the Holy Roman Empire takes on a different dimension: attention must be focused on the territorial states. And in the context of the territorial states the relationship of majority and minority was often reversed. Thus in the kingdom of Bohemia and the margravate of Moravia Czechs and Slovaks constituted a Slav majority vis-à-vis a German minority, which on the other hand was a dominant minority in some areas. But in some of the appendages of the Bohemian crown, such as Silesia and Lusatia, the Germans were not simply a dominant minority but a genuine majority.[8] This situation became even more difficult in the sixteenth century. Bohemia had been ruled by the Polish kings from 1471 to 1525, when they were succeeded by the German Habsburgs, who became territorial overlords in this conglomeration of lands. As elsewhere in the Empire, their rule was limited by strong estates. A similar situation prevailed in wide areas of the southern Low Countries,[9] which belonged to the Holy Roman Empire and had come as part of the Burgundian inheritance to the Spanish Habsburgs as territorial overlords; the same was true of the Franche Comté, in so far as the population was French-speaking.[10] The situation was different in the duchy of Lotharingia, where a ruler who was French in language and culture controlled a German-speaking minority and a majority of French subjects.[11]

Bohemia with Moravia, Silesia and the two Lusatias also presented a different situation since they were outside the military and political circles (*Reichskreise*) of the Empire.[12] The Netherlands formed their own Imperial Circle, the Burgundian, and from 1548 were excluded from the competence of the highest imperial courts.[13] One must also ask to what extent minority is a useful concept for discussion of the border areas between the Holy Roman Empire and Denmark.[14] The duchy of Holstein, with its German population, was an integral part of the Empire but was held in fief by the Danish king. The duchy of Schleswig on the other hand was an integral part of the Danish kingdom and its German inhabitants were intermixed with Danes. But between the two duchies there existed – irrespective of the boundaries of the Empire – a union of the territorial estates which bound together the two duchies 'for ever undivided',[15] a factor that immeasurably complicates the whole problem. However, in all cases it must be stressed that in political and constitutional terms the confrontation between territorial power and the power of estates and diets was far more important than that between Germans and non-Germans.

All these difficulties in defining and describing genuine minorities of a cultural–national type in the century recur in the sector of religion and denomination. Apart from the Jewish population, which is not treated here, the religious question assumed a more general and significant form only in the age of religious divisions. The minority created by Luther's reformation expanded considerably and steadily even after the mid century and into the 1570s, by which time it formed a clear numerical majority within the population of the Empire. It maintained this position until the Counter-Reformation period, when the Catholic population rose by a proportion that cannot be estimated precisely but which was certainly appreciable.[16] It is necessary to distinguish between grass roots response and religious allegiance at the level of princes or of territorial overlords. First, we should look at the relationship of Protestant and Catholic princes in the Imperial Diet. The territorial overlords of necessity remained Catholic to a greater extent than did the ordinary subjects of the Empire.[17] During the expansionist phase of Protestantism many of the subjects of Catholic overlords were Lutheran. In the subsequent period religious allegiances at the levels both of lords and ordinary subjects once again became more closely aligned. Thus the Empire is not an appropriate frame of reference for discussion of the problem of religious minorities.

Once again the territorial states are far more important, though by no means exclusively so. Territorial overlordship generally did not manifest itself in the uniform, comprehensive execution of all public rights and duties – judicial rights, military and taxation rights, feudal ties – but often only of some of them.[18] Territorial authority recognized in one way or another the residual 'autonomous' structures, often not ending at the territorial boundaries but carrying across into the neighbouring territorial lordship and impinging on certain groups of rights there. Very often such categories as 'the lowest level', or 'the border area' remained decisive to such an extent that the phenomenon of divergent religious development in a small-scale regional or local framework cannot be adequately discussed by reference to the modern concept of minority. Protestant aristocratic lordships and Protestant cities in their largely 'autonomous' positions vis-à-vis Catholic territorial overlords (and, less frequently, vice versa) were something quite distinct and different. More than just meeting places of religious dissenters within a homogeneous state, they were commonweals or organized pockets of power with distinctive characteristics developed on the basis of an independent internal order.

At the same time it must be stressed that the significance of the small-scale regional and local autonomous structure decreased very considerably vis-à-vis the territorial state in the course of the sixteenth century. There occurred within the territorial organization a very noticeable intensification and consolidation of power over justice, finance and general administration (*Policey*).[19] This development made the middle level of power, the territorial state, the most important form of political organization in relation to both the Empire above and the small-scale regional and local powers below. With the growth of a territorial church organization from the end of the fifteenth century, the same development can also be traced in the ecclesiastical sphere, where the middle level of power increased in relation to the higher level (the church as a whole and its bishops) and also in relation to the lower level (the large number of local patrons).[20] Taking all this into account, it can be argued that by 1517 the territorial level had already become the most important even in the ecclesiastical sector, although there were still a number of deviations from this trend, which attest to the lasting significance of the extensive 'autonomies' at the lowest level.

Both movements must be borne in mind, if one stresses the territorial dimension of the minority problem in central Europe. First, there is the often overlooked consolidation of territorial lordship in all sectors of public life and especially in the ecclesiastical sector, which gives us a dominant, unequivocal frame of reference (and it is precisely this unequivocal nature which produces the conflicts inherent in this situation); and second, the denominational split as a new element intensifying the constitutional territorial boundaries, and in turn creating majorities and minorities.

The rapid expansion of the Lutheran Reformation from the early 1520s created everywhere in Germany and its territories Protestant minorities in transition – that is, minorities which tended to become actual majorities or, at least, dominant minorities. This occurred at the very latest when the overlord accepted the new religion. The process was very complex. In many political units there was no simple linear development, but rather a meandering movement, which resulted sometimes from several successive changes of religion by individual overlords, producing fluctuating minority situations.[21] Furthermore, the changing intellectual and spiritual climate should not be overlooked. Increasing denominational polarization, caused in no small degree by the intervention of overlords in matters of dogma and theology (especially in the Protestant territories) largely eliminated any mediating position between Catholics and Protestants.[22] On the other hand it must be acknowledged, though not overemphasized, that the formation of minorities of this type presupposes the attainment of a certain intellectual level, which – without doubt – broad sections of the population did not reach, as reports and memoranda on both sides reveal to an alarming extent.[23]

What has been said suggests two groups of questions. First, how did the majority treat the minority? To what extent was integration tried and successful? How did the dominant minority deal with the majority under its control? Inseparably connected with these questions is the other group, which suggests the special flavour of the minority issue, at least in

Germany. How did the overlord arrive at his religious orientation, and how did he treat those parts of the population which did not share his own views? The answers to these two related questions are of central importance: they reflect the particular character of German history.

In some cases it is difficult to decide whether the emergence of a clear Protestant majority among the population preceded the decision of the overlord to accept the Reformation or whether it resulted from this decision. This is especially true in areas such as Hesse, which were very early converts to the Reformation.[24] Often, however, this question can be settled with near certainty. It is clear at least that in most cases the conversion of overlords to the Reformation coincided with the convictions of the majority of inhabitants, irrespective of whether the subjects followed or led the way or whether the 'general trend' provided an additional motive for people to change their religion. This picture is valid for the early and the middle phases of the Reformation. For the later conversions of overlords there is often incontrovertible evidence that the mass of the population had already taken this step, but that the overlords, especially the smaller ones, had for political reasons hesitated to follow their lead. Whatever may have happened there always remained Catholic minorities, even if they were numerically very small and are difficult now for the historian to detect.

With the consolidation of territorial control over the church, Protestant state churches that insisted on denominational exclusivism emerged from the late 1520s. In the territorial states that remained Catholic, majority and minority denominations developed side by side. These could hardly be defined in numerical terms since they varied from place to place, and Protestant concentrations occurred in towns. Here, in the territories that remained Catholic, were the special zones of pragmatic mediation, which sought to join Protestant and Catholic elements in church services and pastoral care. This mediation makes it difficult to unravel the majority–minority question in any meaningful way, since it must have been condoned by the communities.[25] The attitude of these Catholic overlords towards Protestant church practices (and in the case of spiritual overlords often also towards morals) was frequently lax and defused a potentially dangerous situation, which in the event did not become acute until the last quarter of the sixteenth century, during the Counter-Reformation. At this stage the conviction that the state authority had the duty to enforce a precisely defined, specific, exclusive denominationalism, already firmly held by most Protestant and some Catholic overlords (notably the dukes of Bavaria),[26] gained more general support. In the Protestant areas the duty of the overlords in their capacity as emergency bishops (*Notbischöfe*), as *Praecipua membra ecclesiae*, comprised the *custodia utriusque tabulae* with the result that the overlords were obliged to compel their subjects, by force if necessary, to conform at least outwardly to all marks of religious uniformity – to attend divine service, listen to sermons, take the sacraments, and conform to ecclesiastical–political custom. The *patres familias* for their part had to lead their families and servants to the true faith.[27]

Whether the faith enforced in this manner was based on inner conviction or not was in any case not the concern of men but of the spirit of God. Whether the margin that remained between the necessity to conform even in the intimacy of the household and the overpowering might of divine grace could be called 'freedom of conscience' appears, to the modern observer at least, hardly more than a question of terminology. These principles, which regulated the lives of both Protestants and – often with partially different justification – Catholics, constitute the lines of demarcation not only between Catholics and Protestants but also between them and the groups of Anabaptists and Spiritualists, as well as between internal Protestant divisions, which tend to be oversimplified as 'Lutheran' and 'Reformed'.[28] In most cases divergent religious teaching was assessed as a crime of blasphemy, which incurred the death penalty. The Anabaptists were usually treated in this way; Catholics and Protestants, often; and internal Protestant dissidents, sometimes. All this lends support to our methodological approach, which minimizes simple numerical relations and emphasizes those of overlord and subject as the essential context for discussing the question of religious minorities.

The Religious Peace of Augsburg of 1555 cemented these conditions. It secured them in imperial legislation, although modifying them in some points.[29] The Peace conceded freedom of religious choice only to territorial overlords, not to subjects. This principle, which later came to be termed *cuius regio eius religio*, was coupled with the right of subjects to emigrate. But there was one fundamental modification for the ecclesiastical principalities – the territories and states of archbishops, bishops and abbots within the Empire. Catholic prelates who turned Protestant had to relinquish their lordship together with their ecclesiastical office, and the cathedral chapters had the right to elect an orthodox successor. This was the famous *reservatum ecclesiasticum*. The imperial cities, too (cities not subject to a territorial overlord but immediately subject to the emperor) were granted the *ius reformandi* (the right to order the religious affairs of a territory) by the Peace of 1555; but if they had a population of mixed religion they were obliged to maintain the status quo. This was the only form of religious coexistence in the Empire fully guaranteed by imperial law. Much less secure in legal terms, having the force only of a *declaratio* made by the emperor and not included in the Imperial Diet's resolution, was the regulation that the estates of the ecclesiastical dominions – nobility, towns and communities – should be allowed to maintain their dissenting Protestant faith. What emerges is a layered system of legal securities: generally recognized was the *cuius regio eius religio* of the secular territorial overlords, and the principle of coexistence in religiously mixed imperial cities. The reservation in favour of the spiritual overlords was part of the imperial recess: it had reached the statute book not through common consent but through imperial mandate. Thus, at subsequent meetings of the Imperial Diet, the *reservatum ecclesiasticum* was repeatedly discussed.[30] The *declaratio* in favour of the Protestant subjects of spiritual overlords was the weakest guarantee of all. It was kept secret for several years. When it was discovered in 1574 and publicized, it was no longer of any political use.[31]

Apart from the denominationally mixed imperial cities and the less well secured Protestant subjects of spiritual overlords, religious coexistence and hence, religious minorities existed only in exceptional circumstances, arising from actual conditions or from legal agreements within territorial states. All these cases merit our special interest because they manifest the minority problem on the decisive level, namely the territorial one. But it must be stressed that all imperial legislative regulations concerned only Catholics and members of the Augsburg Confession, that is Lutherans in the generally accepted sense. Until 1648 'Sacramentarians' – Zwinglians and Calvinists, and 'Sectarians' – Anabaptists and Spiritualists, could lead an actually or legally secure minority existence only as a result of an intra-territorial arrangement.

The Religious Peace of Augsburg provides general criteria, imperial legal criteria, for determining religious minority questions. In the first instance the issue was the realization of *cuius regio eius religio* as the most important fundamental principle in the secular territorial states. It applied primarily to the relationship between Catholics and Lutherans. The vast majority of secular states, especially the larger ones, were already Protestant before 1555.[32] Catholic minorities, which had existed in these states, disappeared, partly through emigration but more often, in the course of years, through the natural demise of the older generation. It was especially important that no public catechization of young Catholics was allowed. No alternatives were permitted that could have stopped the general trend away from Catholicism. This situation obtained in the large areas of eastern and northern Germany that were under secular territorial rule. There the implementation of *cuius regio eius religio* after 1555 hardly altered the situation at all. Other secular overlords, primarily in southern and western Germany, proceeded only then, under the protection of the Religious Peace, to the Reformation; often subjects had led the way. Conversely, recatholicization took place in some secular territorial states under Catholic rulers, notably in the duchy of Bavaria.[33] And after the turn of the sixteenth century the reconversion of large Protestant sections of the population in the Habsburg lands was undertaken. In many regions these Protestant populations formed numerical majorities, not only in the German Habsburg lands, that is Austria, but also in Bohemia and the dependencies of the Bohemian crown.[34] In the latter territories, the Old and New Utraquists were numerically the most significant groups. They were followed by the Bohemian Brethren and the Lutherans. The Catholics made up only about ten per cent of the population at the end of the sixteenth century.[35] In all these cases recatholicization was accompanied by protracted and severe military conflict, and was effectively completed during the course of the Thirty Years War. Only in parts of Silesia did the Habsburgs make exceptions for the Lutherans of the unchanged Augsburg Confession. The constant advances of the Counter-Reformation led to considerable losses for Protestantism, before and after 1648.[36] Lusatia, which passed between 1635 and 1648 from the Bohemian–Austrian to the electoral Saxon state, could only in this way save its Protestant majority. Earlier in the century only its proximity to Saxony had made possible the success of the Reformation there.[37]

In the secular territorial states Catholic or Protestant remnants could survive only under cover, in isolation, and for short periods of time. Stringent control made it impossible to establish parishes which did not conform to the official creed. Persecution and expulsion followed immediately upon discovery.

Thus the principle of *cuius regio eius religio* was rigidly enforced in the secular territorial states. In general the *ius reformandi* was tied to territorial lordship. In imprecisely defined lordships, however, the question of creed could become decisive for the emergence of a more clearly defined territorial power. In these areas the *ius reformandi* – in the absence of any previous clearly defined territorial claim – was tied to the higher jurisdiction and therefore simultaneously repressed other privileges, such as patronage.[38] In this manner the religious problem became linked to decisive developments in the constitutional sphere. In other situations it was a question of determining who could establish himself with what title as overlord in the sense of the Religious Peace stipulations.[39] In a few instances overlordship and imperial immediacy of a territory resulted from a decision by the Imperial Cameral Tribunal (for example, in the county of Ortenburg).[40] Wherever lordship was clearly defined the overlords enforced their faith as that of the territory. If the territory changed hands by hereditary succession or reversion to the feudal lord, by sale, pawning or redemption, by marriage or annexation of the land, this could mean a change in the religion of the area concerned; and it did mean this in many cases.[41] Even if only the ruling member of a dynasty changed religion, the territory had to follow suit. There are examples of this happening, especially in southern Germany. Some areas changed their creed several times between Protestant and Catholic, as in the case of Neuburg palatinate and the margravate of Baden.[42] In this manner many secular territories produced changing minorities in great profusion, even in the decades before the Thirty Years War. The war itself, of course, brought frequent religious changes in individual territories and cities.

This picture is true at least of the main conflict between Catholics and Protestants. Exceptions are rare in the sixteenth and seventeenth centuries. But they could arise under certain circumstances in smaller secular territories, for instance where two branches of the same dynasty adhering to different creeds (such as the counts of Öttingen and Pappenheim) treated the *ius reformandi* differently and not consistently, or where common rule in villages or territories was shared by several dynasties (*Kondominate Ganerbschaften*).[43] In some cases therefore the local divisions of inheritance had no influence on religion, while in others they led to divisions in individual towns and villages or resulted in the simultaneous exercise of two religious practices within the same church.[44] But to find a significant exception it is necessary to look forward to the late seventeenth or early eighteenth centuries – the conversion of the Lutheran elector of Saxony, Augustus II, to the Catholic faith as a consequence of his election to the Polish crown in 1697; the territory remained Protestant.[45]

Thus in the sixteenth and seventeenth centuries Catholic and Protestant minorities within secular territorial states with a different official creed were the complete exception. If they existed at all, they were almost always temporary minorities in transition, no longer tending towards majority status, but rather constantly threatened with exile. In many Protestant states the relationship between Lutheran and Reformed was somewhat different. The Calvinists, or Reformed church, were insignificant at the time of the Religious Peace of Augsburg of 1555, and so were not considered there. Later they expanded, won the support of many overlords for their cause, and claimed rights against the Lutherans under the *cuius regio eius religio* clause. There were numerous successful and unsuccessful attempts by overlords to introduce into their Lutheran territories the Reformed confession, Reformed worship and Reformed church organization, which could have comparable consequences for their subjects. In the period up to the Thirty Years War these so-called second reformations, and the often virulent reactions which they encountered, introduced the *ius reformandi* of Protestant overlords into areas where it had played no part in regulating conflicts between Catholics and Protestants in the years following 1555. The areas included the Rhine and Upper Palatinate, Saxonia, Nassau, Sayn-Wittgenstein, Solms, Ysenburg, Wied, Hanau, Bremen, Bentheim, Anhalt, Hesse-Kassel, Brieg, Baden-Durlach, Lippe, Holstein, and Brandenburg.[46] Internal Protestant antagonisms were no less acrimonious than those between Protestants and Catholics. Persecution, compulsion, removal from office, chicanery vis-à-vis preachers, teachers, professors, mayors and councillors were accepted features of daily life. But outside these social groups expulsions were relatively rare and execution remained the exception.

The rigours of the *cuius regio eius religio* system were relaxed much sooner in internal Protestant disputes, however, than in the Catholic–Protestant context of the conflict. The subjects of the counts of Ortenburg could successfully defend their Lutheran faith in 1589 and 1597 in the face of attempts by their overlords to introduce Calvinism. They owed the success of their stand to the likelihood of support from the otherwise feared Catholic dukes of Bavaria.[47] The changed situation emerged clearly in 1615, when the Reformed Hohenzollern dynasty did not succeed in inducing their Lutheran hereditary lands of Brandenburg to alter their religion. The subjects mounted a determined resistance, a fact of the greatest significance for the later development of the Brandenburg–Prussian state.[48] Not to be overlooked are the religious conflicts among the various Lutheran orientations in the sixteenth century. They produced various minorities as soon as an overlord championed one or the other side on the principle of *cuius regio eius religio*. Here, too, one finds chicanery and the exile of leading personalities. In other situations, individual cities of one religion struggled with their territorial lord of another religious persuasion. This occurred in Lutheran Lemgo, the most important city of the Reformed county of Lippe.[49]

The principle of *cuius regio eius religio*, therefore, was stringently enforced in the secular territorial states between the different branches of Protestantism. But there were exceptions here too – not *de jure* but *de facto*. One must distinguish between dissent against the will of the overlord and dissent with his approval and sometimes even under his considerable influence. Against the will of the Lutheran counts of East Frisia, a permanent, strong, Reformed element emerged in their lands under the leadership of the mighty trading city of Emden with its syndic Johannes Althusius, the famous political theorist.[50] In western Germany, too, aristocratic lordships and civic communities in secular states with differing creeds existed side by side, such as those in the Lower Rhine region in the territories of the dukes of Jülich, Cleves, Berg and Mark. Here one finds in the early years strong Erasmian tendencies, and later ineffectual policies occasioned by personal failure of the dukes.[51]

Of special interest are the religious relationships in some newly founded towns where in contrast to the previously mentioned examples, the founding lord had for economic reasons envisaged peaceful coexistence of divergent creeds. Examples of this are the North Albingian towns of Altona (1602), Glückstadt (1616) and Friedrichstadt (1621), founded by the counts of Schauenberg, the dukes of Gottorp, and the Danish king in his capacity as Duke of Holstein, respectively. These towns offered a sanctuary not only to different kinds of Reformed Protestants (orthodox Calvinists, Remonstrants) and Lutherans, but also to Catholics, Mennonites and Jews.[52]

As a rule, however, the only recourse for subjects of opposite creeds was emigration. The extent of this exodus *in toto* or in individual territorial states cannot be estimated even approximately. Some data exist, but they do not give total population figures for towns, which are impossible to derive with any accuracy. Population statistics for entire territories are even more difficult to arrive at. In any case it is not possible to determine the numerical strength of an entire minority from the total number of exiles. More than likely the exiles formed only the hard core, and were predominantly those who could reasonably expect to find a refuge somewhere else.[53] The enforcement of exile on a large scale and often at short notice could lead to the economic ruin of those affected by the measures, because they had to sell their real, and parts of their movable, property at great loss and had to pay substantial fines.[54]

Exile was also the fate of Protestants in some of the spiritual territories, especially in southern Germany and primarily in Franconia – here above all in the territories of the bishops of Würzburg, Bamberg and Eichstätt as well as in the state of the abbot of Fulda.[55] In southern Germany the number of Protestants had continued to grow considerably after 1555. Whereas a number of nobles of these territorial states succeeded, in the course of the delimitation of territorial boundaries, in becoming free imperial knights and thereby gaining the right of choice in matters of religion,[56] other aristocratic lordships and all the urban communities remained within the jurisdiction of the respective spiritual territorial states. The *declaratio* of Emperor Ferdinand envisaged the guarantee of religion at least for those Protestant groups that had existed in such spiritual states before 1555, but this guarantee counted for nothing when zealous Catholic bishops started the Counter-Reformation, especially since not even the Protestant princes insisted upon its fulfilment. Only in Fulda in 1602 did the abbot have to guarantee his nobility religious freedom and the right to choose the pastors for the territories under their jurisdiction. Elsewhere the Counter-Reformation was imposed. This development first led to a polarization that removed the grey zones of compromise between Protestant and Catholic. Then, in a second phase, the *ius reformandi* was placed at the service of the Tridentine reformers. In either case Protestantism disappeared. Sometimes it was absorbed non-violently into Catholicism by popular missionary effort, sometimes Protestants were expelled from the territory.[57] The 'notables' of the Franconian towns and villages especially (mayors, councillors, elders, jurors) were subjected to the latter treatment. The mass of the population remained behind.[58] But it was nevertheless a considerable exodus from small towns, when twenty, forty, eighty or 120 families – sometimes a quarter or a half of the whole population – turned their backs on the homeland in order to seek refuge in neighbouring territorial states. Only small Protestant remnants could survive.[59]

The predominant trend in the spiritual states of western and northern Germany was different. In them, too, Protestant teaching continued to spread after 1555. Their populations in towns and country turned Protestant largely through peaceful means. The cathedral chapters, composed of local nobility, elected Protestant or denominationally indeterminate bishops, often sons of neighbouring Protestant dynasties. In some of them the ecclesiastical overlords and their subjects eventually adhered to the same Lutheran creed, as in the territories of Bremen, Verden, Minden, Halberstadt, Magdeburg, Ratzeburg and Schwerin. There were some Catholic remnants, for instance in the territorial states of the archbishop of Magdeburg and of the bishop of Halberstadt.[60] In others the Counter-Reformation succeeded almost completely, as in the territories of the archbishops of Cologne and Treves.[61] In the other cases where the spiritual overlords actively supported the Counter-Reformation, they were not as successful as their south German and Rhenish counterparts, because Protestant aristocratic lordships within the territorial states were often able to maintain themselves as religious minorities, as in the territories of the bishops of Paderborn and Münster (in the district of Niederstift), the abbot of Corvey, and the abbesses of Essen and Werden.[62] In the fourth group of spiritual overlordships, genuine coexistence, that is guaranteed by law and contract as opposed to simple factual existence, was enforced. Thus strong and genuine Protestant groups were able to survive in the territories of the bishops of Osnabrück and Hildesheim. This coexistence of denominations in Osnabrück[63] led to a unique regulation in the Peace of Westphalia of 1648, which stipulated that the territorial overlordship should be filled by the alternating succession of a canonically elected bishop and a member of the Welf dynasty, each governing for life. The 'Eternal Capitulation' of 1650, in fifty-eight articles, recognized the free choice and exercise of religion and was valid until 1802, when Osnabrück was secularized.

In the territories of the bishops of Hildesheim of major importance was the fact that substantial parts of the territory had been pawned to the future Protestant overlords of the duchy of Brunswick-Wolfenbüttel just before the Reformation, and, like the city of Hildesheim, had become Protestant.[64] The city obtained a guarantee for the Lutheran creed in 1555, and the redemption which occurred at a later stage was facilitated by similar guarantees, again in this territorial state leading to the coexistence of Protestants and Catholics under the protection of an intra-territorial treaty, which remained valid until the early nineteenth century.

Another example is offered by the city and territory of Erfurt, in central Germany. As early as 1529 the coexistence of the two creeds was regulated by treaty. It provided a guarantee for churches and of university chairs for Catholics in a predominantly Protestant city, which the archbishop of Mainz as overlord could not later reduce to Catholic conformity. The Eichsfeld in Thuringia, which also belonged to Mainz, was strongly recatholicized, although around 1550 it had been almost entirely Protestant.[65] Thus there were in northern and central Germany examples of the denominational coexistence of Catholics and Protestants regulated by generally agreed treaties in the ecclesiastical territories. The passage and maintenance of each successful treaty was facilitated by power-political factors such as the proximity of Protestant territorial overlords like the Welfs or the Saxons. If we look at developments in the ecclesiastical states in terms of the provisions made at Augsburg in 1555, it is clear that the 'ecclesiastical reservation' was less vigorously applied than the principle of *cuius regio eius religio*, and that the so-called *declaratio Ferdinandea* played absolutely no role at all.

After the Religious Peace of 1555, there was a well-regulated coexistence of Protestants and Catholics in the imperial cities, which were already religiously mixed. One should not forget, however, that of the estimated 3,000 cities and civic communities in the sixteenth-century Empire, only about eighty according to the *Matricula Imperii (Reichsmatrikel)* were Imperial Free Cities.[66] Actual coexistence of denominations occurred in less than ten imperial cities, namely Augsburg, Ulm, Ravensburg, Biberach, Donauwörth, Kaufbeuren, Leutkirch, and Dinkelsbühl. The others were mostly purely Protestant, though a small number were Catholic. The Religious Peace offered a chance to the denominationally mixed imperial cities, but hardly more than a chance. In some of them reverses and changes of religion occurred until coexistence became stabilized. Such coexistence was in many ways fraught with struggle, in spite of the Religious Peace.

There were quarrels over churches, benefices, schools, and the appointments of preachers and teachers. The incorporation of city churches in monasteries located outside the cities presented great difficulties.[67] Public display of spiritual conviction, such as the Corpus Christi processions, could have frightening consequences. In Donauwörth, where religious parity was assumed but where the city was actually Protestant, such manifestations actually led to the enforced termination of the imperial liberties.[68] Religiously motivated raids and even murder committed against members of the opposite creed were not infrequent occurrences. And the development of rather unusual minorities was possible. Powerful territorial overlords in the vicinity of imperial cities could prevent the implementation of the Reformation in the city's territory,[69] thereby creating opposing religious minorities or, in the case of new acquisitions, causing the imperial city to renounce its rights of *ius reformandi*.[70] In other cases patricians of religious minority persuasion could ensure that their own creed, even though it contrasted with the majority creed in the city, was officially recognized in the villages of their manors.[71] But again it needs to be stressed that relationships in the religiously mixed cities were regulated on the whole on the basis of the imperial legislation of 1555.

Inevitably this study of a minority problem has been concerned with the religious history of Germany, and with the complexities of the atomized states that characterize the German past. It is this that gives the religious minority question its special character. By contrast with the racial or linguistic–ethnic minority, the religious minority seems to originate in a conscious act of individual decision, however it was arrived at. But in the Holy Roman Empire the over-riding power of territorial overlords in religious matters makes minorities seem to be the result of quasi-mechanistic processes outside the sphere of individual decision. That is only one side of the picture, but compared with other minorities it may well be the specifically German feature.

By the same token one needs to remember that the atomization of the minority problem had its advantages, too, which even contemporaries observed. Often a move across the village stream or into a suburb outside the gates under another overlord sufficed to avoid religious repression. Often the nearest neighbouring village offered the opportunity of 'running out' (*Auslaufen*), that is, secretly attending church services to take the holy supper, or arranging for burial in a cemetery, which the native town may have refused. A nearby town in another territorial state with which one had old-established trading connections might offer new prospects, as might the small courts with their bureaucracies, pastors and schoolmasters. And yet, every new beginning was difficult and fraught with risks, professional rivalry, and genuine fear among co-religionists from whom protection was sought. All this presented serious problems, even for one who was only a few miles away from his place of origin, in the case of small-scale territories.

With the Thirty Years War the age of religious division reached its climax and began to fade. At its end we find toleration, enforced more by circumstances than by any changes of heart, beginning to emerge, though certainly not generally recognized in principle. Unresolved problems were not removed thereby, but in some respects discord was lessened. Although the Peace of Westphalia of 1648 specifically confirmed the Religious Peace of Augsburg, it interpreted it in such a manner that the problem of religious minorities appeared in a different light.[72] The principles of *cuius regio eius religio* and the *reservatum ecclesiasticum* were retained in 1648. But the status quo of 1 January 1624 was taken as the confessional norm thereafter, which fairly reflected the actual situation at the end of the war. With this decision many old minority problems were removed or defused. All these stipulations did not apply to the Habsburg lands, however, where persecution of Protestantism continued, with the exceptions mentioned above. This date (1624) was also to apply to the religious practices within a territorial state, where divergence from the official religion was recognized for the private sphere as well as in public church services. But also – and this truly pointed the way to the future – wherever single individuals had adopted and professed a divergent religion after 1 January 1624, private worship could be conducted in the home and children could be educated by private tutors or sent to a school in a different state. Divergent spiritual life was therefore recognized. Those who adhered to a religion other than the official state religion were not to be subjected to any civic disadvantages. From the time of the Peace of Westphalia, subjects were no longer obliged to change their religion whenever their ruler changed his from Lutheranism to Calvinism or vice versa.

On the whole the Reformed creed was recognized in the Peace. But Mennonites and Spiritualists were not. All they could do in the second half of the seventeenth century was to consolidate their position *de facto* where possible, in the very slowly changing intellectual climate that culminated in the Enlightenment. The Peace of Westphalia was not a product of the Enlightenment. It resulted rather from the consequences of a hopeless religious situation, which could not be resolved peacefully; it resulted from a military situation, from an economic and social catastrophe. Nevertheless, it is integrally related to the Enlightenment. The variety of religious experience, which had emerged finally as a result of attempts at mediation, the distinction between public and private worship, between religious and civic existence, were all significant steps forward into a new age. Although the confessional imprint still dominated life for many decades, signs of the new were everywhere to be seen.

I have tried to convey an impression of the problems of religious minorities in central Europe in the sixteenth and early seventeenth centuries, characterizing the Catholic, Lutheran and Reformed churches in their various situations as majorities and minorities which changed and were reversed several times. The coexistence of the large minorities determined the structure and character of the age; they manifested themselves as a stage of transition into a new age.

This is not intended to mean that groups that remained in permanent minority status, small in number and without the support of an overlord, like the Anabaptists, do not also merit our attention. To determine their minority status it is necessary to differentiate between those who lived in communities, like the Hutterites in Bohemia, and the scattered Anabaptists who lived originally in towns and later, in the second half of the century, in the villages of southern and central Germany.[73] There they lived dispersed among Protestants. Austere in their personal lives and contemptuous of the world, they rejected the existing secular authorities and refused to pay taxes, to participate in wars, or to swear oaths. This led to their rejection by the majority population and almost always to persecution by the secular authorities.

The methods and intensity of persecution, on the other hand, differed widely. Of the total number of 715 death penalties pronounced against Anabaptists – a minimum figure which has been verified for central and southern Germany between 1525 and 1618 – 80 per cent occurred in the years 1527–33. Catholic overlords were responsible for 90 per cent of the executions; Protestants, for only 10 per cent.[74] In Protestant territories exile was the prevalent punishment, and in later years it was generally adopted. Quite different were the conditions among the so-called Hutterites, who were under the protection of manorial lords in Moravia. Right up to the Thirty Years War, they lived in their rigidly organized authoritarian colonies and were highly esteemed as artisans, who produced wealth for their protectors. With the destruction of noble privileges after 1621, they lost the basis of their organization and were forced to leave the area of the Holy Roman Empire.[75]

In mentioning the Hutterites and their community existence, we have already touched upon economic reasons for the toleration of Anabaptists. As hard-working settlers and reliable tax-payers, they were accepted, tolerated and allowed to settle under the protection of German and Polish noblemen in the delta of the Vistula, within the realm of the Polish crown near the border of the Holy Roman Empire.[76] They were also able to maintain themselves dispersed among the peasants of northwestern Germany. Here they were tolerated *de facto* rather than formally recognized. The fact that this area was thinly populated provided an opportunity, not present in densely populated areas, of avoiding contact and subsequently conflict with neighbours.[77]

The advent of the Enlightenment changed much of the situation that I have described. But as late as 1732 the archbishop of Salzburg expelled his Protestant subjects, though it was even at the time considered an anachronistic measure.[78] It would be necessary to look clearly at Catholic and Protestant territorial states and populations as well as at social and intellectual changes in order to put into perspective the practical impact of the Enlightenment and to evaluate the significance of the eighteenth century in the development of our subject. However, what had been the exception in 1648 became more and more tolerated, if not the rule. A new age emerged in central Europe – with new minority problems.

Notes

I am grateful to Dr C. Robinson-Hammerstein of Trinity College, Dublin, and Dr W. Sheldon of Marburg for translating this essay from the original German, and to the Goethe Institute, Manchester, for a generous contribution towards travel costs, which permitted me to participate in the conference at Coleraine.

1 For the constitutional structures of the Holy Roman Empire see G. Oestreich, 'Verfassungsgeschichte vom Ende des Mittelalters bis zum Ende des Alten Reiches' in *Gebhardt. Handbuch der deutschen Geschichte* (Stuttgart, 1970) II, pp. 361 ff.; H. Conrad, *Deutsche Rechtsgeschichte* (Karlsruhe, 1966) II, pp. 66 ff.
2 For a short history of the boundary of the Empire see Conrad, pp. 106 ff.
3 *Handbuch der Geschichte der böhmischen Länder* (Stuttgart, 1974) II, pp. 158 ff.
4 H. Pirenne, *Histoire de Belgique* (6th edn, Brussels, n.d.) II; R. Parisot, *Histoire de Lorraine* (Paris, 1922) II; H. Witte, 'Zur Geschichte des Deutschtums in Lothringen', *Jahrbuch der Gesellschaft für Lothringische Geschichte und Altertumskunde* II (1890); C. Aimond, *Histoire des Lorrains* (Bar-le-Duc, 1960).
5 B. Schumacher, *Geschichte Ost- und Westpreussens* (4th edn, Würzburg, 1959), pp. 139 ff.

6 *Handbuch der historischen Stätten. Oesterreich* (Stuttgart, 1970) I, pp. 694 ff.
7 Conrad, pp. 110 ff.
8 L. Petry and J. J. Menzel (eds), *Geschichte Schlesiens* (Darmstadt, 1973) II; R. Lehmann, *Geschichte der Niederlausitz* (Berlin, 1963).
9 Pirenne, II, pp. 265 ff.; B. H. M. Vlekke, *Evolution of the Dutch Nation* (*s.* l., 1963), pp. 94 ff., 124 ff.
10 E. Préclin, *Histoire de la Franche Comté* (Paris, 1947).
11 See note 4, above.
12 Conrad, p. 164.
13 *ibid.* p. 166.
14 O. Klose, ed., *Geschichte Schleswig-Holsteins* (Neumünster, 1972) V 1; O. Brandt, *Geschichte Schleswig-Holsteins* (6th edn, Kiel, 1966).
15 M. Peters, 'Der Ripener Vertrag und die Ausbildung der landstaendischen Verfassung in Schleswig-Holstein', *Blaetter fuer deutsche Landesgeschichte* CIX (1973) and CXI (1975).
16 F. Lau and E. Bizer, 'Reformationsgeschichte Deutschlands bis 1555' in *Die Kirche in ihrer Geschichte* (Göttingen, 1964) III.
17 See below, p. 37.
18 D. Willoweit, *Rechtsgrundlagen der Territorialgewalt* (Cologne and Vienna, 1975), p. 17 ff.
19 Oestreich, pp. 397 ff., 404 ff.
20 J. Hashagen, *Staat und Kirche vor der Reformation* (Essen, 1931).
21 A survey in W. Maurer and H. Hermelink, *Reformation und Gegenreformation* (2nd edn, Tübingen, 1931), pp. 136 ff., 141 ff., 157 ff., 288 ff.
22 E. W. Zeeden, *Die Entstehung der Konfessionen* (Munich, 1965), pp. 72 ff.
23 J. B. Goetz, *Die religioesen Wirren in der Oberpfalz von 1576 bis 1620* (Münster, 1937), pp. 233 ff.
24 W. Sohm, *Territorium und Reformation in der hessischen Geschichte 1526–1555* (Marburg, 1915).
25 For some examples, see *Handbuch der bayerischen Geschichte* (Munich, 1971) III, 1, p. 427.
26 M. Simon, *Evangelische Kirchengeschichte Bayerns* (Munich, 1942); *Handbuch der bayerischen Geschichte* (Munich, 1966) II.
27 J. Lecler, *Histoire de la tolérance au siècle de la Réforme* (Aubier, 1955) I, pp. 243 ff.
28 See below, p. 40.
29 K. Brandi, ed., *Der Augsburger Religionsfrieden. Kritische Ausgabe des Texts* (2nd edn, Göttingen, 1927).
30 G. Westphal, *Der Kampf um die Freistellung auf den Reichstagen zwischen 1556 und 1576* (PhD thesis, Marburg, 1975).
31 Westphal, pp. 21, 190 ff.; Simon, p. 387.
32 G. W. Sante (ed.), *Geschichte der deutschen Länder* (Würzburg, 1964) I.
33 Simon, pp. 206 ff., 294 ff., 374 ff.; *Handbuch der bayerischen Geschichte* II, pp. 632 ff.
34 F. Krones, *Handbuch der Geschichte Oesterreichs* (Berlin, 1878) III, pp. 313 ff.; H. Hantsch, *Die Geschichte Oesterreichs* (4th edn, Graz, 1959) I, pp. 237 ff.; E. Zöllner, *Geschichte Oesterreichs* (5th edn, Munich, 1974), pp. 191 ff.; K. Gutkas, *Geschichte des Landes Niederoesterreich* (2nd edn, St Poelten, 1962) II, 47 ff.
35 *Handbuch der Geschichte der boehmischen Laender* (Stuttgart, 1974), II, especially pp. 158 ff., 179.
36 Petry and Menzel, pp. 92 ff.
37 Lehmann, p. 229.

38 Simon, pp. 277 ff.
39 For examples see *ibid.* pp. 281 ff.
40 *ibid.* p. 379.
41 For examples from the Bavarian region see Simon, pp. 378, 382 ff., 393 ff.; for Westphalia see H. Rothert, *Westfälische Geschichte* (Gütersloh, 1950) II, p. 121.
42 For Neuburg see Simon, pp. 408 ff., 420 ff.; *Handbuch der bayerischen Geschichte* III, 2, p. 1340; for Baden see F. v. Weech, *Badische Geschichte* (Karlsruhe, 1890), pp. 150 ff., 256 ff.
43 Simon, pp. 281 ff. *Handbuch der bayerischen Geschichte* III, 2, p. 927; H.-J. Koehler, *Obrigkeitliche Konfessionsaenderung in Kondominaten . . . am Beispiel der baden-badischen Religionspolitik (1622–1677)* (1975), pp. 82 ff., 145 ff.
44 Simon, pp. 281 ff. *Handbuch*, p. 927.
45 R. Koetzschke and H. Kretzschmar, *Sächsische Geschichte* (2nd edn, Frankfurt am Main, 1965), pp. 267 ff.
46 T. Klein (ed.), *U. Pierius, Geschichte der kursächsischen Kirchen- und Schulreformation* (Marburg, 1970), pp. 5 ff.
47 L. Theobald, *Johann von Ortenburg und die Durchführung der Reformation in seiner Grafschaft* (s. 1., 1927).
48 O. Hintze, *Die Hohenzollern und ihr Werk* (4th edn, Berlin, 1915), p. 165; E. Faden, 'Der Berliner Tumult von 1615', *Jahrbuch fuer brandenburgische Landesgeschichte* V (1954); R. v. Thadden, *Die brandenburgisch–preussischen Hofprediger im 17. und 18. Jahrhundert* (Berlin 1959).
49 E. Kittel, *Geschichte des Landes Lippe* (Cologne, 1957), pp. 103 ff.; Karl Meier, *Geschichte der Stadt Lemgo* (2nd edn, Lemgo, 1962), pp. 123 ff. Another example are the Calvinist villages in the Lutheran county of Oldenburg: G. Ruethning, *Oldenburgische Geschichte* (Bremen, 1911), p. 531.
50 T. D. Wiarda, *Ostfriesische Geschichte* (Aurich, 1794) IV; H. Antholz, *Die politische Wirksamkeit des Johannes Althusius in Emden* (Aurich, 1955).
51 H. Forsthoff, *Rheinische Kirchengeschichte* (Essen, 1929) I, 'Die Reformation am Niederrhein', pp. 245 ff., 461 ff.; O. R. Redlich, *Staat und Kirche am Niederrhein zur Reformationszeit* (Leipzig, 1938), pp. 97 ff.; A. Franzen, *Die Kelchbewegung am Niederrhein im 16. Jahrhundert* (Münster, 1955), pp. 38 ff; J. P. Dolan, *The Influence of Erasmus, Witzel and Cassander in the Church Ordinances and Reform Proposals of the United Duchies of Cleves during the Middle Decades of the 16th Century* (Münster, 1957), pp. 25 ff.; D. Coenen, *Die katholische Kirche am Niederrhein von der Reformation bis zum Beginn des 18. Jahrhunderts* (Münster, 1967), pp. 27 ff., 65 ff.; F. Petri and G. Droege (eds), *Rheinische Geschichte* (Düsseldorf, 1976), pp. 70 ff.
52 H. Hassinger, 'Wirtschaftliche Motive und Argumente fuer religioese Dudsamkeit im 16. und 17. Jahrhundert', *Archiv fuer Reformationsgeschichte* IL (1958); H. Berlage, *Altona. Ein Stadtschicksal* (Hamburg, 1937); D. Detlefsen, 'Die staedtische Entwicklung Glueckstadts unter Christian IV', *Zeitschrift der Gesellschaft für schleswigholsteinische Geschichte* XXXVI (1960); G. Koehn, *Die Bevoelkerung der . . . Exulantenstadt Glückstadt von der Gruendung 1616 bis . . . 1652* (Hamburg, Glückstadt, 1974); F. Pont, *Friedrichstadt an der Eider* (Erlangen, 1913) I; Harry Schmidt, *Friedrichstadt, Vergangenheit und Gegenwart* (3rd edn, Lübeck, 1957); K. A. Carstensen, *Die Gruendung und anfaengliche Entwicklung von Friedrichstadt an der Eider* (Kiel, 1913).
53 For examples see Simon, p. 388. In 1585, 72 of 391 citizens of Karlstadt were Catholics, but only 80 left the town because of their Protestantism. More than 200 remained.
54 *ibid.*

55 Simon, pp. 286 ff., 384 ff.; F. Stein, *Geschichte Frankens* (Schweinfurt, 1886) II, pp. 68 ff.; J. Looshorn, *Die Geschichte des Bistums Bamberg* (Bamberg, 1903) V; G. Frh. v. Pölnitz, *Julius Echter von Mespelbrunn* (Munich, 1934); J. Sax, *Die Bischoefe und Reichsfuersten von Eichstaett* (Landshut, 1885), pp. 453 ff.; F. X. Buchner, *Das Bistum Eichstaett* (Eichstätt, 1937–8) II.

56 V. Press, *Kaiser Karl V., Koenig Ferdinand und die Entstehung der Reichsritterschaft* (Mainz, 1976), pp. 40 ff.

57 *Handbuch der bayerischen Geschichte* III, 1, p. 429.

58 Simon, p. 389.

59 *ibid.* pp. 397 ff.

60 Johannes Meyer, *Kirchengeschichte Niedersachsens* (Göttingen, 1939), pp. 100, 138.

61 L. Ennen, *Geschichte der Reformation im Bereich der alten Erzdioezese Koeln* (Cologne, 1849); P. Weiler, *Die kirchliche Reform im Erzbistum Koeln (1583–1615)* (Münster, 1931), pp. 37 ff., 150 ff.; J. Leonardy, *Geschichte des Trierischen Landes und Volkes* (Saarlouis, 1870).

62 Rothert, II, pp. 194 ff. with a survey on the religious situation in Westphalia at the end of the age of reform; F. Ph. Funcke, *Geschichte des Fuerstentums und der Stadt Essen* (Elberfeld, 1848): the town of Essen remained Protestant; H. Goossens, 'Geschichte der spanischen Einfaelle ... in Essen', *Beitraege zur Geschichte von ... Essen* XII ((1888); F. Koerholz, *Abriß der Geschichte des Stifts und der Stadt Werden* (Werden, 1925); W. Langenbach, 'Stift und Stadt Werden im Zeitalter des 30 jaehrigen Krieges', *Beitraege zur Geschichte des Stifts Werden* XV (1911); W. Bueltermann, *Das Fuerstentum Corvey unter der Regierung Arnolds IV von Valdois (1638–1661)* (PhD thesis, Münster, 1919); L. Leineweber, 'Die Paderborner Fuerstbischoefe im Zeitalter der Glaubenserneuerung', *Zeitschrift fuer vaterlaendische Geschichte und Altertumskunde Westfalens* LXVI (1908), LXVII (1909); H. A. Erhard, *Geschichte Münsters* (Münster, 1837), pp. 446 ff.

63 H. Hoyer, *Untersuchungen ueber die Reformationsgeschichte des Fuerstbistums Osnabrück* (ThD thesis, Göttingen, 1927), pp. 122 ff.; L. Schirmeyer, *Osnabrück und das Osnabrücker Land* (Paderborn and Osnabrück, 1948), pp. 170 ff.

64 A. Bertram, *Geschichte des Bistums Hildesheim* (Hildesheim, 1916) II, pp. 99 ff.; III, pp. 44 ff., 75 ff.

65 T. Klein, 'Politik und Verfassung ... 1485–1572' in H. Patze and W. Schlesinger, eds, *Geschichte Thüringens* (Cologne, 1967) III, p. 288; E. Beyreuther in *ibid.* (1972) IV, pp. 10 ff.; P. Knieb, *Geschichte der Reformation und Gegenreformation auf dem Eichsfelde* (2nd edn, Heiligenstadt, 1909); A. L. Veit, *Kirche und Kirchenreform in der Erzdioezese Mainz ... (1517–1618)* (Freiburg, 1920).

66 For a list of the members of the *Reichstag* see Oestreich, pp. 769 ff.; G. Pfeiffer, 'Der Augsburger Religionsfriede und die Reichsstaedte', *Zeitschrift des Historischen Vereins fuer Schwaben und Neuburg* LXI (1955), especially pp. 292 ff.; *Handbuch der bayerischen Geschichte*, III, part 2, pp. 1033 ff.; Simon, pp. 283 ff.; W. Zorn, *Augsburg, Geschichte einer deutschen Stadt* (2nd edn, Augsburg, 1972); D. A. Schultes, *Chronik von Ulm...*, revised by K. Hoehn (7th edn, Ulm, 1937); F. Fritz, *Ulmische Kirchengeschichte vom Interim bis zum 30 jaehrigen Krieg* (Stuttgart, 1934); J. G. Eben, *Versuch einer Geschichte der Stadt Ravensburg* (Ravensburg, 1835); E. Bruder, *Biberach an der Riß* (Biberach, 1950); M. Zelzer, *Geschichte der Stadt Donauwoerth* (Donauwörth, 1958) I, pp. 231 ff.; F. Junginger, *Geschichte der Reichsstadt Kaufbeuren im 17. und 18. Jahrhundert* (thesis, Munich, 1965), pp. 29 ff., 149 ff.; R. Roth, *Geschichte der ehemaligen Reichsstadt Leutkirch und der Leutkircher Haide* (Leutkirch, 1875) II; C. Buerckstuemmer, *Geschichte der Reformation und Gegenreformation in der ehemaligen und freien Reichsstadt Dinkelsbuehl (1524–1648)* (Leipzig, 1915).

67 For examples see Simon, *passim.*

68 M. Ritter, *Deutsche Geschichte im Zeitalter der Gegenreformation und des Dreissig-jaehrigen Krieges (1555–1648)* (Stuttgart, 1895) II, pp. 213 ff.

69 For examples see Simon, pp. 284 ff.

70 *Handbuch der bayerischen Geschichte,* III, 2, pp. 930 ff.

71 For examples see Simon, p. 285.

72 K. Zeumer (ed.), *Quellensammlung zur Geschichte der deutschen Reichsverfassung* 2nd edn (Tübingen, 1913), nrr. 197 ff.; F. Dickmann, *Der Westfaelische Frieden* (2nd edn, Münster, 1965), pp. 343 ff.

73 C. P. Clasen, *Anabaptism, a Social History* (Ithaca, N.Y., 1972), pp. 305 ff.

74 *ibid.* pp. 358 ff.

75 *ibid.* pp. 210 ff.

76 Hassinger, p. 228.

77 R. Dollinger, *Geschichte der Mennoniten in Schleswig-Holstein, Hamburg und Lübeck* (Neumünster, 1930); J. P. Müller, *Die Mennoniten in Ostfriesland vom 16. bis zum 18. Jahrhundert* (Emden, 1887). For a rare example of toleration and active support by a territorial overlord of minor importance in favour of the spiritualist Schwenckfeldians, see Franz Michael Weber, *K. Schwenckfeld und seine Anhaenger in den freybergischen Herrschaften Justingen und Oepfinger* (Stuttgart, 1962).

78 J. K. Mayr, *Die Emigration der Salzburger Protestanten von 1731/32* (Salzburg, 1931); G. Florey, *Geschichte der Salzburger Protestanten und ihre Emigration 1731/32* (Vienna, 1976).

4

Dominant minorities: English settlers in Ireland and Virginia, 1550–1650

Nicholas Canny

I

The principal purpose of this chapter is to examine the extent to which the New English adventurers in Ireland and Virginia perceived themselves, or were thought by others, to be a minority, to account for this awareness or lack of it, and to explain how this factor influenced their actions and behaviour. The comparison between the English experience in Ireland and Virginia will suggest parallels, but it will also assist our understanding of the greater complexity of the Irish situation, where the New English had to compete with alleged barbarians and also with the descendants of earlier waves of English settlers who had previously been dominant, and who until the mid-sixteenth century persisted as the minority element in Ireland. Most evidence has been drawn from the conquest phase in the two areas (Ireland *c* 1560–1603; Virginia 1607–*c* 1630), but some attention has been devoted to settlement, since to draw a rigid division between the processes of conquest and colonization would be to introduce a false distinction.

The New English with a permanent interest in Ireland in the period of conquest were an extremely small group consisting of senior administrators, bishops, and lawyers in Dublin and the provinces; army officers who wished to convert their position as seneschals and captains of garrisons into hereditary fiefdoms; sheriffs and sub-sheriffs in the provinces who sought to use their power to acquire land for themselves through judicial process; and the settlers on the officially sponsored plantations. All these, with the exception of successive lords deputies, a few senior officials and an occasional bishop, were concerned to establish themselves and their families as landowners or tenants in Ireland, and even the exceptional ones were interested in promoting the interest of their personal followers there. It must have been obvious to, but not always admitted by, those concerned that success in this matter could be achieved only at the expense of the existing proprietors and occupiers of the soil, and that conflict would almost certainly ensue.

The total number of English-born careerists in Ireland, civil as well as military and ecclesiastical, did not exceed sixty in 1560, but they had increased in number to about 200 in 1603, and were then about to multiply at an even more dramatic rate. It was these who advocated and promoted the conquest and colonization of Ireland, and even if not in agreement on how this should be accomplished, they certainly considered the presence of a permanent army in Ireland as essential to their purpose. The nominal strength of the army fluctuated between less than 2,000 in peacetime and 20,000 at the height of the Nine Years War (1594–1603), but it is impossible to calculate the precise number of English soldiers in Ireland at any one time because of the desertion and mortality rates, and because of the falsification of returns made by the captains.[1] The actual settlement of Ireland was also under way before 1603, and it is possible that in excess of 3,000 English people had occupied land in Ireland prior to the disruption of the several English plantations during the 1590s.[2] Thus, the total New English presence in Ireland did not exceed 23,500 before 1603, and the overwhelming majority of these were soldiers who were present in significant numbers only after 1594. When this figure is placed beside a total Irish population of approximately 1·1 million it seems evident that, in statistical terms, the New English were in a distinct minority within Ireland. While the absolute number of British settlers had increased to at least 50,000 by 1641 their relative position had not improved significantly because by then, as a result of natural increase, the total population of the country had reached an estimated 1·7 million.[3]

More precise information is available on the English population in Virginia from the moment of settlement in 1607 until the 1640s, by which time the conquest of Tidewater Virginia had been accomplished. Beginning with the three boat loads that disembarked at Jamestown on 26 April 1607, the number of English in Virginia crept slowly to 1,240 in 1622 to about 1,300 in 1625, 2,600 in 1629, and roughly 8,000 in 1640. It is thought that the Amerindian population in Virginia had been decimated by disease even before the arrival of the English, but the first settlers still thought themselves to be overwhelmingly outnumbered, and in military terms claimed to be opposed by 5,000 Indians 'able to bear arms'.[4] Such was their position, in the early years, that the colonists were dependent upon the generosity of the native population for supplies of food, but after the massacre of 347 English settlers in 1622 it was resolved to abandon the original intention to have an integrated society, and by 1640 almost all the indigenous population had been removed from the plantation area.[5]

II

Those in England who advocated the conquest and settlement of Ireland and Virginia recognized that those sent overseas would, unless due precautions were taken, face the prospect of total expulsion or absorption by the native population. English officials who provided advice on Ireland were acutely aware that what they were sponsoring was, for the most part, a reconquest of the country, which was required because the earlier settlers had succumbed to Gaelic customs and practices. This historical fact was recited by almost every sixteenth-century English commentator on Ireland, as likewise were English misgivings that newly appointed governors and colonists would, like their predecessors, neglect 'the ways and courses to civilize those called the wild Irish', and instead 'following the nature of man, ever inclining to the worse, rather [learn] rudeness and barbarism of the Irish'.[6] The behaviour of English officials and settlers in Ireland during the first half of the sixteenth century did nothing to allay these fears of English sponsors and it was reported repeatedly in England that these too had been drawn to partake in certain prohibited Gaelic practices.[7]

The promoters of the English invasion and the colonization of Virginia were equally uncertain of the outcome, and were clearly anxious lest, once freed from the constraints of English society and exposed to new pressures, their agents in America would give free play to their passions, thus giving rise to tumult, freebooting, drunkenness and desertion to the enemy. Their fears were further intensified when they witnessed the youth and, what seemed to them, the dissolute character of most of those who went to Virginia, and there was general agreement that 'a prodigious prodigal here, is not easily metamorphosed in a Virginian passage to a thrifty planter'.[8]

It was accepted in England that only those in need of employment were likely to be attracted as settlers to either Ireland or Virginia, and since these were generally considered to be lazy, licentious and rebellious,[9] it was consistent that the promoters saw little hope that colonization efforts would bear fruit unless commanded by leaders whose 'eminence or nobility' would restrain the 'servile nature' of the majority.[10] The directions and instructions given to leaders of these enterprises show clearly that the organizers in England looked forward to the development of tightly knit communities, held together by leaders 'of good families and countenance' to whom it was intended to extend wide discretionary powers in maintaining discipline over their followers.[11] Since this point has been developed elsewhere,[12] it will be sufficient for our present purpose to cite the example of the Munster plantation, the regulations for which are fairly typical of those formulated for projected colonies in both Ireland and Virginia. Planters in Munster were prohibited from retaining native occupiers on their estates because it was thought that 'intermixture of the Irish with the English' would serve the future overthrow of the colony. Would-be settlers were required to take up residence in nucleated communities 'without interruption or intermixture of others'; land was to be leased only to those 'born of English parents'; heirs female were permitted to marry only 'those born of English parents or children of patentees'; the employment of Irish servants was denied them, and it was specifically decreed that 'none of the meer Irish ... shall be maintained or permitted in any family there'.[13] What was envisaged by the English officials who designed the scheme was a completely separate society in Munster, which in the early years would need careful nurturing, but which, if the conditions were rigidly adhered to, would eventually flourish and radiate civility throughout the province. No effort was made to disguise the attendant risks, and potential colonists were warned that from the outset they would be opposed 'by the savage people of the country' who 'being stronger than the inhabitant English, the enterprise may be easily qualed'; and they were also reminded of 'the Irish nature whereby the whole state of the country will return unto his unruly course'.[14]

The organizers of English settlement in Virginia similarly recommended that strict discipline be maintained over the colonists, and a military structure was intended from the outset. When the original government failed to function efficiently, even more extensive powers, known as the Laws Divine, Moral and Martial, were granted to the commanders. Planters in Virginia were given more latitude to move from the primary areas of settlement once the economic potential of tobacco was realized, but considerable restraints were still placed upon them until the massacre of 1622 when it became official policy to expel the Indians from the English sphere of influence.[15] Prior to that, it was intended that the colonists establish themselves in nucleated settlements situated in the midst of the native population, who it was hoped would, in time, come to recognize and accept the English culture, religion and economic system. English officials were certainly hopeful that the superior cultural system would prevail, but they were confident that this would happen only if proper restraint were observed by their sometimes doubtful agents of civility, who otherwise would succumb to the allure of their barbaric surroundings. Those who viewed the overseas enterprise from the vantage point of England also accepted that the colonists would, except in a very extreme situation, have to provide for their own defence. This explains why musters, intended to gauge the military capacity of the colonies, almost invariably had their origin in England. The organizers in England also expected that colonies would, in a short time, become self-sufficient, and even render a profit to the mother country: thus just as the monarchy intended that settlement in Ireland would end the drain of that country on crown resources, the members of the Virginia Company in London, and after 1623 the crown officials, looked to their supplement there to render a return on investment in manpower and capital. The promoters of colonization can in one sense be regarded as generally optimistic, but the ambivalence of the official mind on the whole question of colonization is evident from the writing of Fynes Moryson who thought that 'no less caution were to be observed for uniting them [English settlers] and keeping them from mixing with the other [native Irish] than if those new colonies were to be led to inhabit among the barbarous Indians'.[16]

III

The perception of English directors and advocates of conquest and colonization contrasts sharply with that of those actually engaged upon these enterprises in Ireland and Virginia. Their spokesmen were so assured, or so convinced themselves, of their social and cultural superiority that they would admit no possibility of their being attracted by the alleged barbarism of their neighbours. Neither were they daunted by the numerically superior forces of their opponents, and both settlements included individuals who wished to provoke the native leaders to oppose them. These believed that once the leaders were removed by force the native society would be a *tabula rasa*, 'apt to receive what print so ever' the English government might wish 'to put upon it'.[17] In the case of Ireland these aggressive ones were the most consistent advocates of a plantation policy, and they were assured that newly erected colonies would both survive and exert a beneficial and civilizing influence over the indigenous population.[18]

It may have been this conviction that – regardless of numbers – a superior culture would inevitably prevail over an inferior one, that made it possible for planters to generally ignore the conditions laid down by the authorities in England. In almost every plantation in Ireland the regulations relating to close habitation, defence, and the employment of native tenants and labourers, were disregarded by the patentees.[19] Even those English who acquired isolated property or livings in the midst of Gaelic or Gaelicized parts of Ireland remained convinced that, when expediency dictated it, they could stride the cultural frontier without diluting their Englishness. Captain William Piers, for example, who had an interest in Carrickfergus either as a trading centre or military outpost from 1555 into the 1580s, presented the public face of advocate of English colonization in Ulster, while, simultaneously, he became intimately acquainted with his neighbouring Gaelic lords and even fostered some of their children.[20] Successive presidents in Connacht, notably Sir Nicholas Malby and Sir Richard Bingham, also thought themselves capable of living in two worlds without jeopardizing their own claims to civility. Bingham acknowledged that of the seventy-five people 'daily feeding in his house', one third were natives of Connacht; while Malby denied that he had any of 'his children to foster to the Irishry', he did concede that many chieftains 'did seek to have them', and that the statute to which his accuser referred permitted 'an English man to foster with the Irishry for the advantage of the princes service'. Many captains of remote garrisons throughout Ireland married native wives, and they at least argued that this in no way compromised their loyalty or effectiveness.[21]

This type of behaviour did not escape criticism in London, or even Dublin, but the essential point is that the offenders themselves saw no danger in maintaining intimate contact with the native inhabitants. The English experience in Virginia provides plentiful examples of this same overwhelming confidence in the immunity of their own civility from contagion. Even while the settlement was confined to Jamestown, some of the leaders, and especially Captain John Smith, sought to maintain regular contact with the Indians and in times of extreme scarcity the colonists were sent to live among their neighbours.[22] Once large-scale tobacco growing had been introduced, the planters in Virginia tended to disregard the requirement that they live in confined quarters, and instead 'planted dispersedly in small families, far from neighbours ... out of the eye of the magistrate'. It was said of the Virginia settlers that 'such was the conceit of firm peace and amity, as that there was seldom or never a sword worn, and a piece seldomer'. Even situated 'scatteringly and straglingly' as they were, their houses were none the less 'set open to the savages who were always friendly entertained at the tables of the English'. Some of the Indians who were employed as servants were instructed in the use of firearms, and it was alleged that 'they became so good shot, they were employed for fowlers and huntsmen by the English'.[23]

Lest it be thought that planters in Ireland and Virginia saw no obstacles in the way of conquest and colonization, attention must be drawn to the frequent cries of despair that were forwarded to London. One factor that received hardly any attention from officials in England but was of major concern to those placed overseas, was the extent to which they, much more than the native inhabitants, suffered from the disease environment. In Ireland during the sixteenth century the ranks of the English army were depleted more by disease than warfare, and some spoke of the country as 'a sepulchre . . . and a place of hazard'. The 'decaying of the companies of sickness' was all the more terrifying when the precise cause of death was unknown, and when it was noticed that men 'newly supplied' from England were most susceptible to contagion.[24] The high death rate caused by unidentified diseases to which 'unseasoned' recruits were most suscep- tible was also one of the principal factors that sapped the confidence of the English in Virginia. The gravity of the situation there was, however, relaxed somewhat when the process of settlement took over from that of conquest, and for Ireland it was likewise noted that where 'hardly one in six' conquests survived the hardships of war, of those who went as settlers ('not one in twenty of them usually miscarried'.[25]

Soldiers, adventurers and settlers in both areas were also disheartened by the lack of social amenities, by the general absence of compatible female companionship, and by the failure of their chosen place of settlement to live up to the description provided in the propaganda literature.[26] Some officials also complained that their overseas service did not receive adequate recognition at home.[27] Occasionally in the immediate aftermath of a calamity, such as Hugh O'Neill's defeat of the English at the Yellow Ford or the Virginia massacre of 1622, individuals feared that the entire English presence would be wiped out by native forces, but these expres- sions were infrequent and settlers, for the most part, looked with con- fidence to the future even in the face of adversity.[28]

IV

Having thus outlined the two positions it remains to be explained why the minority factor that loomed so large in official thinking on colonization did not appear of any particular relevance to those engaged upon English overseas enterprise. The most fundamental difference was that English conquerors and colonists refused to accept that in an emergency they would have to depend on their own resources. Rather, they thought of colonies as a mere extension of England which would, if necessary, come to their assistance. This point was perhaps put most forcefully by Robert Payne who, in allaying the fears of would-be settlers in Munster against the possibility of Spanish attack, made it clear that he considered such an eventuality would be met by the combined resources of the two kingdoms, as is evident from his remark that 'you cannot view her majesties able subjects less than six million of men'.[29]

In this context it is important to recognize that adventurers in both Ireland and Virginia anticipated greatest difficulty from Spain, and expended far more energy in catering for the possibility of Spanish invasion than in defending themselves against the prospect of attack from the neighbours whom they had disturbed.[30] Thus the colonists, unlike the officials in England, saw the principal threat to their security as coming from outside rather than from within the country of settlement. Their perception of this matter was different from that of their mentors in England because they had the utmost contempt for the political organization and military capacity of their local adversaries. Throughout the sixteenth century the English in Ireland derided the military efforts of the Gaelic Irish, and attributed the few successes that they recorded to skills that their leaders or soldiers had acquired from the English, or to foreign assistance.[31] Similarly in the case of Virginia, Henry Spelman who had lived among the Indians for some years reported that 'as for armour or discipline in the war the[y] have not any'. This opinion was endorsed by the missionary Alexander Whitaker who described the Indians as 'a people to be feared of those that come unto them without defensive armour, but otherwise faint-hearted . . . and easy to be subdued'. Having convinced themselves of the military ineptitude of their adversaries, the adventurers were satisfied that, relatively few as they were, they could overawe them and 'become masters of their country . . . which might with few hands employed about nothing else be in short time brought to pass'.[32] Where officials in England cited historical precedent to suggest that small numbers of Englishmen would be in danger of total overthrow unless they followed strict rules, those in the colonies were able to counter by reference to Roman colonizing experience, to the Norman conquest of Ireland, to the achievements of the Spaniards in Mexico and Peru and to their own recent success.[33]

The settlers' confidence that backsliding would not occur and that the more highly developed culture would inevitably prevail was also justified both by historical precedent and by reference to their own observation and experience. The Romans, it was thought, had not only subdued the ancient Britons but had taught them 'to know the powerful discourse of divine reason (which makes us only men and distinguishes us from beasts)'.[34] English adventurers in Ireland and Virginia were agreed that the native inhabitants, for the most part, lived in a beastly condition, but they stated themselves to be convinced that once dominance was established the civilizing and uplifting process would follow. The barbarism of the native inhabitants was usually attributed to particular elements within the alien culture – Gaelic chieftains or Indian priests – but once these were forcefully removed, it was argued, there was considerable hope of civilizing the majority who were thought 'generally very loving and gentle . . . [and] are easy to be brought to good, and would fayne embrace a better condition'.[35] Even in their state of barbarism glimmerings of light were detected, as when William Strachey, in asserting that force was required to amend the 'horrible heathenishes' of the Indians, marvelled at 'how religious and manly' were 'these simple and innocent people . . . kneeling when we kneel, and lifting up their hands and eyes when we pray, not so docible [educable] as willing to receive our customs, herein like raised and unblotted tables apt to receive what form, so ever shall be first drawn thereon'.[36]

A few among the colonists (such as the planter William Herbert as well as archbishops Thomas Lancaster and John Long in Ireland, and John Rolfe and George Thorpe in Virginia) were so assured of the inevitable success of the superior culture that they hoped that good example, preaching and instruction would alone be sufficient to lure the natives from their alleged barbarism. These humanitarians were supported by the majority in advocating the instruction of native children who would be removed from their barbaric environment; but they were unique in that they conceived as possible the mass conversion of barbarians by developing their natural reason and thus leading them to an appreciation of revealed truth. Both Herbert and Thorpe attributed lack of progress in the matter of conversion to the hardness of heart of the English settlers who were 'not so charitable to them as Christians ought to be'.[37] Thorpe himself sought 'to gratify them [the Indians] in all things, for the winning of them with degrees', and he thought it best to begin by introducing their kings to the material benefits of the superior civilization, thus exposing them to 'the book of the world as being nearest to their sense'. Having entered into discourse with one chieftain, Opechancanough, Thorpe found 'that he had more motions of religion in him than could be imagined in so great blindness, for he willingly acknowledged that theirs was not the right way, desiring to be instructed in ours'.[38]

Those, like Thorpe, who were convinced that example and persuasion alone were sufficient to effect the conversion of barbarians (and others when expediency dictated it), were much addicted to extending the symbols of civility to the ruling segment of the alien society. Thorpe was happy to see Indian chiefs 'more and more to affect English fashions', and thought they would be 'much allured to affect us by gifts if the company would be pleased to send something in matter of apparel and household stuff'. As part of his educational programme Thorpe provided King Powhatan with an English-style house, and the settlers were amused by Powhatan's amazement with the lock and key 'as locking and unlocking his door an hundred times a day, he thought no device in all the world was comparable to it'.[39] The English in Virginia also contrived to have Powhatan and other Indian chiefs submit 'themselves and their lands' to the English monarch, and Powhatan was offered 'a copper crown as vassal of King James'. This episode illustrates the childish simplicity that the English attributed even to the rulers of American Indian society. Powhatan was first presented with gifts of a basin, ewer, bed and furniture for his house, and these having been put on display, 'his scarlet cloak and apparel (with much ado) [was] put on him ... but a foul trouble there was to make him kneel to receive his crown. He neither knowing the majesty nor meaning of a crown, endured so many persuasions, examples and instructions as tired them all.'[40]

The enactment of this pageant is of course reminiscent of much of what had previously occurred during the Elizabethan conquest of Ireland. The submission of Indian chieftains to King James, the efforts to persuade Indians to give over their children for upbringing among the English, and the sending of some of these children to England for education, all have parallels in Ireland. Likewise there were innumerable examples of English officials presenting robes, chains, jewellery and plate – items which they themselves referred to as 'trifles' – to Gaelic chieftains in the hope that these would elicit a loyal response. Neither were the wives of lords and chieftains neglected, and English officials forwarded regular requests to Queen Elizabeth asking her to bestow on such women 'some cast suit of apparel from her highness'. Towards the end of the sixteenth century, the emphasis was placed more on the presentation of portraits of Queen Elizabeth – sometimes of doubtful provenance – in the hope that her image would kindle a loyal response in the breasts of simple-minded barbarians.[41]

The English in Ireland also used devices from Gaelic institutional life to symbolize their own ascendancy. Lord Deputy Sidney came by the knowledge that the O'Molloys had, centuries before, acted as traditional standard-bearers to the *Árd-ri* (High-King) and thereafter one of the O'Molloys was kept on the government pay roll as standard-bearer to the lord deputy. In similar fashion Sir John Perrott had Turlough Luineach O'Neill, at the parliament of 1585 and 'other times', carry 'her Majesties sword before me ... when before he had held his sword many times against her Majesties forces'; Perrott also gave 'money to rhymers to set forth her Majesties most worthy praises'.[42] It might be argued that resort to such stratagems was an indication of weakness rather than strength, but either way they constitute evidence that English colonists and officers in Ireland and Virginia thought themselves to be dealing with an opposition totally lacking in political sophistication. Since they were thus effectively demonstrating that the leaders of the Gaelic Irish and the American Indians were as credulous as the poorer and unlettered elements in England, this in itself was sufficient argument that the superior culture would inevitably prevail.

This description indicates that adventurers and settlers in Ireland and Virginia were, as J. H. Elliott has said of the Spaniards in Mexico, 'from the moment of arrival, involved in a process of self-discovery, and they were developing a historical past which both enabled them to develop a sense of present identity and look with confidence to the future'.[43] They were unable to accept the English official view of them as an embattled minority because to have done so would have implied that they were likely to remain in that position for a long time to come, and even suggested that when the uplifting process had taken place there was no guarantee that they, or their descendants, would be in the dominant social position to which they aspired. Even more fundamental was the recognition by the more perceptive ones that they did not command the economic resources necessary for erecting the types of settlement favoured by the English officials. Consequently they were forced to offer some rationalization for attempting to introduce dispersed settlement among a more numerous population.

It was well recognized by Englishmen, both at home and abroad, that there were two forms of colonization possible in a country that was previously inhabited. One allowed for the possibility of Englishmen being substituted for the indigenous ruling elite and retaining the subservient population as a workforce, while the other required a total clearance of the native population and the introduction of a completely English society to take its place.[44] The officials in England favoured the latter of these two possible courses, while the adventurers and colonists favoured, or at least attempted, the former. In the case of Ireland, when Sir Arthur Chichester was asked why he himself was not an undertaker in Ulster he responded 'that to build castles and forts was chargeable, neither then if there should be a manor erected with twenty or forty tenants, would they and it secure their goods'.[45] Captain John Smith verbalized the same response for the Virginian settlers when he observed that 'it is much better to help to plant a country than unplant it and then replant it'. The Spaniards had, he claimed, no option but to pursue the latter course in the West Indies where the Indians 'were in such multitudes', but such stern measures were not called for in Virginia where the Indians, being 'such a few and so dispersed, it were nothing in short time to bring them to labour and obedience'.[46] In pursuing this course of action against the wishes of the authorities in England, the adventurers were forced to ignore the fact that they were in a small minority, or at least discount the dangers which English officials claimed to be inherent in such a position.

V

Once the English in Ireland and Virginia had satisfied themselves that they were dealing with barbarians, they were unable to conceive of themselves as a minority group. To have done so would have implied that they were competing for power and privilege with a majority, and such competition was unthinkable with any other than social and cultural equals. This essential point is borne out by the Irish experience in the sixteenth century, when the New English had to some extent seen themselves as a disadvantaged minority, but in relation to the Old English within the Pale rather than to the far more numerous Gaelic and Gaelicized element without.

Throughout the sixteenth century English-born officials in Dublin complained repeatedly that they were unable to fulfil the duties of their office, either because of non-cooperation from the Irish-born officials, or because of threats of recrimination should they disclose any of the corrupt practices that they claimed were prevalent.[47] Those English who had acquired property within the Pale claimed that they were being discriminated against both by judges and juries, and could not get fair trial either at the local or the central courts. Allegations were made that they suffered from the hostility of their neighbours, who made this manifest on the occasion of raids when 'there was neither cry made by any of the country, nor any man of this country birth that came to their rescue'.[48] One even complained that discrimination was such that all Irish lawyers refused to plead his case, and it was generally agreed that, without an English-born chancellor who would be able to redress their grievances, 'it were but folly for any English man inhabiting here to have matter in question in the laws of their realm'.[49] On the higher political level it was seen that they were again disadvantaged because 'the number of the English councillors is far less than that of the Irish', and the situation in parliament was even worse since all attempts to introduce English-born members were opposed on technical grounds.[50] The most fundamental grievance of the New English was that, although a political and patronage system, comprehensible in English terms, existed in Ireland, they were excluded from it.[51]

Various remedies for their plight were advanced by the New English over the years, but each had its shortcomings. It was generally accepted, both in England and among English-born officials in Ireland, that judicial and administrative posts should fall to Englishmen as vacancies occurred, thus guaranteeing the New English community fairer treatment in the law courts, and simultaneously making available men suited for service as councillors. Service in Ireland had, however, few attractions for successful lawyers in England, and the problem of maintaining an English-born chancellor was resolved only by having a bishop of the established church serve in a dual capacity.

Another solution, favoured by most of the English in Ireland, was the resolute pursuance of a forceful policy, in complete disregard of the wishes of the Old English community, aimed at excluding from office all but committed Protestants. In the event of this giving rise to treasons and conspiracies it was recommended that the offenders be punished with the full rigour of the law.[52] However, when stern action was resorted to, the more usual response of the Old English was not to rebel, but to send representatives to voice their grievances in England. Successive delegations proved they could argue their case persuasively in constitutional terms and impress the queen that it was her officials and not they who had acted unreasonably. Furthermore, from the 1570s onwards, the Old English exploited divisions among the English governing group to serve their purpose,[53] and throughout the sixteenth century they courted the favours of successive governors in Ireland. Thus the one occasion on which the New English in Ireland were truly disturbed was when, following the split between Sir John Perrott and Archbishop Loftus, the lord deputy gained support from the Irish-born councillors in Dublin and took to describing his adversaries in unflattering terms such as they had continuously used for depicting the Old English officials.[54] Even when in extreme circumstances the Old English resorted to unorthodox methods, such as the anonymous attack made in the 1560s on the governing establishment, this too caused disquiet among the New English because the authors displayed political sophistication in confining their attack to the advisers of the lord deputy while praising him for his personal integrity.[55]

It was this talent of the Old English to appear reasonable, accommodating, and concerned for the queen's interest that was seen to be their most effective weapon, and the English-born officials constantly sought to render it a blunt instrument by questioning their loyalty and very civility. The frustration of the New English was best expressed by Robert Rosyer who complained of the Old English 'what with their humble letters, their caddows, their hobbies, and their hawks, they by that means can make much friendship, more than any Englishman, with honest face will seem to do'.[56] This frustration stemmed from the fact that the generally cautious behaviour of the Old English left their adversaries with little concrete evidence with which to discredit them. The lawyer Andrew Trollope, for example, who came to Ireland predisposed to criticize the Old English, was clearly disconcerted when his purpose was thwarted by the hospitable treatment accorded to him on his arrival in Dublin. He could do nothing but argue that the private disposition of the Old English belied their gracious appearance. He alleged that even 'councillors and judges' of Irish birth, who 'would have the world ... think that they be good subjects', did not, 'if they can choose', attend church or receive communion, and no learned Englishman could advance himself in Ireland 'except he be the better friended or able to match them'.[57]

These examples serve to show that, ironically, the New English in Ireland feared civility more than barbarism and could conceive of themselves in a minority situation only when pitted against individuals as politically capable as themselves. The same held true when the New English contemplated reformation in religion. Here they saw the Catholic Old English as unmitigated opponents of Protestantism but, while refusing to concede that the Gaelic Irish were even Christian, they anticipated little difficulty in eventually converting them to the Protestant faith once political domination had been achieved.[58] Developing from this, however, was the prospect that as English authority was extended throughout the island, and as the Gaelic Irish were forced to choose between barbarism and civility, those of them who became civil, and hence politically conscious, would identify with the Old rather than the New English. Their fear of this development was so obvious that it was said of the New English that they did not really seek to reform Ireland 'least being civil her enemies would be the stronger and so grow to her Majesties greater detriment'.[59] Sir John Perrott professed himself bound by secular as well as moral considerations to reject this doctrine, but it was, seemingly, so widespread among his fellow countrymen in Ireland that he could refer to it as 'the old common objection ... whether it be safety or danger, good or ill, for England to have Ireland reformed, least growing to civility, government and strength, it should cast off the yoke, and be the more noisome and dangerous neighbour to England'.[60] The actual behaviour of Englishmen in sixteenth-century Ireland is proof of the ambivalence with which they regarded Gaelic and Gaelicized lords becoming civil. Sir Richard Bingham as president of Connacht had little fear of facing far superior numbers in battle, and seemed pessimistic for the future only when Richard Burke of Mayo challenged his rule on constitutional grounds and emphasized his own English lineage. Bingham retaliated by ridiculing Burke's claims to civility, and averred that his speech was no different 'from the railing of the collier against the lord mayor of London'. Nevertheless, Bingham was obviously disconcerted, most especially when the government in Dublin appointed commissioners to investigate Burke's allegations and grievances.[61]

It may well be the fear of the New English that political consciousness was beginning to glimmer in the primitive Irish mind that accounts for their morbid concern with the ritual mutilation performed by the Irish on the corpses of soldiers killed in battle – rituals that were quite obviously in direct imitation of English practice. Similar concern was voiced when the Irish, again in imitation of the English, expressed their defiance of English rule by resorting to symbolic actions, such as the assumption of Gaelic titles for the English ones that had been granted them, the discarding of English garments in favour of Gaelic attire, the smashing of English coats of armour, and the desecration of portraits of Queen Elizabeth.[62] There are also some suggestions from Virginia, particularly in the aftermath of the 1622 massacre, that the English thought the Indians would have been incapable of executing such a well-thought-out scheme were it not for the education they had acquired from themselves.[63] When, towards the end of the sixteenth century, the Gaelic resistance to the Elizabethan conquest became formidable, and actually threatened the survival of the state in Dublin, the New English attributed the greater effectiveness of their opponents to their having adopted English methods of warfare. It was consistent with this thinking that the English in Ireland generally refused to see Hugh O'Neill as a Gaelic chieftain but rather as a renegade English captain like Thomas Stukely or William Stanley, who owed everything he had to the queen's munificence and who had betrayed this trust in favour of a foreign potentate.[64]

While the outcome of the Elizabethan conquest of Ireland was generally satisfactory from the settlers' point of view, some believed that their worst fears had materialized, and that common opposition to themselves had forged an alliance between the Old English and Gaelic Irish. Some explained this confederacy exclusively in terms of expediency, but one observer attributed the fact that 'the ancient dislike and contempt' of the Old English for the Gaelic Irish was 'laid aside' at least in part to the advanced civility of 'the meer Irish [who] by their travel abroad are civilized, grown to be disciplined soldiers, scholars, politicians, and further instructed in points of religion, than accustomed'.[65] By then, however, the much dreaded alliance was of little concern to most of the New English who, as a result of plantations, had become the dominant elite in the kingdom, and were on the point of gaining a majority in parliament. Furthermore, by a rigid enforcement of the Oath of Supremacy, the New English had gained a virtual monopoly of posts in the judiciary, the administration and the council, and of patronage. The Old English, and those of the Gaelic Irish who made common cause with them, were still capable of soliciting support in England but the New English were more secure than they had been before and were clearly more confident of their political futures than they had been in the sixteenth century. Most important, however, was the fact that English law was everywhere in force and the established church introduced in all parts of the country, so there was reason to hope that the native population would eventually be drawn towards English culture, civility and religion.[66] The New English in Virginia had, after 1622, steered a different course, but there is evidence that some of the planters there relented this decision and regretted that they were not able to employ a native labour force, which would have been much less costly than the importation of indentured servants.[67]

VI

The thrust of this chapter has been to show that the concepts of minority and majority had little meaning for English settlers in either Ireland or Virginia, and no meaning whatever once a position of dominance had been achieved. Those in England who directed the operations had reason to believe that their early misgivings had been well founded, and they persisted in their view that dominance alone was little guarantee of security if their settlers were outnumbered by the native population. Throughout the first half of the seventeenth century settlers in Ireland and Virginia were persistently criticized by officials in England because they had failed to introduce the prescribed social order, because they had been corrupted by their environment, or because they had succumbed, to some extent, to the barbarism of their neighbours.[68] These criticisms were, however, never acknowledged by the settlers themselves, and in the case of Ireland, even after the 1641 rebellion, the settlers refused to concede that their being a minority living in dispersed settlements was primarily responsible for their overthrow.

This, in fact, was the fundamental point at issue between Richard Lawrence, representing the official English view, and Vincent Gookin, the Irish planter, when they debated the propriety of transplanting the native Irish population to Connacht. Lawrence, like the planters in Virginia after the 1622 massacre, advocated the virtual removal of the native population from three provinces 'as essential to the future peace and safety of the English interest there'. Instead of the dispersed order, which Lawrence condemned, he prescribed 'that the English inhabitants ... should live together in distinct plantations or colonies, separated from the Irish', and he would countenance no more than one fifth Irish in any one plantation. If this were adhered to, there was, he averred, nothing to fear from the native Irish because their success in 1641 had been made possible by the English 'promiscuous and scattered inhabiting amongst the Irish who were in all places far the greater number, and in most a hundred to one'.[69] Gookin, on the other hand, saw the rebellion as 'the provocation of the Divine Majesty by sins of the English' who, when the means had been available in peacetime, had failed to use their dominant position to introduce the native population to civility and Protestantism. The minority factor was, he claimed, totally irrelevant and he thought 'the Irish cohabiting with the English was a means probably to have quashed the rebellion'. Thus assured, he, like most of the existing planters, looked to a continuation of mixed settlement in the belief that 'we may safely taste the good of the Irish without fearing the ill'.[70]

This chapter has, hopefully, done something to explain the existence and survival into the 1650s of these two diametrically opposed perceptions, and in the process perhaps vindicated the view of R. C. Collingwood 'that the enlargement of historical knowledge comes about mainly through finding how to use as evidence this or that kind of perceived facts which historians have hitherto thought useless to them'.[71]

Notes

Research on this topic was made possible by the award, through An Bord Sco-laireachtaí Cómalairte, Dublin, of a Senior Fulbright–Hays Fellowship for the academic year 1974–5, and a grant from the Royal Irish Academy for 1976–7 under the exchange scheme arranged between themselves and the British Academy; a special word of thanks is due to the staff of the Public Record Office of Northern Ireland who were extremely generous in providing an extended loan of material on microfilm.

1 Cyril Falls, *Elizabeth's Irish Wars* (London, 1950), pp. 39, 56, 57, 61.

2 D. B. Quinn, 'The Munster Plantation: Problems and Opportunities', *Journal of the Cork Historical and Archaeological Society* LXXI (1966), pp. 19–41, especially p. 30.

3 The figure of 50,000 is arbitrary, based on the possibility of 30,000 settlers in Ulster, 15,000 in Munster, and scattered numbers throughout the country. This is based on the assumption that most settlers were young single men and this accounts for the discrepancy with the estimates cited in D. B. Quinn, 'The Munster Plantation' and M. Perceval-Maxwell, *The Scottish Migration to Ulster in the Reign of James I* (London, 1973). On the population of Ireland see T. W. Moody, F. X. Martin, F. J. Byrne (eds), *A New History of Ireland* III, *1534–1691* (Oxford, 1976), pp. 388–9; and the revision suggested in Nicholas Canny, 'Early Modern Ireland: an Appraisal Appraised', in *Irish Economic and Social History* IV (1977), pp. 63–5.

4 Edmund S. Morgan, *American Slavery, American Freedom: the Ordeal of Colonial Virginia* (New York, 1975), p. 136; Francis Jennings, *The Invasion of America: Indians, Colonialism, and the Cant of Conquest* (Chapel Hill, N.C., 1975), pp. 15–31; *Haklytus Posthumus, or Purchas his Pilgrimes* (Glasgow edn, 1906, referred to hereafter as Purchas, *Pilgrimes*) XIX, p. 222, marginal note.

5 Morgan, p. 101.

6 E. C. S., *The Government of Ireland ... under Sir John Perrot, 1584–8* (London, 1626), pp. 65–6.

7 'Notes and propositions for the reformation of Ireland ... as the substance of Sir Henry Sidney's own speeches brought together', June 1571 (PRO, S.P. 63/32/66); Ed. Tre[mayne] 'Undated book on the government of Ireland' (BL, Add. MS. 48015, f. 276).

8 Nicholas Canny, 'The Permissive Frontier: the Problem of Social Control in English Settlements in Ireland and Virginia, 1550–1650', in K. R. Andrews, N. P. Canny and P. E. H. Hair (eds), *The Westward Enterprise: the English in the Atlantic, Ireland and America, 1550–1650*   (Liverpool, 1978) pp. 17–44; 'Virginia's verger' in Purchas, *Pilgrimes* XIX, p. 236.

9 A. L. Beier, 'Vagrants and the Social Order in Elizabethan England' *Past and Present* no. 64 (1974), pp. 3–29; J. F. Pound and A. L. Beier, debate on the above, in *Past and Present* no. 7 (1976), 126–34.

10 Sir Thomas Gates *et al.*, petition to Virginia council, 1619 (PRO, 13/15/2, no. 247).

11 Privy council to Sir John Stowell *et al.*, 24 February 1586 (PRO, S.P. 63/122/80).

12 Canny, 'The Permissive Frontier', pp. 17–20.

13 Grant of the queen to the undertakers, 27 June 1586 (PRO, S.P. 63/124/95).

14 Act for planting of habitations in Munster, 21 December 1585 (PRO, S.P. 63/121/41).

15 Canny, 'The Permissive Frontier', pp. 39–42.

16 Fynes Moryson, 'The Commonwealth of Ireland', in C. L. Falkiner, *Illustrations of Irish History* (London, 1904), p. 298.

17 Nicholas Canny, *The Elizabethan Conquest of Ireland: a Pattern Established, 1565–76* (Hassocks, 1976), p. 119; Geoffrey Fenton to Burghley, 6 December 1583 (PRO, S.P. 63/106/4).

18 Fenton to Burghley, as above; this paper was unfortunately completed before K. O. Kupperman 'English Perceptions of Treachery: 1583–1640: the Case of the American "Savages"', *Historical Journal* XX (1977), pp. 263–87 appeared in print, but her paper supports many of the points being made here; see especially pp. 266–70.

19 *A New History of Ireland* III, pp. 187, 174–6; M. Perceval-Maxwell, *The Scottish Migration*, pp. 138–59, 184, 228; Quinn, pp. 36–8.

20 Arrearages due by Captain William Piers, 21 February 1580 (S.P. 63/73/53); 'Records of Carrickfergus as transcribed, 1785, by Richard Dobbs' (PRONI, Class T., 707), pp. 3, 5, 15; articles by Captain William Piers for the reformation of the north, 10 August 1581 (S.P. 63/85/7); Lord Deputy Grey to privy council, 12 August 1581 (S.P. 63/85/13).

21 Charges of Perrot and Bingham's reply, 2 June 1587 (PRO, S.P. 63/130/2, f. 9. r); Edward Whyte to privy council, 12 April 1582 (S.P. 63/91/24, f. 59, v); Malby's reply to above (S.P. 63/91/25, f. 64, v); Wallop to Walsingham, 15 May 1582 (PRO, S.P. 63/92/42); see also note of abuses done by Malby, July 1576 (S.P. 63/72/24).

22 Morgan, pp. 73–6.

23 George Sands to Sir Miles Sandys, 30 March 1623 in Susan Kingsbury (ed.), *The Records of the Virginia Company of London* (4 vols, Washington, 1906–35, referred to hereafter as *R.V.C.*) IV, pp. 70–72; Edward Waterhouse, 'A Declaration' in *R.V.C.* III, p. 550; *Travels and Works of Captain John Smith*, ed. Edward Arber and A. G. Bradley (Edinburgh, 1910), pp. 615–20; *Minutes of the Council and General Court of Colonial Virginia*, ed. H. R. J. McIllwaine (Richmond, 1924), p. 28.

24 Lord Justice Pelham to Burghley, 29 December 1579 (PRO, S.P. 63/70/68); St Leger to Fenton, 24 March 1582 (S.P. 63/91/23, i); Lord Deputy Grey to Walsingham, 18 July 1581 (S.P. 63/84/26).

25 Morgan, pp. 158–64; Richard Lawrence, *The Interest of England in the Irish Transplantation, Stated* (Dublin, 1655), p. 18.

26 George Percy, 'Observations', 1607 in L. G. Tyler (ed.), *Narratives of Early Virginia* (New York, 1907), p. 20; Henry Spelman to Sir Henry Spelman, 15 August 1615 (Oxford, Bodleian, Tanner MS., 74, ff. 49–51); letter to John Pory, 1619 in *Narratives of Early Virginia*, p. 286; George Thorpe to John Smyth, 19 December 1620 (*R.V.C.* III, pp. 417–18); Thomas Niccolls to Sir John Worsenholme, 2 April 1623 (*R.V.C.* IV, p. 231).

27 Edward Denny to Walsingham, 8 September 1580 (PRO, S.P. 63/76/18).

28 R. Dudley Edwards, *Ireland in the Age of the Tudors* (London, 1977), speaks, p. 166, of 'the sense of siege which had settled on' Dublin following the Yellow Ford; Edward Hill to Mr John Hill, 14 April 1623 (*R.V.C.* IV, p. 234); Captain John Smith also recalled the trauma of having lived 'neere 37 yeares [1597–1633] in the midst of wars, pestilence and famine, by which many an hundred thousand have died about me, and scarce five living of them [that] went first with me to Virginia', *Travels and Works of Smith*, p. 945.

29 Robert Payne, *A briefe description of Ireland* (London, 1590), p. 12; even a settler such as Richard Boyle in Munster who devoted considerable attention to defence against possible insurrection was concerned only to be in a position to defend his lands until English assistance would reach him; T. O. Ranger, *The Career*

of Richard Boyle first Earl of Cork in Ireland, 1588–1643 (D.Phil. thesis, Oxford, 1959), p. 124.

30 W. F. Craven, *The Dissolution of the Virginia Company* (reprint, Gloucester, Mass., 1964), p. 198; Fitzwilliam to Burghley, 1 May 1571 (Oxford, Carte MS., vol. 131, no. 101).

31 Sir Nicholas Malby thought 'that without the help of the English races the Irishry is not to be respected nor to be thought dangerous', to Walsingham, 31 August 1580 (PRO, S.P. 63/75/82).

32 Henry Spelman, 'Relation of Virginia' in *Travels and Works of Smith*, p. CXIII; Alexander Whitaker, *Good News from Virginia* (London, 1613), p. 40; L. B. Wright, *Elizabethans' America* (London, 1965), p. 221.

33 On the Romans see William Strachey, *The Historie of Travell into Virginia Britania* (London, 1612), ed. L. B. Wright and V. Freund (London, 1953), p. 25; on Norman precedent, *A Letter Sent to I.B.* (London, 1571) sig. B³; on the Spaniards, *Travels and Works of Smith*, pp. 600, 955; on recent spectacular successes Thomas Churchyard, *A Generall Rehersall of the Warres* (London, 1579), sig. Q⁴, and Fenton to Walsingham, 29 September 1586 (PRO, S.P. 63/125/32).

34 Strachey, p. 25; see also R.I., *Nova Brittannia* (London, 1609), in Peter Force (ed.), *Tracts and other Papers Relating Principally to the Origin, Settlement and Progress of the Colonies in North America* (Washington, 1836) I, p. 14.

35 Canny, *The Elizabethan Conquest*, pp. 116–36; R.I., *Nova Brittannia*, p. 11.

36 Strachey, p. 23.

37 Brendan Bradshaw, 'The Elizabethans and the Irish', *Studies* (spring, 1977), pp. 38–50; Lancaster to Walsingham, 12 October 1580 (S.P. 63/77/29); Long to Walsingham, 20 January 1585 (S.P. 63/114/39); John Rolfe, 'A true relation of the state of Virginia (1616–17)', BL, Royal 18.A, XI, ff. 10–10ʳ; Rolfe to Edwin Sandys, 8 June 1617 (*R.V.C.* III, pp. 70–73); George Thorpe and John Pory to Sir Edwin Sandys, 15 May 1621 (*R.V.C.* III, pp. 70–73; George Thorpe and John Pory to Sir Edwin Sandys, 15 May 1621 (*R.V.C.* III, pp. 446–7).

38 Letter of Thorpe and Pory, as above; Edward Waterhouse, 'A Declaration' in *R.V.C.* III, p. 552; *Travels and Works of Smith*, p. 565.

39 Edward Waterhouse, 'A Declaration' in *R.V.C.* III, p. 552.

40 Virginia's Verger' in Purchas, *Pilgrimes* XIX, pp. 228–9; Captain John Smith disapproved of this 'stately kind of soliciting' because it made Powhatan 'much overvalue himself', *Travels and Works of Smith*, p. 121.

41 'Sidney's Memoir', in *Ulster Journal of Archaeology*, first series, VI (1858), p. 187; Nicholas Bagenall to Walsingham, 7 April 1581 (S.P. 63/82/18); Perrott to Burghley, 28 December 1590 (PRO, S.P. 12/234/67); *Cal. S.P. Ire., 1588–92*, p. 273.

42 Hugh O'Molloy to Burghley, December 1585 (PRO, S.P. 63/121/34); Perrott to Burghley, 28 December 1590 (PRO, S.P. 12/234/65); *The Life, Deedes and Death of Sir John Perrott* (London, 1728), p. 312; Englishmen also asserted their supremacy by destroying religious and secular objects of symbolic importance to the Irish.

43 J. H. Elliott, 'The Triumph of the Virgin of Guadalupe', *New York Review of Books* XXIX, no. 9 (26 May 1977), pp. 28–30.

44 Canny, *The Elizabethan Conquest*, p. 74.

45 Thomas Blenerhasset, *A Direction for the Plantation in Ulster* (London, 1610) sig. A3ᵛ.

46 *Travels and Works of Smith*, p. 955.

47 See Fitzwilliam to Burghley, 23 March 1572 (Oxford, Bodleian, Carte MSS.,

vol. 57, no. 157, fol. 324) where he remarks that the office of rembrancer is not fit for 'such as will be corrupted or afraid of Ireland men's displeasure'.

48 Loftus and Wallop to privy council, 6 October 1581 (PRO, S.P. 63/86/10); Gerrard to Walsingham, 4 March 1579 (S.P. 63/66/1).

49 *Life of Peter Carew*, in *Cal Carew Mss., 1515–74*, p. XCIX; Mathew King to Cecil, 7 May 1562 (PRO, S.P. 63/6/7).

50 Fenton to Walsingham, 6 Aug. 1582 (PRO, S.P. 63/94/88); Brian Farrell, *The Irish Parliamentary Tradition* (Dublin, 1973), pp. 68–101 for studies by Brendan Bradshaw and Hugh Kearney on the Irish parliament during the early modern period.

51 See for example Wallop to Walsingham, 29 July 1582 (PRO, S.P. 63/100/55).

52 Wallop to Walsingham, 6 March 1583 (PRO, S.P. 63/100/5).

53 See Walsingham to Sidney, 10 June 1577, in Arthur Collins (ed.), *Letters and Memorials of State* (London, 1746) I, p. 193, where the secretary warns the lord deputy of the influence of Ormond at court.

54 Perrott was alleged to have said in 1586 'What care I for the council? They are all of them but a sort of beggers and squibbs, puppies, dogs, dunghill churls – yea even the proudest of them came hither with their hose patched on the heels,' *Cal. S.P. Irel., 1586–8*, p. 212.

55 Lord deputy and council to privy council 31 January 1572 (PRO, S.P. 63/35/11), with enclosure signed Thom Troth and John Justifier.

56 Robert Rosyer to Burghley, 25 September 1586 (*Cal. S.P. Ire., 1586–8*, p. 155).

57 Andrew Trollope to Walsingham, 12 September 1585 (PRO, S.P. 63/85/39).

58 Canny, *The Elizabethan Conquest*, pp. 123–5; 'Irish Ecclesiastical Affairs, 1619' in Grosart (ed.), *Lismore Papers*, 2nd series, II, p. 201.

59 'The efficient and accidental impediments of the civility of Ireland', 1579 (PRO, S.P. 63/70/82).

60 E.C.S., *The Government of Ireland under Sir John Perrot*, sigs D–D².

61 *Cal. S.P. Irel., 1588–92*, pp. 177, 271.

62 Canny, *The Elizabethan Conquest*, pp. 143–5; *Cal. S.P. Irel., 1588–92*, pp. 142–3.

63 Edward Waterhouse 'A Declaration' in *R.V.C.* III, 541–71; note also the concern of the English when King Powhatan, no longer impressed with his gift, refused to negotiate further 'unless they brought him a coach and three horses, for he had understood by the Indians which were in England, how such was the state of great werowances and lords in England to ride and visit other great men,' Purchas, *Pilgrimes* XVIII, p. 65.

64 See, for instance, the comment on O'Neill in E.C.S., *The Government of Ireland under Sir John Perrot*, p. 63, and Thomas Gainsford, *The True, Exemplary, and Remarkable History of the Earle of Tirone* (London, 1619).

65 'A Discourse of the Present State of Ireland, 1614' in *Desiderata Curiosa Hibernica* (2 vols, Dublin, 1722) I, pp. 430–31.

66 It is not being denied that individuals felt threatened by their being outnumbered so heavily – see Mr Stowell to Laurence Parsons, 17 April 1619 (NLI, Lismore MSS 13, 237 (1)) where he speaks of being 'so oppressed on every side with evil neighbours'.

67 See *Minutes of the Council and General Court*, 11 October 1627, p. 155.

68 See Canny, 'The Permissive Frontier', pp. 42–4.

69 Richard Lawrence, *The Interest of England in the Irish Transplantation, Stated*, (Dublin, 1655), pp. 16–18; for the similarity with Virginia, post-1622, see Francis Wyatt's statement, soon after the massacre, 'our first work is expulsion of the savages to gain the free range of the country for increase of cattle, swine & c

which will more than restore us, for it is infinitely better to have no heathen among us' (BL Wyatt MS., no. 3).

70 Vincent Gookin, *The Author and Case of Transplanting ... Vindicated* (London, 1655), pp. 38, 40–41.

71 R. G. Collingwood, *The Idea of History* (Oxford, 1946), p. 271.

5

A contrast in crises: southern Irish Protestantism, 1820–43 and 1885–1910

Ian d'Alton

The means by which, in an increasingly democratic society, a dominant minority comes to terms with the end of its ascendancy is of interest to students of minority problems. Irish Protestantism, in its manifestation in the southern areas of that island, offers an illustration of a gradual transformation from dominant to non-dominant status. Though its peak of unfettered power had passed, in 1800 the Protestant nation still held sway over all facets of life in the island. As one observer wrote, 'it is socially proud because it has all the landed property of the country'.[1] One hundred and twenty years later its political philosophy was in ruins, its position in the country no longer pre-eminent. Despite this the Protestant community in southern Ireland has survived – its religious institutions free, the economic position of its adherents quite intact. And since 1920 the Protestant and Catholic nations in what is now the Irish Republic have tended to grow closer together. The foundations of this present assimilation were laid during the nineteenth century.

The purpose of this chapter is to describe how, and offer an explanation why, this movement should have occurred. It draws for illustration largely on the experience of Protestantism in one region of southern Ireland since it is felt that a more coherent and real image emerges thereby. The southern Irish Protestant tended to have been excessively localized in his political outlook and social and economic behaviour. The area chosen, then, is Cork city and county. These administrative units covered about 2,800 square miles of contrasting countryside, desolate mountain areas and an extensive sea coast. There were numerous small towns in the county; but the main quasi-industrial base was in the city of Cork – the island's second city – which had a population of some 90,000 in the early nineteenth century.[2]

I

The population pattern in the nineteenth century, produced in the main by Elizabethan plantations and inflows of Cromwellian ex-soldiers, is a starting point for any descriptive analysis of the minority. Its numerical inferiority to southern Catholicism was clearly recognized long before the early nineteenth-century censuses definitely established that fact. But that did not matter. As long as landed property essentially represented power complacency and indifference were features of Protestant opinion. Not so on the other side of the sectarian divide. If a Roman Catholic bishop of Cork thought that 'independent of every other consideration, the ascertaining of the population ... is a matter of great curiosity', one of his parish priests was in no doubt that 'not of much less importance that the number of Catholics be known, than that the number of Protestants be strictly ascertained'.[3] When Thomas Newenham established in the 1810s that Protestants were fewer in Cork than hitherto imagined, it was an unpalatable revelation and even dangerous.[4] In an age when memories of the Irish rebellion of 1798 and the French Revolution were still fresh, over-reaction to agrarian agitation and resistance to tithes could be reinforced by such knowledge.[5]

It should be realized that the Protestant population was not spread smoothly over the southern landscape. The remote reasons for this are rooted in the sixteenth and seventeenth centuries. In the nineteenth an uneven spread was a significant determinant of the level and type of social and political activity. Comparative densities give some indication of the differences. In Cork county, for instance, the average ranged from one Protestant to every 1,500 acres in the mountainous areas of the northwest, to densities ten times as great in the southwest. In the northern third of the county Protestants formed little more than 2 per cent of the total population in the 1830s, in the eastern third about 4 per cent, and in the southwest, 16–27 per cent. Of the total *Protestant* population of the county in 1834 one tenth was resident in the northern third, one third in the eastern third, and the remainder in the southwestern third.[6] This would lend support to an assumption that a greater level of political activity and more social confidence might be discovered in the last area. It was certainly no coincidence that edginess amongst Protestants was at its most obvious in the sparsely populated and isolated areas of northwest Cork in the 1820s and 1830s.[7]

Another significant social feature of southern Protestantism was that it was not composed entirely of, nor completely dominated by, the rural landowning classes. It often encompassed entities that were different from and even hostile to the rural landed connection. Within Cork county in 1834 only about one quarter of Protestant families belonged to the substantial landed classes. In southwest Cork there were large numbers of Anglican and Methodist tenant farmers. Of the small towns perhaps Bandon, with its idiosyncratic folk Protestantism close to the northern Irish model, is best known. In the town of Kinsale there subsisted a small, inbred community of Protestant fishermen that brooked little interference with its strange ways.[8] In the other small towns there lived and worked Protestant merchants, shopkeepers and professional men. The largest cohesive non-landed Protestant group in the county was found in Cork city. It was populous (about 12,000 in 1834), compact and possessed a complete class structure. Two groups within this structure should be mentioned – the run-down merchant families who controlled the municipal corporation in their own economic interests; and the poor freemen – about 800 Protestants in the lower unskilled occupations – who relied on the corporation for charity and upon whom that body depended for electoral purposes.[9]

Whatever the composition of the putative rank and file, the leadership of political and social fashion in early nineteenth-century Ireland was vested securely in the landed classes. And because it was rarely threatened directly by the growth of Catholic economic power in that period, landed ascendancy could afford the luxuries of political infighting and social squabbling. Not all members of the urban Protestant group were as insensitive to the changes in the political, social and economic balances following the post-Napoleonic war depression. In many respects urban Protestantism was in the van of political experiment and innovation at that time. For instance, while from the Act of Union to 1818 politics in Cork city faithfully reflected the state of affairs in the country at large, in the election held in the latter year the basis of political debate underwent a change. The aristocratic county families who had controlled city politics for decades found their hegemony questioned by a Protestant political party of merchant families. 'The scandalous coalition of the nobles, forcing into the heart of the city, county speculations' was roundly denounced.[10] The 1818 election marked the start of a period of political uncertainty which lasted until 1830. During this era there was an attempt to create a polity of rising men of business to replace what was seen as the dead hand of familial landed aristocracy. The appeal was to the merchants – whig and tory. It failed. The centrifugal forces of sectarian politics were too strong to allow a party political system based on dissimilar economic developments to arise.

The period, then, was characterized by a concentration on the aristocratic tinkering with city politics, the taming of the city freemen (many of whom belonged to the rural landed classes) by the city Protestant political leadership, and ultimately by the creation of a strong tory Protestant voting base.[11] This latter was achieved by an appeal from the leadership to the Protestant bourgeoisie on quasi-class grounds and to the poorer freemen on a ticket of Protestant evangelism.

It is suggested that, because of urban Protestantism's more intimate social and economic contacts with Catholicism at similar class levels, its adjustment to changes in the political as well as the socio-economic climate was more measured and realistic than that of rural landed society. Faced with a priest-organized revolt in the 1820s against traditional forms of political control, the reaction of the landed classes – pale imitations of O'Connellism in the county Brunswick Clubs before 1830 and in the national Protestant Conservative Society after 1832 – was ineffective. By and large the gentry and aristocracy, save those like the duke of Devonshire and Lord Kingston, did not have the nerve to operate a system of unashamed political oppression.[12]

Other means of politically controlling Protestants were few. Any attempt to use the established church in the manner in which O'Connell used the Catholic would have been stoutly resisted. In the first place the fact that the local clergy were drawn mainly from the middle and lower Protestant social groups precluded their exerting much decisive influence within local politics. In the second the church held in a sometimes fragile unity a Protestantism that was deeply and fundamentally divided on the question of

Catholic emancipation. After 1829 circumstances were somewhat different; and the church under attack provided a powerful rallying point for all political opinions. The Irish church in this period proved an important social prop for southern Irish Protestantism. It was an avenue to employment; it symbolized the minority's dominant position and was something to defend; and its temporal organization, excessively decentralized, bolstered the localism inherent in southern Protestant society – a society that was not particularly spiritually minded, it would seem. Even during the heyday of the evangelical revival, church attendances were low, if vestry minute books are to be believed. The religious revival can be seen at its most effective among the urban community and those church members lower on the social scale. These were the people – minor gentry, farmers, shopkeepers – who consistently attended vestry meetings and became churchwardens, overseers of Sunday morality and the bastions of the Bible societies.[13] It seems that only when prestige or patronage was involved – for instance in the allocation of pews or dispensing of livings – did the upper strata appear to take any more than a cursory interest in the temporal or spiritual affairs of the church.[14]

If the personnel and policies of the established church at a local level merged indistinguishably into the general Protestant social structure, the same might be said of Protestant Dissent. Largely an urban phenomenon in southern Ireland, early on Dissenters seemed anxious not to disrupt a mutual alliance against encroaching Catholic economic power. Both Anglican and Dissenter were fearful of the rise of urban democracy under O'Connell. By 1841 in Cork the Protestant *non*-tory was a rare political animal.[15]

The secret of maintaining group morale in rural areas in which the Protestant population was scattered and isolated was not discovered in this period. As all leaders and little rank and file, county Protestant society found it extremely difficult to effect a useful and viable political organization. Ad hoc bodies to meet particular needs, or to fight specific elections were all that could be managed. Again, the leaders of county society maintained their social and political hegemony by virtue of their possession of land. In the Irish context landed society began to lose its grip on the tenants' votes in the 1820s. To fall back on Protestant voters was a necessary and natural development. But such voters accounted for only a small proportion of the total. The arithmetic was simple; the conclusions, for the landed classes, were devastating. The position within the larger urban areas was strikingly different. In Cork city, for instance, there existed a large, compact body of Protestants – in prospect all voting on the same side. Divided before 1829 by warring aristocratic factions and differing views on Catholic emancipation, that body became much more united in the 1830s and 1840s. Two gentlemen, Joseph Leycester and James Chatterton, were mainly responsible. The pair represented a coalition of the differing social and political strands within city Protestantism; they set the pattern for the gradual development of a Protestant political party. Leycester typified city commerce, high church toryism and the power of the municipal corporation. Chatterton came of an old and respected suburban liberal family, with a part-landed, part-army background. Together they contested parliamentary elections in Cork city from 1835, the double-seat constituency allowing the coalition to function satisfactorily.[16] Their creation of a political Protestantism was aided by two organizations – the Orange Order and the Protestant Operative Association. The latter was a society of working-class Protestants which surfaced in Cork in the 1830s. It represented a political manifestation of the current evangelical revival and offered evidence that city political Protestantism was not just an unstable overlay on a slippery floor of Roman Catholic votes.[17]

Of greater significance was the Orange Order. Attention has been concentrated on the Order's more spectacular northern Irish manifestation. The Order in the south, however, acted as a particularly important buttress to group morale during the 1820s and 1830s. Before 1830, Orangeism in Cork was composed of two principal elements. The first, the folk Orangeism of places like Bandon, was rare in the south. In that town each July the Battle of the Boyne was re-enacted; and the custom of a sham fight lasted until 1809. The planting of trees decorated with paintings of King William continued until the 1830s. The practice of holding special church services remained until the mid-century at least. In essence – as a nineteenth-century observer pointed out – Orangeism as a folk cult, as a social comfort to a minority group and as an affirmation of community roots, was considered unexceptional and was even tolerated to a peculiar degree by local Catholics.[18]

The second element was found in the larger urban areas. In Cork city the lodges were composed of lower-middle-class elements with strong attachments to the dominant parties within the unreformed municipal corporation. Before 1832 the lodges were little more than drinking clubs; as in Bandon, they fulfilled a purely social need. And because of the social composition of the membership the Order was not 'respectable' in the Cork city of the 1820s. One result may have been that within the lodges could be found the nucleus of the anti-aristocratic party in the city. Another was that the lodges were not accepted as the channel through which ultra-Protestant opinions were expressed. It is of interest to observe that when it was desired to set up an anti-Catholic emancipation movement in Cork in 1827 the existing Orange institutions were not utilized.[19]

A distinct change took place in the character of the southern Order after 1832. In the words of a deputy grand treasurer of the Grand Lodge of Ireland, 'the general feeling there was, that the Orange institution was the best and most effectual means of checking it [repeal], and about 120 gentlemen of the first rank in the country became members of the Grand Lodge'.[20]

In Cork this acceptance of the Order was symbolized by the formal adherence of the county tory leader, Lord Bandon, in 1834. The pre-1834 essentials of the lodges themselves seem to have remained unchanged by the sudden influx of gentility; but there was a new spirit of confidence and a willingness to stand up and be counted, exemplified by the extensive courting of publicity in local Protestant newspapers in the 1830s.[21] These changes in Orangeism were indicative of an unconscious beginning of adaptation to a minority position. The role of the Order was seen as defensive, its object the maintenance of morale. Orangeism, it was said, stood for 'simply bringing together so many Protestants, for ... the indulgence of conference and companionship ... so comforting to Protestants at such a season of gloom and trouble – and so auspicious of Protestant resource'.[22]

Parliamentary electoral politics were only the tip of the iceberg as far as members of county Protestant society was concerned. Of much greater importance was their local position – as magistrates and grand jurors, and as members of corporations, boards of guardians and numerous voluntary organizations. In this local sphere, armed with a generally superior education, southern Protestants most fiercely attempted to maintain their power and prestige throughout the period. There were some setbacks, notably in the unfettered administration of justice and in the control of the corporations; but in general there was no question of them becoming irrelevant to the mainstream of Irish life, or even of losing a substantial part of their power at local level.

The watershed in the political development of southern Protestantism came in the period from 1828 to 1832. Catholic emancipation proved at once to be a defeat and at the same time a victory for those who were intent upon building a political credo on Protestantism. It is hardly necessary to elaborate upon the aspect of defeat. The victory, though, even if camouflaged, was significant. The question of emancipation had divided vertically the body of Protestants on a fundamental principle. For all its defects, the passage of the Act in 1829 removed the cause of that division. Similarly, the Irish Parliamentary Reform Act released much ultra-Protestant sentiment from the political bondage of borough proprietors and the arrangements of whig and tory landed aristocracy.[23] In such a manner did many of the so-called 'reform' measures of the 1830s ease the transition from ascendancy power to minority participation. As southern Protestants began to congregate on the same side of the political fence in the late 1820s and 1830s they had perforce to come to terms with the realization that they must take sides in a permanent minority grouping. As the century progressed the role of the landed classes as the dominant national political force was, in many ways, reduced; but a healthier spirit of competition for representative positions within the Protestant side of municipal, local and parliamentary politics grew up. Municipal reform in 1841, while depriving a small unrepresentative clique of economic power and privilege, was the mechanism by which Cork city political Protestantism was infused with a new spirit. The annual elections prescribed by the Irish Municipal Reform Act ensured that a near-permanent political organization not based on patronage had to be created and maintained.[24] That feature – notably lacking in Cork before 1841 – also ensured that a debate regarding the nature and direction of urban Protestantism remained active and continuous.

The reformist measures and the consequent rise of Catholic political power changed somewhat the direction of political Protestantism. Activists felt freer to pursue a policy of Protestantism as the foundation for a trinity of individual moral worth, collective social virtue and public stability. The drive towards a Protestant unity continued. Commencing in the 1830s there was a conscious effort by the tory gentry to attract their whig counterparts into a firm political partnership. Whig and tory, after all, were united in their belief in the moral primacy of the landed classes. Their brand of localism, based on complex patterns of status, landownership, patronage and kinship, was uniform. Emancipation and parliamentary reform had divided them: but in an atmosphere of attacks upon the established church and the body politic in the 1830s a steady, if slow, drift of whigs into the tory camp took place.[25]

Despite the indications that southern Irish politics were setting firmly into a majority–minority mould, based on an essentially sectarian division, another basis for political cooperation was being tentatively canvassed. The first elections held under the provisions of the Irish Municipal Reform Act were contested by a party calling itself Conservative and putting forward policies in Cork that hardly appealed to a sectarian electorate. That party saw itself as the custodian of the municipal purse, its role that of watchdog on behalf of the ratepayers. The impetus for its formation came from within the Peelite wing of the Protestant political party in the city. This led the Catholic *Cork Examiner* newspaper to remark in 1842: 'We are at a loss to understand now what conservatism means. . . . Do they mean to follow out the conservatism of Peel? Why, Peel is a free trader and reformer, and has cut dead all the fanatic followers of old toryism and all the stupid worshippers of things as they are.'

Perhaps this should be viewed as a sign of political maturity among urban Protestants. As early as 1841 they were making a distinction, perhaps not publicly, between occupying a permanent minority position at a local level and being part of a larger United Kingdom majority. As long as that latter majority supported them, a sense of group confidence remained. To make the most of their influence and to safeguard their existing powers and privileges was the object. That this could be achieved by concentrating on economic issues within local politics while at the same time espousing a sectarian toryism for dealing with the national question did not imply any hypocrisy or conflict of ways and means.[26]

II

For Irish Protestants, the awareness of a minority position and an increasing impatience and indifference demonstrated by government and public opinion in Britain created a crisis of morale in the period 1820–40. It was a crisis from which southern Irish Protestantism appeared to emerge strengthened. From 1825 to 1835 virtually every facet of Protestant ascendancy came under public and parliamentary scrutiny. It responded by an attempt at the creation of a political party that used a profession of religious belief as its basic tenet and that had as its professed object the maintenance of English government in Ireland. This was a shorthand way of expressing, on the part of the landed rural classes, the continuation of their local economic and social structure and on the part of urban Protestants, a stable local economic climate and mercantile hegemony.

While in the 1820s the maintenance of the union between the two kingdoms and the continuation of Protestant power and privilege might have seemed inextricably bound together, already by the late 1830s the proposition was not at all self-evident. Events between the Famine and the 1880s served to emphasize this point. The pattern of history from the mid-century – the handling of the Famine itself, its economic consequences for the landed classes, the urban–rural split over free trade, disestablishment of the Irish church, Gladstone's tinkering with land law and custom, the inch-by-inch erosion of local power – indicates that southern Protestantism, in terms of its local position, might have been becoming a little sceptical of the value of the connection. (Indeed, discontent did surface briefly after disestablishment – but it quickly faded.)[27] On the eve of Gladstone's realization of the propriety of Home Rule for the Irish, southern Protestantism might have been expected to examine its position carefully. A debate within Protestantism as to its future political direction might have been expected. But this was not allowed. One suspects that there may have been many more reasonable men on the southern unionist side than has been apparent. Those well-disposed to try the experiment, and that much larger group totally indifferent to it, were fiercely criticized later by Lord Castletown as 'a nice lot of cowards' for their failure to come forward publicly.[28] But they were wise. The hysterical reaction of ultra-unionists could be vicious and dangerous. As a result, those Protestants who actively espoused the Home Rule cause found themselves political pariahs and social outcasts; and a political debate *within* southern Protestantism never really commenced.[29]

Despite the signs pointing towards the political unity of like-minded southern Protestants (observed in places like Cork from the early 1830s) it took an indication of the Union being in serious danger to accelerate the process. In May 1885 the Irish Loyal and Patriotic Union (ILPU) was formed – a specific attempt to allow Irish Protestants to support a broad political concept, the maintenance of the Union.[30] The practice of minority politics was being learnt at a rapid rate in the 1880s. This and the formation of a single organization with a simple aim, to act as the mouthpiece of the minority, were important developments.

Yet almost immediately a serious mistake was made. In the aftermath of the 1884 Parliamentary Reform Act and faced with the certainty of defeat at the polls, the ILPU decided to sponsor fifty-two contests in the south at the general election of 1885. The result was a bloody rout, with fifty candidates defeated, most ignominiously; but in the words of one of them 'abject surrender' was not southern unionist policy in 1885.[31] Henceforth, however, except for isolated local instances, direct confrontation with the nationalists in parliamentary elections was avoided. An unwritten lesson, that minorities should not demonstrate their weaknesses publicly, had been well learnt. Another lesson, quickly comprehended, was to exploit as fully as possible any weaknesses in the majority's local armour. Nationalist splits in the 1890s and 1910s provided an opportunity for southern unionists to act as a wedge between the two wings, driving them apart by attaching themselves now to one side, now to another. Political

Protestantism in Cork city became adept at this. Acting through the medium of municipal politics Cork unionists first supported the Parnellite nationalists. As soon as it became apparent that they were being taken for granted, the unionists switched sides and supported the anti-Parnellites! The concrete result was the election of a unionist mayor, the first for some twenty years. Again, during the O'Brienite (moderate nationalist) split in the 1910s Cork unionism occupied a central position within local politics. A minority of 15 per cent of the population at the beginning of the twentieth century could find its sense of group importance inflated in those special circumstances.[32]

A third manifestation of a heightened sense of minority defence was pragmatism in the approach to local politics. Some evidence of this has been mentioned in the case of nationalist splits. When a nationalist-inspired ratepayers' defence association was formed in Cork city in 1898 to counter the threat of a free-spending labour-dominated corporation, the unionists were quick to aid the nationalists in what was clearly seen as the protection of mutual economic advantages.[33]

A fourth result of minority awareness was concentration on economic and social politics – to exclude Home Rule from the agenda, as it were. This was the object of men like Sir Horace Plunkett at a national level and Sir George Colthurst at a local level in Cork. It offered the landed gentry the best hope for a continuation of their relevance to Irish society at a local level.[34] Even in the 'Home Rule' election of 1885 in Ireland, some unionist candidates attempted to contest it on other grounds – the industrial development of Ireland, amelioration of the plight of the agricultural labourers, the reform of local government. Again, a number of unionist members of the landed gentry contested the elections for the new county councils on the basis of the people's economic advancement. In Cork county the approach was so popular that some unionists obtained over 20 per cent of the vote. Yet the willingness to show that they were concerned with an Ireland not bound by former constraints seems not to have lasted among Cork landed unionists. The county council elections held in 1901 found few unionist candidates offering themselves to the electorate.[35]

Southern Protestantism was much concerned to maintain its relevance to Ireland and Irish society in general during this period. At the same time it was acutely conscious of its relation to the British polity and its position within the Empire's governing clique. In this sphere, perhaps, there occurred the most embarrassing divergence between the Catholic and Protestant segments of the nation. Nationalists could not understand the unionists' reaction to Victoria's jubilees or the enthusiasm engendered by the South African war and organizations like the Primrose League. Here there was the greatest gulf of understanding, despite those Catholics who also saw the Empire offering opportunities.[36] Certainly the unionists' most insidious enemy during this latter stage of the Union was a conservative government with a conscience. Any such government spelt danger since it meant that the House of Lords – the ever-vigilant protector of the Irish Protestant – was effectively anaesthetized. The elegant, brutal rationalities

of the 'Souls' who governed Ireland between 1886 and 1904 were as un-
settling to Irish unionism as to nationalism. Gerald Balfour's local government policy, given Protestantism's peculiar sensitivity on its local position,
was more likely to kill unionism by ungratefulness than Home Rule by
kindness. And linked to this, of course, was the question of unionist morale.
By the 1890s, if events in Cork are any indication, it was becoming pain-
fully obvious that to the minority near-victories uplifted morale more than
did near-defeats. When the Union appeared more secure than ever, in the
early 1900s, the result was a tired and apathetic response to local government and radical land purchase measures.

With the new century it *seemed* that the differences between the minority
and majority populations in southern Ireland were at a most profound
level. The Protestant position had changed little since the 1830s. Nationalism, however, had accrued to itself a new dimension and was busy building
a cultural counterpart to the sectarian bulwark that was already an insur-
mountable barrier between the two communities. By and large the vast
majority of southern Protestants could not comprehend (or professed not
to comprehend) the town-led, idealistic, linguistic view of Irish nation-
hood. Such cloudy generalities usually embarrassed and irritated men and
women used to the realities of life often uncomfortably close to nature
on Irish estates or to the problems of making the commercial mill grind
out a penny or two. The unionists were always happier when they could
get their teeth into a juicy Home Rule bill. Then their experts – constitutional, financial and political – could discuss, dissect and finally dis-
miss it. In 1886, 1893 and 1912 minority politics had a definition and a
direction. The problem of the maintenance of group morale – the central
question – is clearly seen. Without a bill the unionist position was in danger
of disintegrating; with a bill there was the possibility of losing all.

III

A sense of isolation and uselessness becomes more prevalent among the
landed classes than among urban Protestants in the years immediately preceding the First World War. The latter had, after all, close commercial
and social contacts with the majority and had been adjusting more sensi-
tively to the changes in the economic and political balance since the 1840s.
Their pretensions were less, their touch more sure. They, rather than the
landed gentry, came to represent the resilience of southern Protestants in
these years. The visibility of urban Protestants, especially their prominent
position within commerce and industry, went neither unnoticed nor un-
challenged by urban Catholicism.[37] The result was often a tension between
the communities that was not mirrored (at any rate after the land question
had been virtually settled) in the rural situation. In the country, the
majority had simply become indifferent to the minority by the early 1910s.
Perhaps this represents the distinction between the 1830s and 1910s in
rural southern Ireland. Earlier, Catholics could not afford to ignore the
small elitist community which held so many of the channels of advancement in its hands. They could in the latter period, since the residue of

national influence and local power held by the landed classes was smaller. It is suggested that the pace of the political nationalist movement was regulated throughout the nineteenth century by government and the movement itself and by the rate at which they were prepared to divest southern Protestantism of its powers. When these were all but gone, the central demand for self-government stood untrammelled by any other.

Despite an occasional flare of sectarian strife, the transformation of southern Protestantism from dominant to non-dominant minority status has successfully taken place. In part this has been due to an identity of economic interests between the majority and the minority. In part it has resulted from a low – some would say a cringing – profile adopted by the Protestant community in the south. Since 1922 its reluctance to advertise itself has been a minority's sensible defence of its position rather than a mark of disapproval of the Irish state. Those who could really not bear the change had left in the early 1920s; those who remained were freed from an albatross of history. The irredentist element in this minority has been negligible, both in influence and numbers.

The image of southern Protestantism as seedy, tired, run-down, pathetic, is surely not a true view. That there were individuals and families so circumstanced, there is no doubt. They are to be found in any community. But the evidence of the 1830s and 1910s, instanced in Cork at any rate, would not suggest that this was southern Protestantism's view of itself. The reality may have been an amalgam of the type of life-style, of community existence engendered in Somerville and Ross's *Experiences of an Irish R. M.* and *The Real Charlotte*.[38] Unselfconsciously, perhaps, southern Protestants were more at one with Ireland and the Irish than many were prepared to admit. In so many areas of life the Protestant and Catholic positions were but two sides of the same coin: completely separate development was never a feature of this particular minority–majority problem. An intimacy and respect born of close and keen conflict in the nineteenth century has been southern Protestantism's salvation in the twentieth.

Notes

1 D. Madden, *Ireland and its Rulers; since 1829. Part the First* (London, 1843), p. 4.
2 R. Hayward, *Munster and the City of Cork* (London, 1964), p. 47; J. Windele, *Historical and Descriptive Notices of the City of Cork* (Cork, 1839), p. 2; J. Donnelly, Jr, *The Land and the People of Nineteenth-Century Cork* (London, 1975), p. 2; T. Freeman, *Pre-Famine Ireland* (Manchester, 1957), pp. 224–5.
3 Newenham Papers, in possession of Cork Archives Council, Courthouse, Cork; T. MacCarthy to T. Newenham (n.d. but probably 1805–6); W. O'Brien to MacCarthy, 24 May 1807.
4 Newenham's work formed the basis of Edward Wakefield's estimations of population in the latter's *Account of Ireland, Statistical and Political* (Dublin, 1812). See also T. Newenham, *Progress and Magnitude of the Population of Ireland* (London, 1805), and *A Statistical and Historical Inquiry into the Population of Ireland* (London, 1805).

5 G. Broeker, *Rural Disorder and Police Reform in Ireland 1812–36* (London, 1970), pp. 205–16.

6 The statistics are compiled from *First Report of the Commissioners of Public Instruction, Ireland* (Brit. Parl. Papers, 1835 (45, 46) XXXIII), appendix, 78c–156c.

7 Seen in the famous 'Doneraile conspiracy' trials of 1829 in which Daniel O'Connell took a prominent part for the defence – *Cork Constitution* newspaper (hereafter *Cork Con.*), 18 August 1829.

8 National Library of Ireland (hereafter NLI), MS. 675, Returns of the Parish of Ballymodan (Bandon), 1834; J. Craig, *Real Pictures of Clerical Life in Ireland* (London, 1875), pp. 334–5; C. Shannon, *The Kingston Family in West Cork* (Armagh, 1929); J. White, *Minority Report* (Dublin, 1975), pp. 17–21.

9 Evidence given to the parliamentary commissioners appointed to inquire into the Irish municipal corporations, *Cork Con.*, 8–15 October 1833.

10 Anon., *A Synoptical Exposé of the Proceedings of the late City Election* (Cork, 1818), pp. 11–14, 34.

11 Anon., *A Full and Correct Report of the Proceedings at the Election for the City of Cork* (Cork, 1818); Anon., *A Full and Accurate Report of the Proceedings at the Election for the City of Cork* (Cork, 1820); Anon., *A Full Report of the Proceedings at the Election for the City of Cork, 7–9 July 1829* (2nd edn, Cork, 1829); Anon., *The Entire Proceedings of the Election for the City of Cork* (Cork, 1830); evidence of B. Gibbings to the commissioners appointed to inquire into the Irish municipal corporations, *Cork Con.*, 12 October 1833.

12 For Lord Kingston, see R. King-Harman, *The Kings, Earls of Kingston* (Cambridge, 1957), pp. 79–85; E. Bowen, *Bowen's Court* (London, 1942), pp. 8, 187–90. The Brunswick Clubs are discussed nationally in H. Senior, *Orangeism in Ireland and Britain 1795–1836* (London, 1966), p. 226; NLI MS. 5017, Letters ... relative to the Brunswick Constitutional Clubs. The first club in Ireland was formed in Cork city in 1827 (*Cork Mercantile Chronicle*, 21 February 1827).

13 Details of the structure of the Anglican church in Cork are in W. Brady, *Clerical and Parochial Records of Cork, Cloyne and Ross* (3 vols, London, 1861–64). For church attendances, see NLI MS. 9508, Union of Aghern and Britway, vestry minute book, lists of communicants, 1834; NLI MS. 5074, Register of the parishioners of Dunmanway, Co. Cork, 1848; PRO (I) MS. 6083, Parish of Cloyne, miscellaneous book. For the activities of a rural Bible society, see Fanlobbus Parish Records, in possession of the Rector, Dunmanway, Co. Cork, vestry minute book 1794–1870, pp. 131–3.

14 For pews, see Representative Church Body Library, Dublin 14, M/54, Ballymartle Parish, vestry minute book, 1791–1874, various entries; Douglas Parish Records, in possession of the Rector, Douglas, Co. Cork, vestry minute book 1791–1874, entries for 4, 9 May 1814 and 14 June 1824; Cork Archives Council, Courthouse, Cork, Castlehaven vestry minute book 2, 1825–70, 28 April 1828.

15 C. Irwin, *A History of Presbyterianism in Dublin and the South and West of Ireland* (London, 1890), pp. 213–14; PRO (L.) HO/100/216, ff. 64–5, R. Sainthill to the lord lieutenant of Ireland, 23 March 1826; *Cork Con.*, 26 June 1834 (editorial advice to Irish Dissenters to cast their lot in with Anglicans), 23 September 1841 (report of a speech by a leading Methodist minister); *House of Commons Committee on the State of Ireland* (Brit. Parl. Papers 1825 (129) VIII), 388, evidence of Reverend J. Burnett (independent minister, Cork).

16 E. O'Kelly, *The Old Private Banks and Bankers of Munster* (Cork, 1959), p. 95; *Cork Con.*, 6 January 1835; NLI Microfilm P. 3064, diary of Otho Travers, entry for January 1835.

17 Reports in *Cork Con.*, 22, 25 July 1837 indicate the nature of the southern Protestant Operative Associations. See also B. L. Peel Papers, Add. MS. 40613, ff.

82–3, George Shea (secretary, Cork Protestant Operative Association) to Sir R. Peel, 16 March 1845.

18 G. Bennett, *The History of Bandon, and the Principal Towns in the West Riding of County Cork* (Cork, 1869), pp. 297–301, 508; NLI Shannon Papers, MS. 13304 (2)/297, Lord Bandon to his mother, 15 July 1809; State Paper Office, Dublin Castle, S.O.C. Papers, 2293/6, magistrates of Bandon to Sir William Gregory, 18 July 1821.

19 Cork City Public Library, T. C. Croker Papers, I, 126, R. Ryan to T. C. Croker, 3 March 1823; N. L. Beamish, *Peace Campaigns of a Cornet* (London, 1829, not published, copy in Cambridge University Library); *The Freeholder* newspaper, 21 April 1827.

20 *Report from the Select Committee appointed to inquire into the Nature, Character, Extent and Tendency of Orange Lodges, Associations, or Societies in Ireland* (Brit. Parl. Papers 1835 (377) XV), 201, evidence of H. R. Baker; also appendix, p. 40.

21 See *Cork Con.*, 6, 11 and 27 July, 1 August 1833; 1, 8 July, 14 August, 25 September, 9 October, 11 November 1834; 12 March, 26 September 1835; 18 February, 17 March 1836; 25 July 1837 for reports of Orange activities in Cork. A letter in *Cork Con.*, 26 September 1834 stated that 'the number of Orangemen in the city and county of Cork has more than *trebled* within the last two years'.

22 *Cork Con.*, 1 August 1833, opening of the new Orange headquarters in the city.

23 This is particularly seen in Bandon and Youghal. In the latter, the duke of Devonshire's tight whig control produced a Protestant backlash in 1829 and moves towards Protestant political unity in 1835; see *Cork Con.*, 6 August 1829 (editorial), 7 February 1835. In the face of a revolt by the tory corporation against an electoral arrangement with the duke of Devonshire, Lord Bandon was forced to relinquish political control of Bandon in 1833 (evidence of J. Swete and E. Docherty to the commissioners appointed to inquire into the Irish municipal corporations, *ibid.*, 24 September 1833).

24 BL Add. MS. 40467, f. 72, J. Besnard to Lord Stanley, 19 February 1841; *Cork Con.*, 19 August 1841.

25 A tory play for the whigs was especially made during the 1835 elections (*Cork Con.*, 3 January 1835). The newspaper printed an important editorial on the defection of Arthur Hyde – 'long regarded as the head of the whig commoners of the county' – to the tories (*ibid.* 1 July 1837).

26 For the 'economic' conservative party in the city see *Cork Con.*, 21 August 1841, letter from A. Beale. For the later development of a similar group on the liberal-repeal side see M. Murphy, 'Municipal Reform and the Repeal Movement in Cork 1833–44', *Journal of the Cork Historical and Archaeological Society*, 2nd series, LXXXI (1976), pp. 10–12; *Cork Examiner* newspaper (hereafter *Cork Exam.*), 20 August 1842 (editorial).

27 A concise account of this interlude is in F. S. L. Lyons, *Ireland since the Famine* (London, 1971), pp. 139–40.

28 University College, Cork, O'Brien Papers, MS. AR 91, Lord Castletown to William O'Brien, 15 April 1910.

29 The victimization of Rev. R. A. Anderson, an Anglican rector and vocal supporter of Home Rule, was a particularly unpleasant example (*Cork Exam.*, 9 January 1891). Protestant Home Rulers in Cork city in 1885–6 were also subject to much abuse and vilification.

30 P. Buckland, *Irish Unionism* I (Dublin, 1972), pp. 2–3.

31 For a more detailed discussion of these contests and the general electoral activity of southern unionists during the years from 1885 to 1910 see Ian d'Alton, 'Cork Unionism: its Role in Parliamentary and Local Elections 1885–1914', *Studia Hibernica* XV (1975), pp. 143–61.

32 *Cork Exam.*, 7 July 1892; *Cork Con.*, 24 June 1895, 7, 9 December 1910.
33 *Cork Con.*, 4 February 1899 and *Cork Exam.*, 24 January 1899, reports of meeting of the reformed Cork corporation.
34 Plunkett's philosophy is clearly set out in his *Ireland in the New Century* (London, 1904), Colthurst's in a speech reported in *Cork Con.*, 26 March 1899.
35 *Cork Con.*, 7 March 1899.
36 For a further discussion of this and the refusal of the southern unionist to accept the genuineness of the nationalist movement see Buckland, pp. 10, 143–4.
37 For an interesting point of view of the relatively high visibility of Dublin Protestants – past and present – and the Catholic reaction, mainly through the Knights of St Columbanus's organization, see J. White, chapter 13.
38 The air of extroverted, bemused, unselfconscious gaiety in the 'R. M.' works is complemented, not contradicted, by the tortured wish for self- and community-destruction so evident in *The Real Charlotte*. Both express legitimate facets of the landed Protestant view of itself. A superlative discussion of *The Real Charlotte* is in O. MacDonagh, *The Nineteenth Century Novel and Irish Social History: some Aspects*, The O'Donnell Lecture, National University of Ireland (Dublin, 1970), pp. 15–18.

6

Catholics in the north of Ireland, 1850–1921: the urbanization of a minority

A. C. Hepburn

I

> This town is governed by Protestants, but the bone and sinew of the town is Roman Catholic. What I mean by this is that this is a Roman Catholic town.

So declared Bernard Hughes, owner of a large bakery and sole Catholic member of the Belfast corporation, before the royal commission appointed to enquire into the Belfast riots of 1857.[1] The majority of the working class, he asserted, was Roman Catholic, a community numbering in all more than 50,000 persons. This estimate, had it been correct, would indeed have brought the Catholic proportion of the city very close to 50 per cent. In fact it was probably quite a substantial overestimate, for the first official census of religious distribution, taken four years later in 1861, showed Catholics to number a little over 41,000, or 34 per cent of the city's population.[2] But Hughes's tone is an accurate reflection of public feeling in the 1850s. Both Catholics and Protestants were highly conscious of the fact that the Catholic community had for some time been growing at an increasingly faster pace than the Protestant, in what was by mid-century the fastest growing town in the United Kingdom. 'The Romish mobs have triumphed in our town', screamed the *Belfast Newsletter* in the same year, after the rioting of rival mobs had caused the magistrates to ban inflammatory Protestant street-preaching, 'Belfast ranks now with Kilkenny, Cork or Limerick.'[3]

Belfast of course grew enormously in the nineteenth century, from around 19,000 in 1800 to 378,000 in 1911.[4] The consequent eruption of wealth and opportunity, as well as industrial poverty and squalor, gave the city a newly dominant position not only in Ulster's economy but also in its politics and society. In the simplest terms this may be measured by Belfast's expanding share of the population of the six-county area that now constitutes Northern Ireland – in 1821, 3 per cent, in 1861, 9 per cent, and by 1911, 31 per cent. A recent essay has analysed the impact of this growth on community relations and demonstrated how the respective hopes and fears of Bernard Hughes and the *Newsletter* did not come to fruition, how the Catholic proportion of Belfast fell from its highest recorded level of more than a third in 1861 to less than a quarter in 1911.[5] In the six-county area as a whole, where the total population declined by over 10 per cent during the same period, the Catholic population experienced an absolute decline of almost 25 per cent. In relative terms this reduced the Catholic proportion in the area from 41 per cent to what has become its stable twentieth-century level of 34 per cent. Two thirds of this decline is accounted for by the relative loss of numbers in Belfast. In this specific sense, then, the city was truly the cockpit of community conflict in late nineteenth-century Ulster.

In terms of the various definitions of minority employed in the modern world, both Catholics and Protestants constituted minorities in the north of Ireland prior to the coming of partition in 1921. Protestants might have found the United Nations 'European' definition suitable to their circumstances.[6] They thought they were different from Catholic Irishmen and wished to remain so; they saw the 'homeland', which they and their ancestors had controlled for more than two centuries, under threat of erosion by the dynamic force of industrial urbanization, spreading Catholic nationalism into the new power-centres of the province. Just as forced industrialization by Fascist Italy created a new Italian-dominated urban society in the midst of the predominantly German and rural South Tyrol,[7] so the more spontaneous economic changes in Victorian Ulster threatened to throw up a new metropolis where the Catholic 'bone and sinew' would come to dominate, not through wealth but through numbers – what we may term a 'colonialism of the dispossessed'. The difference between the two cases was, of course, that in Ulster the power to direct economic and political development, as well as traditional rural predominance, was in Protestant hands. Thus a complete reversal of the trend that Bernard Hughes identified in 1857 was easily generated from within Ulster society. Urban Protestantism in the Victorian period evolved, from simpler rural precedents, processes which could informally but highly effectively resist the erosion of the 'homeland' that would otherwise have stemmed from the principles of equal human rights and fairness in public and private appointments. The ascribed threat was Irish nationalism, but the badge of nationality was religion. There was no room for discrimination between Catholics who were nationalists and those who were not: in the nature of things a Catholic presence in Belfast could no more make a contribution to the preservation of the Ulster Protestant community than an Italian presence in Bolzano could help preserve the German character of the South Tyrol. The attitude of the Orange Order – 'a religio-political system' as William Johnston called it – both reflected and encouraged this feeling.[8] Many of us find the measures that were employed unattractive. But what was achieved by their employment was in fact very similar to the demands and goals of many minority groups in the modern world.

It is within this context, as a minority within a minority, that the Catholics of Ulster must be studied. Whether as would-be assimilators or would-be assimilated, their attitude to their Protestant neighbours has in the main been that of 'no real difference between us'. They are a minority in Louis Wirth's 'American' sense,[9] in as much as they have been discriminated against because of a Protestant presumption that their flourishing presence represented a threat to the future of the Protestant community.

The political development of the Catholic community in the period, forming as it does a part of the wider history of Irish nationalism, is well known. This chapter will concentrate on the impact of the situation in the north of Ireland on the demographic and socio-economic circumstances of the Catholic community.

To take the broad outlines first of all. The population of the six counties became increasingly urban in the later nineteenth century: whereas only 20 per cent lived in towns of more than 1,500 population in 1861, 48 per cent did so in 1911. Apart from the 218 per cent increase in Belfast during the period there was also an absolute increase of 42 per cent in the total population of the 37 next largest towns in the area. We have seen that in Belfast the Catholic proportion fell by a full 10 per cent during the period. In rural areas, however, it dropped by only 2 per cent, and in the next 37 towns by only 1 per cent. At this level the Catholic decline in Belfast appears exceptional. But if we disaggregate the data for the other towns a more complex picture emerges. In the expanding mill town of Portadown, the Catholic proportion fell by 12 per cent, in Coleraine and Ballymoney by 7 per cent, in Ballymena by 6 per cent and in Larne by 5 per cent. In Downpatrick it increased by 7 per cent, in Newry by 10 per cent, and in Strabane by 12 per cent. Age structure and the balance of population in the local hinterlands certainly played their part in some of these fluctuations. But there was also something of a move towards segregation *between* towns, as Catholic towns became more Catholic, and Protestant towns grew more Protestant. In particular, most of the expanding industrial towns became more Protestant, Belfast most obviously, but also Portadown, Larne, Ballymena and Lisburn. Even in Derry city, with its large and depopulating Catholic hinterland of Donegal, the impact of the rail link across Protestant north county Derry tipped the balance enough for the Catholic proportion in the city to fall by 2 per cent during the period. Lurgan was in fact the only industrial town to experience any increase in the Catholic proportion of its population. In its case, proximity to the more intensely Protestant Portadown, and the relatively well-entrenched Catholic position in the handloom sector of the Lurgan weaving industry, resulted in the development of a local segregation between the two towns that has become very much more pronounced in the twentieth century.

Residential segregation *within* towns has been a more obvious feature of urban Ulster. Given a community divided in terms of church and school attendance, it is to be expected that residential patterns will reflect this to some extent. But the intensity of the segregation, especially in working-class areas, has been remarkable. It has been argued that the very existence of this degree of segregation, the tradition of intense loyalty to a locality which identifies itself in terms of its opposition to another locality, with ritual flashpoints and battlegrounds known to all, was in itself an important cause of disturbances.[10] This can hardly explain the origin of such districts, although it may be that the cultural factor has been a key feature in perpetuating conflict. But while tight residential segregation was a necessary pre-requisite for the characteristic Ulster riot, it is equally the case that segregation has been the most popular mechanism for *avoiding* the sharper penalties of community conflict. If occasional pitched battles and protracted riots have taken place, they are simply a measure of the degree to which the mechanism is less than fully effective.

The sort of data that modern geographers have used to calculate precise measures of segregation are not available for Victorian Belfast.[11] The corporation submitted evidence to the 1864 enquiry which shows that the Catholic proportion of parliamentary electors by ward ranged from 31 per cent in Smithfield through 16 per cent in St Anne's to approximately 12 per cent in each of the other three wards.[12] But this is far too crude a measure to give any real indication, especially since one of the intentions of the ward system which survived until 1896 was to cut across any solid block of Catholic voters. We know that Smithfield market and nearby Hercules Street was a Catholic district in the early nineteenth century, and that the working-class area known first as the Pound and later as the Falls grew out of it. Sandy Row was known as a Protestant mill workers' district by the same period. What we do not know is the proportion of the city's population that lived in such segregated enclaves. Neither is it entirely clear how tight the segregation was in mid-century. The 1857 commissioners received evidence from one John Hackett (leader of the 'Republican Gun Club') that before the riots of that year his own street in the heart of the Pound had been composed almost equally of Catholics and Protestants. There were also a number of Catholics living in Sandy Row, some of them partners in mixed marriages, others simply workers living close to their mills.[13] But, the commissioners reported, 'since the commencement of the late riots the districts have become exclusive, and by regular systematized movements on both sides, the few Catholic inhabitants of Sandy Row have been obliged to leave it, and the few Protestant inhabitants of the Pound district have been also obliged to leave that locality'. In that year, the report continued, 'street-preaching drastically changed its character, and was used to mark out the people and divide them'.[14] Major riots again swept Belfast in 1864 and 1872, so that by the time of the even greater disturbances which followed the defeat of the Home Rule Bill in 1886, the driving out of obnoxious individuals from the heart of these districts was no longer a prominent feature, because virtually no such individuals remained. Attacks on private houses were confined to areas of disputed territory between the two communities. Only the public houses were by then Catholic in the Protestant areas of west Belfast, and twenty-eight of these were the objects of attack during the 1886 disturbances.[15]

Intermarriage between Catholics and Protestants, which might have been expected to erode segregation in a tightly packed urban community, never did so. After the expulsion of mixed couples from Sandy Row it became customary for such couples to reside in Catholic areas. By 1908, when the Irish hierarchy began to enforce the Tridentine decree *Ne Temere* (which sanctioned the marriage of Catholics to partners outside the faith only where the marriage celebration was exclusively Catholic, and where it was agreed that all children of the marriage would be raised as Catholics) the Catholic church and Sandy Row were effectively at one in the view that 'mixed marriages were Catholic marriages'. Such mixed marriages as did occur, therefore, were entirely swallowed up by the pattern of segregation, and never occurred in large enough numbers in any generation to upset it. In the 1960s the level of Catholic–Protestant intermarriage in Northern Ireland remained negligible.[16]

Segregation in employment was another distinctive trend during our period. In view of the predominantly Protestant control of public and large areas of private employment in Belfast, this most often meant in practice discrimination against Catholics. One of the largest public employers was the Belfast corporation, with only three Catholic councillors ever before the boundary reorganization of 1896, which created two predominantly Catholic wards.[17] The return of corporation officials furnished to the riots commissioners in 1886 shows that only five out of a total of ninety-five officers were Catholics, earning an average salary of £95 per annum, compared to the Presbyterian average of £183 and the Episcopalians' £153.[18] The lord mayor claimed in 1911 that Catholics were fully represented at 24 per cent of the entire corporation workforce, but even then their average pay was £60 per annum against the Protestants' £104.[19] As for white collar officials, the census tables for 1911 show only a slight change from the 1886 position: of the 360 men and women employed in local government and poor law administration only 9 per cent were Catholics, whereas central government officers and clerks in the city were 28 per cent Catholic. In Derry city at the same time the number of local government officials was much smaller, but again Catholics, at 20 per cent of the total, were 34 per cent under-represented.

In the private sector, measurable evidence of employment practices is rare. The ability of foremen to detect job applicants of the wrong persuasion or to put them at the top of the list for redundancy was not a skill which required employers to keep records on the religious balance of their workforces. But the evidence of large employers before the various riots commissions of the period contains a certain amount of piecemeal information. Sir Edward Harland reported in 1886 that his shipyard workforce (which in good years numbered 5,000, but which in the slump of the mid-1880s had been cut massively to 3,000) included only 225 Catholics, half of whom had not reappeared for work in the first three months after the disturbances at the yard.[20] A Catholic riveter who had worked at the yard almost from its foundation in the 1850s claimed in evidence that he had been obliged to leave three times during his career because of intimidation.[21] The Catholic proportion of shipyard workers in the city overall, which in 1881 was over 11 per cent (and may in 1861 have been relatively much larger)[22] had by 1901 fallen to a bare 7 per cent. In 1857 the owner of a large mill in the Sandy Row area told the commissioners that he believed the widespread attacks on Catholics at the Blackstaff crossing had arisen out of a combination at the mill to exclude Catholics.[23]

There were also large Catholic employers, although far fewer in number. Bernard Hughes claimed in 1857 that his bakery employed 150 men, two thirds of them Catholics.[24] But in 1886 cross-examining counsel claimed that no Protestants could get work there.[25] The same counsel claimed that Ross's mill, on the Falls Road, with 600 hands, employed only Catholics. The manager, although he denied that this was the case, could cite only the example of two Protestants who were employed in positions of authority.[26] The truth seems to be that, increasingly, and most thoroughly in times of strife, managers and foremen took the line of least resistance: where one community dominated a workplace, its position was allowed to drift towards exclusivity insofar as the demand for labour permitted. Sir Edward Harland, who had closed his gates in a bid to halt sectarian rioting in 1864, and who was still prepared to use the lockout for strike-breaking purposes in 1884, refused to close his gates following the outbreak of disturbances in 1886. (He denied, furthermore, that it was within the management's power to prevent the wholesale filching of 'Belfast confetti' from company premises for us as missiles.)[27] During the same disturbances the manager of Ewart's mill, who claimed a Catholic proportion of approaching 20 per cent in his 3,000-strong workforce, refused to allow an RIC patrol into the factory to identify those who had attacked Catholics during a lunch-hour riot.[28]

The generation of rioting in Belfast, from mid-century up to 1886, established widespread segregation, and thus discrimination, in employment, just as it intensified segregation in housing. Having failed to stop sectarianism, large employers found it easier to acknowledge and accept it. Only firms where for some reason, perhaps geographical accident, the workforce was more evenly balanced, had any real interest in using their influence in favour of harmony and cooperation. Thus Combe, Barbour & Combe, employing some 1,400 mill hands in North Howard Street, situated on a section of what is today the Falls–Shankill 'peace line', had a workforce estimated at 40 per cent Catholic, which during times of strife could leave work by a different gate.[29] It was no coincidence that a firm with this kind of balance was singled out, alone of all the large employers, for praise from the commissioners for the behaviour of its management during the 1886 disturbances.[30]

A recent study based on the printed census reports for 1871–1911 has suggested that while there were some signs of relative growth in the small Catholic white collar class during the period, and in the less readily classifiable category of public house keepers, there was if anything a relative decline in the position of Catholic industrial workers. This was most notable among fitters and carpenters from 1881 onwards, and paralleled by an increase in the proportion of Catholics in heavy unskilled jobs like dock work.[31] Comparable figures for other towns are not listed in the census reports, except for Derry city in 1901 and 1911, where the Belfast trend is confirmed. Even in just one intercensal period the under-representation of Catholics among commercial clerks in Derry decreased from minus 32 to minus 23 per cent, while their representation among engine-makers and fitters declined from minus 8 to minus 18 per cent. Carpenters remained a steady minus 12 per cent, while the heavy over-representation among dockers and publicans actually increased. Perhaps surprisingly, however, the *scale* of under- and over-representation in Derry was greater than in

Belfast: clerks in 1911 at minus 23 per cent against minus 9 in the larger city; fitters at minus 18 against minus 12; dockers at plus 36 against plus 17. The reasons for this are not entirely clear, but one factor may be termed 'urban maturity'. Because Belfast's Catholic population increased far less rapidly than its Protestant counterpart between 1861 and 1901, a relatively large element was at least second generation urban by the early twentieth century. In Derry, on the other hand, Catholic growth had continued to match that of Protestants between 1871 and 1901, so that a bigger proportion of Derry Catholics were probably urban newcomers, particularly ill-equipped to compete for social mobility against the odds (table 6.1: Figures for the smaller industrial towns of Lurgan and Portadown are included for further comparison).

TABLE 6.1: Catholic growth rate in relation to Protestant growth rate, selected towns by decade. 1861–1911 (percentage)

	1861–71	*1871–81*	*1881–91*	*1891–1901*	*1901–11*
Belfast	−14	−17	−15	−14	−1
Derry	−14	+1	+1	0	+4
Lurgan	+7	−9	−1	+3	+8
Portadown	−26	−17	−12	−11	0

At the upper end of the social scale, Catholics certainly constituted no more than a small proportion. The Catholic bishop of Down and Connor estimated in 1864 that there were in the city 'seventy or eighty or ninety Catholics who could spare out of their income £100 without injuring their family prospects or interfering with their work. That included persons with £2,000, £3,000, £4,000, or £5,000 capital.'[32] But there can be no doubt that Catholics as a group were the worst-off section of the northern community during the immediate post-Famine period. The problem is to assess the extent to which this continued to be the situation, the extent to which a certain amount of Catholic success and mobility is concealed by the overall low status of Catholics, and the extent to which the projection of a Catholic–Protestant dichotomy was politically motivated in the first place, inasmuch as the wider economic gulf may have lain between the Episcopalians and Catholics on the one side, and the more prosperous Presbyterians on the other.

II

A source of enormous potential, still very much underused, is the manuscript material for the censuses of 1901 and 1911, which survives in the Public Record Office of Ireland – a huge and, until the arrival of the computer, unwieldy mine of information on the social circumstances of the mass of the population. From this source the towns of Lurgan and Portadown have been selected for study. Both linen towns, six miles apart, and in more recent times forming nuclei for the projected new city of Craigavon, they were after Belfast and Derry the largest towns in Ulster. They may be taken as reasonably typical of that section of Ulster society which experienced industrial change in the nineteenth century. A 10 per cent sample of households was randomly drawn for each town, producing 272 households (1,319 persons) for Lurgan, and 244 households (1,159 persons) for Portadown. A comparison of the main statistics of the sample with the population parameters from the printed census suggests that, in general terms, the sample is reasonably representative of the overall population. In addition, the rateable valuation, or PLV, for each sample household was traced in the valuation books held at the Public Record Office of Northern Ireland.

Lurgan in 1861, with a population approaching 8,000, was 35 per cent Catholic and Portadown, smaller at just over 4,000 population, was 34 per cent Catholic. By 1911 both towns had grown to about 12,000, but while Lurgan's Catholic community had grown by 67 per cent against the Protestants' 58 per cent, Portadown's Catholics grew by only 39 per cent against a Protestant figure of 149 per cent. In Portadown, as in Belfast, reassertive Protestantism (gaining particular strength in this area from its proximity to the fountainhead of rural Orangeism) effectively discouraged the migration of Catholic industrial labour into the town, and reversed a previous trend. The remainder of this chapter will examine the impact of these developments on the structure of the two towns in 1911.[33]

Taking residential segregation first of all, figure 6.1 illustrates the degree of residential segregation between Protestants and Catholics in the two towns (based in this case on a 100 per cent sample). The Lurgan graph illustrates a very high level of segregation, with the great majority of householders residing in streets more than 90 per cent occupied by their co-religionists. The Portadown graph indicates rather less segregation: predominantly Catholic quarters did exist, but the less sharp gradient on the right of the graph suggests that by no means all Catholics lived in such quarters. Measured by the index of dissimilarity, the segregation level for Lurgan was 80 per cent, and that for Portadown 54.[34] (For comparison, the figure found by Poole and Boal for Belfast in 1969 was 71.)[35] Bearing in mind that the central business district occupies a substantial part of the overall area in towns of this size, the index for Lurgan is about as high as it could be; only the shopping streets of the town centre were not highly segregated. In fact the situation for Portadown was not entirely dissimilar. The different shape of the graph reflects the fact that the Catholic industrial working class, which is indicated mainly by the small block on the left of the graph, did not grow, so that those Catholics who lived in the mixed town centre constituted a greater proportion of the whole. The familiar animosities which made Lurgan intensely segregated kept Catholic growth out of Portadown altogether.

There is some indirect support for this view in table 6.2i and ii: the Portadown Catholic population in 1911 was older than its Lurgan equivalent, and closer in its broad structure to the Protestant populations. The fertility ratio in table 6.2iii indicates the same relatively static structure, although the Catholic sample size here is rather small. The more reliable 'Craigavon' data suggests that in general there was a higher fertility rate

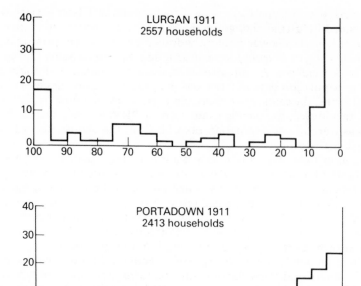

The horizontal scales measure the religious distribution of streets, in terms of percentage Catholic. The vertical scales indicate the proportion of householders living in such streets.

Figure 6.1. Segregation by street

among Catholics during the years immediately prior to 1911, although the difference was by no means as great as that found by Kirk for 1961. We can, however, move to less speculative measures of fertility, for the 1911 census was the first to require married women to state the number of children born to them of their present marriage. In a society characterized by low levels of divorce and illegitimacy, this is a reliable measure of overall fertility. By taking all married women in the sample aged over forty-five, we can obtain a reliable estimate of the mean size of completed families. Combining the figures for the two towns to produce the largest possible sample, we find (table 6.2iv) that the mean number of children born to the older generation of Episcopalian women was almost certainly larger than that born not only to Presbyterians, but also to Roman Catholics. What seems to emerge overall, then, is that until about 1900 the large family was the norm for all denominations, with the Presbyterian average slightly lower, but after that date came a change in the Protestant pattern which was not paralleled on the Catholic side.[36] In table 6.2v and vii we can discern the same tendency towards Catholic–Episcopalian similarity

TABLE 6.2: The social structure of Lurgan and Portadown, 1911

	Roman Catholic	All other denominations	Church of Ireland	Presbyterian
i. *Age ratios* Number of persons aged 31–60 per thousand persons aged 0–30				
Lurgan	385	455	451	—
Portadown	446	446	434	—
ii. *Mean average age*				
Lurgan	23·9	27·2	27·1	27·7
Portadown	27·6	27·8	27·6	31·1
iii. *Fertility ratios* Number of children aged 0–4 per thousand women aged 15–49				
Lurgan	553	424	431	446
Portadown	292	336	322	222
'Craigavon'	451	376	371	358
Lurgan 1961*	546	336	331	321
iv. *Completed family size* Mean number of children born to married women aged 45 and over in 1911				
'Craigavon'	5·37	6·15	6·66	4·53
v. *Mean female age at time of present marriage*				
Lurgan	23·7	23·8	23·0	26·0
Portadown	26·7	24·4	23·3	28·6
vi. *Marital status of persons aged 20–29* (% *married*)				
Lurgan	35·6	34·6	29·4	30·3
Portadown	24·0	26·7	29·7	19·0
vii. *Length of tenure at 1911 residence: 'Craigavon' heads* (%)				
3 years or less	16·9	15·0	17·5	9·1
4–8 years	28·4	21·5	20·1	20·0
9 years or more	54·7	63·5	62·4	70·9
viii. *Mean no. persons per household* 'Craigavon'	5·14	4·66	4·77	4·40
ix. *Households with more than six persons (as* % *of all)* 'Craigavon'	29·8	20·5	22·4	15·5

---

* Lurgan data from T. Kirk, *The Religious Distributions of Lurgan with Special Reference to Segregational Ecology* (MSc thesis, Queen's University, Belfast, 1967), p. 63.

TABLE 6.2 (contd): The social structure of Lurgan and Portadown, 1911

	Roman Catholic	All other denominations	Church of Ireland	Presbyterian
x. *Households with one or more co-resident kin* (%)				
'Craigavon'	29·1	19·7	19·5	19·0
xi. *Households with one or more domestic servants* (%)				
Lurgan	1·0	4·1	2·7	9·1
Portadown	4·2	8·2	4·7	16·1
xii. *Mean number of persons per room*				
Lurgan	1·29	0·96	1·01	0·83
Portadown	1·10	0·84	0·92	0·67
'Craigavon'	1·22	0·89	0·96	0·75
xiii. *Overcrowding: households with $1\frac{1}{2}$ or more persons per room* (%)				
Lurgan	37·9	22·5	26·8	12·1
Portadown	31·2	17·3	21·7	0
'Craigavon'	35·8	19·7	24·1	6·9
xiv. *Illiterate (persons aged 9 or over)* (%)				
Lurgan: total	23·2	10·1	12·7	5·7
sample	25·9	9·6	11·4	6·3
Portadown: total	15·7	9·7	12·4	3·6
sample	13·8	10·6	13·2	4·1
xv. *'Dependents' (as % of population)*				
'Craigavon'	48·2	50·4	50·6	48·8
Belfast 1911	50·3	53·7	55·1	55·9
Derry 1911	53·3	56·2	54·6	55·8
xvi. *Industrial distribution of workforce* (% over- or under-represented in relation to overall distribution in workforce)				
Retail dealing:				
Lurgan	−29	—	+24	0
Portadown	−3	—	−17	+16
General labour:				
Lurgan	0	—	+10	−2
Portadown	+2	—	+8	−1
Linen manufacture:				
Lurgan	+12	—	−7	−4
Portadown	0	—	+5	−5
Sewing, stitching, etc:				
Lurgan	−3	—	−1	0
Portadown	+3	—	−4	−3

TABLE 6.2 (contd): The social structure of Lurgan and Portadown, 1911

	Roman Catholic	All other denominations	Church of Ireland	Presbyterian
xvii. *Social class index (heads)*				
Lurgan 1911	1·75	2·06	1·93	2·26
Portadown 1911	2.0	2·19	1·88	2·92
Lurgan 1961*	1·70	—	1·82	2·18
Portadown 1960*	1·71	—	2·15	2·22
xviii. *Mean PLV*				
Lurgan	3·75	6·50	5·95	8·33
Portadown	5·53	8·06	6·91	15·03
'Craigavon'	4·31	7·38	6·46	11·28
xix. *Households valued at less than £4 (% over- or under-represented)*				
Lurgan	+14·2	—	−5·3	−2·7
Portadown	+10·1	—	+2·4	−7·0
xx. *Households valued at more than £8 (% over- or under-represented)*				
Lurgan	−31·2	—	+5·5	+27·9
Portadown	−7·4	—	−10·8	+10·9
'Craigavon'	−19·0	—	−3·0	+16·4

*Lurgan data from T. Kirk, *The Religious Distributions of Lurgan with Special Reference to Segregational Ecology* (MSc thesis, Queen's University, Belfast, 1967), p. 59. Portadown data from D. P. Barritt and C. F. Carter, *The Northern Ireland Problem* (2nd edn, 1972), p. 54.

and Episcopalian–Presbyterian difference in the data on marriage, and again the difference in pattern between Lurgan and Portadown Catholics.

Turning now to information about the household, table 6.2vii indicates a high level of residential stability. Somewhere in the region of 60 per cent of families in the two towns occupied their 1911 address for nine years or more. No large difference between religious denominations is apparent in this respect, although it seems that Presbyterians were less likely to move within three years than any other group, and that Catholics were more likely to move within nine years than the other groups. Table 6.2viii and ix reflect similarly narrow differences: taking 'Craigavon' as a whole (for the differences between the two towns were slight in these respects) it is fairly certain that Catholic household size was on average slightly higher than for all Protestants, and probably higher than that for Episcopalians. With slightly less confidence we may assert that Episcopalian households were larger than Presbyterian ones. Interestingly, the overall proportion of large households, those with more than six persons, is much higher at 23 per cent than Clarkson's finding for Armagh city in 1770 of 13 per cent, as is the 'Craigavon' figure of 22 per cent for households having some co-resident kin, compared with Clarkson's three per cent.[37] Table 6.2x indicates very clearly that the nuclear family was by no means the undisputed norm in industrial Ulster.

Other household characteristics can give some indication of relative prosperity. In studies of this type carried out on nineteenth-century

English towns, the proportion of households with resident servants has been a widely used indicator. Twelve per cent of Nottingham households and 20 per cent of York households in the mid-nineteenth century were found to include servants.[38] Table 6.2xi suggests that while servants were found in Presbyterian households on almost a similar scale, their presence among Catholics and Episcopalians was very rare indeed. Another indicator of social conditions is the density of occupation of dwellings and the proportion of dwellings that might be classed as overcrowded. Table 6.2xii and xiii give some measure of these items. Again the Catholic community compared unfavourably with Protestants in general, but a glance at the right-hand columns indicates that diversity within the Protestant sector was almost as great as that between Protestant and Catholic. For 'Craigavon' as a whole, we may say that overcrowding was a serious problem for both Catholic and Episcopalian communities. No town in England in 1961 had more than 16 per cent of its households living at this density.[39]

Literacy was a characteristic to which the Irish census paid particular attention. It was the only variable in the published report that was regularly cross-tabulated with religion. The political motive for this is obvious, and the differential was widely exploited by unionists north and south. But for our purposes the availability of data on this item for the entire population provides a convenient spot-check on the reliability of the sample. It should be noted that 'literacy' for this purpose was assessed by the head of each household, and we cannot entirely exclude the possibility that the pressures against admitting illiteracy may have been stronger in some sections of the community than in others. It is clear from table 6.2xiv that illiteracy was significantly higher in Lurgan than in Portadown, but that almost the whole of the difference in the overall figure between the two towns was accounted for by the difference in the Catholic proportions. Whereas the difference between Catholics and others in Lurgan was very substantial, that in Portadown was much more slender. In the latter town, indeed, the real gap was between Episcopalians and Presbyterians.

Perhaps the main area of interest in the study of religious differences in Ulster has been the imbalance in the distribution of jobs. We have already attempted to gain some idea of the broad outlines from the published data for Belfast and Derry. Even from the unpublished material it is difficult to build up a reliable picture of the comprehensive situation because of the problem of classifying occupations from the range of subjective job descriptions given by respondents in the census returns. But some general features emerge clearly enough. Table 6.2xv, first of all, measures that proportion of the sample population which gave no occupation, that is, the dependent population. The data for 'Craigavon' reveals figures slightly lower at all points than the juxtaposed population data for Belfast and Derry cities for the same year, caused no doubt by the comparative lack of any substantial white collar class with non-working wives and daughters. The same factor also explains the differences between denominations within each town. In all these cases a bigger proportion of Catholics than of any other denomination were members of the workforce. Unemployment, of course, is another matter, and is unfortunately beyond the scope of this kind of analysis for this period.

Table 6.2xvi makes some attempt to classify the Catholic and main Protestant workforces by industrial distribution. Many sectors of employment were too small to permit analysis, but the four sectors included in the table accounted for 79 and 72 per cent of the Lurgan and Portadown workforces respectively. Firstly, Catholics were hugely under-represented in the retail trade, that is the main commercial sector, of Lurgan, whereas in Portadown they were close to parity. In the basic linen industry occupations, however, they were clearly over-represented in Lurgan, but again close to parity in Portadown. The explanation is not that it was easier for Catholic traders to flourish in Portadown, but that the large Catholic working class of Lurgan was not paralleled on the same scale in Portadown, so that the small shopkeeping and white collar class of Catholics formed a *relatively* large part of the latter community. There was a Catholic industrial working class in Portadown, but as we have seen it was a small and relatively static one. Its entry into industry met more Orange resistance than was the casè in Lurgan, and it was not over-represented in the linen industry in the same way.

The social class index indicates the same trend. This index is derived from occupation only, using the Registrar-General's 1950 scheme for the social classification of occupations into five groups, from business and professional to unskilled manual, and then weighting the classifications to form an index figure (Social classes I and II have been grouped together).[40] The results are given in table 6.2xvii. Also included in the table for the purposes of comparison are data for the same two towns for 1960–61, compiled from the work of others. The three main denominations are all clearly differentiated from each other, but the widest gap is not between Catholics and all the Protestant groups but, again, between Episcopalians and Presbyterians. The figures from the modern period are remarkably similar. The apparent absolute decline in the Catholic position is probably accounted for less by declining circumstances than by a move away from linen occupations (almost all of which the Registrar-General classed as skilled, Class III) into more modern industries where the work is classified as 'semi-skilled', even though it is in most cases lighter, better paid, and no less skilled than factory linen work. The Presbyterian superiority is apparent in both towns in both time periods, and only the Episcopalian position in Portadown seems to have undergone any significant change.

The other main measure of socio-economic status available to historians is rateable (poor law) valuation, or PLV. Use of this indicator rests on the assumption that most people live in as good a house as they can afford. In Ulster this has to be modified to the extent that religious segregation limited the choice of residence. This factor may have been quite important in towns with, in absolute terms, small Catholic communities like Lurgan and Portadown. With this qualification in mind, therefore, let us look at tables 6.2xviii–xx, which indicate the mean average valuation by denomination and the degree of over- or under-representation of each denomination in the highest and the lowest valuation groups. In table 6.2xviii, the most pronounced characteristic is the difference between the Presbyterians and the rest, most notably in Portadown, but less spectacularly in Lurgan also. The table demonstrates how it is essentially the high Presbyterian level that accounts for the clear-cut Catholic–Protestant differential. In Portadown Catholics and Episcopalians are relatively very close together, and indeed table 6.2xx suggests that Episcopalians were more heavily underrepresented among the highest echelon of ratepayers than were Catholics. But overall the picture is of an Episcopalian community distributed relatively evenly throughout the spectrum, with the Presbyterian and Catholic distributions biased towards the top and bottom ends respectively.

The first lesson to be drawn from this type of census analysis is that interpretation of the results is not a straightforward matter. As implied earlier in this chapter, it was not the aim of popular Protestantism in the period to create a Catholic helot class (although it may be argued that something of the kind was beginning to emerge as a by-product), but rather to maintain control of the Protestant 'homeland' by diverting Catholic urban migration, as far as possible, out of the province altogether. Thus a 'Portadown' outcome represented a greater success for this policy than a 'Lurgan' outcome, even though the findings outlined above suggest that the material circumstances of Catholics were on average better in Portadown.

Catholics did constitute an 'American' type minority in the sense outlined earlier, but they did so partly because their marginally inferior socioeconomic situation was reinforced strongly by their ascribed status in the province, by the way in which monolithic political Protestantism sought to present itself as socially and economically monolithic as well, for example, in the way that Belfast corporation presented its PLV tables to the 1864 commission with subdivisions of 'Protestants' and 'Roman Catholics'. In a different political universe, the socio-economic circumstances outlined for these two towns could have formed an equally convincing basis for a Catholic–Episcopalian group consciousness vis-à-vis a Presbyterian elite. Data from Newry suggest that there was no social basis in our period, however, for the older liberal alliance of Catholics and Presbyterians against the established church (table 6.3). In its last phase that alliance was essentially a vestigial combination of the two extremes of the social spectrum; only the richer Presbyterians were at all likely to vote in the same camp as their Catholic neighbours. Thus during the period 1850–1921, the battles of the seventeenth and eighteenth centuries were refought to establish old hegemonies in new settings. Catholics became an urban minority in mid- and late nineteenth-century Ulster in the same sense that they had previously been a rural one.

TABLE 6.3: The Presbyterian vote in Newry, 1868[41]

	Number of Votes	Mean PLV	% in each PLV category Above £15	Below £15
Presbyterian liberals	30	£36·7	26	5
Presbyterian conservatives	171	£17·8	74	95

But for politicians in 1921, Ulster Protestants were the perceived minority in Ireland – a minority which the British government decided, from 1913 onwards, to recognize. The Sinn Fein solution to the northern Catholic problem was simply the converse – to deny political recognition to Protestant irredentism. There was no contingency plan. Only occasionally did a northern bishop express concern about the position of Catholics if partition should come.[42] Even rarer was the emphasis placed on the plight of Ulster Catholics by the Falls Road émigré, Sean MacEntee, when he opposed the passage of the treaty in the Dail.[43] For the most part Sinn Fein politicians in the south tacitly wrote off their co-religionists in the north as the price of freedom, just as the six-county unionists extorted the ultimate sacrifice from their fellow-covenanters in Cavan, Donegal and Monaghan.[44] For Michael Collins and his colleagues the solution was not a minority treaty for Ulster Catholics, but a wide-ranging boundary commission. The two policies were not in practice compatible. Only the Craig–Collins agreement of March 1922 indicated a possible move towards protection of northern Catholic group interests, including economic interests, in a partitioned Ireland.[45] But it was very much an *ad hoc* effort to deal with short-term troubles in Belfast. It was never fully implemented, and the development of the civil war in the south took any pressure for compromise off the shoulders of the northern government, and effectively preoccupied the Free State leaders with internal matters. The commitment of the British government (and tacitly of the Irish Free State) to Ulster Protestants as a 'European' type of minority was construed by them to be incompatible with requiring the new regime to make sympathetic provision for Ulster Catholics (what is nowadays called 'affirmative discrimination') as an 'American' type of minority. It was a decision that bought them fifty years of time. Like Faustus at the end of the day, they may now feel that the price was too high.

Notes

I am indebted to the following for assistance in the preparation of this chapter: to the Wolfson Foundation and the New University of Ulster research fund for financial support; to Dr S. J. Connolly and Mr A. K. Wilson for research assistance; to the staffs of the Public Record Office of Ireland and the Public Record Office of Northern Ireland for guidance in the use of census and valuation records respectively; and to the manager and staff of the New University of Ulster Computer Centre for advice and assistance in processing those records.

1 *Royal Commission of Inquiry into the Belfast Riots* (Brit. Parl. Papers, 1857–8 XXXVI), evidence, p. 241.
2 Except where otherwise stated, the population figures in this paper are taken from the published census of Ireland, 1861–1911.
3 *Belfast Newsletter*, 5 September 1857.
4 I. Budge and C. O'Leary, *Belfast: Approach to Crisis* (London, 1973), p. 28.
5 S. E. Baker, 'Orange and Green: Belfast, 1832–1912' in H. J. Dyos and M. Wolff, (eds), *The Victorian City: Image and Reality* (London, 1973) II, pp. 789–814.
6 See above, p. 2.
7 See below, p. 189.

8 Speech to the Grand Orange Lodge of Belfast, *Belfast Newsletter*, 15 May 1861.
9 See above, p. 1.
10 See for example J. Darby, *Conflict in Northern Ireland* (Dublin, 1976), p. 26.
11 See M. A. Poole and F. W. Boal, 'Religious Residential Segregation in Belfast in mid-1969' in B. D. Clark and M. B. Gleave (eds), *Social Patterns in Cities* (London, 1973), pp. 1–40.
12 *Belfast Riots Inquiry Commission 1864*, (Brit. Parl. Papers, 1865 XXVIII), evidence, p. 363.
13 *Belfast Riots Inquiry 1857*, evidence, pp. 134–8.
14 *ibid.* report, pp. 2, 13.
15 *Report of the Belfast Riots Commissioners* (Brit. Parl. Papers, 1887 XVIII), report, p. 11.
16 B. M. Walsh, *Religion and Demographic Behaviour in Ireland*, Economic and Social Research Institute pamphlet (Dublin, 1970), p. 28.
17 Budge and O'Leary, p. 118.
18 *Belfast Riots Inquiry, 1886*, evidence, pp. 585–7.
19 Calculated from data in Budge and O'Leary, pp. 122, 133.
20 *Belfast Riots Inquiry, 1886*, evidence, pp. 263–77.
21 *ibid.* p. 492.
22 The 1861 census report included a cross-tabulation of occupation by religion at the provincial level only. It showed 664 persons employed as 'shipbuilders' in Ulster, of whom as many as 25 per cent were Catholics. Some of these were probably employed in Derry, and a handful may have been small boatbuilders at the various Ulster ports, but the great bulk of this number must have been made up of Harland & Wolff employees.
23 *Belfast Riots Inquiry, 1886*, evidence, pp. 28–9.
24 *Belfast Riots Inquiry, 1857*, evidence, pp. 240–43.
25 *Belfast Riots Inquiry, 1886*, evidence, p. 518.
26 *ibid.* p. 545.
27 *ibid.* pp. 492–3.
28 *ibid.* pp. 314, 490.
29 *ibid.* p. 314.
30 *ibid.* report, p. 14.
31 S. E. Baker, 'The Conflict Produced by Nineteenth-Century Immigration in Edwardian Belfast' (unpublished paper).
32 *Belfast Riots Inquiry 1864*, evidence, pp. 42–6.
33 In some places I have made anachronistic use of the term 'Craigavon' to mean simply the urban districts of Lurgan and Portadown combined.
34 The index of dissimilarity is a simple calculation which gives a figure of zero when two groups are distributed randomly in a population, and a maximum score of 100 where segregation is complete. In practical terms it may be treated as measuring 'percentage segregated'. See K. E. and A. F. Taeuber, *Negroes in Cities: Residential Segregation and Neighbourhood Change* (New York, 1965), pp. 325–8.
35 Poole and Boal, p. 24.
36 In 1961, the mean completed family size in Northern Ireland was 4·69 children for Catholics and 2·88 for all other denominations. Walsh, p. 10.
37 L. A. Clarkson, 'Households and Families in Armagh City, 1770' (paper read to the Irish Economic and Social History Conference, September 1976).
38 A. Armstrong, *Stability and Change in an English County Town: York, 1801–51* (Cambridge, 1974), p. 179.
39 B. T. Robson, *Urban Analysis* (Cambridge, 1969), p. 87.
40 I have adopted the simple weighting method of scoring four points for each

householder in Classes I and II, two points for Class III, and one point for Class IV or V, as used by T. Kirk, *The Religious Distributions of Lurgan with Special Reference to Segregational Ecology* (Queen's University, Belfast, M.Sc. thesis, 1967), pp. 58–9.

41 This table is based on data drawn from the Newry poll-book for 1868, a copy of which is in the Public Record Office of Northern Ireland, T.2336. I am grateful to Mr G. J. Slater for drawing this item to my attention.

42 For example the bishop of Raphoe to John Redmond, 9 October 1913, in D. Gwynn, *The Life of John Redmond* (London, 1932), p. 231.

43 Dail Eireann, *Treaty Debates*, pp. 152–8 (22 December 1921).

44 For the bitter correspondence relating to this episode, see P. J. Buckland (ed.), *Irish Unionism: a Documentary History* (Belfast, 1973), pp. 413–16.

45 For the text of the Craig–Collins agreement see D. Macardle, *The Irish Republic* (4th edn, 1951), pp. 966–8.

7

Towards caste: blacks in eighteenth-century America

Duncan J. MacLeod

The growth of antislavery apart, the history of American slavery has rarely been written with an eye to chronology and in terms of change and continuity. We now know enough about the eighteenth century to attempt such a task. What follows is largely a synthesis of work already published but from it one can detect a change in the status of blacks that is of considerable interest to those who would write black history within the general context of minority studies. For this purpose it is convenient to divide the eighteenth century into three periods. The first phase takes us up to the 1720s, the second thence to the era of the American Revolution, and the third from the Revolution into the early nineteenth century. Clearly there are continuities which make these divisions unsatisfactory; equally clearly the divisions apply more satisfactorily to some regions and some aspects of the story than to others; but they are none the less useful.

I

The most striking feature of the first of these three phases is the extent to which Britain's North American mainland colonies shared a similar experience. During the first three quarters of the seventeenth century the black population of those colonies rose only slowly. From the 1690s to the 1720s the rate of increase picked up and came everywhere to exceed that of the white population. Between 1680 and 1720 New England's blacks rose in number by more than 50 per cent each decade and by 1750 they comprised over 3 per cent of the total population. In the middle colonies the peak period of growth was between 1700 and 1720: by the latter date blacks were more than 10 per cent of the population while in New York the figure was over 15 per cent. The experience of the upper south followed a similar pattern. From 7 per cent in 1680 the number of blacks rose until they represented in 1720 some 24 per cent of the total. The increase was most dramatic in South Carolina. Blacks had been an important element of the population there from the first days of settlement comprising some 17 per cent of the early settlers. By 1720 they outnumbered whites by more than two to one.

It is important to grasp the essential similarity in this respect of the colonial experience, because later events have tended to obscure it.

Between 1680 and 1720 the percentage increase in the black population was of the same order of magnitude in the colonies of New England, of the middle region, and of the upper south. The middle colonies were to become increasingly differentiated from the upper south, less because they lacked slavery than because their slavery peaked early. It was the *continuation* of a substantial slave trade into the upper south that generated the divergence: the initial impetus towards slavery was not a southern phenomenon alone but an American one.[1]

The increase in the size and significance of slavery prompts three questions. Why did it occur? What effects did it have on the treatment and status accorded blacks? Did it lead blacks to new conceptualizations of their role and social position?

An answer to the first question is suggested by the near universality of the increase. Whatever else slavery may have been, or became, it was a labour system. Its growing significance across a wide range of economic and social circumstances forces us to seek an explanation in the fluctuating relationship between the supply and demand for labour. The colonies were always short of labour. The settlement of semi-tropical regions in the south and the growth of a tobacco plantation agriculture further north led to increased requirements for agricultural workers. In the middle states and New England it was the growth of commerce and the consequent growth of port cities that multiplied the demand. The corresponding increases in the wealth of planters and merchants led also to a greater demand for house servants. But whatever the precise circumstances, the burgeoning economic development of the colonies led to a generalized concern about securing adequate supplies of labour.

In the late seventeenth and early eighteenth centuries the supply of white labour appears to have contracted. The reasons are obscure but the evidence does permit some reasoned guesses. The stagnation of population growth in England from the 1660s reduced some of the pressures upon land and upon the rural poor. The contemporary stagnation in wheat prices ought also to have reduced the pressure upon the poor in general. The need to emigrate was probably lessened thereby. Emigration was in any case made more difficult as a result of the European wars of the period. It was the disruption of the supply of labour from traditional sources as much as an increase in demand for it that led Americans to seek an alternative source of supply. Slavery was by then a normal and long-standing component of the societies of the western hemisphere and it was natural to look to black slaves to fill the gap left by white servants.

White servants had traditionally included in their number many skilled and semi-skilled artisans and craftsmen. Slave owners were compelled by the growing shortage of such skills – relative, that is, to the opportunities for deploying them – to train slaves in similar skills. The growth of slavery in the early eighteenth century, especially in the middle and eastern states, but also in Charleston, South Carolina, had a very strong urban component. In 1690 blacks constituted about one third of the population of Charleston. By 1709 they had come to roughly equal the white population of the city and maintained that parity through the revolutionary era. They monopolized a large number of the skilled trades and white artisans were bitterly to lament the fact for several decades. New York City also witnessed an explosion in the size of its black population. From about 750 in 1700 the number of blacks rose to nearly 2,300 in mid-century. During the first two decades of the century the growth in their numbers far exceeded that of whites and by 1720 blacks constituted nearly one quarter of the city's population. Thereafter, the influx of whites tended to exceed that of blacks and by mid-century blacks represented only 16 per cent of the total. The rise in Newport, Rhode Island, occurred a little later but by mid-century blacks there numbered over 1,000, that is about 16 per cent of the population. The growth of Boston's black population was scarcely less conspicuous. Rising in numbers from some 400 in 1708 to 2,000 in 1720, blacks in the latter year were one sixth of the city's population. Over the next three decades or so they suffered a proportionate decline until in mid-century they were only 8 per cent.[2]

The decline in the significance of slavery in middle-colony and eastern cities began after the Peace of Utrecht. Less interrupted by European wars, the immigrant trade could once again resume its earlier course. Conditions in Britain, moreover, began again to worsen with a resultant higher desire to emigrate. More significant was the opening of new centres of emigration in Ireland, Scotland and Germany. In Boston, for example, there were three Irish immigrants for every black one after 1715. Slavery was to remain an element in the social and economic life of the middle and eastern colonies but it had passed its peak. Only in Rhode Island did it continue to grow. Elsewhere, blacks declined as a proportion of the total population and slavery declined in economic importance. The material conditions of blacks as a group appear also to have worsened as a result of the failure of many slaves to complete approved apprenticeship schemes. They were thereby restrained from passing on their skills and the black foothold in the skilled trades became more difficult to sustain.[3]

In the upper south the picture was a little different. Tobacco was the major regional crop and its continued expansion to meet growing demand depended upon the arrival of new labourers. But two facts appear to have operated in this region to complement the general shortage of English servants experienced by all would-be employers. While it is likely that the pressure upon the English rural poor lessened in the later years of the seventeenth century, it is almost certainly the case that the pressure upon the smaller freeholders increased. Those who wished to preserve small freeholdings, and those who wished to turn modest mercantile wealth into landed property, found it a poor time to do so. Yet the ownership of land had more than economic value. It carried with it status and, to a limited extent, power. And while four or five hundred pounds might not go far in England they would go a considerable distance in Virginia or Maryland. They would buy there a decent plantation complete with slaves. Thus the supply of white labour began to dry up at the precise moment that men with capital were eager to invest in colonial agriculture.[4]

There were also internal factors predisposing Virginian employers towards slave labour. Edmund Morgan has vividly portrayed the hardships of servant life in seventeenth-century Virginia. He has also demonstrated that as the general mortality in the colony decreased, and servants ever more frequently survived their term of service and became freemen, so they became increasingly discontented at the continued attempts to exploit them. Much of that discontent boiled over during Bacon's rebellion.[5]

Patterns of exploitation had become increasingly complex. The ruling class had sought to maximize its control of labour and its profits by extending periods of service on the flimsiest grounds – by creating an artificial scarcity of land which drove people back into a species of servitude, by inflicting severe penalties for the killing of hogs, which might make work unnecessary, and by several other means. Slavery was an obvious alternative to all of these. The labour barons of the 1620s, and the land and labour barons of the 1660s and 1670s, treated their servants with sufficient harshness and sufficiently like commodities to render unlikely any squeamishness regarding slavery. But the enslavement of English people would require conscious actions unlikely to be approved by parliament and certain to close the supply of labour. Buying African slaves was another matter and some had existed in the colony from the 1620s. The delay in the build-up of slavery had arisen from a number of reasons. Slaves cost more than servants at the same time as the high mortality rate made it unlikely that more work could be extracted from them. It was not, moreover, until about 1660 that the comparative costs of sugar and tobacco converged sufficiently to make it more profitable for traders to sell slaves in Virginia than in the British West Indies. While the Dutch were happy to oblige at that time they were interdicted from so doing by the Navigation Laws and it was only in later years when the Royal African Company and private interlopers stepped in that a stable supply of slaves could be guaranteed.

A more reliable supply situation coincided with increasing possibilities of slaves producing profits from the cultivation of tobacco. Their working lives grew longer and lower mortality rates enhanced the relative advantages to employers of labour of black slaves over white servants. Since the proportion of women carried in the slave trade was greater than that in the servant trade the prospects for capital gains arising from the natural reproduction of the slave force began to grow even better.

The more well-to-do Virginians, in other words, sought a means to continue their engrossment and exploitation of labour which did not have the unsatisfactory side effects of generating a social and political discontent they were unable to control. Their solution was to enslave as large a proportion of the labour force as possible and to sink their differences with the upwardly mobile freeman class. For while the continued growth of staple crop agriculture made it easy for freemen to prosper it did not lead to a reversion to the use of white labour when the supply of such might once again have become plentiful. In the middle and eastern colonies the dependence upon black labour had been a stop-gap measure; in Virginia, on the other hand, internal considerations made it more desirable than the alternative of white immigration. Further to the north the growth of the black population had peaked by the 1720s; in the upper south this period of growth proved to be but the prelude to the sustained development of a thoroughgoing slave society.

In South Carolina the early settlers had arrived from Barbados as often as from England and they had frequently taken their slaves with them. Blacks and whites had laboured together to establish the new colony. Increasingly as land was cleared in lowland areas so the cultivation of rice began to play a major part in colonial economic development. The problem of labour shortage was enhanced in South Carolina by the unattractiveness of its climate to many whites. With so many of the white settlers having their origins firmly rooted in a slave society, moreover, it was natural that they should have recourse to slavery, especially as Barbados was the nearest source of supply. Production for a market in conditions of a limited supply of free labour and a plentiful supply of slave labour could, in the context of time and place, produce only one conclusion. By the third decade of the century blacks greatly outnumbered whites and did so in some lowland areas by as many as a hundred to one.[6]

How, then, did whites accommodate themselves to the new situation? One of the more obvious ways in which they did so – more obvious, that is to the historian – was through the passage of increasingly more comprehensive legislation defining the relative positions of the two groups. This is not the place to analyse that legislation, but some comments on its main features are in order because they say much about the total social situation. First, the various colonial codes were more similar than dissimilar. Second, they reflected the problems inherent in any attempt to define persons as things. There was confusion as to whether slaves should be considered as real or as personal property; there were doubts about the extent of an owner's legitimate powers over his property: did they extend, for example, to its destruction or to its alienation through manumission? The codes were brought piecemeal onto the statute books except in South Carolina, where Barbadian precedents were enacted with some coherence. But they universally recognized that slaves were property of some kind, that their management was largely the prerogative of their owners, but that governmental intervention between owner and slave was in some respects inevitable and proper. The codes were harsh, especially in the southern colonies, but so too was the legislation concerning white servants and apprentices.[7]

For our purposes, however, two features of the codes need special emphasis. First, they defined the position of a labouring class in terms designed to secure the interests of the employers. Secondly, although they reflected racial prejudices of long standing they did not codify those prejudices. Put another way, the racial features of the codes were incidental to their regulation of labour. Without the existence of racial prejudices it is doubtful that slavery could so easily have developed or that such codes could have been passed. Their object however was not to define social distinctions based upon race but to define class distinctions based upon function. Not until the revolutionary era were the codes formulated between 1690 and the 1730s to be revised at all extensively and not until then was legislation consciously to concern itself with racial and class considerations on more or less equal terms.

Labour competition appears to have provided much of the context for relations between blacks and whites. White craftsmen in Charleston and in northern cities fought against the penetration, and in the former case the engrossment, of many trades by blacks. In Charleston the conflict was to remain a central one into the revolutionary era. Elsewhere it was to be muted within a more pervasive ethnic consciousness. In Boston and Newport, Philadelphia and New York City, black competition was often to seem of minor importance compared with the new immigration of Scots–Irish, Scots and Germans. But it persisted nonetheless. John Adams was to claim that the abolition of slavery in Massachusetts in the 1780s reflected the hostility of whites to the protection accorded slave artisans: without a formal abolition, he suggested, the people would have taken matters into their own hands.[8]

Labouring conditions also appear to have provided the context within which blacks responded to changed circumstances as far south as South Carolina. They seem to have resented the switch away from the rough functional equality with whites which characterized the early frontier experiences of that colony. Peter Wood argues that after about 1720 they became more assertive of their position. An alternative reading of his evidence suggests that the process was more defensive than innovative: they were resisting an erosion, consequent upon the spread of the plantation, of their former more favoured position.[9]

Slavery was but one of a number of subordinate statuses in the early colonial south. Blacks were accustomed to working alongside white indentured servants, transported criminals, and apprentices. All were subject to the discipline and whims of their masters and mistresses to an extent scarcely credible today. Blacks reacted adversely to the growing debasement of their position relative to these other groups, but that debasement was a function less of slavery as such than of their increasing concentration upon the plantations. It was felt more in the south than elsewhere.

II

The shift in the middle decades of the eighteenth century towards a plantation focus reflects the growing importance, in this story, of the south. Within the south the process was not, however, uniform. In the lower south the move was towards highly specialized plantations of considerable size with widespread owner-absenteeism. Charleston provided, moreover, an urban setting for much of the region's cultural and political development. Elsewhere, and especially in the Chesapeake Bay area, the plantation developed as a diversified economic unit which also served as a surrogate for towns. The demographic structure of the slave population also differed. In the lower south the proportion of African-born slaves was higher than elsewhere and that African-born contingent was more heavily concentrated geographically. The result was that a framework existed within which African cultural forms and values could more easily be preserved.

In the upper south African-born slaves were rarely concentrated together in such numbers. Indeed the large planters, who often acted as agents for slave traders, tended to disperse them by sale in small groups. As a consequence they were isolated linguistically and culturally in a manner not experienced by their southern counterparts.[10]

The tobacco plantation reached the apogee of its development in the mid-eighteenth century. In its most complete form it was a petty autarchy, self-sufficient in food, cash crops, and the skills needed for it to function effectively as an independent entity. Its independence was partially a matter of geography. The great plantations of Virginia were located along the banks of the York, Rappahannock, James and Potomac rivers which divided the Tidewater into great peninsulas. Ocean-going ships tied up at their wharves and the planters acted as agents for the sale of the produce of their less fortunately located brethren as well as for the ships' captains. They dealt directly with English merchant houses. In acting to create their modern baronies they responded to social and political motives as well as economic ones. And their actions had economic, social and political consequences. They affected the manner in which owners thought of their slaves and the ways in which slaves reacted to their plight.[11]

The search for autarchy produced a society in which the control of and concern for the poor was decentralized, devolving as it did upon the slaveholder. He experienced thereby a substantial increment in his functions and powers. Regarding his plantation as a total entity he came to conceptualize it as an extended family. In so doing he was merely extending a prevalent mode, for servants and apprentices had long been regarded as belonging to and in the family that controlled their destinies. At least one historian has persuasively argued that if slavery was ever characterized by paternalism then this was the time and place. The plantation was to provide a setting within which blacks could acculturate themselves to the American experience in a large number of ways because its very autarchic nature compelled diversification. It also served as a surrogate for towns by becoming a centre of colonial culture and political life. Because plantations needed skilled workers, and because they dominated the economic life of the region, slaves came to dominate the skilled trades. Because their owners dominated the political and cultural life of their colonies some of them also came into contact, albeit tenuously, with the main intellectual currents of the day.[12]

But in some important respects the situation of plantation slaves was inferior to that of their urban counterparts. The latter operated within a more cosmopolitan context. Cities were entrepôts through which ideas flowed as freely as goods. But the plantation fragmented the labouring class. It offered diverse opportunities at the expense of isolating one group of slaves from another. The scope for developing larger horizons and generating a broad class or racial perspective on their position was extremely limited. The paternalism of the slaveholders – a paternalism that should not be confused with kindness – was, moreover, suffocating. It demanded a sense of loyalty, gratitude, and duty from the slaves just as it required obligations on the part of the masters. By conforming to the demands made of them in this respect slaves might materially enhance the ease and comfort of their lives. But only by resisting them, perhaps, could they maintain their dignity and psychic well-being. A recent study has suggested that it was the more acculturated slaves who found this situation most difficult to accept. They were more likely to resist the authority of their masters and mistresses and more likely to flee the plantation. But although they were largely responsible for Gabriel Prosser's rebellion in 1800 they more usually resisted in an individualistic way. They ran away singly or in pairs; they tried to pass themselves off as freemen and hired themselves out. Only rarely did they act collectively and seek to establish outlying communities such as were created by the maroons of Surinam and Jamaica. In part, of course, this was a product of a different geography, in part a matter of demography; but it was also a function of acculturation itself. The greater the degree of assimilation the more likely they were to resist slavery without rejecting the total society of which it was a component part.[13]

In the lower south the situation was different. The rice plantation was more specialized and provided less opportunity for the development of a wide range of skills. The concentration of blacks was greater while whites did all they could to escape the low country's insalubrious climate. There could be no paternalist ethos in the context of widespread absenteeism. Just as the pressures towards assimilation were less, so were the opportunities for collective behaviour greater. Large numbers of slaves from similar regions of Africa worked and lived together. When they sought to escape the confines of slavery they very often did so in groups; their aim was usually to establish outlying communities or to escape to the Spanish settlements to the south. The Stono rebellion of 1739 was just such an attempt. The work of Angolan slaves, its object was a group escape from slavery. In many important respects the experience of the lower south approximated to that of the West Indian islands. There it was the unassimilated who sought a collective escape.[14]

The middle period, then, was one in which the status of blacks as slaves was firmly established. It witnessed the transformation of the southern colonies from societies with slaves into slave societies. It saw also the development of two possible modes of black resistance to the trend. In the lower south blacks seem to have been able and desirous of developing along a path that was in part a projection of their African heritages. But the attempt to define themselves in terms of a separate culture was an option which depended upon the circumstances of large specialized plantations, a substantial African-born element, and absenteeism. After the end of the eighteenth century those factors were no longer to coexist nor were they individually to define large areas of the south. In the upper south, on the other hand, blacks – or at least those for whom evidence exists from which their responses can be inferred – increasingly assimilated the dominant cultural forms of the society in which they found themselves and sought less to resist or by-pass them than to enjoy them more fully. As members of an oppressed group they endeavoured to escape oppression in order that they might enjoy the same rights as those enjoyed by their oppressors.

The middle years of the eighteenth century saw a decline in the social and economic importance of slavery in New England and the middle colonies; the establishment of a slave society in the upper south in which blacks were becoming increasingly assimilated; and the rapid growth of a slave society in the lower south in which blacks predominated in numbers and remained largely unacculturated. Nowhere, however, were there systematic attempts to conceptualize the meaning of the existence in America of a large black minority. Slavery was defined and the definition spilled over into some uncoordinated treatment of blacks as such, but that was as far as it went. Slavery was, moreover, still one among many forms of servitude. It was not in this period that there developed a firm concept of a black minority as opposed to a slave class.

III

Long before the final quarter of the eighteenth century all the ingredients existed in America of a thoroughly racist society and they were reflected in the colonial slave codes. Those codes banned, for example, inter-racial marriage but not inter-racial sex. But they were not justified or rationalized in these terms. They were advanced and accepted as methods of social and economic control, as pragmatic measures. They were discriminatory but not sacred. One must emphasize, too, that slavery and the colour line largely coincided. Free blacks were far from numerous and many spent a considerable portion of their lives in effective slavery: bastards had to serve until the age of thirty-one, for example, and many free blacks indented themselves to whites for long terms. What was it about the revolutionary era that stirred up this pot of ingredients and drew from it that coherent racist doctrine which was to become sacred, was to become a significant totem in American society?[15]

I think developments in four directions were primarily responsible. Let us look first at the question of revolutionary ideology. Interpreting the imperial conflict as an attempt by England to make them slaves, it was inevitable that the colonists should eventually bring into the discussion the chattel slavery they themselves practised. There being no compelling reason to resist the logic of revolutionary rhetoric in the northern states slavery was everywhere abolished there, although the process of abolition was sometimes slowed by considerations of property rights. In the southern states there were powerful economic and social reasons for following a different course. Property rights were more extensively involved, of course, and it was not unreasonable to fear economic catastrophe if so fundamental an alteration were made in existing patterns of labour relations. But these arguments were politically inadequate. Few slaveholders doubted the legitimacy, or even the justice of slavery, but they apprehended dangers from the actions of their leaders. The dangers were of two kinds. First, those leaders might act directly against slavery as Jefferson seemed to the delegates from South Carolina and Georgia to be doing in his draft Declaration of Independence. Second, the routine operation of sound American principles might undermine slavery. In a decision paralleling that of the Massachusetts Supreme Court, for example, George Wythe in the Virginia Court of Chancery ruled that the Virginia Bill of Rights had effected a general emancipation. Although his decision was over-turned in the higher court the potential for disaster was revealed. Slave-holders were in any case compelled to a defence of slavery by the need to convince themselves and others of their true attachment to American principles: otherwise they must stand branded as hypocrites. Usually, although not always, they acknowledged the ultimate iniquity of slavery while affirming its present necessity. Nor were their arguments all racist. The existence of an extensive landless proletariat was, for instance, incom-patible with the idea of republicanism as all Americans then defined it. And what else could the mass of freed men be if a general emancipation was accomplished? More fundamentally, however, southerners developed the argument that black and white could not live freely together because of racial differences. Blacks, it was asserted, were inferior in intellect, in their capacity for survival in a competitive economic society, and in that observance of moral values upon which civilized society ultimately de-pends. The term 'All men ...' in the Declaration of Independence had to be interpreted as all *white* men.

From this line of thinking there emerged the clear outlines of a hostile stereotype of blacks. They were deemed to lack intelligence; they were alleged to be idle, dishonest and savage; they were described as sexually promiscuous and a threat to white womanhood and the purity of the white race. The need to develop such systematic views was impelled in part by the need to repel attacks on slavery coming largely from outside the region. But it arose more significantly from the tension generated by articulating libertarian ideals within a slave society. In seeking a reconciliation between these contradictory trends southerners preserved their commitment to republicanism by formally reading blacks out of the polity, thereby separating black slavery from white freedom.

The second aspect of the era that concerns us was the creation of a new political framework. Southern control over southern institutions had not been complete during the colonial period. But independence from Great Britain accentuated rather than resolved the problem. Now the southern states found themselves linked in union with quite dissimilar states, which were led by their commitment to freedom to abolish slavery within their own confines. The sense of a special American destiny to establish free-dom-oriented goals and structures made this new linkage potentially dangerous for the south.

Relations between north and south were from the beginning bedevilled by the existence of slavery. Any central government would have to represent in some admixture the population, wealth and power of its con-stituent parts. How was slavery to enter into the calculation? It was a prob-lem during debates over the Articles of Confederation; it was an even big-ger problem in respect of the constitution that emerged from the 1787 Philadelphia convention. The compromises inherent in that document seemed to guarantee southern interests, but the scruples that prevented the term slave or slavery appearing in it, the heat of debate generated by the issue, and the willingness and ability of northerners to interpret the document in an antislavery sense, all raised doubts. Whenever the new Congress established by that constitution undertook the following years to raise the question of slavery in any form, the debate was acrimonious and laden with threats to the Union. From the beginning, moreover, it emerged that sectional balance within the Union would depend upon a more or less equal sharing-out of western territories between north and south, between slavery and freedom. The south refused ever to concede that it had surrendered any of the powers necessary to maintain an autonomous control over its own institutions. But legalistic arguments of this nature were not wholly effective. To repel assaults made in the name of American principles merely by professing self-interest would hardly prove satisfying or permanent. Southerners responded instead by setting out the dangers to be apprehended from a general emancipation. Their arguments centred upon the nature of blacks and the depredations they could be expected to commit upon any society foolish enough prematurely to liberate them.

Thirdly, the idea of a revolutionary solution to the problem of slavery was not lost upon any of the parties. That the American example was relevant to the slaves was never doubted and Lord Dunmore, royal governor of Virginia, rammed the point home by enlisting slaves under his loyalist banner with the promise of freedom. Of course, slave societies had become inured to the idea of revolt. Revolts were everywhere feared and they were also expected but few doubted that they could be suppressed. The age of revolutions, and especially of the French Revolution, altered perceptions of revolt which had hitherto obtained. Welcomed in its early stages as evidence of the influence of American ideals, the French Revolution turned sour for most Americans as the Terror unfolded and as Napoleon's imperial ambitions emerged. But it was less events in France than events in the French West Indies that alarmed southerners. The slave revolts in Martinique, Guadeloupe and St Domingue injected a new order of magnitude into modern slave rebellions. St Domingue eventually secured its independence and housed the first autonomous black republic in the western hemisphere. It did so only after a decade and a half of bitter, bloody fighting and constant massacres. In a three-cornered fight between blacks, mulattoes and whites all parties were guilty of the most horrendous cruelties. Refugees fled to the United States and insurrectionary fears circulated, seeming to gain credibility from Gabriel Prosser's rebellion of 1800.

It was the horrors perpetrated by blacks that most impinged upon the American imagination. Yet one lesson seemed to stand out above all others. The revolt stemmed, it appeared, from actions taken in Paris. St Domingue was the richest colony in the hemisphere and it had been thrown into ruin through the ill-considered actions of those determined to interfere in the relations between black and white without being fully appraised of the realities of the multiracial situation. The most horrid revolts were to be feared less from slavery than from antislavery.

Finally, the feature of the Haitian imbroglio which impressed itself most fiercely upon southern consciousness was the role of the free mulattoes. It was the claims of this caste for the same political rights enjoyed by whites, and their eventual willingness to ally with the slaves, that explained the inferno. Did the United States have such a caste? Many historians, most notably Carl Degler, have argued that American slavery was differentiated from that in other western hemisphere countries by the difficulty of securing freedom. Manumission was legally circumscribed in the southern mainland colonies. Degler has argued, furthermore, that as a result of the greater assertiveness and equality of English women, compared with their Latin counterparts, inter-racial sex was less openly enjoyed by their husbands. The result was that masters might fornicate with slave women but they were less likely to make the matter overt by liberating or giving special privileges to their mistresses and offspring. Certainly at the outset of the American Revolution slavery and the colour line approximated to one another closely, although those who were free were predominantly mulattoes. The Revolution promoted important changes here also.[16]

Antislavery pressures arose in the late eighteenth century from a number of sources which need not concern us here. It is sufficient to note that by 1804, with the exception of Delaware, the eastern and middle states had all provided for the abolition of slavery and that religious pressures, coupled with revolutionary considerations, had culminated in a temporary loosening of manumission laws in the south. From between 3,000 and 5,000 in 1780, free blacks had risen in number to 60,000 in 1790 and over 180,000 in 1810. The great majority were to be found in the upper south and in the middle states. The coincidence of slavery and colour had been broken as also had the overwhelming predominance of mulattoes among the free coloured community. This new class in the population was viewed by whites with increasing fear and distaste as potential aides to a slave insurrection, as promoters of unrest and discontent amongst the slaves, as receivers of goods stolen by slaves from the plantations, and as a poor, work-shy, criminal element which constituted a drain upon society. Soon after the turn of the century renewed restrictions upon private manumissions began to find their way back onto the statute books.[17]

Thus the reconciliation of revolutionary pretensions with southern slavery, the defence of the southern position within the Union, the resistance to antislavery, and fears about the fastest growing sector of the population – the free blacks – all acted to focus attention upon negroes who were free. Their character was scrutinized and found wanting: they were poor, idle and vicious. They served to refute the charge that similar vices observed upon the plantations were the consequences of slavery: on the contrary, they were adduced as evidence that they were innate to blacks. Discrimination against blacks was henceforth to follow an explicitly racist orientation as well as a class one: indeed, where slavery no longer existed it followed a wholly racial line. Whites had come to define blacks as a minority that differed from themselves in physiological, biological, and cultural characteristics.

What of the blacks? A great number of them took advantage of the opportunities offered by the Revolution to secure their freedom. They served in the armed forces, especially on the British side, and many eventually found their way to Sierra Leone by way of Nova Scotia as a consequence. Others remained in the United States and were joined by those manumitted by their masters or emancipated by abolition laws. They resisted growing encroachments upon their liberties and rejected the hostile picture whites drew of them. But with some exceptions their actions were not directed towards the development of a separate culture and society but towards the winning of an acceptance by whites that the revolutionary creed spoke for all men. True, they reacted against discrimination by forming their own separate institutions – churches, schools, benevolent societies – but they also resisted attempts by whites to define America as a white man's country and to colonize blacks abroad. In so far as there was pressure towards the development of separate cultures it was the product of self-assertiveness in the face of white hostility and discriminatory practices. The main impetus came from a conviction that the American creed was a universalist one that could serve them as easily as it served whites.

By the end of the eighteenth century blacks had become a minority group defined by colour but no longer by condition. It is important to note, though, that the definition was made by the dominant majority, not by the black minority, which exhibited no major internal tendencies to develop along a separate path, no concern to maintain or extend separate language skills, cultural forms or value systems. Blacks did not seek the preservation of their minority status within a pluralistic society. On the contrary, they desired full incorporation into the extended American society. They wished to share in the obligations and prizes incurred and bestowed by a young and vital nation. Over the next two centuries their faith in their American destiny was sometimes to be shaken and they would look inward upon themselves, but the thrust imparted by the Revolutionary era has remained the dominant mode of behaviour, if less often of expression.

Notes

1 The percentages are derived from *The Statistical History of the United States from Colonial Times to the Present* (New York, 1976), series Z–19, p. 1168. The rate at which the black population increased is a measure of the general growth in the popularity of slavery in the mainland colonies but it does not measure adequately the popularity itself. Using Philip Curtin's estimates of the increase in the slave population due to importations and natural increase respectively, one can do so (Philip D. Curtin, *The Atlantic Slave Trade: a Census* (Madison, 1969), table 40, p. 140). If one assumes that the natural increase in the slave population was proportional to the number of slaves one can derive figures for the importations in each region. Using the mid-point of each twenty-year period as the base for such calculations the following table was derived. It expresses importations in terms of the total population and thus measures, however crudely, their impact upon the labour market.

Importations of slaves per 1,000 residents

	1700–20	1720–40	1740–60	1760–80
New England	9·3	11·6	1·9	−6·5
Middle Colonies	66·7	11·4	20·3	1·6
Upper South	146·8	148·8	170·6	72·2
Lower South	890·6	374·6	263·7	178·5

It is clear that during the first half of the century the experiences of the middle region and the upper south diverged sharply as the middle colonies came to approximate the behaviour of New England. Even this measure, then, helps to confirm the *shape* of my argument. The accuracy of the figures should not be too readily assumed but there is no reason to doubt the relative orders of magnitude they suggest.

2 Carl Bridenbaugh, *Cities in the Wilderness: the First Century of Urban Life in America 1625–1742* (Oxford, 1971), pp. 95, 200, 201, 249, 409; Bridenbaugh, *Cities in Revolt: Urban Life in America 1743–1776* (Oxford, 1971), pp. 88, 333.

3 Bridenbaugh, *Cities in the Wilderness*, pp. 201, 250, 409.

4 F. M. L. Thompson, 'The Social Distribution of Landed Property in England since the Sixteenth Century', *Economic History Review*, 2nd series, XIX (1966), pp. 505–17; J. P. Cooper, 'The Social Distribution of Land and Men in England, 1436–1700', *Economic History Review*, 2nd series XX (1967), pp. 419–40.

5 Edmund S. Morgan, *American Slavery, American Freedom: The Ordeal of Colonial Virginia* (New York, 1975), pp. 215 ff. The next three paragraphs follow closely the argument in Morgan's chapter 11 ff.

6 The best treatment of slavery in early South Carolina is Peter H. Wood, *Black Majority: Negroes in Colonial South Carolina from 1670 through the Stono Rebellion* (New York, 1974).

7 See the discussions in Winthrop D. Jordan, *White Over Black. American Attitudes toward the Negro, 1550–1812* (Baltimore, 1969), pp. 111 ff., and David Brion Davis, *The Problem of Slavery in Western Culture* (London, 1970), pp. 274 ff.

8 Bridenbaugh, *Cities in Revolt*, pp. 88, 274, 286; Massachusetts Historical Society *Collections*, 5th Series, III, pp. 401–2.

9 Wood, chapter 7.

10 See the discussion in Michael Mullin (ed.), *American Negro Slavery: a Documentary History* (New York, 1976) pp. 8 ff. See also the account by Wood, *Black Majority* and Morgan, *American Slavery American Freedom*.

11 The autarchic nature of the tobacco plantation in the eighteenth century is well understood and is most succinctly suggested by Mullin and Morgan, above, and by Daniel J. Boorstin, *The Americans: the Colonial Experience* (London, 1965), pp. 118–69.

12 Mullin, 14 ff., Morgan, 363 ff.

13 Gerald W. Mullin, *Flight and Rebellion. Slave Resistance in Eighteenth Century Virginia* (Oxford, 1972).

14 Wood, *passim*; Mullin, *American Negro Slavery*, p. 12 ff.

15 What follows is based on the account in Duncan J. Macleod, *Slavery, Race and the American Revolution* (Cambridge, 1974).

16 Carl N. Degler, *Neither Black nor White: Slavery and Race Relations in Brazil and the United States* (New York, 1971), pp. 235–9.

17 Macleod, pp. 162–9; Ira Berlin, *Slaves without Masters: the Free Negro in the Antebellum South* (New York, 1974).

8

Red, black and white in nineteenth-century America

Christine Bolt

I

In 1894 the prominent anthropologist, Franz Boas, argued that there were 'few countries in which the effects of intermixture of races and of change of environment upon the physical characteristics of man can be studied as advantageously as in America, where a process of slow amalgamation between three distinct races is taking place'.[1] But the interactions between these three are still imperfectly understood. There has been relatively little concern to compare the respective fortunes of Indians and Africans in the United States, and the policies and attitudes developed towards them by white Americans, no doubt because of the magnitude of such an undertaking.[2] Those works which do throw light upon these themes, while pointing out the pervasive nature of white prejudices and the general priority given to political or social, rather than humanitarian or theoretical, considerations in the framing of public policy concerning minorities, tend to stress the differences between red and black and the responses they provoked.

Of course the two races were very different in their original cultures, their numbers and physique. The native Americans possessed the bargaining counters of land, military strength and local knowledge, the negroes had the assets of adaptability and usefulness. Both were enslaved, but the Indians proved more difficult to hold, as well as being less numerous and less familiar with agricultural labour. If the native Americans, like Africans, were described as savages, by the nineteenth century only the Indian still retained claims to nobility, however vulnerable; the red men were also considered by scientists as superior in brain power and appearance, and by most Americans as having some cultural attainments worthy of respect. The history of the original inhabitants of America was investigated sooner, and with greater zeal, than the languages and cultures of uprooted Africans, if only to demonstrate the venerable heritage of the new republic and because the piecemeal 'conquest' of the Indians over two centuries, together with the failure of Indian slavery, required a longer show of toleration for their alien ways. This ignorance of Africa and equation of most negroes with slavery meant that Americans might be more tempted to think in terms of a single 'negro problem' than they were of a uniform

Indian challenge, while the different context in which the two minorities were encountered – Indians generally as defenders of the untamed wilderness, despite the dependence of many tribes on agriculture, and negroes as a crucial component of commercial farming – obviously meant that they were separated in the public mind.

Moreover, those who made a serious study of such matters emphasized the permanence of racial types, although it is debatable how far scientific and popular attitudes interacted, at least before the Civil War. Nor have Indian men usually been regarded as a threat to white women, despite their failure to spare them in warfare, even if there is some evidence that the Plains tribes were thought to be dangerously lecherous (and not just by the female commentators whom Professor Fiedler sees as so misleading on this subject). In a turbulent society, martial activities among the tribes, though opposed, were appreciated more highly than traditions of peaceful resistance among black slaves. Finally the two races have had a very different legal status and relationship with the federal government, albeit there has been no consistent commitment to Indian separation, while the ostensible commitment to assimilating the negroes has not ruled out savage policies of social segregation. This difference has been sustained in part by an appreciation of contrasting black and red responses to the white majority. Although black nationalist movements have a long history in the United States, the free black community strove to live in a manner acceptable to other Americans, as did the majority of negroes when freedom was secured, demanding and expecting in consequence all the rights enjoyed by their fellow citizens. As the black leader, Frederick Douglass, declared of his race in 1854, 'civilization cannot kill ... [the negro]. He accepts it – becomes part of it'.[3] Conversely, while Indian groups were willing to adopt aspects of white civilization, those in the west were determined, if possible, to retain their distinctive languages and customs in geographical isolation from other Americans, and in the east small bands survived with similar cultural autonomy into the twentieth century.

None the less a graded caste system did not develop in the United States, although distinctive black-coloured-white groupings emerged in some southern cities, and a black-red-white separation existed in the Carolinas. If contrasting emotional reactions and intellectual speculations about the two major non-white minorities produced a contrasting literary and artistic imagery of red and black, the need of the dominant white population to retain and justify the power it had grasped, as well as the need for labour and peace of mind, dictated that both groups should be 'civilized' – that is, christianized, taught English and educated after the white fashion, persuaded to conform to white ways of dressing, eventually admitted to civil rights and then obliged to make their own way in a competitive world. Indians and blacks alike suffered from European colour prejudices, contempt for non-Christians, and fears of the unrestrained sexuality attributed to those who wore few clothes and permitted somewhat freer relations between the sexes, especially before marriage, than were tolerated in their own polite circles. Both peoples helped white settlers to redefine the essence of their own civilization and afforded them a means of reasserting class distinctions in a world whose size and bounty threatened established ways, a land where the poor could rise and outcasts be at home.

The elaboration of prejudices brought from Europe to justify slavery on the one hand and expropriation on the other, thus increasing the economic fortunes of white men, though well advanced by the middle of the eighteenth century, was only perfected from the revolutionary period onwards. Racial attitudes hardened as slave numbers grew and Indian wars proved endlessly inconclusive, as settlers poured westward, and when, for the first time, 'societal racism' came under organized attack from men who believed in environmentalism and natural rights – from missionaries and other opponents of Indian removal and from the abolitionists.[4] In that situation poor southern whites and slave-owners were able to come together in what G. M. Frederickson has termed a '*herrenvolk* democracy', ironically supported by white northerners who applauded their increasingly strident assertions about the innate inferiority of negroes, without necessarily seeing slavery as the best solution. And to those faced with the realization that the Indians remained 'uncivilized' while the expansion of white civilization could not be restrained, scientific teachings on race offered simultaneously an explanation for failure and a rationale for removing the remaining tribes west of the Mississippi. In a white man's country, such as America was self-consciously becoming in the first half of the nineteenth century, any shade other than white bestowed no major advantage.

The point about the homogenizing tendency of white prejudices in times of crisis may be taken a little further through a brief account of the objectives of those who claimed to be the friends of the coloured races, but who none the less were very much men and women of their own times.[5]

II

On the face of it humanitarians did distinguish clearly between 'the plight' of Indians and that of negroes. They organized separately to aid the two minorities, and by the end of the eighteenth century black slaves were claiming the most attention.[6] In many ways it was disastrous that the world-wide antislavery movement and the problems posed by the negroes and native Americans came to a climax at about the same time. Since the amount of time and money which could be spared for oppressed groups was strictly limited, given the fickle nature of public interest, the inadequacy of white reformers, the hostility of many Indians, and the fine balance between the political parties, it should not be too surprising that black Americans attracted more attention. And while the Indian policies of the 1830s incurred disapproving comments from European visitors, they precipitated no such 'moral embargo' against the United States as that operated by western countries which had abolished slavery or slave trading in the early nineteenth century. Again, whereas freedmen's aid societies flourished before the Civil War had ended, really effective Indian reform organizations did not appear until the 1880s, even though the fate of both races was in fact similar during the two preceding decades.[7] According to Loring B. Priest, the post-war Indian reformers, whatever their earlier connections with antislavery, were obliged to start afresh in building up a constituency sympathetic to an equally unfortunate minority.[8] Throughout Reconstruction financial and western pressures on Congress, continuing Indian disturbances, the clamour of women for the vote, a sense of gratitude to the blacks for wartime services and the need to secure their political allegiance once more ensured that priority was given to negro claims.

Yet, despite these difficulties, reformers did seek to present the two minorities in a similar fashion, appealing to comparable racial stereotypes and, in each case, to prevailing values and social requirements. Assimilation was always their ultimate objective, though it might regrettably have to be achieved in stages – through slavery and then through segregation in east or west, allowing red and black to rise at their own pace. Soldier and educator Captain Richard Henry Pratt, an advocate of intermarriage between red and white, seemed unhappy about the prospect of instructing Indians and negroes together at Hampton Institute, Virginia, because he hoped to see native Americans educated at the public schools and was fearful that the heavy social prejudices against blacks would be transferred to any group with whom they associated.[9] No doubt his unhappiness was shared, since Hampton remained the only bi-racial educational institution of its kind. But Pratt himself, who deplored segregation for either Indians or blacks, remained best known for his work at Carlisle Indian school. Such race schools, for all their stern regulations, provided the best opportunity for non-whites to obtain a conventional education until the changing outlook of twentieth-century whites slowly permitted their officially unsegregated participation in the public school system.

Many contemporaries believed that the condition of the negroes had retrogressed since the abandonment of slavery, and made this alleged development one more excuse for repression and regulation. Bearing this in mind, reformers were careful to admit – while denying retrogression – that they had learned from the mistakes of Reconstruction and that the full civilization of the Indians must precede the granting to them of civil rights.[10] However, just as the abolitionists had stressed that slaves, like women, deserved special sympathy and manifested special qualities, and some feminists had equated their claims for equal rights with those of the black population, so the Indian and negro were linked together as twin reproaches to the individual of conscience: as one group received better treatment, then in equity, it was argued, so should the other. Since the native Americans were less numerous than the freedmen, assistance to them would cost less. Both stood in need, for it was confidently predicted that each race might die out; yet neither required paternalistic treatment which would stifle enterprise and the ability to survive still further. Hence the Bureau of Indian Affairs was as obnoxious as the Freedmen's Bureau to certain philanthropists.[11]

Concern with the new turn given to racist ideology and reform organizations by the Civil War, the popularization of Social Darwinism and the increasing influence of ethnologists and anthropologists, themselves affected by evolutionary teaching, should not obscure the fact that continuities in reformer as well as racist thought, dictated always by the needs of white society, were more striking than any new departures.

III

Despite their common predicament, it has not been easy for negroes and Indians to come together to advance their interests, sometimes because of mutual antipathies, as witness the reluctance of certain modern Pan-Indian movements to collaborate with negroes; more usually because contacts between them were strictly limited.[12] Yet the experiences of the two races have not always been starkly opposed, as an examination of the history of the Five Civilized Tribes will reveal.

These tribes all lived in the south and were consequently well aware of the increasing importance of slavery among the whites. They also valued the institution on their own account. The Cherokees, Choctaws and Chickasaws ultimately desired slaves for cotton cultivation and other despised agricultural tasks. Furthermore negroes, like white men, were prized as agents and interpreters, and slaveholding was most common among the mixed-bloods of the various tribes, who were clearly influenced by white example. None the less there does not seem to have been a parallel interest in slavery as a means of asserting the total superiority of one race over another.

Among the Creeks and the Seminoles of Florida, long a haven for runaway slaves, relations between Indians and negroes were particularly harmonious, despite the use of Creek mercenaries in the Seminole wars. In Florida there was a determined common resistance to removal further westwards, with all its attendant risks. The Seminoles, as a small and poor tribe, stood to benefit from additions to their numbers, and the negroes, many of whom proved redoubtable fighters, found allies to help them evade recapture. The slaves, who had also been legally purchased from the Spanish, English or Americans, were allowed to live in separate villages, own property and move around freely, and were rarely sold in return for specified 'tribute' or labour. Eventually some of these slaves gained their freedom, and slaves who fled to the Seminoles when the wars with the United States began frequently did so with a view to securing their emancipation. The risk was justified, since the majority were allowed to go with the Indians and older refugees into exile beyond the Mississippi. For the Indians, unfortunately, the long conflict between white slave hunters, Indians and negroes only strengthened white determination to expropriate Indian land and pacify the southern frontier.[13]

In the light of these findings it is tempting, as uneasy missionaries did, to romanticize the relationships between red and black, but the strongest bonds between them were probably self-interest, and hostility towards the white man. Black preference for slavery among Indians rather than whites may thus be explained in terms of the greater status and opportunities afforded for advancement, while from colonial times Indian tribes took slaves, often ransoming or selling them to American traders, in addition to welcoming runaway black slaves and occasional captives as a source of labour, wealth and prestige. Moreover, the two races were united by comparable treatment at the hands of whites, who enslaved and circumscribed them with discriminatory laws, and by whom they were feared as savages, potential allies in a forcible bid for liberty or revenge.[14] White fears in turn led to the adoption of successful defensive measures, including the use of black slaves to hunt out and harass the Indian owners of land allotted under the removal policy and the paid employment of certain Indian tribes to catch runaway black slaves or suppress slave unrest.[15] Ironically black troops would later be used to help put an end to Indian warfare in the west.[16]

The slave narratives, which have been comparatively little used for the study of Indian–negro relations, reinforce such indications of a complex relationship between red and black Americans. They reveal both that individual Indian masters could be harsh and thoughtless, and that the manner of treatment differed from tribe to tribe. Mary Grayson, a black slave born in the Creek nation, testified that 'all the negroes I knew who belonged to Creeks always had plenty of clothes and lots to eat, and we all lived in good log cabins we built', working 'the crops like they belonged to us'. But she went on to add that the Chickasaws used their slaves more sternly, 'like the people in Texas and other places', and apparently the Cherokee owners were equally strict.[17]

After removal, slavery persisted among the Five Tribes, and even increased in severity. White influences may again have been a factor, given the location of the Indian Territory and the fact that key agency posts were held by men from Texas and Arkansas. Yet the survival of the institution among the Indians, and some resistance to the activities of abolitionists among them, did not bring unqualified support for the Confederacy. Many other considerations influenced tribal actions during the Civil War.[18] Furthermore the Indians themselves believed their system to be less harsh than that of the whites, despite the contrary opinion advanced by pious white critics convinced of the ameliorating effect in the south of white women and Christian society.[19]

The Reconstruction years saw a deterioration in relations between red and black in Indian Territory, and these have not yet been adequately examined. By treaties with the United States, the Five Civilized Tribes were required to extend full citizenship rights to their ex-slaves who, contrary to the wishes of some white reformers though not to those of President Johnson, were excluded from the benefits of the national civil rights legislation.[20] The sudden transformation of race relations by force, and the feeling that they were being asked to act more generously towards their freedmen than whites were prepared to do, partly explain Indian discontent.[21]

Another cause for alarm was the designation of Indian Territory as a home not only for displaced Plains tribes but also for negro settlers.[22] This was a pet project of white politicians, and in the later nineteenth century blacks did indeed migrate to the Territory, a movement which did not seriously arouse Indian antagonism until the Oklahoma Territory was opened to white settlement in 1889, and the influx was swelled immediately afterwards by fresh attempts to move black families into the region.[23]

The Five Tribes responded differently to the Reconstruction treaties, according to the numbers of freedmen in their midst and their former relationship with them. Generally the half-breeds were hostile to the new order, while the Creeks and Seminoles appeared to be least resentful of the freedmen.[24] The Choctaws and Chickasaws, who had owned many slaves, were given the choice of incorporating or resettling their negroes. Both tribes opposed adoption – the Choctaws resisted until 1885 and the Chickasaws never complied.[25] The Cherokees were divided, as they had once been over slavery, contesting innumerable cases concerning the rights of freedmen returning from wartime exile, and granting their adopted negroes a share in tribal finances only in 1888.[26]

The first years of readjustment were the worst, as the federal government appeared to be favouring the blacks unduly, and bad conditions aggravated lawlessness among the Choctaw and Chickasaw freedmen, which in turn bred a kind of Indian Ku Klux Klan. An emancipated slave living near Fort Gibson later recalled that 'the negroes who were made Cherokee citizens were so intimidated by intermarried whites and Cherokees that they were afraid to venture out on the streets after dark'. Long after material prosperity had returned, the presence of the negroes complicated law enforcement problems and political disputes in Indian Territory.[27] Reports reached the federal government in the late 1870s that even among the compliant Seminoles the freedmen were still not assimilated, although a more encouraging account of negro conditions was given a decade later.[28]

However, the petitions from the freedmen to Washington, requesting removal or full citizenship rights and the individual allotment of land, were evidently influenced by land-hungry whites. The prospects of land ownership and general advancement seem to have been better for negroes in the Indian Territory than elsewhere in the United States. Outside the Territory, W. McKee Evans's account of the Lowry Gang of North Carolina during Reconstruction indicates there was some possibility for a union of the poor and exploited, regardless of race, in that turbulent era. The Lowrys brought together red, black and white outlaws, and were protected by a local community suspicious of the existing authorities and grateful that raids were directed against prosperous conservatives. After the gang was defeated, the state Democrats interestingly reverted to divide-and-rule tactics among negroes and Indians, by concessions designed to make the latter a 'middle-status' group, above the blacks but below the white population.[29]

But what did the two races really think of one another? The studies referred to here are primarily concerned with the Indians, and such information as they offer relates to behaviour rather than racial attitudes, though the two are obviously if not automatically linked. We know that many negro communities, before and after emancipation, lived quite separately from the rest of their tribe. While such separation understandably developed in slavery, was it perpetuated because of habit, or the resentments of Reconstruction, or mutual antipathies? Blacks may well have been influenced by white racial views, as the southern Indians were. At the 1891

Lake Mohonk conference a Lieutenant Wortherspoon, commenting on the fate of Geronimo's Band in custody under the war department in Alabama, was obliged to admit that when the Indians were hired out locally, black as well as white carpenters refused to work with them.[30] Writing about negro settlements in Indian Territory at the turn of the century the influential black leader, Booker T. Washington, welcomed this separation as he accepted racial segregation and conformity to white ways among the negroes of the south. Although there were 'still ... among the "natives" some negroes who cannot speak the English language, and who have been so thoroughly bred in the customs of the Indians that they have remained among the hills with the tribes by whom they were adopted', as a rule 'the negro natives do not shun the white man and his civilization, but, on the contrary, rather seek it, and enter, with the negro immigrants, into competition with the white man for its benefits'.[31]

IV

During the colonial period there was considerable miscegenation between red and black, both slave and free, which has been attributed to the absence of physical repulsion, the scarcity of negro women, the lack of legal or social obstacles, and shared antipathies towards the white man, beginning in slavery.[32] Under these circumstances there was a natural coming together of the remnants of eastern tribes with another abused minority group, and reports of such mixing can be found from Maine, Rhode Island, Massachusetts, New York, New Jersey, Delaware, Ohio, Tennessee, the Carolinas, Georgia, Mississippi, Florida and Virginia.[33] These contacts continued throughout the nineteenth century, no doubt for the same reasons, so that by 1928 one scholar who polled a sample of American negroes found that some 27·3 per cent of them claimed Indian ancestry. (According to the official census figures, by contrast, in 1910 only 0·8 per cent of the Indian population was reported to be negro–Indian, and 0·7 per cent to be of white, negro, Indian descent, although Reuter argues that the totals are inaccurate because of Indian unwillingness to admit negro blood.)[34] The generally more robust negro physique may have been a positive attraction, while the marriage of negro slaves to free Indians may have been valued by the former principally as a means of securing their own freedom, or that of their children. Certainly there is evidence that in the numerous suits brought from colonial times until the Civil War to establish the race and therefore status of petitioners, proof or appearance of Indian descent often meant freedom.[35] Where the consequence of red–black mingling was the ascendancy of the more numerous negro element, local white resentment of its enjoying Indian rights – including entitlement to land and tax exemption – might be considerable, and mixed communities were also seen as possible refuges for runaway slaves and dangerous free negroes.[36]

Yet it is evident that the native Americans could be as fascinated with African blackness as Europeans – witness in ante-bellum Texas the grisly experiments of Comanche raiders on negro captives, whom they often held to ransom, to determine 'whether or not their dark colour extended to parts beneath the surface'.[37] Most Indian tribes initially regarded even other Indians as quite distinct from themselves, if not positively alien, while Pan-Indianism was in fact fostered by white policies and pressures. Thus Indian assertions of superiority to the newcomers should not surprise us, however much they irked contemporaries, and pleasure in Indian physical attributes appears to have played some part in such assertions. According to John Dunn Hunter, who in 1823 published his controversial account of captivity among the Kansas and Osage tribes:

> The Indians call themselves red men, in contradistinction to whites and blacks, wherever such are known to exist. Generally they pride themselves much on their color; its coppery darkness being considered a peculiar mark of excellence. . . . The Indians universally believe that the Great Spirit, when he created all things, exercised a partiality in their favor, which was indelibly registered in their color. Next in order to themselves some class the whites, while others suppose the blacks to be superior to them: they generally believe this partiality extended to the whole descending series of organic and inorganic things, according to the perfections they respectively display.[38]

It has also been noted that Governor Pownall of Massachusetts, some sixty years earlier, when dividing mankind into three distinct races, 'ascribed such a belief to the Indians', who were influenced not only by the colour of these races but by 'the form of their skull, and their hair'.[39]

There remains considerable controversy about the degree, nature and consequences of racial mixing among the Five Civilized Tribes, not least because marriages were not legally recorded. The Choctaws and Chickasaws seem to have been strongly opposed to these liaisons, and the Cherokee felt much the same, whether influenced by southern attitudes, fears of negro fecundity, or 'the pride of race, which our people have so long cherished', though there is some evidence that they took place just the same and first-hand testimony on the matter is hard to come by.[40] The Seminoles and Creeks were more tolerant, leading to what Annie Abel, reflecting the prejudices of her own day, called the 'pitiful racial deterioration' of the Creeks.[41] Since during the Seminole wars General Jessup had observed that the two coloured races in Florida were 'rapidly approximating', and those conflicts were partly provoked by the refusal of Seminole fathers to surrender to whites the children born of fugitive slave women whom they had sheltered and married, close relations predictably continued in Indian Territory, albeit some racism developed within the tribe.[42]

Contemporary observers were not always so jaundiced in their comments as Miss Abel. Kansas senator J. H. Lane, an advocate of colonizing non-whites in Indian Territory, was even convinced that 'the finest specimens of manhood I have ever gazed upon in my life are half-breed Indians crossed with negroes. It is a fact . . . that while amalgamation with the white man deteriorates both races, the amalgamation of the Indian and the black man advances both races.'[43] Ignoring the obvious satisfaction of a politician who was apparently convinced that he had found a justifiable excuse both for negro and further Indian removal, it may be that Lane had seized upon a curious adaptation of Victorian scientific teaching. If the Indian was indeed less 'inferior' than the negro in terms of facial angle, prognathism and brain weight, then perhaps miscegenation would not come amiss.[44] But by the same token, he should also have justified mixing the physically not too dissimilar red and white races.

Although historians have neglected the study of whites who took Indian partners or ways as presumably untraceable, fragmentary evidence of their activities exists. In the early history of Virginia there were some efforts to encourage miscegenation, with a view to christianizing and civilizing the natives, improving political relations between the races, and relieving a shortage of white women. In 1611 it was reported that forty or fifty Virginia settlers had married Indian women and that English women were consorting with the natives – though this seems to have been rare, mainly because white females were initially scarce and not involved in the occupations where an Indian spouse was an advantage. Early Puritan records, as well as those of New York and, more importantly, Georgia and the Carolinas, indicate a comparable state of affairs.[45]

Whereas the English were more hostile to mixing than the cosmopolitan and numerically vulnerable Spanish or French, attraction and self-interest might conquer religious taboos and the sense of difference, as the fair-haired, blue-eyed Mandans reported by the Lewis and Clark expedition, and the relations of their own party with the Indians would seem to testify.[46] Captivity narratives were always popular in the New World, and some captives chose to embrace the lifestyle and persons of their captors permanently – probably because they were taken young and held long, discounting white disapproval in the case of ultimate release. (Recent works on this subject do not entirely illuminate their motives and have a tendency to romanticism.)[47] And a man as ambivalent in his racial views and policies as Thomas Jefferson could suggest, on many occasions, that Indians and whites should 'intermix, and become one people' – that people, of course, upholding white civilization.[48]

Did the proportion of such alliances to the total population fall dramatically after the passage of prohibitory laws by Virginia and North Carolina, or simply as the proportion of white women in the New World increased? Had the number of alliances ever been large? The answer to the last question would seem to be no, for the shortage of white females prevailed for only a few decades, and family settlement was encouraged in parts of the east, while the Indian population was quickly outnumbered and reduced. There was no place for mixed-bloods in white society, their value and opportunities springing rather from association with Indian communities, even if whites unreasonably resented such associations as much as they deplored tribal reluctance to embrace their 'superior' civilization. Moreover, even in the colonial period few settlers lived near Indians, let alone became sufficiently acquainted with them to contemplate matrimony. This separation was plainly more important than any mutual antipathies, although they clearly existed.[49] The common image of the natives as bestial, cruel, possibly cannibalistic was never the whole picture, and in any event it altered with knowledge. Attitudes towards Indians, as towards any minority group, changed according to social circumstances, but there was no constant expression of physical revulsion, fear and guilt such as we see regarding the negro. Indians might allegedly prostitute their women for liquor, hospitably offer them to strangers, permit casual pre-marital intercourse and strip their captives, but they were not as a race felt to be lustful or easy, and not universally regarded as rank or hideous, with their straight hair and tawny colour. Mixed bloods, after all, might not look so very different from white men, and whites congratulated themselves on their ability to pick out 'not only the best-looking squaws, but also the finest physical specimens of the race'.[50] For their part the Indians seem to have taken into their midst, on their own terms, the strong, the useful and the attractive from among those who came their way and, secured by in-group pride, not to have felt the need for elaborate racial theories. Acting thus they did not yield the general superiority of white civilization but merely the occasional acceptability of its agents, just as they coveted white trade goods without consenting to welcome the non-material aspects of settler culture.

The decline in intermarriage and 'sexual commerce' owed more to shrinking need and opportunity than to changing racial attitudes – that is to Victorian moralizing on their bad effects and conviction that pure blood was the best, however useful such moralizing was in sanctifying the inevitable. None the less wherever the two races met during the nineteenth century – throughout the eastern states, on the boundaries of and within the Indian Territory – mixing took place and was recorded with due disquiet. While practising miscegenation fur traders rarely urged it and were often disappointed in their half-breed progeny, who seemed to sense their status as 'marginal men' – distinguished, as mustees, from mulattoes but likewise included in the slave codes, and thought to combine the worst qualities of both races.[51] Missionaries to the various tribes were in the awkward position of having to deplore irregular liaisons between the races while benefiting from miscegenation: it was the mixed-breeds who, for obvious reasons, gave the most encouraging reception to the religious and educational activities of the missionaries.[52] And if feelings of superiority generally encouraged men of God to set a good example to neighbouring whites in sexual matters, they might succumb to temptation. Reporting to the Lake Mohonk conference in 1886 Miss Alice Robertson, born in Indian Territory and the daughter of an Indian missionary, asserted in a wonderful piece of special pleading that she had 'known a great many missionary families brought up among the Indians, and I have yet to know one in which at least one member has not intermingled with the Indians. I have one sister whose husband is an Indian and an aunt whose husband is an Indian. This shows that there is nothing inferior in the Indian. I don't know any such general rule of marrying among the negroes.'[53]

Indian reformers were similarly in the position of having to live up to their own high ideals, to respond, as it were, to the Iroquois plea to the French Jesuit priests: 'if you love, as you say you do, our souls, love our bodies also, and let us be henceforth but one nation.'[54] There is disagreement as to whether, when humanitarians of the second half of the nineteenth century urged assimilation of the native Americans, they meant this to be confined only to the political and economic realms: they, like their contemporaries, often believed in the degeneracy of hybrids and regarded 'squaw men' as a most uncivilizing influence.[55] But not all could bring themselves to rule out miscegenation entirely. An executive committee member of the Indian Rights Association suggested in 1886 that amalgamation could not be prevented and would not be harmful with so small a group as the Indians: mixing was, after all, tolerated with the larger black minority. He neither recommended nor feared miscegenation, which could be safely regulated by 'the tastes and prejudices of individuals'.[56] Theodore Roosevelt, though acknowledging that half-breeds and squaw men were complained of on the reservations, thought them healthier and generally more advanced than other Indians, some showing fully as much ability as whites and having 'an enormous advantage over the mixed bloods of negro and white ancestry in that they have comparatively little race prejudice to combat'.[57] He was right about Indian ambivalence on this subject. Even among the Five Civilized Tribes half-breeds and intermarried whites, like the adopted negroes, served to avert the necessity for complete Americanization of the rest of the tribe. In other words they could trade and negotiate with outsiders, or perform tasks shunned by the full-bloods, but their value was clearly questioned when their numbers grew threateningly large.[58] Yet however uncommon legal marriages may have been, by the twentieth century Madison Grant was noting the frequent assertion that half the Indian population had white blood. (The real figure was closer to a third: in the 1910 census 33·1 per cent of the Indian population was declared to be of white–Indian blood at a time when 35·2 per cent of the total were estimated to have mixed parentage. It is further suggested that perhaps four fifths of the mixed-bloods were at least half white.)[59]

Mixing between white and black, more frequently discussed because of the rapid expansion of the black community up to independence and the vulnerability of negro slaves to white manipulation in sexual as in other aspects of life, nevertheless requires further study. Even for reformers who linked the mistreatment of Indians and blacks in America, amalgamation with the latter might be regarded with dismay, in recognition, perhaps, of the still stronger prejudices of other whites and received 'scientific' opinion, as well as of the greater numbers liable to be involved. Thus abolitionists were reluctant to endorse miscegenation if this played into the hands of their political enemies, urging abolition as a means of ending illicit intercourse between the races and averting a terrible sexual revenge by black men against white women. As a result white southerners would be saved from debilitating sexual indulgence and intermarriage might even decline. However the blunt commitment to miscegenation, when desired, of men like William Lloyd Garrison, Wendell Phillips and Theodore Tilton, could only confirm the worst fears of southern racists.[60]

Amalgamation of the black and white races was generally deplored more strongly than red–white assimilation, not least since numbers and proximity made it more likely; the charms of New Orleans and Charleston 'coloured' women notwithstanding, the offspring were liable to be displeasing. However, many of the 'causes' for concern were identical –

the fact that so many matches were not legally sanctified, and that mixed breeds might be intellectually superior to pure bloods (a familiar explanation of their prominence in the nineteenth-century black or Indian community, before and after the Civil War) yet were morally vicious or weak ('the tragic mulatto' was a popular theme for American writers), restlessly caught between two worlds and disturbing the non-white masses. The adoption of coloured children of whatever type was never popular with white parents, though Indians were willing to adopt white children just as they absorbed other outsiders. In fact American mulattoes – unlike their brethren in, say, Jamaica – while frequently valuing their ties with the white man did not seek to establish themselves as an intermediate caste. Like the Indian half-breeds, though they might act as spokesmen for the race, acceptable to whites who gave them publicity and declared them to be leaders, their ultimate loyalties lay outside the white world.[61]

Slavery was the major differentiating factor. The laws against inter-marriage that had slowly developed in the seventeenth century had been particularly concerned to prohibit black–white crossing and to further strengthen the slave system by ensuring that mulatto children followed the status of the mother, most alliances being between black women and white men. But we know that, despite determined efforts by black men and women to protect themselves against abuse of privilege, miscegenation remained as an indictment of the white slave-owner and a source of shame to his wife, and as an occasional link between otherwise distinct working-class groups in American cities, even if some white women formed attachments to black men in defiance of community condemnation.[62] Inter-racial sex was manifestly not confined to those lower orders among the whites whose bestiality or at least complacency in such affairs was a common upper class fantasy, though we have little direct evidence as to motive, if it is a relevant consideration where emotions are concerned. All that we may conjecture, bearing in mind the sexual *mores* of Anglo-Saxons in other parts of the world, is that force, personal insecurity, mistrust of their own women who, like savages, had to be protected against biological weakness or decadent lust, and fears about the degrading or democratizing effects of sex between the unequal, were factors so far as white men were concerned, concealed from colonial times behind monotonous pronouncements on the lasciviousness of black women and the irresistible potency of the black man. It is a nice irony, little documented, that these fixations about the sexual prowess of other races, born of distance, curiosity and wishful thinking, were also entertained by blacks about whites.[63]

During the Reconstruction years and beyond, as intermarriage was banned, legalized and then banned again, following both northern and southern precedent, it is usually accepted that miscegenation declined, especially outside the cities. But this decline surely owes less to laws than the increased physical and mental separation between the races, particularly in the south, and was in any event exaggerated by whites reluctant to acknowledge the existence of a mulatto class. Freedmen acted quickly to legalize slave marriages and, although most of them remained in agricultural employment in the south, they were no longer subject to that minute supervision in daily life which many southerners would have liked to reimpose, and which had facilitated inter-racial sex. If blacks asserted their claims for equality through the medium of southern politics, with some success where they offered no numerical or other threat to white supremacy, they also increasingly looked to the management of their own affairs without white interference. Violent sexual contacts did not cease, of course, as the grim testimony before the commission investigating Ku Klux Klan outrages makes plain. The alleged but seldom substantiated threat of black outrages against white women, reflecting ancient fears about how slaves would behave when free, was made the excuse for the Klan, lynching and the ruthless extension of segregation in American life.[64]

Debates about the size of the mulatto population are complicated by the method of enumeration by inspection, a technique which probably led to undercounting. (In the case of the Indians, not adequately estimated until after 1890, appearance, self-declaration, the community verdict and inclusion on tribal or agency rolls have been the guides, producing similar problems.) However between 1850 and 1890 the number of mulattoes rose from 159,095 free, and 246,656 enslaved, to 1,132,060; or from 11·2 to 15·2 per cent of the total 'black' community, in a period when the overall population was increasing from 23,192,000 to 62,948,000, and black numbers went up from 3,638,808 to 7,488,676.[65] These figures, possibly unreliable and unimpressive in terms of grand total, would none the less appear to confirm the truism that laws to enforce 'morality' may win support from the dominating sectors of society yet are seldom enforceable. And this confirmation is not invalidated by the fact that much of the increase in the mulatto class – which took place throughout the country, but especially where there was a high proportion of whites in the population – may be accounted for by the mingling of blacks with mixed-bloods. The statistician F. L. Hoffman, pronouncing in 1896 on the sad decline of both the Indian and negro population, urged as at least a partial remedy that 'intercourse with the white race must absolutely cease and race purity must be insisted upon in marriage as well as outside of it.'[66] Earlier in the century Abraham Lincoln, who was himself opposed to miscegenation, had come much nearer to practicalities in advancing that counsel of despair, colonization. The 'separation of races', he declared, 'is the only perfect preventive of amalgamation.'[67]

Notes

1 Quoted in J. D. Forbes (ed.), *The Indian in America's Past* (New York, 1964), p. 142.
2 But see for instance W. D. Jordan, *White Over Black: American Attitudes Toward the Negro, 1550–1812* (Chapel Hill, N.C., 1968), especially pp. 2, 82, 89, 162–3, 169, 239–40, 477–81; C. Degler, 'Slavery and the Genesis of American Race Prejudice', *Comparative Studies in History and Society* XI (October 1959), pp. 49–66; G. B. Nash, *Red, White and Black: the Peoples of Early America* (New York, 1974); and Nash, 'Red, White and Black: the Origins of Racism in Colonial America' in G. B. Nash and R. Weiss (eds), *The Great Fear: Race in the Mind of America* (New York, 1970), pp. 1–26; F. M. Binder, *The Color Problem in*

Early National America as Viewed by John Adams, Jefferson and Jackson (The Hague, 1968); M. T. Bailey, *Reconstruction in Indian Territory: a Story of Avarice, Discrimination, and Opportunism* (Port Washington, N.Y., 1972), *passim*; D. F. Littlefield, *Africans and Seminoles: From Removal to Emancipation* (Westport, Conn., 1977); R. Halliburton, Jr., *Red Over Black: Black Slavery Among the Cherokee* (Westport, 1977); W. G. McLoughlin, 'Red Indians, Black Slavery and White Racism', *American Quarterly* XXVI, no. 4 (1974), pp. 367–85, which focuses on the Cherokee; B. W. Dippie, *The Vanishing American: Popular Attitudes and American Indian Policy in the Nineteenth Century* (Ph.D. thesis, University of Texas at Austin, 1970), chapter 6; L. A. Fiedler, *The Return of the Vanishing American* (London, 1972), pp. 26, 40, 52, 70, 82–3, 117–18, 136, 177–8; E. Parry, *The Image of the Indian and the Black Man in American Art, 1590–1900* (New York, 1974); and for periodical and dissertation literature in particular see F. P. Prucha (ed.), *A Bibliographical Guide to the History of Indian–White Relations in the United States* (Chicago and London, 1977), pp. 51–3, 352–4.

3 P. S. Foner, (ed.), *The Life and Writings of Frederick Douglass* (New York, 1950) II, p. 308.

4 See the illuminating article by G. M. Frederickson, 'Toward a Social Interpretation of the Development of American Racism' in N. I. Huggins, M. Kilson and D. M. Fox (eds), *Key Issues in the Afro-American Experience* (New York, 1971) I, pp. 240–54. From the huge literature on white racial attitudes the reader should consult: Jordan; D. B. Davis, *The Problem of Slavery in Western Culture* (Ithaca, N.Y., 1969 edn) and *The Problem of Slavery in the Age of Revolution, 1770–1823* (Ithaca, N.Y., 1975); B. Sheehan, *Seeds of Extinction: Jeffersonian Philanthropy and the American Indian* (Chapel Hill, N.C., 1973); R. Slotkin, *Regeneration Through Violence: the Mythology of the American Frontier, 1600–1860* (Middletown, Conn., 1973); R. H. Pearce, *The Savages of America: a Study of the Indian and the Idea of Civilization* (Baltimore, 1953); G. M. Frederickson, *The Black Image in the White Mind: the Debate on Afro-American Character and Destiny, 1817–1914* (New York, 1971); and L. Friedman, *The White Savage: Racial Fantasies in the Postbellum South* (Englewood Cliffs, N.J., 1970).

5 The wider ramifications of relations between the three races will be discussed in a larger work by the present author, primarily focused on Indian history, now in preparation.

6 On the considerable religious and abolitionist interest in the Indians which did exist see forthcoming article by C. Bolt, 'The Antislavery Origins of Concern for the American Indians'; T. E. Drake, *Quakers and Slavery in America* (New Haven, 1950), p. 10; and S. V. James, *A People Among Peoples: Quaker Benevolence in Eighteenth Century America* (Cambridge, Mass., 1963).

7 C. Bolt, 'Return of the Native: Some Reflections on the History of American Indians', *Journal of American Studies* VIII, no. 2, pp. 254–8.

8 L. B. Priest, *Uncle Sam's Stepchildren: The Reformation of United States Indian Policy, 1865–1887* (New Brunswick, 1942), pp. 58, 174–5.

9 E. G. Eastman, *Pratt: the Red Man's Moses* (Norman, Oklahoma, 1935), chapter 6; and R. H. Pratt, *Battlefield and Classroom: Four Decades With the American Indian, 1867–1904*, ed. R. M. Utley (New Haven, 1964), pp. 7–8, 10, 213–14, 312.

10 On degeneration theories see H. Gutman, *The Black Family in Slavery and Freedom, 1750–1925* (Oxford, 1976) pp. 531–44; on the danger of premature civil rights see Priest, pp. 175–6.

11 For expressions of these various views see: *Proceedings of the Fourth Annual Mohonk Conference, October 12, 13, 14, 1886* (Philadelphia, 1887) pp. 10, 27,

42; W. Barrows, *The Indian's Side of the Indian Question* (Boston, 1887) pp. 138–74; Drake, p. 10; *Mohonk Conferences on the Negro Question* (New York, 1969 edn); Eastman, p. 64; Pratt, pp. 7–8, 213–14, 336; Priest, pp. 174–6.

12 On Indian hostility to, and aloofness from, negroes in modern times see H. Hertzberg, *The Search for an American Indian Identity: Modern Pan-Indian Movements* (Syracuse, N.Y., 1971), *passim*; V. Deloria, *Custer Died For Your Sins: an Indian Manifesto* (New York, 1969), chapter 8; and J. O. Waddell and O. M. Watson, *The American Indian in Urban Society*, (Boston, 1971), pp. 175, 239.

13 E. McReynolds, *The Seminoles* (Norman, Oklahoma, 1957), pp. 74, 116 and *Oklahoma: a History of the Sooner State* (Norman, Oklahoma, 1964), pp. 187–8; articles by Kenneth W. Porter: 'Negroes and the Seminole War, 1817–1818', *Journal of Negro History* XXXVI (July, 1951), 'Florida Slaves and Free Negroes in the Seminole War, 1835–42', *ibid.* XXVIII (October, 1943), 'Negroes and the Seminole War, 1835–1842', *Journal of Southern History* XVII (July, 1932), and 'Relations Between Negroes and Indians within the Present Limits of the United States', *Journal of Negro History* XVII (July, 1932); and on the Creeks, see A. Debo, *The Road to Disappearance* (Norman, Oklahoma, 1967), p. 115.

14 L. J. Greene, *The Negro in Colonial New England* (New York, 1969), pp. 128, 160; A. Lauber, *Indian Slavery in Colonial Times Within the Present Limits of the United States* (New York, 1913), pp. 189–95, 253–64, 269–82, 289–92; K. W. Porter, 'Indians and Negroes on the Texas Frontier', *Journal of Negro History* XLI, 1956; C. N. Degler, pp. 49–66; on negro captives, J. N. Heard, *White Into Red: a Study of the Assimilation of White Persons Captured by Indians* (Metuchen, N.J., 1973), p. 46; and see Nash, *Red, White and Black*, pp. 291–6.

15 M. E. Young, *Redskins, Ruffleshirts and Rednecks: Indian Allotments in Alabama and Mississippi* (Norman, Oklahoma, 1961) pp. 75–6. South Carolina Indians in particular were used against black slaves: see B. Quarles, *The Negro in the American Revolution* (Chapel Hill, N.C., 1961), p. 125, and J. H. Johnston, *Race Relations in Virginia and Miscegenation in the South, 1776–1860* (Amherst, Mass., 1970), p. 282.

16 See W. H. Leckie, *The Buffalo Soldiers* (Norman, Oklahoma, 1967), and A. L. Fowler, *The Black Infantry in the West, 1869–1891* (Westport, Conn., 1971).

17 Quoted in B. A. Botkin (ed.), *Lay My Burden Down: a Folk History of Slavery* (Chicago, 1969), pp. 131, 134; for evidence of individual cruelty see narrative quoted by C. V. Woodward in 'History From Slave Sources', *American Historical Review* LXXIX, no. 2 (April, 1974), p. 479. See also Halliburton, pp. 142–3.

18 A. Debo, *Road to Disappearance*, pp. 126–7; M. T. Bailey, pp. 23–4; and A. Abel, *The American Indian as Slaveholder and Secessionist*, (Cleveland, 1915), *passim*. See also Halliburton, chs. 7–9; Littlefield, pp. 74, 78–9, 81, 180–89, 200–201.

19 Chickasaw testimony quoted in J. H. Malone, *The Chickasaw Nation: a Short Sketch of a Noble People* (Louisville, 1922), pp. 41–8; W. H. Dixon, *White Conquest* (London, 1876) I, pp. 275–7, 282–4; and Captain Richard Pratt, quoted in Priest, p. 176.

20 R. W. Mardock, *The Reformers and the American Indian* (Columbia, Mo., 1971), pp. 36, 55–7; A. Abel, *The American Indian Under Reconstruction* (Cleveland, 1925), p. 29; Priest, pp. 58, 263–4; and W. E. B. DuBois, *Black Reconstruction in America* (New York, 1969), p. 282 on Johnson's veto of the Civil Rights Bill in March 1866 for fear that under it 'Chinese, Indians and Gypsies, as well as Negroes, might be made citizens.'

21 Abel, *Reconstruction*, p. 211; and Malone, p. 416.

22 McReynolds, *The Seminoles*, p. 314; and Bailey, p. 63.

23 C. G. Woodson, *A Century of Negro Migration* (New York, 1969), p. 143, and

R. W. Logan, *The Betrayal of the Negro* (New York, 1967 edn), pp. 141–4; A. Debo, *The Rise and Fall of the Choctaw Republic* (Norman, Oklahoma, 1961), pp. 179–81; G. S. Woodward, *The Cherokee* (Norman, Oklahoma, 1963), p. 323; and Debo, *Road to Disappearance*, p. 265.

24 Debo, *Road to Disappearance*, pp. 170, 253; Abel, *Reconstruction*, p. 295; Bailey, pp. 97, 123; McReynolds, *The Seminoles*, p. 320; Littlefield, pp. 193, 203.

25 Debo, *Choctaw Republic*, pp. 101–2; Bailey, pp. 149–53; Malone, pp. 415–19.

26 Woodward, p. 285; Bailey, pp. 178–82; Abel, *Reconstruction*, p. 299.

27 Abel, pp. 272–3; Debo, *Choctaw Republic*, pp. 100–101, 103; H. Aptheker, *A Documentary History of the Negro People in the United States* (Secaunus, N.J., 1972 ed), II, pp. 619–22; Woodward, p. 210; Debo, *Road to Disappearance*, pp. 222, 224, 230–31, 237, 247, 253–7.

28 Abel, *Reconstruction*, p. 324; Woodson, p. 144.

29 *To Die Game: the Story of the Lowry Band, Indian Guerillas of Reconstruction* (Baton Rouge, La., 1971), pp. 64–5, 73–5, 90–91, 114, 142, 144, 158, 173, 253 f.

30 Cited in L. A. Burgess, *The Lake Mohonk Conferences on the Indian, 1883–1916* (PhD thesis, Claremont Graduate School, 1972), p. 104.

31 Booker T. Washington, *The Outlook*, 4 January 1908, quoted in Aptheker, pp. 871–3.

32 Greene, pp. 198–201; John H. Russell, *The Free Negro in Virginia, 1619–1865* (Baltimore, 1913); and Lauber, pp. 107, 287.

33 J. H. Johnston, pp. 272–92; and Jordan, p. 169.

34 See M. J. Herskovits, *The American Negro: a Study in Racial Crossing* (New York, 1928), p. 10. Herskovits does not, however, give proper details of his sample. The census figures are quoted and glossed in E. B. Reuter, *The Mulatto in the United States* (Boston, 1918), pp. 78–9, 82. Some 8·3 per cent of the Indian population was 'not reported' in this census in terms of ancestry.

35 See the often quoted Indian response to the negro slave York, taken on the Lewis and Clark expedition, in Bernard DeVoto (ed.), *The Journals of Lewis and Clark* (Boston, 1953), pp. 48–91; McReynolds, *The Seminoles*, p. 74, on the fate of the offspring of Indian slave matches; and on legal cases to establish freedom see Johnston, pp. 195, 281, and Duncan J. MacLeod, *Slavery, Race and the American Revolution* (London, 1974), pp. 110–11, 114–16, referring to suits brought in Virginia where (unusually) Indian slavery, once established, had been outlawed by the colonial legislature.

36 Johnston, pp. 276–7, 280–81.

37 McReynolds, *The Seminoles*, p. 263.

38 John Dunn Hunter, *Memoirs of a Captivity Among the Indians of North America*, ed. Richard Drinnon (New York, 1973), pp. 92–3. And see McLoughlin, pp. 378–9.

39 Quoted in and observed by MacLeod, p. 175.

40 Debo, *Choctaw Republic*, p. 109; Johnston, pp. 284, 290–92; F. L. Olmsted, *The Cotton Kingdom* (New York, 1966 edn) p. 322; Hortense Powdermaker, *After Freedom: A Cultural Study of the Deep South*, ed. E. M. Rudwick (New York, 1966), p. 4; Malone, pp. 417–18; Reuter, p. 85; Johnston, p. 292.

41 Abel, *Reconstruction*, p. 9; see also Halliburton, pp. 36–7; Littlefield, p. 202.

42 See Porter, 'Florida Slaves and Free Negroes', for Jessup's comment, and testimony of Harriet Martineau on the problem of Seminole slave matches in W. G. Simms, 'The Morals of Slavery', *The Pro-Slavery Arguments, as Maintained by the Most Distinguished Writers of the Southern States, Containing Several Essays on the Subject, by Chancellor Harper, Dr Simms, and Professor Dew* (Philadelphia, 1852), pp. 237–8. See also Littlefield, p. 199.

43 Quoted in Abel, *Reconstruction*, pp. 253–4; an identical judgement is to be found

in the less cynical George Catlin's *Letters and Notes on the Manners, Customs and Condition of the North American Indians* (London, 1841) II, 227.

44 J. S. Haller, *Outcasts From Evolution* (Urbana, 1971) pp. 140–41.

45 Nash and Weiss, p. 20; G. B. Nash, 'The Image of the Indian in The Southern Colonial Mind', pp. 76–7, 85, in E. Dudley and M. E. Novak (eds), *The Wild Man Within: an Image in Western Thought From the Renaissance to Romanticism* (Pittsburgh, 1972); W. A. Washburn, 'A Moral History of Indian–White Relations. Needs and Opportunities for Study', *Ethnohistory* IV, no. 1 (winter, 1957), pp. 50–51; Johnston, pp. 269–70; J. D. Forbes, pp. 142–63; and Nash, *Red, White and Black*, pp. 278–85.

46 De Voto, pp. 315, 329.

47 See especially Heard, pp. 98–9. Women redeemed from captivity west of the Mississippi seem to have been unwilling wives of warriors, because of ill-treatment, pp. 100–101.

48 Binder, pp. 100, 113; and Jordan, p. 480; Jefferson spoke of the two races blending, amalgamating, identifying and consolidating, obviously meaning cultural as well as physical mixing.

49 It is, of course, possible to find assertions that mixing did not take place because of white hostility or Indian aversion to the prospect of becoming the lowest element in white society; see, for instance, R. R. MacMahon, *The Anglo-Saxon and the North American Indian* (Baltimore, 1876), pp. 20, 28–9. See also Lauber, p. 252. The evidence about attitudes, as well as behaviour, is contradictory.

50 See, for instance, testimony in *The Indians of the Yukon and Tanana Valleys, Alaska* by M. K. Sniffen and Dr Thomas Spees Carrington (Philadelphia, Indian Rights Association, 1914), p. 34.

51 Jordan, pp. 168–9; Lauber, p. 253; L. O. Saum, *The Fur Trader and the Indian* (Seattle and London, 1965), pp. 206–10, 236; there were some happy fathers of mixed breeds, such as Sir William Johnson – see Johnston, p. 269.

52 Robert Berkhofer, *Salvation and the Savage: an Analysis of Protestant Missions and American Indian Response, 1787–1862* (New York, 1972), pp. 21–2, 47, 112–14; and Johnston, pp. 271–2.

53 *Proceedings of the Fourth Annual Lake Mohonk Conference*, p. 43.

54 Quoted in W. E. Washburn, *The Indian in America* (New York, 1975), p. 93.

55 Mardock, p. 3; Priest, pp. 147, 158–9. Priest suggests not all reformers looked askance at miscegenation; see also F. P. Prucha, *Americanizing the American Indians: Writings by the 'Friends of the Indian', 1880–1900* (Cambridge, Mass., 1973), pp. 60–62; E. A. Gilcreast, *Richard Henry Pratt and American Indian Policy, 1877–1906: a Study of the Assimilation Movement* (PhD thesis, Yale University, 1967), p. 102; and M. F. Armstrong, *Hampton Institute, Its Work for Two Races* (Hampton, 1885), p. 23.

56 *Proceedings of the Fourth Annual Lake Mohonk Conference*, p. 9, testimony of Mr P. C. Garrett of Philadelphia.

57 *Report of Hon. Theodore Roosevelt Made to the United States Civil Service Commission, Upon a Visit to Certain Indian Reservations and Indian Schools in South Dakota, Nebraska, and Kansas* (Philadelphia, Indian Rights Association, 1893, Tract no. 4, 2nd series), pp. 8–10.

58 Woodward, pp. 86, 120; Debo, *Road to Disappearance*, pp. 38–9; 69, 140, 212–13, and *Choctaw Republic*, pp. 37, 77–8; Malone, pp. 483–4; Littlefield, p. 202.

59 *The Conquest of the Continent: or the Expansion of Races in America* (New York and London, 1933), p. 292; Reuter, pp. 78–9.

60 On abolitionist prejudices see, for example, W. H. and J. H. Pease, 'Antislavery Ambivalence: Immediatism, Expediency, Race', *American Quarterly* XVII (winter, 1965), pp. 682–95; for Republican fears about being regarded as un-

sound on miscegenation see E. Foner, *Free Soil, Free Labor, Free Men: The Ideology of the Republican Party Before the Civil War* (London and Oxford, 1970), chapter 8; for a perceptive discussion of abolitionists and sexual matters, which influenced this paragraph, see R. G. Walters, *The Antislavery Appeal: American Abolitionism After 1830* (Baltimore, 1976), chapter 5, especially pp. 73–6.

61 See Young, pp. 8–10, 22–3; Heard, chapter 10; the Peases, p. 689, note abolitionist disavowal of such 'non-middle-class shenanigans as adopting colored children'; on mulatto loyalties to the black community, despite the development of caste attitudes among some, see Johnston, pp. 296, 302–3, and E. D. Genovese, *Roll, Jordan, Roll: The World the Slaves Made* (New York, 1974), pp. 429–31; on the physical inferiority but intellectual superiority of mulattoes to pure blacks see the comments of statistician F. L. Hoffman in 'Race Traits and Tendencies of the American Negro', *Publications of the American Economic Association* XI, nos 1–3 (New York and London, August 1896) pp. 184–5; the theme of 'the tragic mulatto' is discussed by S. A. Brown, 'Negro Character as Seen by White Authors', *Journal of Negro Education* II (1933), pp. 179–203; the importance of leaders of mixed parentage in R. Bardolph, *The Negro Vanguard* (New York, 1961), pp. 15–16, 67–8, 87, 89 ff., 113, 124, 129; J. R. Williamson, 'Black Self-Assertion Before and After Emancipation' in N. I. Huggins, I, pp. 216–18.

62 Genovese, pp. 413–31; Johnston, pp. 172–268, 293–314.

63 For a typical statement on the monstrous nature and limited number of liaisons between white (lower-class) women and black men see P. A. Bruce, *The Plantation Negro as a Freeman* (Williamstown, Mass., 1889 and 1970), pp. 53–5. C. C. Hernton, *Sex and Racism in America* (New York, Garden City, 1965), is the standard work on this subject.

64 On post-war developments see, for instance, DuBois, pp. 159, 453, 492, 549; J. R. Williamson, *After Slavery: the Negro in South Carolina During Reconstruction, 1861–1877* (Chapel Hill, N.C., 1965), pp. 295, 297–8; V. L. Wharton, *The Negro in Mississippi, 1865–1890* (New York, 1965), pp. 87, 150, 227–9; and M. L. Callcott, *The Negro in Maryland Politics, 1870–1912* (Baltimore, 1969), chapter 7; on the north's early opposition to miscegenation, see L. F. Litwack, *North of Slavery: the Negro in the Free States, 1790–1860* (Chicago, 1965), pp. 16, 35, 60, 104; for a rejection of the white excuse for lynching see Frederick Douglass, 'Lynch Law in the South', *North American Review* CLV (1892), pp. 17–24; for an indication of the sexual abuses permitted under cover of the Klan and after emancipation see Gutman, pp. 383–402.

65 Johnston, pp. 236, 312–13; and E. B. Reuter, pp. 105–26, especially p. 117; the negro population declined as a proportion of the whole between 1790 and 1930 partly because of white immigration and partly because of a high death rate.

66 Hoffman, pp. 326–8.

67 Quoted in DuBois, p. 146.

9

Towards equality: blacks in the United States during the Second World War

Donald R. McCoy and Richard T. Ruetten

The United States, from its beginnings, has been a land of minorities, and one of its continuing problems has been the quest of these minorities for equal rights. Wave upon wave of immigrant, racial, and religious minorities have struggled to secure the rights promised them in national and state constitutions. These battles, as much as any other American phenomenon, represent the *leitmotiv* of the nation's development.

Between the First and Second World Wars the struggle for minority rights was relatively subdued, partly because of the virtual strangulation of immigration after 1914 and partly because of the degree of success in satisfying most ethnic and religious groups. Great civil rights contests were in the offing, however, if for no other reason than that the racial minorities – blacks, Mexican-Americans, Puerto Ricans, Indians, and Asian Americans – had not achieved anything approaching equal rights or even sufficient power to fight for them effectively. It is with blacks during the Second World War that this chapter will deal, in the hope that an examination of their fortunes then will serve as a measure of their position both earlier and later in the twentieth century.

I

Blacks have been central to the problem of securing rights in America during the past 115 years. In 1930 they constituted the largest racial minority, with over twelve million in the United States and its dependencies.[1] At the most generous estimate all the other racial minorities combined amounted to less than one third the number of America's blacks. Blacks were, however, central for other reasons. For one, no other group was so restricted. Many minority people could return to a homeland; some could occasionally find refuges in the United States where there were better opportunities for advancement; and none encountered patterns of discrimination and segregation as rigid as those fixed for blacks. Moreover, blacks had been the prime cause of the nation's greatest equal rights struggle, during the Civil War and Reconstruction, which led to the Thirteenth, Fourteenth, and Fifteenth Amendments to the Constitution and various civil rights statutes. Enforcement of the bright constitutional promises of the 1860s and 1870s faltered as time passed. The statutes were also drained of their vitality by adverse administrative practices and judicial decisions, which by the time of Woodrow Wilson's presidency had reduced blacks to economic and political impotence. Retrieval of the rights proclaimed during the 1860s was a goal for blacks that other minorities could share only with less fervour and symbolic significance. A last important reason was that blacks had come to America as slaves, a status they endured for generations. Even after emancipation, they had been afforded scant opportunity to make a decent place for themselves. As a result of their colour and former condition of bondage, they were conspicuous as no other minority, and they encountered almost universally insulting attitudes about their character and potential.

Some blacks benefited economically during the First World War and the 1920s, thanks to the restrictions on immigration and an increase in their migration to the cities and out of the south. Yet by 1930 they found themselves as segregated as ever and confronted with the prospect of losing recent economic gains in the developing depression. There were, nevertheless, some favourable changes during the 1930s, despite economic losses. Franklin D. Roosevelt's New Deal administration attempted to give blacks a fairer share of federal government employment, assistance, and services. There were even isolated instances of the desegregation of federal facilities, and the New Deal reversed the twenty-year-old trend of appointing fewer blacks to federal office. There were also advances among blacks, in the levels of education, skills, health, trade union membership, farm ownership, cultural achievement, organization, and agitational, legal, and pressure tactics.

All this is noteworthy, for it was not attributable alone to the *noblesse oblige* of certain officials and the willingness of President Roosevelt to court what there was of a black vote. Blacks themselves exploited the new situation in order to fight for their rights. They also took strength from such diverse sources as Ethiopia's resistance to Italian aggression, the athletic triumphs of world-champion boxer Joe Louis and Olympic star Jesse Owens, and the achievements of singers Marian Anderson and Paul Robeson. And blacks were less alone than ever before in their struggle, as certain whites – including religious figures, scholars, and Marxists – became increasingly interested in racial justice during the time when Nazism most viciously showed the face of racism.[2] Of course, the gains of the 1930s were greater in psychological effect than in substance. Yet hope had dawned among many black Americans, and that hope along with increased militancy and the slender gains of the 1930s would serve as the springboard for the civil rights contests that would soon stud the American scene.

The year 1940 marked the beginning of a new age in race relations in the United States. This was dramatically signalled in the first great outpouring of non-fictional literature dealing seriously with racial questions – literature that included Claude McKay's *Harlem: Negro Metropolis*, E. Franklin Frazier's *Negro Youth at the Crossroads*, and Ruth Benedict's *Race: Science and Politics*. There was the first issue of *Phylon*, founded by W. E. B. DuBois with the aims of attacking racial prejudice and segregation and of instilling racial pride among blacks. There was also, in fiction, that great dividing point between the old and the new, Richard Wright's biting, best-selling novel of black suffering, *Native Son*. With its appearance, black writers were not only welcomed by publishers, but they could address the harshest realities of life among their people.

Despite these developments and the accomplishments of the New Deal, the condition of American blacks in 1940 was pitiful. Soul-searing poverty and back-breaking labour were the lot of the great majority. Almost everywhere in the United States blacks experienced segregation, and the separate facilities available to them were generally so shabby that not even the most vivid imagination could consider them equal. Conditions were better outside the south, but only marginally so. Nevertheless, the 1930s had served as the overture to the opportunities that emerged during the following generation to fashion a potent civil rights movement and to advance substantially the status of America's blacks. What happened during the years 1940–45 was the crucial first act in this drama.

With the coming of war in Europe in September 1939, blacks, like their fellow citizens, were divided on whether they favoured some American participation. As the war continued in Europe, it was obvious that America was becoming involved and that blacks would have to make the best of the situation. Black newspaper columnist George S. Schuyler wrote, 'If nothing more comes out of this emergency than the widespread understanding among white leaders that the negro's loyalty is conditional, we shall not have suffered in vain.'[3] Blacks, confronted with the war, were to decide to fight for equality of military service and work opportunity.

Black America's main battle force was the National Association for the Advancement of Colored People, which had gained some influence with its 50,000 members by 1940. Yet the NAACP had been too often sedate, reflecting the thinking of its long-time white leader, Arthur B. Spingarn. Change came, however, in 1940. Spingarn was kicked upstairs to the organization's presidency and blacks William H. Hastie and Thurgood Marshall took control of the powerful legal committee. At the same time another black, NAACP Secretary Walter White, became more forceful on policy matters. With such black leadership during the war, the NAACP was willing to risk criticism that it was hampering the war effort by striving for black advancement.[4]

II

One of the major black goals was the achievement of equal treatment in the armed forces. Since 1900 the role of blacks in the army and navy had become smaller than during the last part of the preceding century. Blacks in the army on the eve of the Second World War were largely confined to four unspecialized units with a total of 3,640 men and three officers. The navy restricted its few black sailors to servant positions and the marine corps was lily-white. With the expansion of American defence forces in prospect, blacks began to demand the enlistment of their people into every part of the services. One response was the stipulation in the Selective

Service Act of September 1940 that there would be 'no discrimination ... on account of race or color' in conscripting and training men for military service. This provision, however, despite protests from blacks, was generally ignored during the war.[5]

More immediate in 1940 was black discontent over the possibility that soldiers of their race would serve only in labour battalions. In reaction, the White House in September 1940 asked the Department of War to indicate that blacks would have equal opportunities with whites throughout the army. President Roosevelt conveyed his concern to the cabinet on 13 September, adding that the army had informed him that about 10 per cent of its strength in all branches would be black. Apparently with an eye on the November presidential election, he recommended that the army publicize this plan.[6]

In seeking a suitable military role for blacks, NAACP Secretary Walter White arranged for a conference with President Roosevelt, Navy Secretary Frank Knox, and Assistant War Secretary Robert Patterson. The black delegation consisted of White, A. Philip Randolph of the Brotherhood of Sleeping Car Porters, and T. Arnold Hill of the National Urban League, who agreed to press for the use of black officers and men throughout the military services and on an unsegregated basis. The meeting took place at the White House on 27 September 1940. Patterson reported that the army would use blacks throughout its branches and that it would soon call 600 black reserve officers to active duty. When Knox protested that desegregation would not work in the navy because of the close living conditions on board ships, Roosevelt not only suggested that a start could be made by stationing black bands on some ships, but he also urged the appointment of black advisers in the war and navy departments.[7]

The meeting encouraged Walter White, but his optimism was soon shaken. On 8 October Assistant Secretary Patterson sent Roosevelt a draft of War Department policy stating that the number of black soldiers would be proportionate to the blacks in the general population, black units would be formed in each major service branch, black reserve officers would be assigned to black units, officer candidate school training would be available, the air corps would be opened to blacks, and black civilians would be given equal employment opportunity at army installations. There would, however, be no mixing of black and white personnel within regimental organizations because that 'would produce situations destructive to morale and detrimental to the preparations for national defense'. President Roosevelt approved the draft document, which meant that blacks would participate widely in the army, though on a segregated basis. Additional developments before the presidential election were the promotion of the ranking black army officer, Benjamin O. Davis, Sr to brigadier general and the designations of William H. Hastie as civilian aide to the secretary of war and of Major Campbell Johnson as the black adviser to the Selective Service director.

The army policy and the appointments were, of course, election campaign gestures. Although falling short of what black leaders anticipated, the concessions widened the opportunities for blacks of service in the army and gave them a small built-in pressure group. Yet the navy still restricted them to its stewards' branch, the marine corps remained all white, and service continued to be segregated throughout the army. Moreover, the army was not as good as its word, for it did not draft a proportionate number of blacks until 1943 and its air corps procrastinated on training and using blacks.[8]

Blacks were not to be calmed by unkept promises. Their newspapers were replete with stories about service inequities and assaults on black men in uniform, and blacks increasingly denounced military segregation. As George S. Schuyler put it in January 1941, 'we should demand that the government disband all so-called negro regiments and units, and that negro and white youths be assigned to the same regiments, battalions, squadrons, companies, troops, platoons, and squads'.[9] Despite mounting black pressure and protests, however, no further changes occurred in the military until well after the Japanese attack on Hawaii in December 1941. Once the United States entered the war, black leaders made it clear that they would pursue victory not only over the nation's enemies abroad, but also over those who would deny their race equal rights at home. Although there would be pressure for blacks submissively to close ranks with whites against the common foe, black leaders and writers refused to be silenced in their campaign for racial equality. And a nation that said it was fighting for global democracy could scarcely force its own people to cease struggling for democracy at home.

The military services remained one of the chief targets. Although blacks were not united on what they wanted from the army and navy, they agreed that there should be proportionately as many blacks in the military services as there were in the nation's population. They also agreed that their people should be placed throughout the army and navy. Beyond that many blacks contended that they would not find equality in the services unless segregation was scrapped, a position that gathered increasing support.[10] Practically, there was much to be said for the anti-segregationist position. The army had been unable to take a proportionate number of blacks because of the difficulty of staffing segregated units with experienced black officers and of providing separate facilities. Then too, the conviction of many War Department officials that black soldiers were characteristically less effective than whites posed obstacles to the efficient processing, training, and assigning of troops. The blacks' low average educational attainments and their poor morale consequent upon their segregated army experiences complicated the situation. Yet the War Department would not entertain the idea that integrated units might solve some of these problems. The army clung to its belief, as Assistant Secretary of War John J. McCloy said, in 'the unwisdom of having any such unit', for fear of untoward repercussions.[11]

Yet the army was stepping up its efforts to use black soldiers within the framework of segregation. War Secretary Henry L. Stimson in 1942 insisted upon the formation of black divisions and sought the training of additional black officers, including aviators. Plainly, he was doing this on orders from the President, for, as he jotted in his diary, 'as it has been determined that we shall have [black soldiers], I propose that we shall educate them to the highest possible standards and make the best we can of them'.[12] That the army was on the spot was indicated in an April 1942 memorandum from General R. W. Crawford to Assistant Chief of Staff Dwight D. Eisenhower. He wrote that 'the utilization of colored units is a problem that defies rigorous analysis because of the intangible nature of such factors as racial prejudice, social implications, combat efficiency, and international relations'. The educational deficiencies of black soldiers also hampered the army in using them adequately. Crawford's memorandum pointed up the nub of the problem: the army could not, while it maintained segregation, eliminate official discrimination, for segregation was discriminatory.[13] The War Department was unwilling to risk even gradual desegregation for fear not only of combat inefficiency and unhappy political repercussions but also of white and black troops fighting each other instead of the enemy.

An important point in the crusade against discrimination was William H. Hastie's resignation as the War Department's black adviser in January 1943 in protest against the resistance of the army air forces to the decent use of blacks. This resistance was seen in segregated training for pilots, the establishment of black aviation squadrons that performed common labour, and the plans for a segregated air force officer candidate school, contrary to the army's policy. Judge Hastie also complained of, among other things, the War Department's frequent failure to consult him on its racial policies. For example, when in August 1942 the Advisory Committee on Negro Troop Policies was established, Hastie was neither informed nor made a member of it. His resignation apparently led to some favourable action. His successor as civilian aide, Truman K. Gibson, Jr was invited to attend meetings of the Negro Troop Policies Committee. Moreover, the army better provided for promoting eligible black officers, announced that the new officer candidate school would not be segregated, and expanded opportunities for specialized air force training. And there were soon other, more important developments. By 1943, partly because of its increasing manpower needs, the army was taking more than 10 per cent of blacks among its new conscripts and had ordered its branches to increase their proportionate troop strengths.[14]

These and other changes resulted mainly in response to pressure from the NAACP and other black organizations, the black press, the White House, the Selective Service system, and the War Manpower Commission. As powerful as any outside pressure, however, were the inter-racial riots in the army. Chief of Staff George C. Marshall in July 1943 called this 'an immediately serious problem', and issued orders to deal with 'the causes of irritation or unrest'. 'Breaches of discipline', he insisted, 'must be handled firmly, legally, and without compromising any standards of conduct', regardless of race. Moreover, 'adequate facilities and accommodations will be provided Negro troops'. In this and other directives the army's answer was to give more attention to black units in terms of enforcing discipline and of affording equality of treatment. Pamphlets were issued emphasizing that the black should be treated on the basis of his individual merits and a superb film, Frank Capra's *The Negro Soldier*, was widely shown to military and civilian audiences.[15]

If the army was difficult to deal with on racial matters, the navy was impossible well into the war. The seafaring service did not take conscripts until 1943 and so had no obligation to try to strike a racial balance among its personnel. Moreover, it refused to accept black volunteers except as messmen. After the attack on Hawaii, the pressures on Navy Secretary Knox grew, not only from blacks but also from the army, which concluded that it was under greater pressure because the navy was doing nothing. War Secretary Stimson urged President Roosevelt to command the navy to take conscripts and thus blacks. Roosevelt rejected this request, but he did press the navy to allow more general service. Finally, in April 1942, the Navy Department announced that it would 'experiment' with black naval and marine enlistments for service in shore stations and harbour craft. For the time being that had to satisfy blacks, for Secretary Knox was unwilling to yield further.[16]

By the end of 1942 only some 7,000 blacks had been enlisted for general naval duty. Whether or not Secretary Knox was pleased with this experiment, the fact was that discrimination existed in promotions and duty assignments, and the navy refused to commission blacks as officers. The service, however, was soon to make significant changes, largely because its personnel needs were mounting while available white manpower was dwindling. Therefore, early in 1943 the navy announced that it would take conscripts, up to 10 per cent of whom would be black. By the end of 1943 there were 101,573 black sailors, although they never constituted as much as 5 per cent of naval personnel.[17]

There were other changes in the navy. During the first quarter of 1944, the navy made blacks eligible for advancement on the same basis as other sailors, announced plans to man two anti-submarine vessels largely with blacks, and authorized its first black officers. More important were the results that flowed from James V. Forrestal's succession to the secretary-ship after the death of Frank Knox in April 1944. Under the new leader-ship, the navy assigned blacks to duty on a desegregated basis on an ever-increasing range of naval vessels and by summer 1945 had desegregated all recruit and specialized training units. Forrestal, moreover, urged the treatment of all personnel on the basis of merit. He also used Urban League Secretary Lester Granger to inspect naval installations at home and over-seas. Granger's reports and recommendations on black personnel laid the groundwork for much of what the navy under Forrestal did subsequently regarding race relations. And those achievements were impressive, especially in razing the wall of segregation, which the navy had come to realize was wasteful of time, money, and personnel.[18]

As for the army, its policy continued to be, as Assistant War Secretary McCloy said, 'segregation without discrimination'. This may have satisfied white racists, but it goaded blacks to oppose segregation, especially as it was in practice often accompanied by discrimination. Moreover, reports from Civilian Aide Truman K. Gibson, Jr and General Benjamin O. Davis, Sr contended that segregation was at the root of the discontent of black soldiers and their often mediocre performance. Evidence was growing, particularly after the emergency use of mixed units in the 1944 Battle of the Bulge, that integration not only improved the efficiency of black troops, but also melted away the white snows of prejudice. For example, army research surveys of whites who served in mixed combat units showed that 77 per cent had become more favourable to having blacks in their companies. This information had little impact, however. For several years after 1945 the army, caught between the spur of black discontent and the bridle of white prejudice, continued to embrace the concept of 'segregation without discrimination'.[19]

Despite the unsolved problems of the treatment of black servicemen, it must be emphasized that there were highly significant advances. By 1945 almost 189,000 blacks served in the navy and marines, including sixty-five officers. During 1940–45, 922,965 blacks served in the army and of these 7,767 were officers. What war service meant for blacks must be considered in the context of the problems they encountered or brought with them. The low educational attainments of many imposed limits on their opportunities for assignment to skilled jobs. Nevertheless, substantial numbers of blacks did acquire skills that they might otherwise not have gained. In addition, an army sample towards the war's end showed that 42 per cent of black soldiers wore technician's, corporal's, or sergeant's stripes. Service also permitted many black soldiers and sailors to widen their horizons. By June 1945, for example, almost 75 per cent of black troops were overseas.[20] Of course, for many men military experience was more basic. Many blacks enjoyed higher economic returns in service and most received better medical care than they had as civilians. Almost 100,000 black soldiers and sailors passed through schools that brought them up to functional literacy. Moreover, military experiences whetted the taste of many servicemen for further knowledge. An army study of March 1945 indicated that 43·5 per cent of black soldiers wanted to continue their education after leaving the service.[21] In short, military service was a boon for many black Americans at least in terms of expanding their fund of experience and skills and challenging them to advance themselves.

III

A no less important wartime goal of blacks was to expand their civilian employment opportunities. The coming of war in Europe soon brought the end of depression as the nation's defence requirements and foreign demands for American goods swelled the job rolls. Blacks found, however, that the new prosperity was eluding them. Although this was in part because relatively few were skilled workers, it was largely because many factories would not hire blacks. The reason underlying this were that whites purportedly would 'not work with blacks', that labour unions would object, and that industrial facilities designed to perpetuate segregation were too costly.[22] Blacks quickly united to demand equal job opportunities. The NAACP, the Urban League, and the black press were the most prominent minority forces that sought racial justice in employment during the war. As industry expanded, black organizations and newspapers fully reported the extent to which their people were excluded from new jobs and they vigorously pressed industry and the government for remedies. In August 1940 their campaign was accelerated when the NAACP distributed to its branches its first list of industries holding defence contracts. The association asked its local affiliates and other interested organizations to send representatives 'to visit the plants and to confer with chambers of commerce and employment agencies in a concerted nationwide effort to secure employment of negroes'.[23]

These actions paid some small dividends, partly because of the Roosevelt administration's political sensitivity during an election year. Before the November election, the administration appointed a black consultant, Robert C. Weaver, to the government's National Defense Advisory Commission. The commission itself announced that there should be no discrimination against workers on the grounds of age, race or sex and revealed that it had persuaded the American Federation of Labor and the Congress of Industrial Organizations to work against racial discrimination in defence employment. In addition, the Office of Education directed that there should be no racial or religious discrimination in the use of vocational education funds, and President Roosevelt condemned racial discrimination before Congress. Even Congress went on record favouring prohibition of discrimination in the use of defence training funds. These developments, however, led to no great changes. In April 1940, 22 per cent of the blacks on the job market were unemployed compared to 17.7 per cent of whites. By October the percentage of jobless whites had declined to 13 while unemployed blacks had decreased by only 0.10 per cent. The proportion of blacks allowed into the government's vocational training programmes was also unimpressive.[24]

Blacks were becoming impatient and all the more insistent in their employment demands. Despite their loyalty to Roosevelt and his party at the polls in November, the administration made no immediate response. Black leaders countered by shifting into a higher gear of militancy. The NAACP called for blacks to demand 'the wiping out of the color line' in defence employment, and a national conference of blacks proposed the holding of 'huge defense meetings' in various cities and in Washington to demonstrate black concern over employment problems.[25] Local action began in Kansas City. In November 1940 the Urban League had reported that only three of the city's twenty-seven defence plants were hiring blacks for jobs other than janitors and watchmen. Kansas City's blacks consequently called a mass meeting for 8 December to demand work in defence industries. Sponsored by fifty local organizations, the meeting drew 5,000 blacks and captured headlines in the national black press. The Kansas City mass meeting was the first big local demonstration on defence employment and training problems, and there was some truth in the later claim of the Kansas City *Call* that it 'was the spark which set afire the determination of negroes all over the country to have jobs in defense industry on the same basis as other Americans'.[26]

Largely as a result of fresh agitation, more opportunities for defence jobs began to open. This amounted, however, to little more than throwing a handful of peas into an apple barrel. The United States Employment Service reported that between October 1940 and March 1941 blacks represented only 6,150 of the 150,000 male workers placed in twenty major defence industries.[27] Blacks therefore continued to apply pressure on industry and government in the form of editorials, petitions, lobbying, and local mass meetings. By the end of January 1941 A. Philip Randolph of the Brotherhood of Sleeping Car Porters suggested another kind of protest – a march on Washington by 10,000 blacks under the slogan, 'we loyal negro American citizens demand the right to work and fight for our country.' This was the way, said Randolph, to bring 'definite and positive pressure of the negro masses' to bear upon government.[28] Although other forms of action continued, Randolph's March on Washington Movement was to become the most militant and prominent black effort to gain a decent role in the defence programme. By late April, the movement's goal had crystallized: the President should issue an executive order prohibiting discrimination in defence industries, government agencies, and the armed services. Randolph set 1 July as the date for the march, announced that 50,000 blacks would participate, and on 29 May wrote to President Roosevelt of the movement's plans and demands.[29] The NAACP and the Urban League contributed money, and march committees were established in more than a dozen large cities. Randolph, apparently now speaking of 100,000 marchers, toured the south organizing march committees. The Sleeping Car Porters formed the movement's organizational skeleton, but how many marchers the brotherhood, the NAACP, or the local committees could have provided remains unclear.[30]

While black leaders were organizing the march, government officials were becoming concerned. Under-Secretary of War Robert Patterson explained that his department had 'done everything feasible to see that no discrimination is practised against negroes' in government employment. The President's wife, Eleanor Roosevelt, tried unsuccessfully to persuade Randolph to call off the march. Franklin Roosevelt entered the picture directly on 12 June, when he told the Office of Production Management that he expected it 'to take immediate steps to facilitate the full utilization of our productive manpower'. He also arranged for Mrs Roosevelt, Civil Defense Director Fiorello LaGuardia, National Youth Administration Director Aubrey Williams, and Social Security Board Coordinator Anna Rosenberg to meet with Randolph and the NAACP's Walter White on 13 June. At that conference the two black leaders refused to call off the march. White held out for a face-to-face meeting with the President, and Randolph asserted that the march would not be abandoned 'unless we have accomplished our definite aim which is jobs and not promises'. The next day Aubrey Williams telephoned Randolph conveying Roosevelt's personal request to call off the march and his promise to see Randolph and White on 18 June. Their decision was to meet the President, but not to abandon the march on Washington.[31]

At the 18 June meeting Roosevelt and his aides failed to persuade Randolph and White to cancel the march without the issuance of an executive order. Before leaving for another conference, the President therefore asked the group to draft a suitable order. The group then settled down to determine, as one of the participants, War Secretary Stimson, said condescendingly, 'what could be done to help these colored people out of a bad job'. The task required several meetings, during which the MOWM leaders presented detailed demands. They wanted the abolition of discrimination in hiring by defence contractors and in federal job training programmes as well as the elimination of segregation in the civil and armed services. They also demanded that the Employment Service abandon racial distinctions in job referrals and that the President ask Congress to amend the National Labor Relations Act to deny its benefits to unions that refused membership to blacks.[32]

Government representatives whittled down the demands, but finally on 24 June, a week before the planned march, agreement was reached. Executive Order 8802, which Roosevelt issued the next day, commanded vocational training programmes to halt discrimination and provided that all new defence contracts would stipulate that contractors were 'not to discriminate against any worker because of race, creed, color, or national origin'. Moreover, a Committee on Fair Employment Practices was established in the Office of Production Management to redress grievances of job discrimination by defence contractors and federal agencies. Randolph responded by calling off the march on Washington.[33]

The whole process was a classic case of political bargaining. For thirteen months blacks had brought increasing pressure to bear for participation in the defence programme. The government, set in its ways and sensitive to white racist pressure, busy with other domestic problems and the developing world crisis, had resisted. Concessions had been made along the way, but they satisfied neither the needs nor the demands of black Americans. The vision of a mass demonstration of blacks in Washington was one that the administration could not accept. In order to avoid embarrassment at home and abroad, the government had to do something and the result was Executive Order 8802. The order provided less than had been sought, but it was an important step forward. Not only had the government for the first time pledged to use its authority to combat job discrimination, but also for the first time blacks had used the tactic of mass militancy to gain action from the federal government.

Although impressive results were not immediately forthcoming from the issuance of Executive Order 8802, forces were gathering that would use it to advance the employment of blacks. Pressure on government and industry was still the order of the day for black leaders, all the more so as the supply of unemployed whites dwindled. Moreover, trade unions, spurred by their more egalitarian members and by black organizations, began to help. The upshot was a tremendous growth in the membership of blacks in unions, from 600,000 in 1940 to 1·25 million in 1945.[34]

Some federal agencies also encouraged the development of more equal job opportunities. Among such agencies, the Fair Employment Practices Committee probably deserved the greatest share of credit. Yet its history was a troubled one. It started with great promise late in 1941, holding hearings and issuing directives in cases of complaints about discrimination in hiring. Perhaps the FEPC was initially too successful, for unexpectedly in July 1942 the agency was transferred to the War Manpower Commission where it found its efforts increasingly frustrated. After its chairman and two other members resigned in disgust in 1943, minority groups exerted great pressure on President Roosevelt to restore the FEPC to potency. He responded in May by creating a new FEPC located within the Office of Production Management, but subject only to the President's authority. The new committee was strengthened by clarification of its powers and by provisions that government contractors had to insert non-discriminatory employment stipulations in their subcontracts.[35] This FEPC survived until 1946 and it relentlessly maintained pressure for the removal of discriminatory union and hiring practices and publicized the economic plight of racial minorities.

Whatever the cause – government efforts, black and white citizen pressure, a change of heart by unions and employers, or increasing labour shortages – employment of minority-group Americans rose strikingly during the war. From July 1942 to January 1945 the percentage of non-white employment in war industries grew from 5·8 to 8·2, and the number of black civil servants increased from 82,000 to 274,000 between 1938 and 1944.[36]

Other economic data were similarly encouraging. The resources of the nation's eleven black-owned banks swelled from $6,497,000 in 1939 to $28,584,815 in 1945 and non-white farm ownership in the south grew from 25 to 28 per cent between 1940 and 1945. Moreover, the average black male income as a percentage of white male income rose from 41 to 54 between 1939 and 1947. Blacks were also moving into previously untapped job fields. Between 1941 and 1945, there were at least 174 black policemen and five policewomen in forty-six southern and border-state cities and seventy-nine blacks appointed to teach in white colleges and universities.[37] No revolution had been wrought, but blacks, thanks in no small part to their own efforts, had made some significant steps towards employment equality.

The quest for economic opportunity also led to a heavy geographical movement of blacks and other racial minorities during the war, when some 2,729,000, or almost 20 per cent, of the non-white population migrated. Of these, 964,000 moved within states, 578,000 between contiguous states, and 1,187,000 between non-contiguous states. Urban non-white population expanded about 2·5 million and the percentage of the nation's non-whites living in the south shrank from 75 to 63.[38] The significance of these population shifts was to become increasingly clear during and especially after the war, in terms of black aspirations and political strength.

Of course, there was more to the black movement towards equality than fairer treatment in the armed services and in employment. Black Congressman Adam Clayton Powell, Jr summed it up in 1945, declaring that 'The new negro has come forward.... He believes that the Four Freedoms [and] the Atlantic Charter ... apply to him as well as to the white folks on the other side of the tracks. What's more, he has made up his mind to fight for those promises.' What it meant, in effect, was that blacks wanted a part in everything from which they had previously been excluded. Of course, they were divided on tactics and on priorities, but there was abundant evidence that Powell's 'new negro' was emerging into society in search of equality and justice. This was mirrored in the continuation, at least as a social myth, of the March on Washington Movement, widespread individual and local black protest, and the growth and heightened activities of the NAACP, Urban League, and black newspapers during the war. The spirit behind these developments was indicated in the editorial comment of the St Louis *American* that 'the brothers and sisters are no longer singing "Will there be any stars in my crown?" They are concerned about some of heaven here below.'[39]

Scholars and authors during the war forwarded the work of chipping away at the foundations of racism. There were especially the fruits of the Carnegie Corporation's comprehensive study of the American black, which appeared in a number of volumes during the war years. The study's keystone volume, Gunnar Myrdal's *An American Dilemma*, was particularly influential. Among the many other noteworthy works of fiction and non-fiction that dealt seriously with racial issues were Gwendolyn Brooks's *A Street in Bronzeville*, J. Saunders Redding's *No Day of Triumph*, St Clair Drake and Horace Cayton's *Black Metropolis*, Carey McWilliams's *Brothers under the Skin*, and Hortense Powdermaker's *Probing our Prejudices*.

The stage, cinema and radio constituted another area of heightened interest in race and of increased striving by blacks for advancement. Before 1940 blacks were usually found only on the peripheries of show business, but the war brought new opportunities both for productions and roles on Broadway. Particularly notable were *Native Son*, *Anna Lucasta* and *Strange Fruit*, the performances of Paul Robeson in *Othello* and Canada Lee in *The Duchess of Malfi*, and the work of Katherine Dunham in the dance. Among motion pictures with large black casts and great audience response were the musicals *Stormy Weather* and *Cabin in the Sky*. There were also a number of films, for example, *Sahara* and *The Ox-Bow Incident*, in which blacks were portrayed in dignified, non-musical roles, marking a drift away from unfavourable stereotypes of blacks. Radio had offered scant opportunity for blacks before the war, but by 1945 most of the prominent black singers and almost all the name bands were being heard on radio. Even several documentary programmes concerning blacks were aired. The popular Walter Winchell regularly attacked discrimination and prejudice in his commentaries, and in February 1944 the Town Hall of the Air presented a free-swinging symposium on 'Let's Face the Race Question'.[40]

Facing the race question had become an important issue in the United States, all the more so because of the white backlash resulting from the greater mobility of minorities. This backlash was seen early in the war in assaults on black servicemen and civilians. As the black press eloquently revealed, blacks did not suffer silently. Nevertheless, racial violence and tensions reached alarming proportions in a series of riots during the middle of 1943. The bloodiest of them was in Detroit, where in the worst race riot in a generation 34 people were killed and at least 1,000 injured.[41]

The riots led to some important developments. Labour, particularly the CIO, mounted an extensive publicity campaign against discrimination, and hundreds of white, black, and inter-racial committees sprang up to work against the outbreak of fresh rioting. Government became more alert to calming racial tensions. Where they had even a shred of jurisdiction, several federal agencies intervened to reduce tensions. The International City Managers Association circulated a pamphlet, *The Police and Minority Groups,* aimed at preventing disorders by improving group relations.[42]

Perhaps most important in seeking harmony were the citizens' and religious groups, which were often inter-racial in composition. Between 1943 and 1945 at least 267 communities established race relations committees and governors formed similar commissions in thirty-three states. Moreover, some 118 national organizations were concerned with reducing inter-racial problems. There were also the scores of pronouncements and endorsements of national Protestant organizations on the need for racial justice as well as the Catholic inter-racial councils, clerical and student conferences, and several inter-racial community centres. The most substantial consequence of the efforts of these citizens' and religious groups was education. Even though much of it resulted in convincing the converted, it also gave direction to those who were just awakening to the problems of racism, encouraged whites and blacks to work together on civic matters, and applied additional pressure upon government, business, and labour to reduce racial discrimination. Outstanding was the work of the American Missionary Association's Race Relations Department at Fisk University, which by 1946 had trained 500 people from thirty-three states to serve as expert consultants on racial issues. Also noteworthy was the trend towards racial minorities and Jews making common cause in their crusades against discrimination. During the years 1945–50 this alliance would be particularly effective.[43]

Politics continued to be an important part of the racial picture, even if only a minority of black adults could vote. They could after all use politics to place pressure upon the government and to make both the major parties vie for their support. This could be done with some success because many blacks, even Democrats, could roundly criticize Roosevelt and the Democrats and because the Republicans cherished the illusion that the black vote would return to them. The result was that the Democrats occasionally made concessions to blacks and the Republicans tried to outstrip the Democrats in performance and promises.[44]

During the Second World War the last important area of change for blacks was in the courts. The NAACP made some small progress in its suits for equalization of the salaries of white and black teachers and the institution of equal educational opportunities. The dramatic breakthroughs were elsewhere, however. In 1941 the Supreme Court, in *Mitchell* v. *United States,* held that a black could not be denied pullman car accommodations when they were available to whites. The same year, in *United States* v. *Classic,* the court found that the federal government could regulate a state primary election when the primary was a basic part of the nomination of candidates for federal office. In *Smith* v. *Allwright*, in 1944, the justices declared that the Democratic party of Texas could not constitutionally bar blacks from participation in its activities. That ruling, along with the repeal of poll taxes in Louisiana, Florida, and Georgia between 1937 and 1945, contributed to the slow expansion of black voters in the south. In 1940 an estimated 250,000 were registered there to vote, while by 1947 the number had grown to 595,000, an increase of from 5 to 12 per cent among southern blacks of voting age.[45]

IV

Historians have written much about the significance of the black experience in the United States during the Second World War.[46] Was it a shining time when blacks gave notice to whites that there had to be a fair racial order, or else ...? Or was it a sham battle with little connection with what happened during the so-called Black Revolution of the 1960s? Or, worse yet, was it only a skirmish in which blacks deluded themselves that they had made progress towards equality? Enough is known about what happened in racial affairs before, during and after the Second World War to say that each of these is a considerable exaggeration.

What, then, can fairly be said? First, it must be remembered that American blacks, thanks largely to the disadvantages placed upon them, had neither sufficient will nor power to do much on their own behalf before 1940. With the war's advent, their leaders saw a chance to move themselves and their people forward towards equality of opportunity and status. It was plain that the United States could not afford to exclude every tenth person from its defence. Moreover, America could not crusade for freedom of speech, freedom of worship, freedom from want, and freedom from fear everywhere in the world and yet deny these ideals to its black citizens. Black leaders and even many in the ranks moved swiftly to exploit this situation. It is idle to argue that in doing so blacks should have followed a different, supposedly more successful strategy than they did. Given the understandable disagreements among them, the relative weakness of their position, and the fact that they suffered from lack of the hindsight which we claim now to enjoy, that would be absurd. Blacks, of course, did not progress as much during the war or the following eight years as they had hoped to or as in justice they should have. It is also probably true that they lost more than they gained during the succeeding eight years, the Eisenhower period. That is, however, no reason to play down the importance of what blacks achieved during the Second World War, for it is clear that they were in a stronger position in 1950 or 1960 than they had been in 1940.

What then was the significance of the racial struggle during the Second World War? For one thing, blacks eliminated as an issue any question of whether they had borne their share of burdens during that national emergency. Nor was the lesson lost that the government was vulnerable to intensive black pressure. What happened, moreover, during 1940–5 –

and indeed even 1945–54 – in terms of employment, education, and the arts gave blacks the skills, precedents, and even economic strength to push all the harder for equality when it became obvious that new tactics and leadership were needed. The grip of racism on whites had also been loosened, so that however difficult the later struggle, the resistance was less than it might otherwise have been.

Just as what has occurred since 1960 will be viewed as a stage in the battle for equal rights, so must the events of the Second World War. And the years 1940–45 marked a crucial stage. Then, for the first time, there was widespread black militancy, pride, accomplishment, and visibility in the broader society. Moreover, racial questions became large public issues, and remained so in the United States. The successes and frustrations of blacks have encouraged them to press on with the struggle for equal rights. A notable point in all this came during the war, when as never before large black forces, under their own commanders, sallied forth with merit and valour to do battle on their own behalf.

Notes

1 United States Bureau of the Census, *Historical Statistics of the United States, Colonial Times to 1957* (Washington, 1960), 11–12.
2 J. H. Franklin, *From Slavery to Freedom* (New York, 1974), *passim*.
3 Pittsburgh *Courier*, 21 December 1940.
4 C. R. Lawrence, 'Negro Organizations in Crisis: Depression, New Deal, World War II' (Ph.D. dissertation, Columbia University, New York, 1952), pp. 76–7, 103; W. Record, *Race and Radicalism: the NAACP and the Communist Party in Conflict* (Ithaca, N.Y., 1964), p. 126.
5 R. M. Dalfiume, *Desegregation of the US Armed Forces* (Columbia, Mo., 1969), pp. 26–7, 34–5, 44; U. Lee, *The Employment of Negro Troops* (Washington, 1966), p. 55 ff.; L. J. Paszek, 'Negroes and the Air Force, 1939–1949', *Military Affairs* XXXI (1967), pp. 1–2; New York *Amsterdam News*, 24 May, 10 and 31 August 1940; *Chicago Defender*, 8 June 1940; C. C. Johnson, *Special Groups* (Washington, 1953) I, pp. 33, 44–7.
6 Dalfiume, p. 37; Lee, p. 75.
7 Dalfiume, pp. 37–8; Lee, pp. 74–5; W. White, *A Man Called White* (New York, 1948), p. 186; Library of Congress, Washington (hereafter LC), A. B. Spingarn Papers, W. White to A. B. Spingarn, 7 October 1940 and enclosed memorandum of 27 September 1940.
8 F. D. Roosevelt Library, Hyde Park, N.Y. (hereafter FDRL), F. D. Roosevelt Papers, Official File 25, R. P. Patterson to F. D. Roosevelt, 8 October 1940; Dalfiume, pp. 39–43, 51; White, p. 188; New York *Amsterdam News*, 2 November 1940; D. D. Nelson, *The Integration of the Negro into the US Navy* (New York, 1951), pp. 12–13; R. M. Dalfiume, 'Military Segregation and the 1940 Presidential Election', *Phylon* XXX (1969), pp. 42–55.
9 Kansas City *Call*, 20 December 1940; Pittsburgh *Courier*, 4 January 1941. For an interesting, if choleric, view of the black press during the war, see Lee Finkle, *Forum for Protest* (Rutherford, N.J., 1975).
10 Pittsburgh *Courier*, 13 December 1941; Baltimore *Afro-American*, 13 December 1941; *Chicago Defender*, 29 December 1941, 7 March 1942, 20 February 1943; White, chapter 26, pp. 206–8; Kansas City *Call*, 26 March 1943; Johnson, I, p. 61; Norfolk *Journal and Guide*, 25 April 1942; Columbia University Oral His-

tory Collection (hereafter CUOHC), Roy Wilkins Transcript, pp. 84–5; Dalfiume, *Desegregation of the Armed Forces*, pp. 46–8.

11 Lee, *passim*; Baltimore *Afro-American*, 17 January 1942; Dalfiume, *Desegregation of the Armed Forces*, chapters 3–4.

12 Yale University, New Haven, H. L. Stimson Papers, Diary (37), 17 January 1942; Roosevelt Papers, OF 18, H. L. Stimson to F. D. Roosevelt, 16 February 1942; Dalfiume, *Desegregation of the Armed Forces*, pp. 54–5; Nelson, p. 14.

13 Stimson Papers, Diary (37), 17 January 1942.

14 National Archives, Washington (hereafter NA), Records of the Office of the Secretary of War, Record Group 107, R. W. Crawford to D. D. Eisenhower, 2 April 1942.

15 *ibid.*, W. H. Hastie to H. L. Stimson, 5 January 1943, G. E. Stratemeyer to assistant secretary of war, 12 January 1943; Dalfiume, *Desegregation of the Armed Forces*, pp. 82–6; Norfolk *Journal and Guide*, 13 February 1943; Lee, p. 414; Jean Byers, 'A Study of the Negro in the Military Service' (mimeo., Department of Defense, Washington, 1950), pp. 9–10, 40–41.

16 Dalfiume, *Desegregation of the Armed Forces, passim*; White, p. 243; Roosevelt Papers, OF 93, P. V. McNutt to H. L. Stimson and Frank Knox, 17 February 1943; NA, Records of the Adjutant General's Office, RG 94, G. C. Marshall to commanding generals, Air, Ground, and Service Forces, 13 July 1943, W. D. Styer to deputy chief of staff for service commands and directors of plans, personnel, and training, 16 October 1944; Records of the Secretary of War, RG 107, J. S. Leonard, 'Digest of War Department Policy Pertaining to Negro Military Personnel', 1 January 1944, enclosed in H. A. Gerhardt to director of training, ASF, 10 January 1944, and 'The Negro Soldier' file; Lee, *passim*; Byers, pp. 45–7.

17 NA, Records of the Bureau of Naval Personnel, RG 24, F. D. Roosevelt to A. W. Mitchell, 3 August 1942, R. Jacobs to C. Polk, 30 September 1942, F. Knox to W. White, 31 December 1942; *Chicago Defender*, 2 January 1943, 22 July 1944; New York *Amsterdam News*, 6 March 1943; Nelson, pp. 16–8, 129–31.

18 Records of the Bureau of Naval Personnel, Circular Letter 6–44, 12 January 1944, Circular Letter 105–45, 13 April 1945; Nelson, pp. 18–20, 47–8; Kansas City *Call*, 5 May 1944; Operational Archives Branch, Naval History Division, Washington, J. V. Forrestal to F. D. Roosevelt, 20 May 1944, W. L. Calhoun to chief of naval personnel, 2 January 1945, R. Jacobs to CIC US Fleet and CNO, 6 March 1945; Byers, pp. 225–6, 231, 234–5; J. P. Guzman (ed.), *Negro Year Book: a Review of Events Affecting Negro Life, 1941–1946* (Tuskegee, Ala., 1947), pp. 369–73; Dalfiume, *Desegregation of the Armed Forces*, p. 102; NA, Records of the Department of the Navy, RG 80, files 54–1–9 and 54–1–13, J. V. Forrestal to L. B. Granger, 1 February 1945, Granger to Forrestal, 3 February, 19 March 1945.

19 NA, Records of the War Department General and Special Staffs, RG 165, S. G. Henry to J. J. McCloy, 19 September 1944; Records of the Secretary of War, RG 107, H. A. Gerhardt to J. J. McCloy, 15 August 1944, T. K. Gibson to J. J. McCloy, 23 April 1945; Lee, p. 160, 578–9; Johnson, II, pp. 170–71; S. A. Stouffer *et al.*, *The American Soldier: Adjustment During Army Life* (Princeton, 1949), pp. 588–94; D. R. McCoy and R. T. Ruetten, *Quest and Response: Minority Rights and the Truman Administration* (Lawrence, Ks., 1973), p. 10.

20 Johnson, I, p. 104, II, pp. 111–12, 115–16; Byers, p. 41; Nelson, pp. 12, 138–40; Lee, p. 414; Stouffer, pp. 497–9.

21 H. Aptheker, 'Literacy, the Negro and World War II', *Journal of Negro Education* XV (1946), p. 602; Johnson, I, pp. 163–4, 174; Nelson, p. 47.

22 Johnson, I, pp. 22–3; R. C. Weaver, *Negro Labor* (New York, 1946), chapter 2.

23 New York *Amsterdam News*, 24 May 1940; Norfolk *Journal and Guide*, 25 May 1940; *Chicago Defender*, 25 May, 8 June, 31 August 1940; H. Garfinkel, *When Negroes March* (Glencoe, Ill., 1959), p. 33; *Crisis* XLVII (1940), pp. 209, 296, 324.

24 L. C. Kesselman, *The Social Politics of FEPC* (Chapel Hill, N.C., 1948), p. 10; L. Ruchames, *Race, Jobs, & Politics, The Story of FEPC* (New York, 1953), p. 11; Baltimore *Afro-American*, 31 August 1940; Weaver, *Negro Labor*, pp. 18–19, 45–6, 131; S. Redding, *The Lonesome Road: the Story of the Negro's Part in America* (Garden City, N.Y., 1958), p. 271; Norfolk *Journal and Guide*, 2 November 1940.

25 Baltimore *Afro-American*, 19 October, 30 November 1940; *Crisis* XLVII (1940), p. 357; *Chicago Defender*, 23 November 1940; Norfolk *Journal and Guide*, 30 November, 7 December 1940; Pittsburgh *Courier*, 7 and 14 December 1940.

26 Kansas City *Call*, 29 November, 13 December 1940, 17 January, 14 February 1941, 28 September 1945; Baltimore *Afro-American*, 14 December 1940; *Chicago Defender*, 14 December 1940.

27 *Chicago Defender*, 21 December 1940, 11 January 1941; Weaver, pp. 20, 30–31.

28 Baltimore *Afro-American*, 4 and 25 January 1941; Pittsburgh *Courier*, 4 January 1941; Kansas City *Call*, 31 January 1941; *Chicago Defender*, 25 January 1941; New York *Amsterdam News*, 25 January 1941; Norfolk *Journal and Guide*, 1 February 1941.

29 LC, Mary Church Terrell Papers, A. P. Randolph to M. C. Terrell, 26 April 1941; Garfinkel, pp. 56, 198; Kansas City *Call*, 9 May 1941; Roosevelt Papers, A. P. Randolph to F. D. Roosevelt, 29 May 1941, enclosed in OF 391, R. P. Patterson to E. M. Watson, 3 June 1941.

30 Garfinkel, pp. 40, 58; New York *Amsterdam News*, 24 and 31 May 1941; Norfolk *Journal and Guide*, 14 and 21 June 1941; CUOHC, Benjamin McLaurin Transcript, pp. 65–6, 302–3; Pittsburgh *Courier*, 14 June 1941.

31 Roosevelt Papers, OF 391, R. P. Patterson to E. M. Watson, 3 June 1941; Ruchames, pp. 17–19; Garfinkel, p. 60; White, p. 190; Kansas City *Call*, 27 June 1941.

32 White, pp. 190–93; Ruchames, pp. 19–20; Dalfiume, *Desegregation of the Armed Forces*, p. 120; Stimson Papers, Diary (34), 18 June 1941.

33 White, pp. 192–3; Ruchames, pp. 20–21; Garfinkel, p. 61.

34 Weaver, p. 28; *Negro Year Book, 1941–1946*, p. 146; F. R. Marshall, *The Negro and Organized Labor* (New York, 1965), pp. 31, 38–48.

35 Ruchames, chapters 2–3, pp. 56–7; Roosevelt Papers, OF 4245G, H. D. Smith to F. D. Roosevelt, 18 June 1942, M. S. MacLean to M. MacIntyre, 3 August 1942; Executive Order 9346, 27 May 1943.

36 Weaver, p. 80; *Negro Year Book, 1941–1946*, pp. 136, 140–41; J. A. Davis, 'Nondiscrimination in the Federal Service', *Annals* CCXLIV (1946), p. 72.

37 J. P. Guzman (ed.), *1952 Negro Year Book: a Review of Events Affecting Negro Life* (New York, 1952), pp. 103, 238; United States Department of Commerce, *4th Annual Report of Banking Institutions Owned and Operated by Negroes* (Washington, 1944), pp. 5–6, and *5th Annual Report of Banking Institutions Owned and Operated by Negroes* (Washington, 1947), pp. 5, 8; *Negro Year Book, 1941–1946*, pp. 16–18, 135, 297, 318; J. P. Davis (ed.), *The American Negro Reference Book* (Englewood Cliffs, N.J., 1966), p. 233.

38 United States Housing and Home Finance Agency, *Housing of the Non-White Population, 1940–1947* (Washington, 1948), p. 4.

39 A. C. Powell, Jr, *Marching Blacks, An Interpretative History of the Rise of the Black Common Man* (New York, 1945), pp. 3, 5, 129; Baltimore *Afro-American*,

30 January 1943, 3 June 1944; Lawrence, pp. 78, 103. The membership, for example, of the NAACP rose from 50,556 in 1940 to 351,131 in 1945.

40 John Lovell, Jr, 'Roundup: the Negro in the American Theatre', *Crisis* LIV (1947), pp. 213–15; *Negro Year Book, 1941–1946*, pp. 439–43, 446–53; C. S. Johnson *et al.*, *Into the Main Stream* (Chapel Hill, N.C., 1947), pp. 205–6; J. T. McManus and L. Kronenberger, 'Motion Pictures, the Theater, and Race Relations', *Annals* CCXLIV (1946), pp. 153–7.

41 *Negro Year Book, 1941–1946*, pp. 255–6; Kansas City *Call*, 25 June 1943; A. M. Lee and N. D. Humphrey, *Race Riot* (New York, 1943), p. 2; White, pp. 233–41.

42 New York *Amsterdam News*, 19 June 1943; Kansas City *Call*, 13 August 1943, 10 November 1944; *Chicago Defender*, 8 January 1944; NA, Records of the Army Staff, RG 319, file dated 16 April 1945 (291.2), Subject: Racial Potentialities; Roosevelt Papers, OF 4245G, J. Daniels to F. Biddle, 28 July 1943; Harry S. Truman Library, Independence, Mo., Jonathan Daniels Oral History Transcript, 14–15, Oscar L. Chapman Papers, W. C. Leland, Jr to O. L. Chapman, 1 May 1944; Department of Justice, Records of the Justice Department, C. Gill to F. Biddle, 21 July 1943, F. Biddle to C. Gill, 24 July 1943, F. Biddle to L. Smith, 6 July 1944.

43 A. A. Liveright, 'The Community and Race Relations', *Annals* CCXLIV (1946), pp. 106, 109–13, 116; Johnson *et al.*, pp. 4, pp. 12–40; H. H. Long and C. S. Johnson, *People vs. Property* (Nashville, 1947), p. v; F. S. Loescher, *The Protestant Church and the Negro* (New York, 1948), pp. 28–38, 121–32; Johnson, I, p. 61; T. J. Harte, *Catholic Organizations Promoting Negro–White Race Relations in the United States* (Washington, 1947), pp. 21, 62–75, chapters 5–6; W. A. Osborne, *The Segregated Covenant: Race Relations and American Catholics* (New York, 1967), pp. 38–9; McCoy and Ruetten, pp. 12, 62–5.

44 White, pp. 262–6; H. L. Moon, *Balance of Power: The Negro Vote* (Garden City, N.Y., 1948), *passim*.

45 *Negro Year Book, 1941–1946*, pp. 62–4, 297–8; D. R. Matthews and J. W. Prothro, *Negroes and the New Southern Politics* (New York, 1966), pp. 17–18; V. O. Key, Jr, *Southern Politics in State and Nation* (New York, 1949), pp. 518–22, 578.

46 See for example R. M. Dalfiume, 'The "Forgotten Years" of the Negro Revolution', *Journal of American History* LV (1968), pp. 90–106; H. Sitkoff, 'Racial Militancy and Interracial Violence in the Second World War', *Journal of American History* LVIII (1971), pp. 661–81; L. Finkle, 'The Conservative Aims of Militant Rhetoric: Black Protest during World War II', *Journal of American History* LX (1973), pp. 692–713; N. A. Wynn, *The Afro–American and the Second World War* (London, 1976); A. R. Buchanan, *Black Americans in World War II* (Santa Barbara, Calif., 1977).

10

Imperial policy and Indian minorities overseas,
1905–23

T. G. Fraser

Between 1968 and 1972 the successive British governments of Harold Wilson and Edward Heath were forced to respond to the appeals of the East African Asians when Kenya and then, in a more draconian manner, Uganda initiated policies of Africanization aimed at reducing, or in the latter case eliminating, these minorities. Braving many criticisms, both governments in the last resort accepted that, as the former imperial power responsible for the creation of these minorities, they retained certain obligations towards them. Amid the clamour of debate, few bothered to recall earlier bitter disputes around the status of Indian minorities, not just in East Africa, when British governments had been less forthcoming. In the aftermath of the abolition of slavery in 1834 the Victorian Empire had witnessed an Indian migration, some free but most through the indenture system, almost as impressive as the movement of population from the British Isles. Where these two communities came into economic and political competition, tensions developed between them in which the Indians were at a serious disadvantage. As their own country lacked an effective voice, their only ultimate safeguard was the imperial government's unquestioned authority over British colonies and the right, impressive in theory but in practice languishing in abeyance, to question unacceptable dominion legislation. India's central position in the Empire meant that the protection of her overseas minorities should have been a matter of the first concern, and this chapter will attempt to investigate how these communities fared in the great period of imperial vigour and transition between 1905 and 1923. Such a discussion would be meaningless without some identification of the nature of the conflicts between the Indians and the European groups who objected to their presence, and this will be done with reference to the minorities in Canada, South Africa and Kenya. However, the principal object remains that of illustrating how the overseas Indians confronted the Empire as a whole with inescapable moral and political dilemmas.

Southern Africa must be considered first for it was in Natal and the Transvaal in the 1890s that first indications were given that an Indian presence among European settlers might provoke conflict. The hostility of the British in Natal and the Boers of the Transvaal towards the Indians who had settled there is simply explained. They feared that political and economic concessions would merely herald similar advances by the African population to the ultimate destruction of their way of life.[1] For a time it seemed that the Indians might be assisted by the imperial authorities, particularly when their ill-treatment by the Boers featured as one of the reasons for the South African war. But the Transvaal's absorption into the Empire after the war, though welcomed by the Indians there, was to bring them no advantage, and events in the unwilling colony were soon to elicit British attitudes which established an unfortunate precedent for Indian minorities throughout the Empire.

In September 1906 the colony's nominated legislative council passed an ordinance which would have forced the registration of the Indian population, but the Secretary of State for the Colonies, Lord Elgin, was persuaded by Gandhi to withhold the royal assent pending further consideration of the measure. What might have been a significant victory was soon nullified by constitutional change. In January 1907 the Transvaal received responsible government and when its parliament met in March its second act was to pass the ordinance Elgin had rejected. It was an embarrassing affair for Elgin and his government. The Transvaal's acceptance of responsible government so soon after a bitter war was lauded as a triumph of imperial statesmanship, and to have refused the royal assent from its parliament's second measure would have been inconceivable. To the anguish of the Indian community the royal assent was given, the first clear indication that the imperial government would be reluctant to override the wishes of the Empire's parliaments in order to protect the Indian minorities.

This impression was soon confirmed by a series of negotiations affecting the small Indian community in Canada. The Indians involved, some 5,000 Jat Sikhs from the Punjab, started arriving in British Columbia in 1905 as an onward extension of an existing migration to British colonies and concessions in east Asia. Their hard-working qualities were initially prized by employers on the farms, ranches and lumber camps, but their presence quickly became a focus of resentment in the community at large. The crisis came in the second half of 1907 when the citizens of Vancouver, which had already been subject to Chinese immigration from the 1880s, watched with alarm as a sudden, unexpected influx of some 1,600 Sikhs reinforced the arrival of 7,000 Japanese immigrants.[2] Labour hostility towards what they regarded as the importation of cheap labour was predictable, but beneath this was a general racial fear among white British Columbians, numbering just over 150,000, that they were remote from sources of migration in Europe but, inconveniently, the terminus of shipping lanes from Asia. Racial feelings became so inflamed, with anti-Asian rioting in Vancouver and dark hints of the province's secession from the dominion, that Sir Wilfrid Laurier's liberal government was forced to act against further Indian immigration.

Laurier's first proposal to London, that the government of India should agree to an annual quota restriction on migrants to Canada, foundered on the opposition of the Viceroy, Lord Minto, who realized that Indians would regard this as an unwarrantable interference with their freedom of movement.[3] His attitude forced Laurier in January 1908 to issue an order in council prohibiting the landing of immigrants unless they had come by a continuous journey from their country of origin, a cleverly contrived device which could not be accused of overt racism but prevented further Indian immigration as there was no direct shipping route to Canada from the sub-continent.[4] It was bitterly resented by the British Columbian Sikhs, few of whom had yet brought over their families from India.

There was no immediate British reaction to this clear act of discrimination against their Indian subjects, members of a community, moreover, who were particularly esteemed for their contribution to the Indian army. If they had wished to help the Indians, the opportunity came in the spring of 1908 when Laurier sent W. L. Mackenzie King to London to negotiate directly for a quota agreement. In constitutional terms the only champion the Indians had was the Secretary of State for India, the veteran liberal John Morley, who might have been expected to sympathize with them. Morley, on the contrary, was convinced that the Canadians were right to exclude Indian immigration, and when he conferred with Elgin and Sir Edward Grey prior to Mackenzie King's arrival, the three men agreed that Britain could not challenge the new Canadian policy.[5] This confirmed the abdication of responsibility towards Indian minorities which had been implied in Elgin's previous decision over the Transvaal, only on this occasion it could not be explained away by special circumstances. When the negotiations took place between King and Minto, who still opposed the quota idea, it emerged that the British were unwilling to become actively involved. Morley pressed his Viceroy to accept the Canadian proposal but did not attempt to assert the constitutional supremacy of his office in the face of the government of India's continued opposition.

All that now remained was clear public definition of the attitudes that had emerged in the British government's reactions to what had happened in the Transvaal and British Columbia. 'The whole question', *The Times* correspondent observed in 1910, 'is one that cannot be allowed to drag on indefinitely without grave danger to the Empire'.[6] The British Columbian Sikhs allowed just such an opportunity when they decided to present a statement of their grievances to the 1911 Imperial Conference. Their document asked the dominion delegates to consider whether there could be

> two definitions for subjects of one and the same Empire? If there is but one recognized definition under the flag over which the sun is supposed never to set, then it is for us to see that *no injustice shall minimize the rights of that citizenship, whether the holder is black or white.*[7]

Such a concept of imperial equality, with its echoes of ancient Rome, found no favour in the dominions or in Britain where a clear distinction, classically defined in 1883 by Sir John Seeley, was made between the white settlements and India.[8] In their response to the memorandum from British Columbia, the India Office admitted this:

> His Majesty's Government fully accept the principle that each of the dominions must be allowed to decide for itself what elements it desires to accept in its

population. .... It is useless to attempt to veil the fact that the policy of building up new nations of European blood within the Empire is absolutely incompatible with the idea that every British subject, whatever his race, shall have free right of ingress to any part of the Empire.[9]

The delegates avoided debating their Indian minorities, withdrawing a rather offensive New Zealand resolution that coloured races should be encouraged to remain domiciled within their own zone in favour of a more anodyne discussion of shipping policy, it being understood that the new Secretary of State for India, Lord Crewe, would present a major statement on British policy towards the overseas Indians. His speech, though rambling and at times scarcely grammatical, was none the less of the greatest importance both for its definitions and for what it left unsaid. Crewe reminded the delegates that emigrant grievances were the one issue that united political moderates and extremists in India, forcing them to ask the obvious question: 'If ... Indians are to suffer from disabilities in various parts of the Empire, what good is the British connection at all?'[10] He made no attempt to answer this question by initiating anything that might assist the minorities, confining himself to a vague appeal that the dominions 'make the entrance of Indians more easy and more pleasant than it has been in the past'.[11] Far from doing anything to help the Indian minorities, Crewe's speech set out two fundamental principles, which together isolated them from any hope of British intervention on their behalf. The first confirmed what had emerged in 1907 and 1908, that 'nobody can attempt to dispute the right of the self-governing dominions to decide for themselves whom, in each case, they will admit as citizens of their respective dominions'.[12]

The second principle represented an even greater retreat from any notion of imperial authority. 'It is', Crewe lamented, 'a distinct misfortune and a derogation from the unity of the Empire if the mother country continually finds itself implicated in difficulties between various parts of the Empire', adding that in future he wished to avoid 'the necessity for our acting as advocates on the one side or the other, or being called in to give an opinion'.[13]

In view of such a speech, it is not surprising that the position of the Canadian and South African Indians worsened in the remaining years before the outbreak of war. In the Transvaal a dour struggle developed between Gandhi and Smuts that culminated in an agreement of sorts in 1914, while in the same year the *Komagata Maru* arrived at Vancouver with a party of Punjabi immigrants who resorted to bloody rioting on their enforced return to Calcutta. The Viceroy, Lord Hardinge, privately castigated Canadian immigration policy as 'difficult to reconcile ... with the inclusion of Indians within the Empire', and in a speech at Madras publicly sympathized with the South African Indians, but he was powerless.[14] The consequences were predictable. The Canadian Sikhs, many of whom were ex-servicemen, helped form the revolutionary Ghadr party, and on the outbreak of war flocked back to the Punjab to present the British with their most serious armed challenge since 1857.[15] In South Africa, of course,

Gandhi was fashioned into the leader who was to inspire Indian nationalism from 1919 until the independence of his country was achieved.

If the position prior to 1914 offered the Indian minorities little hope,
India's assistance in the war adjusted certain perspectives in their favour.
British officials, uncomfortably aware of how emigrant grievances had
fuelled the Ghadr movement in the winter of 1914–15, argued that fairer
treatment for the overseas Indians should be part of India's reward for
her war effort.[16] The increased respect India now commanded was demonstrated by the presence of the Maharaja of Bikaner and the Bengali politician, Sir Satyendra Sinha, at the 1917 Imperial War Conference, thus free-
ing the Indian minorities from dependence on the Secretary of State for
India who might, like Morley and Crewe, do them less than justice. Sinha
was determined that this time their case would not go by default, but he
had two influential opponents, Smuts, whose new role of imperial champion gave him immense prestige, and Canada's Sir Robert Borden. In an
attempt to avoid the possible embarrassments of a public session, the latter
arranged a dinner for Sinha to present informally the Indian migrant case,
as a result of which he was asked to prepare a draft resolution for further
preliminary discussion. His attempt was comprehensive, proposing the
regulation of migration between India and the dominions on the basis of
reciprocity, free travel between India and the dominions for temporary
visitors, guaranteed settlement in the dominions for a limited number of
Indians each year, and the removal of disabilities from existing Indian
minorities – notably that they should be granted the vote and allowed to
bring in wives and minor children. If these proposals had been accepted
and implemented, most outstanding grievances would certainly have been
removed, but they went far beyond anything contemplated by Borden and
Smuts. Faced with their united opposition, Sinha refused to take any trun-
cated version of his resolution to the conference.[17]

The Secretary of State for India, Austen Chamberlain, had somehow
to resolve the impasse, which he did by securing the agreement of the three
main protagonists to a new resolution accepting reciprocity of treatment
between India and the dominions and recommending that the dominion
governments give favourable consideration to a memorandum on the
treatment of Indian minorities, specially prepared by the India Office.[18]
This fell far short of Sinha's hopes, but it did include positive recommendations about the right to travel in the dominions, a restriction educated Indians resented, and the admission of families, the disability at the
heart of Sikh resentment in Canada.[19] When Sinha returned to the offensive at the second Imperial War Conference in July 1918, he was able to
carry these two points, but at the cost of a fundamental concession. Sir
Robert Borden was at last prepared to concede that the wives and minor
children of the Sikhs should be allowed to enter Canada. He knew that
the exodus of Ghadrite revolutionaries in 1914 had greatly reduced the
Sikh population and was genuinely impressed by the Indian war effort;
even so the price he exacted was Sinha's agreement to a preamble to the
resolution recognizing the right of each dominion government to 'enjoy
complete control of the composition of its own population by means of

restriction on migration from any of the other communities'.[20] The Indians hoped that, by surrendering the principle of free migration, they might enable dominion governments to secure equality of treatment for the existing minorities, but in this they were disappointed. The preamble merely gave formal imperial recognition to the existing *de facto* position of dominion autonomy where the entry of Indians was concerned, and as such was to prove useful to the South Africans. None the less, Sinha had achieved something for the Canadian Sikhs, whose place in the forefront of the debate was now taken by the Indian community in Kenya.

Before this new Indian minority crisis could develop, however, India itself experienced revolutionary changes. The Montagu–Chelmsford reforms of 1918, which looked forward to India's ultimate achievement of responsible government 'as an integral part of the British Empire', created a legislative assembly where the disabilities of the overseas Indians were debated and officials questioned on efforts to assist them. Almost immediately the new policy was brought to the brink of ruin by the aftermath of General Dyer's tragic blunder at Amritsar when Congress, mesmerized by Gandhi's messianic leadership, embarked in 1920 on a campaign to end British rule without delay. Not everyone accepted Gandhi's break with an empire he considered satanic. Some of India's ablest politicians, including three who became particularly identified with the overseas Indians, Sinha, V. S. Srinivasa Sastri, and Sir Tej Bahadur Sapru, sought to advance their country by building on the constructive elements of the Montagu–Chelmsford reforms through a moderate political grouping, the National Liberal Federation. Their continued influence with government meant that they could intervene on an issue that excited universal public concern, offering them a major platform to match Gandhi's appeal to the instincts of Hindu India. But failure to assist the minorities would go far to invalidate their basic claim that India's future would best be served through cooperation with the Empire. Edwin Montagu and the Indian liberals had no alternative but to champion the minorities.

In the early 1920s there was renewed harassment of the Indians in Natal and the Transvaal, but the period was dominated by a crisis in Kenya where relations between Europeans and Indians deteriorated to an unprecedented extent. Both groups, of course, were microscopic minorities compared with the African population of just under three million, but the latter were conveniently dismissed as 'primitive races' or 'savages' until in 1923 they were to provide the mechanism for resolving the crisis. The Indians were the larger of the two minorities, but political power and influence rested with the Europeans. An Indian mercantile presence on the East African coast long pre-dated the coming of the Europeans, but the modern community began in 1896, the year after the territory's formal annexation by the British, when Punjabi workers were recruited through the indenture system for the construction of the Uganda railway from Mombasa to Kampala. By the turn of the century these Punjabis were being reinforced by Parsee and Gujarati traders, and by Goans who were welcomed into the lowlier ranks of the administration. As the railway opened up the hinterland, Indians whose indentures had expired established themselves as small traders, penetrating into the highlands beyond Nairobi and as far as the primitive settlement of Entebbe across the Uganda border. In 1910 they numbered 25,000, a diverse and thriving community drawn from many of the most enterprising elements in the Indian population, who not only continued to run the railway but dominated the trading life of the protectorate.[21]

British officials did not conceal their admiration for the Indian contribution to the area's development. When Lord Sanderson's committee investigated the question of Indian migration in 1910, official evidence, including that of the explorer Sir Harry Johnston and the veteran East African administrator Sir John Kirk, was strongly sympathetic to the Indians. 'But for the Indians,' Kirk said, 'we should not be there now,' adding 'drive away the Indians and you may shut up the protectorate.'[22] But the committee also heard evidence from the white settlers that was bitterly hostile to the Indian presence. Numbering only some 450 families at this time, the Europeans' main concern was to defend the highlands beyond Nairobi for their exclusive settlement, while looking forward to the day when Kenya would be recognized as a new white dominion. They feared that Indian enterprise would threaten the creation of a viable white population, as their principal witness, Captain E. S. Grogan, admitted to the committee:

> My point is that if you do introduce the Asiatic, not only does he tend to displace the white but the native as well, because it does not matter what function you put him to perform, he is a more efficient person, that is to say viewed entirely from an economic plain.[23]

By 1920 the aspiration of the whites, now numbering over 9,000, to become a white dominion was even stronger, reflecting similar feelings in Rhodesia. Disregarding any political potential among the Africans, they continued to see the Indians as the only possible threat to their ambition. For their part, the Indians were unwilling to be cowed. Aware of their economic strength and responding to the growth of nationalism at home, they developed political ambitions of their own. In 1919 they were presented with the threat of subordination to the whites when the latter were granted the right to elect representatives to the colony's legislative council. Fearing the consequences of this, the Indians drew up their political demands, which included an end to segregation, the right of unrestricted immigration, the right to buy land in the 'white highlands', and the right to equal representation with the Europeans on a common franchise.[24] This programme was irreconcilable with that of the whites. On this occasion the imperial government could not retreat behind the doctrine of dominion autonomy. Kenya was unquestionably a colony, and the dilemma seemed to be whether to bow before the white supremacist claims of their fellow countrymen, or recognize in the interests of imperial harmony the Indian demand for equality of treatment, a claim which the whites feared would result in the colony's 'Indianization'. The first attempt at a settlement, by Lord Milner in May 1920, favoured the Europeans, confirming their exclusive right to the highlands, and allowing the election of two Indians to the legislative council on a special franchise.[25] Milner's proposals were regarded as an affront by the Indians, and they were so strongly supported by the government of India that the question was referred to a joint committee of parliament, which had still to report when the first post-war Imperial Conference met in June 1921.

When the conference convened, the intensity of the Kenya crisis and continued discrimination in South Africa made the minorities the main issue as far as the Indian delegation was concerned. 'It was felt', wrote the delegation's secretary, G. S. Bajpai, 'that on its satisfactory settlement would depend in no small measure the future of political events in India and her relations with the Empire.'[26] On one side were ranged the chief Indian delegate, the distinguished south Indian liberal leader V. S. Srinivasa Sastri, and Edwin Montagu, who could always be relied upon for a vigorous defence of Indian interests, but who was now at his wit's end trying to salvage his reforms in the teeth of Gandhi's non-cooperation campaign in India and diehard Conservative malevolence at home. Against them were Smuts, who freely admitted that he saw the Empire as 'a federation of white races', and the Colonial Secretary, Winston Churchill, a fervent admirer of his former Boer adversary who had never regarded India with anything other than distaste.

The government of India's strategy was to remind the dominion premiers of the 1918 concession that they could regulate their own population, while pleading for the removal of disabilities suffered by existing Indian minorities 'by merging them in the general body of citizens'.[27] A preliminary meeting with Smuts was enough to disabuse Sastri of any expectation that South Africa might accept this suggested resolution: racial feelings, Smuts made clear, were too much part of the national experience.[28] When Smuts opened the conference discussion a week later, he took his stand on the principle of inequality and was opposed by Montagu and his fellow premiers, but strongly supported by Churchill. The Australian premier, Hughes, suggested an amendment to the government of India's resolution to the effect that 'in the interests of the solidarity of the British Commonwealth, it is desirable that, as a matter of principle, the rights of citizenship of such Indians should be recognized'; but as this was unacceptable to Smuts, Churchill was asked to mediate between the South African premier and Sastri.[29]

He did not meet Sastri, preferring to deal exclusively with Smuts, who produced a further amended resolution, which, while recognizing the rights of Indians to citizenship, wished to add 'that in some parts, such as South and East Africa, there are exceptional circumstances in the way of its adoption'.[30] While Montagu was reconciled to the fact that he could not interfere with the 'free dominions', he was not prepared to bargain away the British cabinet's right to legislate for Kenya, and successfully insisted on its omission. Now in a state of 'profound despair' over the situation in South Africa, he suggested that as a means of giving the Indians there some hope for the future, the words 'at the present time' should be incorporated into Smuts's amended draft.[31] Smuts refused to agree to any of this, and further pressure from Montagu provoked Churchill to the accusation that he was 'splitting hairs'. Montagu's bitter reply reflected the sense of frustration felt by all those who wished to assist the Indian minorities:

> May I be permitted to say how very deeply I feel your accusation of splitting hairs. I took some trouble in my last letter to you to make out my case. It is that General Smuts refuses to give me any hope, either for the present or for the future, either that things will improve or that they will not get worse. I find this contribution to the solidarity of the Empire pathetically inadequate, and I am told by one of my colleagues that I am splitting hairs. . . . If the history in any form has to be published, I am content to accept a more dispassionate verdict on this subject.[32]

When the conference met to discuss the outcome of Churchill's mediation, Smuts indicated that he would accept the Australian resolution, provided it was made clear that it would not apply in his country. Despairing of anything better, Montagu agreed, but insisted on a second reservation recording Indian concern at the South African attitude. The embarrassing haggle appeared at an end when Hughes announced that he could not accept these two additions to his resolution. This provoked the intervention of Lloyd George, who reminded his listeners of India's war effort, and pleaded that her delegates should not have to return with the message that there was no justice to be had in the Empire.[33] His appeal removed the last obstacles to the adoption of the amended Australian resolution which, while recognizing that the incongruity between India's position in the Empire and the treatment of the overseas minorities meant that their rights to citizenship should be accepted, also recorded South African dissent and India's 'profound concern' at the situation there.[34] The outcome could hardly have been less satisfactory for the Indians. Churchill had rebuffed Montagu and snubbed Sastri, while Smuts had retained the initiative throughout. South Africa was to be allowed to go its own way in racial matters irrespective of any arguments of imperial harmony, and her public disavowal of the resolution, while full of portent for her future relations with the Empire, robbed it of any value as far as the Indians were concerned. The resolution gave no comfort to the Indian minorities in Africa or to the beleaguered partisans of imperial cooperation in India.

The fact that the other dominions had subscribed to the resolution offered some hope to the Indian political moderates that they, at least, might show some generosity towards their minorities. In the belief that he could use the personal contacts he had made at the conference to influence the situation, Sastri undertook an official tour of Australia, New Zealand and Canada in 1922, but he was now confronted with local political realities. In Australia Hughes made it plain that he would neither enfranchise the small Indian community nor allow them access to New Guinea. The New Zealand government was equally adamant that they should be excluded from Samoa. Canada proved still more disappointing, for the conservative premier, Arthur Meighen, who at the conference had indicated his willingness to open the question of voting rights for the British

Columbian Sikhs, had since lost power to the liberals under Mackenzie King, a man to whom imperial arguments were as nothing compared with Canadian electoral arithmetic. With a majority over the conservatives of only one seat, he would not contemplate raising an issue as sensitive as Indian voting rights.[35] Although he put a brave face on things on his return to India, Sastri's tour had been a failure which left moderates like himself dangerously exposed. Nothing, it seemed, could now be expected of the dominions and Indians increasingly looked to the threatening situation in Kenya: here, at least, the Indian minority could be defended by the unquestioned power of the imperial government.

In 1922 relations between the British and Indians in Kenya deteriorated so badly that civil war and even insurrection seemed possible. A compromise, the Wood–Winterton agreement, was reached between the Colonial and India Offices, whereby the highlands were to remain a white preserve, but the elections for the legislative council would be conducted on a common franchise, with some 10 per cent of Indian males initially having the vote. The common franchise proved the nub of the question. The white settlers argued that such a system would ultimately destroy their ambition to become a dominion like South Africa, fearing that subsequent expansions of the franchise would lead to their subordination to the Indians. Their reaction to the Wood–Winterton proposals was violent, threats of armed rebellion against British authority not being excluded. The new Secretary of State for India, Lord Peel, who was much less receptive to Indian claims than his predecessor, wrote to the Viceroy, Lord Reading, that the 'obstinacy and prejudice of the white colonists over this moderate compromise is intolerable'.[36]

For the Indians the common franchise, however restricted, was a recognition of their aspiration to equal status and a means through which it might eventually be realized. In India the unbridled opposition of the whites was seen as an affront to national dignity. The government's director of information, Rushbrook Williams, who stood close to the aspirations of the Indian elite, wrote in a contemporary account that 'Indian sentiment, not merely in Kenya but in India itself, was deeply stirred by what was regarded as a deliberate attempt to stamp Indians with the seal of racial and social inferiority.'[37] Well aware of the depth of this sentiment, Reading's government worked hard for the acceptance of the Wood–Winterton agreement in the knowledge that anything less would threaten remaining hopes that Indian national sentiment might be persuaded to work within the empire. If the British government were forced to depart from the agreement, Reading wrote, 'the Indian will then be convinced that the British Empire doesn't mean to treat Indians as she treats the white members of her Empire, and that India can never thus become in truth an equal partner of the Empire'.[38]

None the less, faced with white intransigence, the government began to give way. Rival delegations led by Sastri and the Kenyan leader, Lord Delamere, came to London, but it was soon clear which was the more influential, and at a cabinet meeting on 23 July 1923 the Colonial Secretary, the Duke of Devonshire, persuaded his colleagues to accept a new set of proposals that seemingly conceded the European case, exclusive rights in the highlands and a separate Indian franchise.[39] Delamere's victory over the Indians proved pyrrhic. In his dealings with the Colonial Office he had argued that the native Africans needed protection from Indian traders and moneylenders. The government seized upon this as their justification for retaining the colony directly under the Colonial Office. Such a solution would not only protect the Africans, but, as it eliminated the prospect of responsible government, rendered the nature of the Indian franchise irrelevant.[40] The real significance of the dispute over Indian rights was official recognition that Kenya was an African country, not to be surrendered to either of its minorities, and the avoidance of another Rhodesia in East Africa.

Reading was incensed by the failure of his representations. 'I hope', he telegraphed Peel on 28 July, 'you and His Majesty's Government understand the difficulty in future of impressing upon the Indians the benefits which they derive from an association with the Empire.'[41] In an attempt to calm the prevailing sense of outrage, he chose to record his dissent from the decision in a major speech that day to the final session of the legislative assembly. 'If submission must be made,' he said, 'then with all due respect to His Majesty's Government it can only be under protest.'[42] His unprecedented statement did nothing to inhibit the angry reaction of Indian opinion in the press, the legislative assembly and the provincial legislative councils. For Congress the decision should have come at a fortunate time, as the civil disobedience campaign they had initiated in 1920 was rapidly falling apart. Their immediate reaction was the proclamation of a *hartal*, a day of protest, on 27 August which was observed in Delhi, Calcutta, Madras, Lucknow and Cawnpore.[43] The following month they met in special session in Delhi and naturally Kenya formed part of their discussions. Their resolution drew the obvious conclusion:

> This Congress looks upon the decision of the British government about the status of Indians in Kenya as being in keeping with England's determination to rule India as a subject country, and, therefore, this Congress urges on the people of India to redouble their efforts to wipe off the stigma of subjection as early as possible.[44]

Despite these demonstrations of annoyance, the impression remains that Congress, which had already moved far from any overt imperial sentiment, was not especially interested. The real snub had been administered to the National Liberals, events in Kenya having shown once again that their influence carried little weight with the British government in the face of white determination. Indicative of their disillusion with the Empire was the chairmanship by one of their leaders, Sir Chimanlal Setalvad, of an all-party meeting in Bombay which demanded an Indian boycott of the forthcoming imperial conference and empire exhibition.[45] Sastri, who had made the issue particularly his own, felt especially aggrieved. Interestingly, his reaction differed little from that of Congress. On his return from leading the Kenya delegation in London, he declared that his supporters 'while remaining true to the liberal creed', would work with all parties 'to get their grievous wrongs righted and in the speedy achievement of Swaraj which is the sovereign need of the hour'.[46]

The only prospect of easing this universal discontent lay with the Imperial Conference, which was due to convene in London, but even here hopes were slight. The chief Indian delegate, however, Sir Tej Bahadur Sapru, was a man of strong character and shrewd ability. Widely respected as the ablest jurist in India, he had an urbanity and flair for negotiation which made him more effective than Sastri, who often offended British and dominion leaders.[47] His secretary, Rushbrook Williams, who had been his close friend for nearly ten years, gave him access to some of the most influential men in Britain, notably the indefatigable imperial thinker, Lionel Curtis. Curtis, who had worked closely with Rushbrook Williams on the preparation of the Montagu–Chelmsford reforms, secured the invaluable support of the Round Table group and *The Times*.[48]

Such prestigious allies helped to diminish the delegation's otherwise precarious isolation. Peel, who was suffering Sastri's verbal assaults and implied rebukes from Reading, felt that he had done his best over Kenya and was now distinctly peevish over the whole affair. It was in any case unlikely that the government would reverse or amend their Kenya decision so soon after its announcement. The dominion situation seemed equally unpromising. Mackenzie King had long regarded the Canadian Indians as an electoral liability, and Smuts now pointed smugly to Sastri's unproductive dominion tour as justification for his attitude to the 1921 resolution. The appreciation of India's war effort, which had helped bring some comfort to the minorities between 1917 and 1921, was now replaced by a feeling of sourness caused by Gandhi's boycott of the Prince of Wales's Indian tour.[49] Before attempting to overcome these formidable barriers, Sapru had to contest sentiment at home which was demanding his withdrawal in protest over Kenya, but he was able to convince his own party that he should remain.[50]

Such an action says much for his tenacity, as his initial treatment in London was far from satisfactory. He almost left for home when he discovered that the position of the Indian minorities did not appear on the conference agenda. His departure in anger from the conference would have reinforced the mounting sense of bitterness in India, but this disaster was averted by Rushbrook Williams who managed to impress on Peel the necessity for amending the agenda.[51] Even so, Sapru was kept at a distance, receiving no official papers and having to rely on his secretary for unofficial information.[52] Only on the very eve of the conference did the lobbying on behalf of the Indian delegation begin to yield results. Peel's attitude began to thaw as he appreciated Sapru's qualities, and between them Curtis and Rushbrook Williams established a fruitful relationship with the Colonial Secretary, the duke of Devonshire, and his permanent secretary, Sir James Masterton-Smith.[53]

Realizing that resolutions were in themselves little more than pious expressions, Sapru's strategy was to create a mechanism for implementing what had been agreed in 1921, which might also be used to bring some relief to the Kenya Indians. His proposal was for the establishment of a committee to investigate Indian minority grievances. When he put this idea to the conference the initial responses were discouraging, support coming only from New Zealand, Newfoundland and Ireland, the countries least affected. Bruce of Australia saw no necessity for such a committee while Mackenzie King evaded the issue by arguing that the Indians in his country suffered disabilities only in British Columbia and that Sastri's visit had roused popular sentiment against them. Smuts's dismissal of the idea was predictable, but a more depressing reaction was that of Devonshire who, while accepting the principle of a committee, made it clear that Kenya was to be excluded from its terms of reference.[54] Between them, they had rendered Sapru's proposal meaningless. Nothing could be done with Smuts, but the following morning Rushbrook Williams met Masterton-Smith in a desperate attempt to modify the Colonial Office position by finding a form of words which would not provoke the white settlers while keeping the Kenya issue open. The agreement they reached was vague, deliberately so. It reminded the conference of the recent Kenya decisions, but added the delphic statement that while the Colonial Secretary 'saw no prospect of these decisions being modified he would give careful attention to such representations as the committee appointed by the government of India might desire to make to him'.[55] The statement could be read either way and, suitably interpreted, did not exclude Kenya from the committee's work. Once the agreement of Sapru and Devonshire had been secured, and the latter's earlier comments on Kenya completely rewritten for official publication of the proceedings, Stanley Baldwin was able to announce to the assembled delegates the pact that the two officials had made earlier in the day.

Like Sinha and Sastri before them, Sapru and Rushbrook Williams had been forced to negotiate their way round serious obstacles to achieve something for the minorities. In such circumstances their success was noteworthy, if of necessity incomplete. In overcoming Peel's reluctance to have the subject discussed, they had made it one of the conference's major items, occupying half its published proceedings. The three-day debate seemed to indicate that the Empire no longer lightly dismissed the problem, thus helping to calm the indignation which had followed the Kenya announcement.[56] Sapru's committee was an honest attempt to give some effect to the 1921 resolution. It met in 1924 and if its results were undramatic, it recorded one substantial victory in preventing the enactment of a proposal to give draconian powers over Indian immigration into Kenya.

The Indian minorities never again formed a major topic for discussion at an imperial conference. Their problems did not diminish, but the Empire had other matters to consider. After many years of obstruction by Mackenzie King, the Canadian Sikhs were granted the franchise in 1947 and the dominion now has a large and vigorous Indian community. But it hardly needs repeating that the minorities in Africa have fared less well. Elgin's refusal to disallow the 1906 Transvaal legislation and Smuts's successful repudiation of the 1921 resolution delivered the South African Indians into the unfettered control of Afrikaner nationalism which has been able to accommodate them in the *apartheid* system. The 1923 Kenya decision, recognizing the paramountcy of African interests, ultimately eroded the Indian position in East Africa as surely as that of the Europeans. After independence the new African governments resented the Indian tendency to hold their adopted countries at arm's length and coveted their commercial position for their own people. The result has been the traumatic expulsion of the Indians from Uganda and an uncertain future for those in Kenya. Recent British governments have shown a greater sense of responsibility over these two crises than their predecessors did in the Empire's heyday.

Why, then, did the Empire treat its Indian minorities so shabbily? This chapter has tried to show that in British Columbia, South Africa and Kenya they were associated with a threat to white dominance. The Kenya whites believed that concessions would result in the colony's Indianization; the British Columbians feared that unchecked immigration would lead to their province being swamped by a general Asian influx; while the South Africans knew that privileges granted to the Indians could not ultimately be denied to others. British governments accepted these arguments in the knowledge that discrimination against the Indian minorities not only hindered their work in India but constantly contradicted protestations of the fairness and justice of their rule. In 1858 Queen Victoria had proclaimed that Britain was bound to the natives of India by the same obligations of duty as to all other subjects. It was not to be. The British Empire in this period was, as Smuts said and Indians came to realize, a white man's federation.

Notes

I am grateful to the Marquess of Reading for permission to quote from the viceregal papers of the first marquess; to the Syndics of the University Library, Cambridge, for permission to quote from the papers of Lord Hardinge of Penshurst; to the Controller of Her Majesty's Stationery Office for permission to quote from the papers of the Earl of Minto; and to the Director of the National Archives of India, New Delhi, for permission to consult material.

Several individuals eased the task of preparing this chapter. Dr Richard Bingle and Miss Dorothy Walker of the India Office Library and Records indicated possible sources, and the latter kindly allowed me to read her University of London MA dissertation on Sastri's dominion tour. The late Honourable H. H. Stevens, MP for Vancouver from 1911, and a leading opponent of Indian settlement in Canada, recollected events to which he was witness. My greatest debt is to Professor L. F. Rushbrook Williams, CBE, Director of Public Information, Government of India 1920–26, and Secretary to the Indian Delegation to the 1923 Imperial Conference, for his insights into the conference's work and his explanations of how the overseas Indian problem affected internal politics. Responsibility for the interpretation of the events reviewed is, of course, my own.

Several abbreviations have been used in the references: IOR, India Office Records; NAI, National Archives of India; MC, Minto Collection, National Library of Scotland; HC, Hardinge Collection, Cambridge University Library; AC, Austen Chamberlain Collection, Birmingham University Library; CC, Chelmsford Collection, India Office Records; RC, Reading Collection, India Office Records.

1　See the forceful expression of this in Smuts's address to the 1923 Imperial Conference: 'You cannot make a distinction between Indians and Africans; you would be impelled by the inevitable force of logic to go the whole hog, and the result would be that not only would the whites be swamped in Natal by the Indians, but the whole position for which we have striven for 200 years or more now would be given up.' Imperial Conference, 1923, *Appendices to the Summary of Proceedings* (Cmd. 1988), p. 115.

2　Personal information from the late H. H. Stevens. Morley to Minto, 22 November 1907, MC, MS12742, no. 501. The analysis of the Sikh migration is based on information from the relevant files in the National Archives of India, NAI Home Dept. Pol. A. 1914, ff. 97–144.

3　Morley to Minto, 14 November 1907, MC, MS 12742, no. 484.

4　India Office memo on Indian immigration into Canada, 26 August 1915, in Chamberlain to Hardinge, 10 September 1915, HC, vol. 121, no. 52.

5　Morley to Minto, 25 March 1908, MC, MS 12743, no. 166.

6　Valentine Chirol, *Indian Unrest* (London, 1910), p. 287.

7　Hindu Friend Society of Victoria, B.C., to Colonial Office, 28 April 1911, *Imperial Conference 1911. Papers laid before the Conference.* (Cd. 5746–1), pp. 279–81.

8　This concept was developed in Seeley's *The Expansion of England* (London, 1883), which ran through many editions in late Victorian and Edwardian Britain.

9　Memorandum by the India Office (Cd. 5746–1), pp. 272–9.

10　*Minutes of Proceedings of the Imperial Conference 1911* (Cd. 5745), p. 398.

11　Cd. 5745, p. 398.

12　Cd. 5745, p. 395.

13　Cd. 5745, p. 399.

14　Hardinge to Crewe, 3 June 1914, HC, vol. 120, no. 28; Hardinge of Penshurst, *My Indian Years* (London, 1948), p. 91.

15　For the Ghadr movement see the author's University of London Ph.D. thesis *The Intrigues of the German Government and the Ghadr Party against British Rule in India, 1914–1918*, (1974).

16　See Chelmsford to Chamberlain, 24 November 1916, AC 21/4/3. The ramifications are also dealt with in the *Montagu Chelmsford Report* (Cd. 91019), pp. 18–19.

17　Chamberlain to Chelmsford, 27 April 1917, CC, IOR MSS Eur.E 264/3, no. 23; Borden to Acting Prime Minister, 19 April 1917, and Minister of Finance to Borden, 23 April 1917, *Documents on Canadian External Relations* I (Ottawa, 1967), nos 477 and 479.

18　Chamberlain to Chelmsford, 27 April 1917.

19　*Extracts from proceedings and papers laid before the Imperial War Conference, 1917–1918* (Cd. 8566), Note on Emigration from India to the Self-Governing Dominions, pp. 159–62.

20　Borden to Acting Prime Minister, 27 July 1918, *Documents on Canadian External Relations*, I, no. 501.

21　This account of the origins of the Kenya Indians is based on evidence contained in *Report of the Committee on Emigration from India to the Crown Colonies and Protectorates*, Part II, Minutes of Evidence (Cd. 5193), especially that of Sir Harry Johnston, Lieutenant-Colonel J. A. L. Montgomery, and Sir John Kirk. See also J. S. Mangat, *A History of the Asians in East Africa* (Oxford, 1969).

22　Cd. 5193, evidence of Sir John Kirk, pp. 236–42.

23　Cd. 5193, evidence of Captain E. S. Grogan, p. 263.

24　'The Indian Problem in East Africa', *The Round Table*, 1921–2, p. 349.

25　'Kenya', *The Round Table*, 1922–3, p. 511.

26 Account by G. S. Bajpai, 9 August 1921, in Montagu to Reading, 15 August 1921, RC, IOR MSS Eur.E 238/3.
27 'The Position of British Indians in the Dominions', *Supplement to the Gazette of India*, 8 October 1921, IOR L/E/7/1227.
28 See note 26, above.
29 *ibid.*
30 Churchill to Montagu, 19 July 1921, RC, IOR MSS Eur.E 238/3.
31 Montagu to Churchill, 19 July 1921, RC, IOR MSS Eur.E 238/3.
32 Montagu to Churchill, 26 July 1921, RC, IOR, MSS Eur.E. 238/3.
33 See note 26, above.
34 Conference of Prime Ministers and Representatives of the United Kingdom, the Dominions and India held in June, July and August 1921, *Summary of Proceedings and Documents* (Cmd. 1474), IX.
35 Sastri's own account of his tour is given in two documents he composed on his return to India: his Report is optimistic, but his unpublished Confidential Memorandum tells the real story of the frustrations he met. Both are to be found in IOR L/E/7/1283. See also Miss Dorothy Walker's University of London MA thesis on the subject.
36 Peel to Reading, 27 January 1923, RC, IOR MSS Eur.E 238/6.
37 L. F. Rushbrook Williams, *India in 1923–24* (Calcutta, 1924), p. 111.
38 Reading to Peel, 2 May 1923, RC, IOR MSS Eur.E 238/6.
39 CAB 23/40(23), 23 July 1923.
40 Peel to Reading, 25 July 1923, RC, IOR MSS Eur.E 238/6.
41 Reading to Peel, 28 July 1923, RC, IOR MSS Eur.E 238/17.
42 L. F. Rushbrook Williams, *India in 1923–24*, appendix II, p. 298.
43 *The Pioneer Mail* (Allahabad), 31 August 1923.
44 *ibid.* 28 September 1923. This amendment narrowly defeated a motion demanding complete severance from the empire.
45 *ibid.* 14 September 1923.
46 *ibid.* 7 September 1923.
47 Personal information from L. F. Rushbrook Williams. It is fair to point out that Professor Hugh Tinker, who has also analysed these events, thinks more highly of Sastri. See *Separate and Unequal* (London, 1976), p. 398, note 31.
48 Sapru to Reading, n.d. November 1923, RC, IOR MSS Eur.E 238/25.
49 Personal information from L. F. Rushbrook Williams.
50 See note 48, above.
51 Personal information from L. F. Rushbrook Williams. The latter ensured that Associated Press gave the London and provincial press daily stories about the overseas Indians, thus helping to persuade Peel and other representatives of the urgency of the problem.
52 See note 48, above.
53 *ibid.*
54 Cmd. 1988. The speeches of Devonshire, in its doctored form, and the other participants were reported at length.
55 See note 48, above. Also personal information from L. F. Rushbrook Williams.
56 Rushbrook Williams ensured that Reuters kept India fully informed of Sapru's efforts.

11

Britain and the protection of minorities at the Paris Peace Conference, 1919

Alan Sharp

Although the collapse of Russia in 1917 and the defeat of Austria–Hungary, the Ottoman Empire and Germany in 1918 swept away the old order in eastern Europe, the allied and associated powers were not handed a *tabula rasa* on which to inscribe their new world. The new states of Poland and Czechoslovakia had already proclaimed their existence before the Paris Peace Conference opened, and other nationalities aspired to independence. Eastern Europe was made up of an inextricable tangle of races, religions and nationalities not readily assignable to any one or more states under President Wilson's formula of national self-determination. It was inevitable that minorities would be created and that the allied and associated statesmen would have to assume some responsibility for their protection.

The precedents for the discussion of the protection of national and religious minorities at Paris in 1919 were largely established in the nineteenth century. Although provision for the protection of religious groups can be traced at an international level as far back as the sixteenth century and possibly earlier, such protection depended upon the willingness to act of an interested state, generally one sharing the religion of the minority.[1] In the nineteenth century while religion rather than nationality remained the object of protection, in theory at least, protection became a joint responsibility of the great powers. The major stimulus for this transformation was the gradual dissolution of the Ottoman Empire culminating in the recognition of the sovereignty and independence of Serbia, Montenegro and Rumania at the Congress of Berlin in 1878. In all, including Greece and Bulgaria, five new states were established in eastern Europe during the century and it came to be accepted that such creations were matters of general European interest. The great powers demanded that before a new state was recognized it should give a formal undertaking to comply with certain principles of government, in particular to guarantee religious toleration and to refrain from excluding persons from public office and civic rights on religious grounds.[2]

Thus the nineteenth century established that the protection of the civic rights of minority religious groups was something imposed upon the small states of eastern Europe when the major powers either recognized new states or agreed to large accretions of territory to existing ones.[3] That the powers could or would not always match their own standards of civilized government and that they did not seek to apply them to new recruits to their own ranks – there were no such obligations imposed upon Germany or Italy – emphasizes the point that the Paris negotiators in 1919 trod many well-worn paths in their actions and deliberations.

In those deliberations they were aware of several problems arising out of their post-Berlin Congress experiences. Religious toleration and non-discrimination on religious grounds remained the major areas of protection and it was the Jews, scattered as they were throughout eastern Europe, who constituted the greatest difficulty in this respect. In the case of Rumania in particular the powers saw their efforts thwarted: Article 44 of the Treaty of Berlin, 1879, had forbidden discrimination against Jewish citizens of Rumania, but this was countered by what amounted to a simple declaration by Rumania that no Jew could be a Rumanian citizen. This glaring abuse went unchecked, apart from some desultory and ineffective protests, largely because of great power rivalry and competition for the protection of small Balkan states. If Rumania was the worst example it was not unique. But the Jewish problem grew complicated as various bodies began claiming (or perhaps reasserting) that the Jews were a nation. Although this was not a universal idea among Jews,[4] and certainly not one which found serious support in the British Foreign Office, it was an indication of the increasing overlap in identity of religious and national groups.[5] Clearly the shift towards an emphasis on nationality as the object of protection was increased by the allied commitment in 1918 to make peace upon the Wilsonian precepts of national self-determination.

In Britain the Foreign Office was aware of the complexity of the problems – how to define a national or a cultural minority, and then how to decide which minorities to protect, and how and with what objectives to protect them. On the other hand it is clear from the discussions and events in Paris that Wilson and his colleagues saw the main issue as the protection of the Jews in eastern Europe against discrimination on religious grounds. There are clear and good reasons why this should have been so. In the first place it was the traditional approach, and this was reinforced by powerful direct and indirect pressures exerted by Jewish organizations both in Paris and in the various allied and associated states on behalf of their co-religionists in eastern Europe. There can be no doubt that the major force in determining that minority problems would be discussed at Paris and that, at crucial stages in the negotiations, they would not be overlooked, were these Jewish pressures,[6] and this was reflected in the wording of the final treaties which referred not to national minorities but to minorities of 'language, race, or religion'. As Macartney commented, this Jewish suggestion was based on the argument 'that if you can prevent a Jew from being persecuted on the score of his race, his language, or his religion, you will have made it humanly impossible to get at him at all'.[7]

There are, however, other factors which may help to explain the concentration of Wilson and to a lesser extent, Lloyd George, on this issue. Eastern Europe was an area about which remarkably little was known by the leading members of both the American and the British delegations. 'It sounds like a joke,' noted W. H. Dawson, 'that although President Wilson had been talking privately and publicly for months for the restoration of a modified Poland he is reported to have believed when he arrived in Paris that Prague was the capital of that already informally organized state. It was more excusable that he thought Bagdad to be in Persia and Sarajevo in Serbia.'[8] Smuts did not know whether Moravia was Hungarian or Austrian while Lord Robert Cecil commented at one point, 'What a funny shape Austria must be.'[9] In addition to this general ignorance it is not clear how far Wilson had thought through the implications of his pronouncements on the future settlement. The Foreign Office was not impressed,[10] and this judgement was certainly borne out by the failure of the President

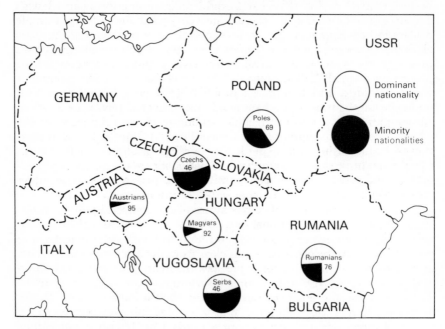

Minorities in Eastern Europe, 1919.

to produce any official American scheme for the League of Nations when the conference opened.[11] How far, if at all, had Wilson considered the innate contradiction between the right of self-determination and the right of a state to maintain its existence in areas like eastern Europe where it was impossible for the territory of any state to be inhabited solely by one nationality?

Among the allied experts, however, there was no doubt that the Paris Peace Conference, in presiding over the final dissolution of the Ottoman Empire and in seeking to apply a new principle of territorial settlement in the former Austro-Hungarian, Russian and German empires, had both a historical and a moral obligation to provide for minority groups in the area. It was never seriously considered that there should be forcible transfers of population – the atmosphere of 1919, despite jibes at the false idealism of the peacemakers, was not that of 1945 – and in any case the problem of the Jews was not amenable to such a solution.[12] Various members of the Foreign Office staff in Paris, notably E. H. Carr and J. W. Headlam-Morley, advocated a special inter-allied commission to consider the question[13] while the territorial commissions all, at some point, indicated that something must be done to protect the minorities which their recommendations must inevitably produce – in all, it has been estimated, some twenty-five to thirty million people, constituting more than 25 per cent of the population of some countries.[14] No definite action was taken, however, until the supreme decision-making body of the conference, the Council of Four,[15] discussed the matter, significantly in terms of the protection of Jewish interests, on 1 May, six days before the draft treaty was handed to the Germans. By then the matter was urgent, for as a Jewish writer impressed upon the Polish commission, on 24 April, once the allies had recognized the independence of Poland by transferring German territories under the treaty to the new state, they would lose any right to impose minority protection upon Poland. If conditions were not imposed at this stage Poland would argue that minority matters were of purely domestic concern.[16] Struck by the force of this argument, and by a British reminder that there were a plethora of international economic, postal and communications agreements that the new state should also be obliged to accept before its full sovereignty and independence was recognized,[17] the Council of Four now established the New States Committee to deal with both areas of concern.

That this action was belated is indisputable. Headlam-Morley later felt that 'this seems to have been due to the general want of foresight and supervision which characterized the arrangement of business, especially with regard to everything which did not immediately concern the future of Germany. It was nobody's business to provide a preliminary survey of the ground or to sketch out the problems that would have to be dealt with.'[18] None the less the Council of Four still hoped that the New States Committee might draw up provisions for the protection of minorities in Poland, based upon suggestions made by Wilson and Hunter Miller, in time for inclusion in the draft treaty with Germany.[19] This proved impossible. Headlam-Morley explained privately to Sir Maurice Hankey, secretary to the British delegation, that the American drafts had simply taken certain Jewish suggestions in a crude form and that these would require thorough revision, partly because they would offend the Poles and partly because, in his view, they did not give the Jews adequate protection.[20] Instead, therefore, a general clause was inserted into the draft treaty binding Poland to accept such provisions for the protection of minorities as the allied and associated powers might consider necessary.[21]

The New States Committee now began to consider what these provisions should be and by 14 May had established a draft of a treaty with Poland that became the model for all the other minority treaties. Poland was to agree to establish as fundamental laws which could not be abrogated a number of provisions for the protection of the life and liberty of 'all inhabitants of Poland without distinction of birth, nationality, language, race or religion'. Bearing in mind the Rumanian experience, the articles defining citizenship were carefully drawn up to ensure that all genuine inhabitants of Poland as constituted by the peace settlement became, as a matter of course, full and complete Polish citizens. All citizens were to enjoy equality before the law and, for those of non-Polish speech, free private use of their own language and provision for either oral or written use of that language before the courts. They also had the right, insofar as it was enjoyed by other citizens of Poland, to establish religious, charitable and social institutions and schools in which their own language and religion could be exercised.

These provisions were fundamental and applied to the whole of Poland, but there were in addition other stipulations relating only to specified minorities or to particular parts of Poland, and these were not regarded as fundamental. In areas where a considerable proportion of the residents spoke a language other than Polish, primary education could be conducted in that language at the state's expense, and in such areas the minorities were also to enjoy an equitable share of public funds distributed for educational, religious or charitable purposes. As far as German-speaking minorities were concerned these provisions applied only to areas which had been part of Germany on 1 August 1914.

There were also specifically Jewish sections which were not repeated in most of the other minority treaties. Jewish educational committees were to administer the proportional share of state funds for education due to them, and also to manage and organize their schools. The sabbath was protected, except insofar as concerned the obligations of military service, national defence or the preservation of public order. In particular Poland was not to allow elections or electoral registration to take place on a Saturday.

These provisions for the protection of persons belonging to 'racial, religious or linguistic minorities' were to be recognized by Poland as of international concern to be placed under the guarantee of the League of Nations. They could not be altered except by permission of a majority of the Council of the League. Any member of the Council had the right to indicate infractions or danger of infractions of these clauses to the Council which then had the right to take what steps it deemed necessary. Disputes of law or fact arising between Poland and the principal allied and associated powers or a member of the Council of the League could be referred to the Permanent Court of International Justice.[22]

There is much in these provisions that requires comment, but before considering their implications, particularly in the light of British policy, it might be helpful to complete the history of the Paris negotiations. The recommendations of the New States Committee, whose remit expanded to include first Rumania and Greece, Yugoslavia and eventually the defeated states of Austria, Hungary and Bulgaria, were accepted by the Council of Four on 17 May.[23] Rumania, with some support from Czechoslovakia and Yugoslavia, led an attack on the imposition by the powers of these provisions, which seriously abrogated the principles of state sovereignty and implied the inferiority of east European states. In his reply

Wilson maintained the right of the powers to ensure, as far as possible, that the settlement, whose possibility had largely been established by their sacrifices, and for whose continuance they would mainly be responsible, should contain as few areas of friction as possible. 'Nothing, I venture to say, is more likely,' said Wilson, 'to disturb the peace of the world than the treatment which might in certain circumstances be meted out to minorities. And therefore, if the great powers are to guarantee the peace of the world in any sense, is it unjust that they should be satisfied that the proper and necessary guarantees have been given?'[24] Poland signed the treaty with Germany on 28 June 1919 and gradually the other states of eastern Europe bowed to the inevitable and followed suit.

This then, in a simplified and abbreviated form, is what happened in Paris in 1919. It is now proposed to discuss the measures taken in the light of British policy both in general and towards minorities in particular, and in any such discussion the role of Sir James Headlam-Morley must be especially noted. Headlam-Morley, a classical and modern historian turned educational administrator, had become by 1918 the effective head, under Tyrrell's nominal leadership, of the Political Intelligence Department of the Foreign Office, a department whose membership reads like a library catalogue of twentieth-century historians: in addition to Headlam-Morley himself, R. W. Seton-Watson, Arnold Toynbee, E. H. Carr, Lewis Namier and Alfred Zimmern were all employed there on a temporary basis during the war. The department's function was to provide coverage of foreign press reporting, and to provide expert reports on various problems facing different departments within the Foreign Office.[25] Immediately after the Armistice it was decreed that 'the main work of the department will now be the preparation of material for the delegates of the Peace Conference', and an impressive series of papers and memoranda on all manner of subjects was produced.[26]

Headlam-Morley's interest in minorities and their problems seems to have been stimulated by his friendship with Lewis Namier, a fervent Zionist and himself the son of an assimilated Polish Jew.[27] This correspondence during the peace conference was frequent and, without being convinced by Namier's more extreme demands on behalf of the Polish Jews, Headlam-Morley greatly valued his advice and comments. Namier was perhaps the most vehemently anti-Polish member of the Foreign Office,[28] and although Sir Eyre Crowe (assistant under-secretary at the Foreign Office) might 'deprecate the assumption that everything the Polish government does is always wrong and wicked',[29] there was little sympathy for the Poles in high places in Britain, Lloyd George thought them greedy and grasping,[30] Cecil wrote 'they are unsatisfactory people'[31] and, according to Crowe at least, Carr's dislike of everything Polish was well known.[32]

There was, on the other hand, concern for the plight of the Jews in eastern Europe, although Eyre Crowe produced one uncharacteristic outburst in November 1918:

It is as well to remember – with due regard to our pro-Zionist policy and our general sympathy for Jewish communities – that the heart and soul of all revolutionary and terroristic movements have invariably been the Jews, the Bolsheviks and the Turkish Committee of Union and Progress being the most notorious examples. There is also every indication that the extreme socialists in Germany are led and organized entirely by Jews. . . . We are facing a powerful international organization and it is well to bear this constantly in mind.[33]

Hardinge agreed, but Balfour was sceptical: 'I should like to hear more of this international Jewish conspiracy which seems equally interested in accumulating money in the west and cutting throats in the east and which sometimes takes the form of a centralized military and imperialistic despotism (as in Turkey); sometimes of a chaotic welter of proletariat rule (as in Russia).'[34]

Headlam-Morley tended to steer a middle course through these disputes, although he was always more convinced than most of his colleagues of the importance of affairs in eastern Europe.[35] More senior men in the Office were cynical about the value of minority protection. Crowe wrote: 'I am . . . sceptical as to the real value of any stipulations of this sort in general treaties. The Jews in Rumania have derived little benefit from the stipulations of the Berlin Act, just as the negroes in the southern states of North America, who were given the fullest guarantees of equality after the American Civil War, have never in fact been allowed to exercise the rights nominally guaranteed to them.' Hardinge agreed 'that in practice the guarantees are useless', but Headlam-Morley had hopes of the system.[36] Where some of his colleagues undoubtedly saw the collective guarantee of the League of Nations as a useful way of avoiding Britain's responsibilities, Headlam-Morley was both anxious that Britain should play a proper part in the enforcement of the treaties and hopeful that the responsibilities incurred by the League would increase its importance and help to make it a really effective body[37] – though never at the expense of what he saw as Britain's vital interests. In Paris he was to play the major British role in minority affairs.

The primary reason for protecting minorities was, as Wilson stated on 31 May, one of international policy, prompted by the recognition that the existence of disaffected groups within the new boundaries of eastern Europe, and their possible exploitation by kin-states seeking to revise the settlement, constituted the major threat to post-war stability.[38] This accorded well with the British policy advocated by the PID in late 1918: 'Our general object must be the establishment of a stable condition; the great danger to be guarded against is anything which would again threaten to entangle us in a great continental war; it is also in our interest that civil disturbances should, as far as possible, be avoided. What we want is peace and order with open facilities for trade.' These not inconsiderable objectives were, furthermore, hopefully to be achieved in such a way that 'Czechs and Slovaks, Jugo-Slavs, Poles – we may perhaps add even Bulgarians, Magyars, and Germans – will feel that on the part of the British nation there has been an honest attempt to carry through a disinterested policy . . . for in the long run the interests of each nation are not antagonistic to the interests of those of the other nations.'

This optimistic note was maintained throughout much of the paper, but especially in the revealing section on 'The Balance of Power', which the

Foreign Office felt would remain a major plank in British policy. Britain's interest was 'to maintain the full and complete independence, political, military, and economic, of the different states between which the continent is divided' but now these states would be national states. 'This is a great gain,' argued the PID, 'for there is every reason to hope that states based on the conscious existence of a common nationality will be more durable, and afford a firmer support against aggression than the older form of state, which was often a merely accidental congeries of territories without internal cohesion, necessary economic unity, or clearly defined geographical frontiers.'[39]

British policy towards the subject nationalities of eastern Europe had largely been determined by her wider vision of how the war was going. Within this limitation there had been a division of opinion between the younger men in the Foreign Office, Nicolson, Percy and Clerk, who favoured nationalism in eastern Europe and the more senior men, Carnock, Crowe and Hardinge, who favoured the continuation of the Austro-Hungarian Empire. Lloyd George, apparently as late as October 1918, and Balfour, until June 1918, still preferred to see the Czechs and Poles as satisfied subjects of a reformed monarchy. This split was, however, repaired by the spontaneous collapse of Austria-Hungary and the emergence of the successor states. For the PID, notoriously anti-Austrian, this was a welcome event. Others had to make a virtue of necessity.[40]

This document is thus reasonably representative of the general view of the Foreign Office (and of others in decision-making circles in Britain) and raises a number of interesting issues. Britain wanted to maintain a balance of power in Europe, and hoped to exploit national self-determination to strengthen the states system by the creation of consciously national sovereign states. The problem, as the paper admitted, lay in eastern Europe. Here an ethnic and religious jumble meant that one man's self-determination was another's bitter disappointment. It was, as the American Secretary of State later observed, 'a principle loaded with dynamite, raising hopes which can never be realized. . . . What misery it will cause.'[41]

In the view of one Foreign Office expert this problem might be overcome: 'Where the inhabitants of a country, irrespective of race, language or religion are guaranteed equal rights by a written constitution, or are in traditional and effective enjoyment of them, as is the case in the British Empire and in the United States, the claim of self-determination, or as it is called in the United States, the right of secession, can clearly be ruled out.'[42] But the solution raised, as the same writer pointed out elsewhere, a further question: 'The great difficulty arises out of the manner in which its acceptance should be forced on the governments of sovereign states.'[43] British policy was thus based upon a series of complicated paradoxes: national sovereign states were necessary for order in Europe, but the application of national self-determination might lead to international tension or internal anarchy, while it was necessary to infringe the sovereignty of certain states in the very act of bestowing it upon them. Finally, although the British favoured nationalism (in eastern Europe) they also wished to see its strength fade.[44]

A further complication arose from the perennial problem of defining nationality. The Anglo-American and western European view of nationality tended not to distinguish between the concept of a man as a member of a racial group and as a citizen of a state. A perfect illustration arises in Headlam-Morley's account of the drafting of the minority clauses: 'A Welshman', he wrote, 'is not the less an Englishman because of the full recognition which is given in Wales to his own language.'[45] Headlam-Morley was here misquoting Lewis Namier: 'A man may be a Welshman, a Boer, or a French Canadian and claim Welsh, Dutch or French schools under autonomous administration and yet be a good Britisher, though he certainly is not an Englishman.'[46] His comment is a revealing piece of un-witting testimony about the political and subjective view of nationality held by western liberals. No practical distinction was made between personal nationality – in Headlam-Morley's case, the Welshman with his own lan-guage, and political nationality – the fact that he was an equal and willing citizen of Great Britain. This dual meaning of the concept of nationality had arisen out of a relatively stable political and territorial history in west-ern Europe and North America and emphasized the subjective nature of nationalism. As long as someone felt himself to be an American (and had fulfilled the technical and legal requirements) then it did not matter if he spoke German, or Polish or Dutch, he was an American. In eastern Europe however, historically divided into multi-national empires, nationality was seen in personal terms, determined by the relatively objective criteria of race, religion and especially language, and it had little or no political sig-nificance. Thus Namier again: 'M. Dmowski represents the Polish point of view and even the overwhelming majority of Jewish opinion, when in his "Problems of Central and Eastern Europe" he declares that "the Jews do not form part of the Polish nation".' In practice, however, the Poles were not above claiming Jewish inhabitants of disputed areas as Poles.[47]

The Wilsonian concept of national self-determination was based on the western idea of nationalism and tended to make what was essentially a null correlation in the west between political and personal nationalism, in that the former was not affected by the latter, into a positive correlation in which personal nationality was thought to determine political allegiance. For the Americans, at Paris especially, language became the real test of nationality, and the assumption was made that a man speaking Polish was a Polish national and hence wished to become a citizen of a Polish state.[48] The minority treaty itself reflected this confusion in its use of 'national' as a synonym for 'citizen', although plebiscites held in disputed areas after the peace conference did not, in fact, entirely support this correlation.[49]

If one accepts Professor Cobban's view that in Wilson's mind national self-determination was essentially a synonym for popular sovereignty,[50] the question in eastern Europe was which peoples would be sovereign, and which would become subjects of states in which they were not the dominant national group. This question was answered not by the peace conference but by events in eastern Europe where the Poles and Czechs had established their position before the conference opened. Other groups were less well developed or less well organized.[51]

In the Wilsonian concept protection of the cultural and religious identity of minority groups could only assist in the establishment of a stable political state and in the reconciliation of various elements within it. But to the dominant nationality in the new host states, deeply suspicious of the loyalty of newly transferred inhabitants, almost exactly the opposite was true. For Wilson, and the British too, the protection of the rights of a German, newly transferred to Poland, to maintain his schools, charitable and social organizations and especially his language with all its cultural and historical implications, would encourage him to accept the political reality of the Polish state. To the Poles, however, such measures seemed more likely to maintain his aloofness and his connection with his former homeland. Indeed, given that the peace settlement was not universally accepted as permanent and final, such measures seemed to the Poles to help to maintain a German claim upon their newly acquired territories.

Thus a further question was posed: would minority protection lead to political assimilation or to continued and growing alienation? Two schools of thought existed, and the treaties themselves did not make their aims explicit, but there can be little doubt that British policy saw the main purpose of minority protection as assimilation and that Austen Chamberlain was in the mainstream of that policy when he told the Council of the League in 1926 that 'the object of the minority treaties ... was ... to secure for the minorities that measure of protection and justice which would gradually prepare them to be merged in the national community to which they belonged'.[52]

The evidence for this assertion comes in several forms. In the first place there is a general assumption throughout the minutes and memoranda of Foreign Office writers that protection would be limited and, hopefully, temporary. Crowe expressed this in part when he wrote on 19 June 1919: 'I should have thought that a general engagement to respect the religious rights of all subject nationalities and to place no obstacle in the way of national speech and schools is all that is either required or appropriate for inserting in the treaties.'[53] Headlam-Morley felt that in the Balkans 'something will be required either in the form of frankly differential treatment, or in the form of mutual treaty obligations; the essential thing, however, is that whatever is done, it should be made quite clear that it is a special exceptional provision, preferably a temporary one, made to suit a particular exceptional case'.[54]

The aim of assimilation was also implicit in the way in which education was discussed, particularly by Headlam-Morley. In his view, what the various cultural minorities required was a system analogous to that granted to the assimilated Roman Catholics and Jews in England. 'It is just because the Jews do not ask for extended privileges that difficulties do not arise in England.'[55] The protection of language in schools was considered in the same way: 'It is often necessary and desirable that any special language of the peasantry should be recognized and used as the language of instruction in elementary or primary schools, but not in higher places of education; this is the system which in fact exists in Wales and applies to those countries where the minority language is one with inferior cultural value.'[56]

Once again the allusion is to Headlam-Morley's integrated Welshman. Places of higher education were excluded because of 'the well-known fact that in the modern world universities have often become the centres of political agitation'.[57] It was better to avoid creating an educated elite to lead minority groups.

The Foreign Office had great faith in the force of circumstances. 'I should hope that in the future if the passionate nationalism diminishes, as it probably will,' wrote Headlam-Morley, 'all the states will get to see that if the frontiers are all permanently settled and if it is definitely agreed that no change of frontier can be made by methods of war and revolution, without the consent of the League of Nations, it will generally be recognized that it is for the advantage of the state itself to treat these national minorities with the greatest consideration.'[58] Obviously this consideration was reciprocal. 'All these difficulties', wrote Hardinge, 'are likely to disappear as soon as the frontiers have been definitely decided by the peace conference and the Germans of Bohemia realize that they will have to live in amity with their Czech neighbours or go elsewhere.'[59] Hardinge also saw positive advantages for the Sudetenlanders: 'The Germans in Bohemia probably make a lot of money by their exports and will have no desire to saddle themselves with any fraction of German indebtedness.'[60] While of the Jews in Poland Sir Esme Howard wrote: 'If Jews have equal rights and duties they will probably settle down in time as citizens of the country they live in as in Western countries.'[61] Majorities and minorities would have to live together within the new and permanent frontiers of eastern Europe. Unfortunately the frontiers were not accepted as final and so majorities eyed their own minorities with deep suspicion.[62]

The main argument in favour of the assimilative aims of British negotiators is their solicitude for the sovereignty of the new states in the hope of ensuring the permanence that was necessary for integration. Protection was for individuals, not for groups, and there was little sympathy with the ideas of local autonomy for minorities: Hardinge wrote in June 1919 that 'The question of local autonomies is being overdone. Their creation is only likely to make for trouble in the future.'[63] The British especially had no desire to create states within states, and thus they were generally satisfied with the final draft of the protection clauses in the treaty with Poland, since their main emphasis lay in guaranteeing equal, but not extra, rights for the minority citizens of the new state. In particular the British resisted any attempts to have the Jews recognized as a national as opposed to a religious minority with definite political rights guaranteed to a public corporation. To have allowed this would have been to seriously undermine the Polish state since the Jews were widespread and not confined to any one area with Poland.[64] Even when Jewish educational committees were established to run the schools allowed by the treaty, the drafters had been careful to specify that these committees should be elected locally rather than nationally so as to strictly limit this concession to a collective body.

It is this concern to avoid establishing the national minorities as public corporations which accounts for the very strange wording of the second paragraph of Article 9 of the Polish minority treaty.[65] The original American draft had proposed to recognize the minorities as having collective rights but this was firmly resisted by Headlam-Morley. What emerged was a provision that it was hoped would allow minorities to enjoy a proportional share of public funds voted by the Polish state for charitable and religious purposes. Headlam-Morley admitted 'I never thought that this was very well drafted . . .'.[66] Pablo Azcaraté, a former director of the minorities questions section of the League of Nations, having tried to understand and to administer it, agreed that it was 'a clause drawn up in language so confused and sibylline that we were never able to discover its real meaning nor the value of its practical application'.[67]

Even so, despite this solicitude for Polish sovereignty and, by extension, the sovereignty of the other states affected by minority protection, there were still those within the British delegation like Harold Nicolson and Eyre Crowe who were not happy at the outcome. Nicolson wrote:

> However carefully the guarantees of the League of Nations are worded, the mere fact that the great powers impose certain duties upon the several governments in regard to internal administration will always give a handle to agitation and propagandists for keeping alive sectional feeling. The result will be that while endeavouring to prevent the ill-treatment of alien minorities we will in effect arouse in a great number of hitherto contented minorities the feeling that they are ill-treated, that they have always had a grievance and that they now have an appeal to Geneva against their own government.

Crowe too was concerned that 'the danger of giving the league of nations [sic] a kind of roving commission to meddle with the internal government of all these states seems to me a real one. It may accentuate and increase friction instead of preventing it.'[68]

Once again, some of the underlying assumptions of Crowe and Nicolson point to a British desire to see minority groups safely assimilated in the new states, but Crowe also raised another question which was much more directly vital to Britain. As early as 19 November 1918 Alfred Zimmern had pointed out: 'It would clearly be inadvisable to go even the smallest distance in the direction of admitting the claim of the American negroes, or the southern Irish, or the Flemings or Catalans to appeal to an interstate conference over the head of their own government. Yet if a right of appeal is granted to the Macedonians or the German Bohemians it will be difficult to refuse it in the case of other nationalist movements.'[69] As Headlam-Morley commented, 'this principle, if once established, will be liable to be extended and the full internal sovereignty of all states might be endangered. The problem is the most serious one which we have to meet.'[70]

The questions of exactly how the League should be apprised of violations or possible violations of the minorities statutes and, especially, of what bodies should have the right of appeal to the League were thus of the utmost importance. In December 1918 Headlam-Morley pointed out:

> My own feeling is that we cannot ask other nations to accept principles which we would not be prepared to see applied to ourselves. It will, I assume, certainly be a condition of our entering the League that questions such as that of Ireland or the French Canadians are purely internal problems in which the League has

no right to interfere; but if we insist on this, then it will become very difficult to give national minorities in other countries the right of appeal to the League.[71]

On the other hand it was clearly necessary, given the unsatisfactory history of minority protection before 1914, to have some sort of supervising mechanism, and some method of bringing the attention of the guarantor to problems that existed. Headlam-Morley's first reaction, despite its implications, was to allow minorities themselves to appeal to the League,[72] but upon consideration he changed his mind and favoured a right of appeal to the League only by Council members.[73] The final draft of the Polish treaty once again reflected the British interest in limiting restriction on Polish sovereignty and in circumscribing the possibilities for outside interference, to the extent in fact that, in Azcaraté's view, had the League itself not created a right of petition for both states and minorities, then the whole document might have become a dead letter.[74]

From the outset, therefore, the British delegation knew that the minority protection policy was like an unstable stick of gelignite. Their concern for the sovereignty of east European states was thus not entirely disinterested. In addition to strict limitations on the scope of protection they were also anxious to ensure that eastern Europe was the only part of Europe or the European empires where the policy would apply. Headlam-Morley wrote:

> The right view seems to me to be that normally speaking a civilized state can be trusted to deal with those matters by itself; special provisions should only be required when a large foreign population is transferred by the peace treaties as in the case of Rumania and Bohemia and even then protection is duly required in the case of these young and new states in eastern Europe which have not a strong tradition of civilized government behind them.[75]

There was thus little enthusiasm in the British camp for Lord Robert Cecil's draft clause for inclusion in the Covenant of the League condemning religious persecution and intolerance and authorizing the Council to take steps whenever the illiberal actions of the government of any state seemed likely to endanger the peace of the world.[76] Such universal proposals were seen as incompatible with the British conception of the League, but their rejection made it hard to counter suggestions that the western states were using double standards.[77]

As well as resisting universal minority protection on general grounds, the British were particularly opposed to any extension of the principle into western Europe. This was in part inspired by concern at the propaganda value to Germany of certain French and Italian refusals to operate any such scheme in Alsace-Lorraine or the South Tyrol.[78] But their main aim was to avoid Germany herself having to give assurances on her treatment of minorities. The ostensible and plausible reason given for resisting Polish and other demands that similar terms be imposed upon Germany was that the proposed settlement largely removed the subject nationalities of the old German Empire and that therefore such provisions would be superfluous. The underlying fear, however, was one of principle. 'It is I submit', wrote Headlam-Morley, 'contrary to public policy to impose similar clauses on the old established states of western Europe. If they are imposed upon Germany, it will be still more difficult to resist the pressure which is being brought by Rumania and other states to impose similar obligations on all countries.'[79] The Flemish question in Belgium, he thought, should be regarded as 'a purely internal matter with which other states are not concerned'.[80] Headlam-Morley was thus deeply concerned when Lloyd George and Wilson promised the Polish leader Paderewski that a condition of German entry to the League would be her adoption of certain principles with regard to internal German affairs. In his mind this would destroy the principles upon which the New States Committee had been working, those of limiting the area of minority protection to eastern Europe and of limiting the prerogatives of the League to interfere in the internal affairs of member states. Reiterating the point that there were now very few Poles in Germany, except for migratory workers, he emphasized the dangers of extending minority rights beyond established communities to floating populations. 'To take an illustration from our own country, it is one thing to allow Welsh to be used as the language of instruction in Welsh schools; it is something quite different to require the municipality of Liverpool to provide education in Chinese for the Chinese washerwomen who, I believe, pursue their calling in that city.' On the other hand he did feel that there was a case for a mutual agreement between Poland and Germany in advance of the intended plebiscite in Upper Silesia, and he suggested that such an agreement might be taken as a satisfactory redemption of the promise made to Paderewski.[81]

All in all it could be said that the minorities treaties largely satisfied the British and great power point of view. They were confined to eastern Europe and were not universal. Protection was defined almost entirely in legal, political and linguistic terms, and most of the protection was in negative form. There was no concept of economic protection or privilege. The clauses infringed as little as possible the concept of national sovereignty, and they were almost exclusively concerned with guaranteeing that the citizen who was a member of a national or religious minority was not treated worse, as an individual, than a citizen of the majority nationality. In particular the British could congratulate themselves on avoiding dangerous precedents which groups who persisted in ignoring the advantages of the British Empire might use against them.

None the less there was little enthusiasm in the Foreign Office for Britain to play a major role in ensuring the enforcement of these treaties. Headlam-Morley and Namier pressed the Office to act in late 1919 and early 1920 on a question of the definition of citizenship in the new Polish constitution. It was Headlam-Morley's contention that 'if there were any open and flagrant violation of the treaty, then it would clearly be the duty of the British as of other governments, to take up the matter spontaneously',[82] but others disagreed. C. M. Palairet of the Northern Department agreed that the new Polish act of citizenship was in violation of the minorities treaty but argued: 'HMG have therefore the right to bring the matter before the League of Nations, but I do not agree with Mr Headlam-Morley that they have the *obligation* to do so. . . . I do not see why HMG should be called upon to champion the cause of minorities as a matter of course, and to incur the odium of lecturing the various offending governments.'[83] The British record in offering leadership in the League on this question shows clearly that Palairet's view came to predominate at the ministerial level.[84]

At Paris in 1919 Britain was aiming at establishing strong national states in eastern Europe to replace the old multinational empires – although Sir Henry Wilson, speaking at Queens University Belfast on 9 April 1920, did not agree with small states becoming independent. 'He liked to see a small state as part of a great empire.'[85] (Tyrrell in the Foreign Office commented: 'This utterance might have come more appropriately from General Ludendorff'.)[86] Protection for minorities was the price that had to be paid in advance in the hope of securing strong and integrated new states. Unfortunately none of the participants, with the exception of the League of Nations minorities section bravely struggling against insuperable difficulties, responded in the way that Britain had hoped. The new states resented their implied inferiority, the minorities remained firmly unintegrated, kin states continued to exploit minorities in neighbouring states for their own ends, while the outside powers showed no enthusiasm to become involved, an attitude which Britain's own record did little to alter.[87]

The underlying British assumption throughout was that the Versailles settlement represented a final and permanent solution to the problems of eastern Europe. In practical terms, however, Britain was not prepared to make any great efforts to ensure that the new boundaries would be respected, particularly by Russia and Germany. When Hitler's Germany began to intensify and then take advantage of the unstable international climate of the 1930s, minority protection, like the League itself, became a victim. At Munich Britain acquiesced in the exploitation of the Sudetenland minority by a revisionist power – the very situation which her earlier commitment to minority protection had sought to avoid. A. J. Balfour's sardonic comment on the proposal of a luckless military officer may serve as a fitting epitaph, perhaps even an excuse, for British policy, in an area which required superhuman vision and skill: 'General Plunkett's solution of our eastern European difficulties is that we should put the whole area in charge of a genius. We have no genius's [sic] available.'[88]

Notes

I would like to thank Professor Agnes Headlam-Morley for her help and encouragement and for the loan of papers written by Sir James. These were supplemented by the extensive collection of Sir James's books and pamphlets deposited in the New University of Ulster Library. Official records in the Public Record Office are Crown Copyright and are quoted with the permission of the Controller.

1 C. A. Macartney, *National States and National Minorities* (Oxford, 1934), pp. 159–78 and *passim*. J. W. Headlam-Morley in H. Temperley, *History of the Peace Conference of Paris* (London, 1921) V, pp. 112–19. Inis Claude, *National Minorities* (New York, 1969), pp. 6–9.

2 Temperley, V, p. 115.

3 Although in 1834 there was an exception when Holland and Belgium in western Europe also had protection enforced upon them by the great powers.

4 See Isaiah Friedman, *The Question of Palestine 1914–1918* (London, 1973), pp. 25–37.

5 W. Ormsby-Gore, minute, 28 January 1919 commented: 'Mr Lucien Wolff [sic – a Jewish historian and journalist influential in seeking support for east European Jews] ... begins his new volume with the sentence "The Jewish question is part of the general question of religious toleration." It isn't! It is the problem of an ethnographic minority anxious to preserve its cultural identity while enjoying civil and religious equality in states where there is a different ethnographic majority' (114/1/3/710 in FO 608/48).

6 Sir James Headlam-Morley, *A Memoir of the Paris Peace Conference 1919*, ed. Agnes Headlam-Morley (London, 1972), p. 113. Cf. Macartney, pp. 218–40.

7 Macartney, p. 4.

8 W. H. Dawson, *Germany under the Treaty* (London, 1933), p. 31.

9 V. Rothwell, *British War Aims and Peace Diplomacy, 1914–1918* (Oxford, 1971), p. 17. Cf. Cecil's own admission that he knew little about Polish politics. (Minute (n.d.) P.I.D. 22 in FO 371/4359).

10 See Sir Eyre Crowe, minute 30 November 1918: 'I do not believe President Wilson has thought out his nebulous proposals.' Lord Hardinge agreed. (P.C. 54/29 in FO 371/4353). Lord Eustace Percy thought, 22 November 1918, that this situation might be turned to Britain's advantage (P.I.D. 38/38 in FO 371/4354).

11 F. P. Walters, *A History of the League of Nations* (Oxford, 1969), p. 30. S. P. Tillman, *Anglo-American Relations at the Paris Peace Conference 1919* (Princeton, 1961), p. 113. R. B. Henig, *The League of Nations* (London, 1973), pp. 3–4.

12 E. H. Carr minuted, 20 November 1918: 'In general it is desirable that states should hold out inducements to their nationals outside their borders to return to them. ... On the other hand, any sort of compulsion is out of the question, and it does not appear that the allied governments can take any action at all in the matter beyond a friendly hint of the possibility of such a solution in the interests of future peace.' (FO 371/4353).

13 A. W. A. Leeper suggested a special investigation 8 March 1919 (493/1/1/2831 in FO 608/151). Carr wrote, 18 March 1919: 'It looks as if a committee to consider the question of cultural minorities in E. Europe will ultimately be necessary' (129/4/1/4561 in FO 608/61). Headlam-Morley agreed (18 April 1919, *ibid.*). Carr again urged an inter-allied inquiry, 25 April 1919 (129/4/1/8239 *ibid.*), while Headlam-Morley had written to Lloyd George's private secretary, Philip Kerr, 15 April 1919, raising minority problems amongst other urgent issues. (Headlam-Morley, *Memoir*, p. 76).

14 Macartney, p. 211. The Polish commission (13 March 1919) and the Czechoslovak commission (13 March 1919) directed the attention of the supreme council to the problem, which they felt lay outside their competence, while the question of minority protection was raised in the Rumanian and Yugoslav commission as early as 22 February 1919. See Headlam-Morley, 'The Minorities Treaties' (W 4864/185/98 in FO 371/14125).

15 In fact only Wilson, Lloyd George and Clemenceau were in attendance, Orlando having left the conference after Italian claims in the Adriatic had been ignored.

16 Headlam-Morley (W 4864/185/98 in FO 371/14125).

17 The question of when the allies recognized the independence of Poland and Czechoslovakia was vexed, but the Council of Four took their stand on the point that since, until the treaties were signed much of the territory of the new states was part of Germany and Austria, Poland and Czechoslovakia were not yet created (Meeting, 1 May 1919, *Foreign Relations of the United States 1919 Paris Peace Conference* (13 vols, Washington 1943) V, p. 395. Hereafter *FRUS*).

18 Temperley, V, p. 123.

19 Hankey to Dutasta, quoted by Headlam-Morley (W 4864/185/98 in FO 371/14125).

20 Headlam-Morley to Hankey, 2 May 1919 (*Memoir*, p. 92).

21 This became the basis of Article 93 of the Treaty of Versailles. It also covered the economic and communications considerations raised 1 May 1919. *Mutatis mutandis* it was repeated in the other treaties of 1919. (Annex A to Appendix, Council of Four meeting 3.5.19 *FRUS* V, pp. 442–3.)

22 *FRUS* XIII, pp. 798–801.

23 *FRUS* V, pp. 678–81.

24 8th Plenary Session of the Peace Conference, 31 May 1919 (*ibid.* III, pp. 395–7, 406).

25 P.I.D. 775/775 in FO 371/4386. See also Professor A. Headlam-Morley's introduction to Headlam-Morley *Memoir*, pp. xxi–xxiii.

26 P.C. 20 16.11.18 (FO 371/4352).

27 Information from Professor A. Headlam-Morley.

28 J. D. Gregory of the Northern Department, 6 December 1919, (admitting that he and Namier had been 'unspeakable enemies') wrote: 'I think on the whole it has been a great pity that Mr Namier ... was ever introduced into the FO. It was done, I believe, about two years ago at the instance of Mr Philip Kerr and Lord Eustace Percy. It has created a very bad impression abroad and it is generally believed in Poland that he is Head of the FO department which deals with Polish affairs and that the anti-Polish policy with which we are credited is to be attributed to his malign influence.' (FO 800/149).

29 Minute 30 July 1919 (130/5/1/16263 in FO 608/64).

30 Council of Four Meeting 5 June 1919 (*FRUS* VI, pp. 196–7).

31 Minute 25 August 1918 (1460617/3361/W 35 in FO 371/3278).

32 Minute 26 June 1920 (205318/73 in FO 371/3902).

33 Minute 18 November 1918 (P.I.D. 547/547 in FO 371/4369).

34 Minutes, n.d. (*ibid.*).

35 'As everyone knows, the danger point in Europe is not the Rhine, but the Vistula; not Alsace-Lorraine, but the Polish corridor and Upper Silesia.' (Written in February 1925). J. W. Headlam-Morley, *Studies in Diplomatic History* (London, 1930).

36 Crowe minute, 30 May 1919. Hardinge minute, n.d. Balfour initialled these views (114/1/20/11328 in FO 608/51).

37 Information from Professor A. Headlam-Morley.

38 *FRUS* III, p. 406. Cf. P. de Azcaraté, *The League of Nations and National Minorities* (New York, 1972), p. 14.

39 P.I.D. paper 3, 'Europe' (FO 371/4353).

40 Rothwell, pp. 221–8 and *passim*. K. J. Calder, *Britain and the Origins of the New Europe 1914–1918* (Cambridge, 1976), *passim*.

41 Robert Lansing, *The Peace Negotiations, a Personal Narrative* (New York, 1921), pp. 97–8.

42 A. W. A. Leeper Memorandum *c.* 28 November 1918 (P.I.D. 64/37 in FO 371/4354).

43 A. W. A. Leeper minute, 8 March 1919 (493/1/3/2831 in FO 608/151).

44 See Headlam-Morley's minute, 18 March 1919 (41/1/1/4537 in FO 608/9).

45 Temperley, V, p. 138.

46 Minute 14 March 1919 (131/1/1/4875 in FO 608/66).

47 Minute 24 September 1918 (P.I.D. 401/401 in FO 371/4368).

48 A. Cobban, *The National State and National Self Determination* (London, 1969), pp. 57–76 and *passim*. Cf. Macartney, chapters 2 and 3.

49 In Allenstein 46 per cent of the population spoke Polish in 1910 yet only 2 per

cent voted for Poland; in Upper Silesia 65 per cent of the population spoke Polish, yet a majority voted for Germany; while in Carinthia 68 per cent of the population were Slovenes but only 40 per cent voted for secession from Austria. K. J. Newman, *European Democracy between the Wars* (London, 1970), p. 148.

50 Cobban, p. 63.

51 *ibid.* p. 67.

52 League of Nations Official Journal (1926), p. 144. Streseman vehemently rejected assimilation for the Germans of the South Tyrol. A. E. Alcock, *The History of the South Tyrol Question* (London, 1970), p. 39.

53 Minute (493/1/1/12709 in FO 608/151). Cf. Hardinge, *c.* 30 June 1919, 'I am still of opinion that all that minorities can justly claim is religious equality and freedom of speech and education' (*ibid.*).

54 Minute, 27 December 1918 (P.I.D. 68 in FO 371/4355). In a second paper on the same file he added: 'Our hope should be that these states will govern themselves in such a way that they may eventually be free from these restrictions on their sovereignty.' (*ibid.*).

55 Minute 22 January [sic] 1919 (in fact the paper was circulated in March 1919) (131/1/1/4875 in FO 608/66).

56 Headlam-Morley minute 5 March 1919 (3585 in FO 608/151). Some doubts were expressed by Headlam-Morley as to whether Yiddish should be a protected language: 'According to my information Yiddish is merely a bastard form of German, I should not have thought that there was any strong claim to official recognition of it' (*ibid.*). Carr, however sensibly pointed out 'that the fact that Yiddish is said to be a debased form of German, and a philological atrocity, does not seem to me to have any bearing on the question. If the Jews in Poland want to talk Yiddish it should have the same protection as any other minority language e.g. the German language itself . . .' and this appears to have settled the matter. Minute 14 March 1919 (129/4/1/4561 in FO 608/61).

57 Headlam-Morley, 'The Minorities Treaties' (W 4864/185/98 in FO 371/14125).

58 Minute 27 December 1918 (P.I.D. 68 in FO 371/4355).

59 Minute *c.* 23 April 1919 (35/1/2/7470 in FO 608/6).

60 Minute *c.* 14 April 1919 (35/1/2/7018 *ibid.*).

61 Minute 11 April 1919 (131/1/1/4875 in FO 608/66).

62 It was a matter of concern to the states concerned that while they had to acknowledge their duties towards the minorities formally there was no corresponding demand that the minorities should pledge their loyalty to the state (for example Point VII of a Yugoslav note handed to A. W. A. Leeper by M. Trumbic, 30 October 1919 70/211/20025 in FO 608/23).

63 Minute *c.* 5 June 1919 (493/1/1/11/32 in FO 608/151).

64 See minutes by Howard and Headlam-Morley 22 January [sic] 1919 (*ibid.*).

65 This read: 'In towns and districts where there is a considerable proportion of Polish nationals belonging to racial, religious or linguistic minorities, these minorities should be assured an equitable share in the enjoyment and application of the sums which may be provided out of public funds under the State, municipal or other budget, for educational, religious or charitable purposes' (*FRUS* XIII p. 800).

66 Minute 1 September 1919 (120/3/15/18543 in FO 608/54).

67 Azcaraté, pp. 60–61.

68 Minutes 5 August 1919 (120/3/14/17110 in FO 608/54).

69 Paper on the League of Nations (PC 29/29 in FO 371/4353).

70 Minute 20 November 1918 (*ibid.*).

71 Minute 27 December 1918 (P.I.D. 68 in FO 371/4355).

72 Memorandum 16 May 1919 (*Memoir*, pp. 109–10).

73 Memorandum 5 June 1919 (*ibid.* p. 139).

74 Azcaraté, p. 99.

75 Minute 18 April 1919 (129/4/1/4561 in FO 608/61).

76 Headlam-Morley, 'The Minorities Treaties' (W 4864/185/98 in FO 371/14125).

77 Cf. Hardinge's private telegram, 2 February 1919, to Lord Granville in Athens who had suggested a plebiscite to determine the future of Cyprus: 'Obviously the conference has nothing to do with territories owned by the allies before the war. As you will readily understand plebiscites taken in countries in our possession or under our control before the war might be very inconvenient and certainly should not be encouraged' (85/1/1/1321 in FO 608/33).

78 Headlam-Morley minute 18 April 1919 (129/4/1/4561 in FO 608/61).

79 Headlam-Morley minute 2 June 1919 (130/2/1/8453 in FO 608/62).

80 P.I.D. paper on Belgium, in FO 371/4353.

81 Crowe minute 5 August 1919 (135/8/1/16747 in FO 608/70). The Germans and Poles did reach a highly complicated agreement running to 606 articles on minority protection in the Upper Silesian area, which was signed 15 May 1922. Azcaraté thought it over-elaborate. Azcaraté, pp. 140–41.

82 Minute 30 January 1920 (171458/73 in FO 371/3900).

83 Minute 19 March 1920 (P.I.D. 793/698 in FO 371/4385).

84 Claude, p. 48.

85 P.I.D. 876/876 in FO 371/4387.

86 Minute 10 April 1920 (*ibid.*).

87 Claude, pp. 39–50.

88 Minute *c.* 19 March 1919 (114/1/17 (5249) in FO 608/51).

12

Three case-studies in minority protection: South Tyrol, Cyprus, Quebec

A. E. Alcock

South Tyrol

The history of the question, 1918–69
The area known as South Tyrol, now the Italian province of Bolzano, was acquired by the kingdom of Italy from Austria at the end of the First World War as reward for changing alliances and intervening in the war on the side of the allies. Although it was intended that peace should be made on the basis of the self-determination of peoples, in South Tyrol – as elsewhere – practice did not follow theory. By the Treaty of St Germain in 1920 Italy obtained an area of about 4,650 square miles, whose economy was entirely agricultural, with a population of about 250,000, 90 per cent of which was German-speaking and Ladin.[1] Although there were protests, Italy insisted on receiving the area for strategic reasons – to obtain an alpine barrier against the pan-German world. Assurances were, however, given that the Italian government would adopt a very liberal policy in respect to South Tyrolese culture and economic interests.

However, within two years the democratic form of government in Italy was replaced by fascism, one of whose policies was deliberately to denationalize the South Tyrolese in order to render the South Tyrol Italian in fact as well as in name. Among the denationalization measures were the following – that Italian should be the only language in schools and public offices; court proceedings were to be almost entirely in Italian; German family and geographical names were Italianized; South Tyrolese political parties were banned. South Tyrolese who could not speak Italian were dismissed from public offices so that by 1939 these were filled 95 per cent by Italians. On the other hand, immigration into the province from other parts of Italy was encouraged, and an industrial zone was set up in the provincial capital of Bolzano, in order to attract Italians from other parts of the peninsula. By 1939 the population of the province numbered some 335,000 of which only 75 per cent were South Tyrolese.

By the time the Second World War ended the position in the province was as follows: on the one hand, there were the Italians, an urban–industrial people living almost entirely in the three largest towns of the province, enjoying a higher standard of living in respect to housing and wages and benefiting from the entire range of normal and vocational education; on the other hand, there were the South Tyrolese, a backward, agricultural people, isolated on the land, very few indeed possessing any secondary or vocational education, participating neither in the administration nor in the industrialization of the province, and significantly poorer in regard to houses and wages. As a result of the denationalization measures of fascism the South Tyrolese had been retarded in regard to the cultural economic and social development of the land on which they had lived for more than 1,000 years.

At the end of the Second World War the South Tyrolese tried to have the province returned to Austria. Two things worked against them. The first was that the allies did not want to give a slap in the face to a country that had not only, yet again, changed allegiances in the war and had ended up on their side, but which also contained the largest Communist party in Western Europe. In addition, Italian-Americans were one of the most powerful political lobbies in the United States. The second factor was the uncertain future of Austria itself, at that time under four-power occupation and to remain so until 1955. However, at the Paris Peace Conference in 1946 the allies agreed that the new democratic Italian state should give South Tyrol a measure of autonomy, and a treaty to that effect was signed between Austria and Italy (the De Gasperi–Gruber Agreement). Italy was to 'consult' the South Tyrolese in preparing the autonomy statute for the province. Some of the special provisions 'to safeguard the ethnic character and the cultural and economic development [of the South Tyrolese]' were listed in the agreement.

This agreement was a disaster. First, the wording was vague; worse, although it was an agreement between Germans and Italians, its official languages were English, French and Russian since it was annexed to the Italian peace treaty. Second, for the Italians, there was no explicit Austrian renunciation of claims to South Tyrol. The South Tyrol question was therefore still open. Third, for the South Tyrolese, if the agreement could be said to restore their cultural situation, it said nothing either about maintaining the German ethnic character of the province or about ensuring an economic development that would repair the damage and retardation caused by fascism and bring the Germans to economic and social parity with the Italians in the province. And the details of the autonomy they were promised would have to be discussed with the Italians without the prospect of much support from abroad or of being able to exert much political influence within the Italian state.

The autonomy statute issued in 1948 was a reflection of Italian fears. These were two – fear for the security of the state and fear for the Italians in the province. If the province was given a large autonomy a South Tyrolese provincial government might run Italian industry down, evict the Italian civil servants and then call for self-determination under circumstances that would lead to a massive majority demand for return to Austria. The Italians therefore devised a system to take care of these fears. A region designated Trentino–Alto Adige was set up, consisting of the two provinces of Bolzano and Trento.[2] In this region Italians were in the majority since the province of Trento was almost entirely inhabited by Italians.

The region and the provinces were indeed given legislative and executive powers, but in such a way as to ensure that the economic and social development of the South Tyrolese, as well as the future of the Italians of Bolzano, lay in the hands of the Italians. Consultations with the South Tyrolese were held but since the Italians were not obliged to heed their wishes there was little the former could do.

The result was that the autonomy statute, and the way it was applied, froze the already unhealthy, unbalanced relationship between the two linguistic groups in the province. For example, the region enjoyed primary and secondary legislative power in twenty-five sectors,[3] including the income-earning sectors of agriculture and forestry, tourism, and the development of industrial production. The provinces enjoyed primary and secondary legislative power in fourteen sectors, mostly of a cultural nature, but including housing. Insofar as the parliamentary system was concerned, the region and each province had its own diet and the majority party formed the local government or governed in a coalition. The regional diet was composed of the members of both provincial diets. The composition of the diet of Bolzano reflected the ethnic proportions of two thirds German/one third Italian living in the province since 1948, and so the South Tyrolese political party, the Sudtiroler Volkspartei (SVP) formed the provincial government. On the other hand, the regional diet reflected the ethnic proportions of one third German/two thirds Italian living in the region Trentino–Alto Adige. But the fact was that the really important decisions were being taken by the Italian state and by the region.

First, the matters to be given over to the region and the provinces by the state were often so complex that the respective legislative spheres of influence had to be marked out through executive measures issued by the Italian government. But there existed nowhere any information on what bases or principles, and within what time-limits, these executive measures were to be issued.

Second, state laws could be contested only by the region, and not by the provinces before the constitutional court. Therefore the province of Bolzano had to get the region, with its Italian majority, to contest state laws.

Third, the ability to protest against the policies of the region, by abstaining or voting against the regional budget, was rendered worthless. According to Article 73 of the autonomy statute the budget needed to be approved by a majority of the deputies of both provinces voting together and separately, but if such a majority was not forthcoming the said approval could be given by the minister of the interior under the very same article.

Fourth, it was stated in the autonomy statute that the region would 'normally' exercise its executive functions by delegating them to the provinces or the communes. However, according to a ruling of the constitutional court, 'normally' did not mean 'automatically', and therefore it was up to the Italian majority in the region to decide whether the executive functions of the region should or should not be so delegated.

Furthermore, housing governed immigration of Italians from the south into the provinces and conversely the movement of South Tyrolese from the land into the towns so as to create a more flexible economic and social composition of the group. It was thus a key instrument in economic and social mobility. Under Article 2 of the statute this appeared to belong to the primary legislative competence of the province. When the state put forward money for housing programmes in South Tyrol, the provincial government claimed the right to dispose of the money as it wished. The constitutional court, however, ruled that if the provinces had acquired the power to proceed autonomously with their own laws, this did not mean that the power of the state to proceed in those areas, with its own laws and with its own means should be considered diminished.

Finally, there was the question of ethnic proportions in the state bureaucracy. In the De Gasperi–Gruber Agreement the declared aim was 'equality of rights with a view to reaching a more appropriate proportion of employment between the two ethnic groups'. Clearly this was no specific undertaking by Italy to bring about, at stroke of the pen, precise ethnic proportions in state and semi-state offices. On the other hand, it was important that every South Tyrolese should have the right to communicate with government officials in his own language, and the fact was that few Italian officials knew German. Underlying both arguments was a deeper economic and political one. If South Tyrolese occupied posts in the state administration in ethnic proportions then they would come to take the place of Italians. If they did so, the South Tyrolese group would be correspondingly broadened economically and socially, with a further penetration of the economically more rewarding urban–bureaucratic life. But then the Italian group would be correspondingly weakened in one of its bastions in the province. The South Tyrolese argued that for state posts South Tyrolese had to compete against candidates from all over Italy, and there was no guarantee that if successful they would be posted in South Tyrol. The Italian government argued that examinations for state posts took place throughout Italy under equal conditions, and that therefore no special conditions could be made so that a certain number of South Tyrolese could not only be guaranteed places but appointed in South Tyrol.

The unbalancing factor was that vis-à-vis the South Tyrolese, the Italian state was far too strong. Internally the South Tyrolese could not put any political pressure on the Italian government since they possessed only two senators and three deputies in the Italian parliament. In addition, the South Tyrolese needed the Italian government to issue the executive measures to implement the autonomy statute. Externally Austria, under four-power occupation, could hardly be said to exist until 1955 and there were no other powers to take up the South Tyrolese case – certainly the United States, the United Kingdom and West Germany did not want to offend a NATO partner.

The problem was therefore, to all intents and purposes, an internal Italian one, but because the South Tyrolese could not put pressure on the Italian government the latter handled the former carelessly. There was little official discussion between Rome and Bolzano about the development of the South Tyrolese in the Italian state. The Italian attitude was guided entirely by the legal factor – whether Italy had or had not fulfilled the De Gasperi–Gruber Agreement by issuing the autonomy statute. The problems of minority protection in its economic and social aspects, as opposed to its cultural and legal aspects, were not considered. In this, Italian practice did not differ from post-Second World War practice in minority protection, which had concentrated entirely on the legal aspect, and the theory of 'equality of rights' between citizens of the majority and citizens of the minority.

Since the Italians would not talk to the South Tyrolese would they talk to the Austrians? The South Tyrolese produced a draft autonomy statute in 1958 requesting that the province of Bolzano became an autonomous region with all the appropriate powers and thus separate from the province of Trento. Shortly after, to prove the point, the Sudtiroler Volkspartei withdrew from the regional government coalition in which they had been partners with the Italian Christian Democrat party since 1948. The South Tyrolese draft statute was substantially backed by Austria. But in discussions with the Austrians, the Italians adopted the same line: the South Tyrol question was an internal Italian affair and if Austria felt that the autonomy statute was not implementation of the De Gasperi–Gruber Agreement, then she could always appeal to the International Court.

Austria also raised the matter in the Council of Europe, but the South Tyrolese had little confidence in a Europe dominated by Italy's NATO and Common Market partners. They also considered that the International Court could only say whether the autonomy statute fulfilled or did not fulfil the De Gasperi–Gruber Agreement. It would not be able to comment on practice since this was an internal Italian affair. What the South Tyrolese wanted was for Austria to obtain negotiating rights with Italy on all points in dispute of the Paris Agreement, and not merely to hold 'conversations' with Italy, when the latter would be free to decide what to discuss and how far to discuss it. And for this, only the United Nations was considered as offering a chance of success.

Since in the opinion of the Austrian Foreign Office the verdict of the International Court would be that Italy *had* fulfilled the Paris Agreement, Austria brought the South Tyrol question before the United Nations General Assembly in 1960. There was another aspect to this move: the United Nations was not so much under the influence of NATO and Common Market countries and support was expected from the Afro-Asian and non-aligned blocks. At the United Nations, although Austria did not succeed in fulfilling her main aim of getting that organization to recommend that the province of Bolzano be raised to the rank of an autonomous region, the resolution adopted by the General Assembly at least obliged Italy to negotiate with Austria on *all* differences relating to the Paris Agreement. This ended for ever the pretence that the South Tyrol question was an internal Italian affair, and also meant that Austria could now discuss the question of an improved autonomy for the province of Bolzano along the lines of the Sudtiroler Volkspartei's 1958 draft autonomy statute.

Austria expected little from direct negotiations with Italy, but at this moment another factor intervened – that of terrorism. Dynamite attacks had taken place sporadically since 1959, usually aimed at the province's electrical pylon system. But at the beginning of 1961, as a background to the bilateral Austro–Italian negotiations, a systematic campaign of violence and terrorism broke out, involving many different economic targets. This campaign was to last until 1967, causing a number of deaths and considerable economic damage.

The terrorists claimed that it was their acts of violence which changed the attitude of the Italian government, first on discussions with the South Tyrolese and then on the granting of an improved autonomy, a claim that, unfortunately, can hardly be denied. For in July 1961 the Italian government established an internal commission of nineteen members, seven of whom were South Tyrolese, to study the problems involved. The discussions of this commission were carried on parallel with the bilateral Austro–Italian negotiations, and the commission's findings (presented in 1964) were used for further discussions – between the South Tyrolese and the Italian government, between the Italian and Austrian governments, and even between Austrians, Italians and South Tyrolese sitting round the same negotiating table.

Quite early on in these negotiations the South Tyrolese declared that if they should receive the legislative and executive powers they considered necessary for their own protection they would drop the demand for the dissolution of the region Trentino–Alto Adige and the raising of the province of Bolzano to regional status. On the other hand, the character of the terrorist campaign also underwent a change. Originally bombs had been thrown to bring the Italian government to the negotiating table. But as South Tyrolese terrorists were arrested by the Italian police, the terrorist movement was completely taken over by Austrian and West German elements motivated by the aim of the secession of the province of Bolzano to Austria. There were also strong pan-German and neo-Nazi undercurrents in the movement. Terrorist activity now took place to prevent any agreement that would leave the province of Bolzano in the Italian state. Tripartite negotiations continued against this background until 1969.

The solution

The immediate cause of the trouble in the province of Bolzano had been fear – fear for the territorial destiny of the Italian population there on the one hand; fear of economic and social backwardness that put in doubt the ability of the South Tyrolese to compete with the Italians, and thus preserve their identity, on the other hand. Accordingly, any solution envisaged would have to take these fears into account. The result was in the form of a package deal.

First, the autonomy statute of the region Trentino–Alto Adige would be substantially modified so as to give the South Tyrolese and the province of Bolzano a far greater autonomy. However, this autonomy would be so designed as also to protect the Italian population of the province. Second, a timetable would govern the introduction of the new autonomy statute. The Italian government would undertake to bring in the new autonomy statute within one year and put through the necessary executive measures to implement it within eighteen months. Third, within fifty days of the last executive measures Austria would declare the South Tyrolese question closed. Fourth, Austria and Italy would sign a treaty making applicable to the South Tyrol question the 1957 Strasbourg Convention for the Peaceful Settlement of Disputes, hitherto not applicable to disputes originating before its coming into effect.

The whole mechanism would be triggered off by the acceptance by the South Tyrolese of the proposed changes in the autonomy statute, as well as the operational calendar for implementing the package deal, the related guarantees, and the arrangements for closing the question. This South Tyrolese approval was given at a party congress extraordinary in November 1969, and the eighteen-point operational calendar, with its precise timetable governing approval of the arrangements by the Austrian and Italian parliaments, the issuing of the appropriate executive measures, signature of the treaty on the applicability of the Strasbourg Convention, and the giving of the Austrian declaration on the closing of the question, then went into effect.[4]

The new autonomy statute was promulgated on 20 November 1972. Since then most, but not all, of the executive measures to implement the statute have been issued. But if the Italian government did not hold precisely to the timetable set out this has not caused much concern in the province of Bolzano. The South Tyrolese are well aware of the economic and political difficulties that the Italian government has been facing (problems of coalition, the divorce law, neo-fascist terrorist activity, inflation, balance of payments problems). The view of all responsible political circles in the province is that it is far better to overstep the timetable and go thoroughly into the complex matter of the issuing of executive measures than to rush matters through, respecting the timetable, but leaving matters vague, with possible loopholes, and thus liable to undesired political exploitation at a future date.

Before analysing the most important changes in the new autonomy statute and their relevance to the situation in South Tyrol, mention must be made of two important factors underlying everyday life in the province. The German-speaking South Tyrolese number some two thirds of the population of the province and the Italian-language group numbers one third. This means that with voting on the lines of proportional representation the German-speaking group dominates the provincial parliament. Out of the thirty-four seats in the provincial parliament the South Tyrolese have twenty-four[5] and the Italian group ten. South Tyrolese politics since 1945 have been dominated by the South Tyrolese People's Party (SVP), and today the SVP has twenty of the twenty-four German-speaking seats. The other four seats are held by two representatives of the South Tyrolese Social Democratic Party; the (South Tyrolese) Progressive Party; and a German-speaking member of the Italian Communist Party. On the other hand, the Italian group is made up of five Christian Democrats, two Socialists, one Communist, one Social Democrat, and one Italian Social Movement–National Right.

The political initiative in the provincial parliament therefore lies with the SVP, and the way this is taken will be examined below. But the balance between the two groups in the province is expressed not only in terms of political majorities but also through the various sectors of the economy and the administration, reflecting the economic and social development of the province. Over 95 per cent of the agricultural sector lies in the hands of the South Tyrolese (from the point of view of tourism the province is one of the two or three richest in all Italy); two thirds of the commerce is in South Tyrolese hands. On the other hand, industry, especially in the Bolzano industrial zone, is overwhelmingly Italian. In administrative matters, if employment in offices of the provincial administration reflects existing ethnic proportions, public offices and bodies of the state administration in the province such as posts and telegraphs, the state railways, the state radio and television authority and the police, are overwhelmingly filled by Italians. Efforts by the South Tyrolese to obtain *de facto* ethnic proportions in state offices in addition to provincial offices will be examined below. The situation is, therefore, that each group has its own sectors of economic strength and these sectors guarantee the different groups' presence in the province.

The second important factor is that it is considered quite normal for every single person resident in the province to declare to which linguistic group he belongs. The principle of ethnic proportions in employment in the public administration is fundamental to the issue of the protection of minorities, and it would be difficult, if not impossible, for ethnic proportions to be filled if these were not known precisely, quite apart from the point that uncertainty would merely create conditions for exploitable political dissension. The first Italian post-war census of 1951 did not divide the resident population of the province up according to linguistic groups, but the second census (1961) did so and this has been the practice ever since. The usual practice has been for the head of the family to declare to which group his family belongs, but a law is in the process of adoption under which persons aged eighteen and over may make their own declaration. The declaration of the head of the family is particularly important when it comes to the question of the school, Italian-speaking or German-speaking, to which his child should be sent.

The main difference between the old and the new autonomy statutes is that much more power in the income-earning sectors now lies with the provinces of the region and no longer with the region itself. Among the matters for which the Province of Bolzano now has primary legislative competence are comprehensive town and country planning, protection of the environment, the handicrafts sector, building, tourism and the hotel trade, agriculture and forestry, and school construction. The province now has secondary legislative competence for commerce and the development of industrial production.

The new arrangements provide for five guarantees that minorities in the region and the provinces are not placed at a disadvantage. First there are the regional and provincial budgets. At the request of a majority of the councillors of any one linguistic group the individual chapters must be voted on by linguistic groups. Those not obtaining a majority in each group must be submitted to a commission which decides the estimates. If it cannot come to a decision, the draft budget is sent to the regional court of administrative justice, which must finally decide on the estimates within thirty days. Second, there is the above-mentioned court. Acts by the public administration considered to offend the principle of the ethnic equality of all citizens may be brought before the court by regional, provincial and municipal councillors. Appeals against decisions of the court may be filed with the council of state in Rome, which must have a South Tyrolese member participating in its decision. Third, if any bill is considered as violating the principle of ethnic equality, the majority of the councillors of one of the language groups may call for a vote by language groups. If this is rejected or should the bill be passed despite the opposition of two thirds of the language group that called for the vote, the bill could be brought before the constitutional court. Fourth, the provinces may now contest state laws before the constitutional court instead of having to go through the region. Fifth, there is an obligation for the minority group to be represented in the regional and Bolzano governments on a basis of ethnic proportions. Thus the government of Bolzano consists of a German-speaking president, a vice-president and seven out of ten assessors (or ministers) responsible for the various sectors of the economy, while the Italian-language group has a vice-president and three assessors.

However, the obligation of both groups to participate in the government administration does not carry with it the obligation to have a coalition government policy. Thus, should the SVP decide on a policy with which the Italian assessors do not agree, there is nothing to prevent the SVP majority (twenty seats out of thirty-four) from putting through the necessary legislation. It would then be up to the Italian councillors as a group to decide whether that legislation is detrimental to the Italians in the province, and take the necessary action.

In this way, democratic government by a parliamentary majority automatically takes place without hindrance by a minority which may or may not be linguistic. If the parliamentary minority is linguistic it can always defend itself before the constitutional court, but only after the democratic process has been followed. It cannot block *a priori* the will of a parliamentary majority, and this point should be remembered when the case of Cyprus is considered. Provincial legislation is prepared by four parliamentary commissions, (general affairs, agriculture, finance and labour), the composition of which is also on a basis of ethnic proportions. Finally in the 117 municipal councils (communes) in Bolzano, each language group has the right to be represented on the executive if it has at least two members.

Under the new arrangements the province has increased sources of finance, including the appropriate percentage of the state budget, and nine tenths of the yield of a number of state taxes, including income and automobile taxes. It disburses the funds at its disposal on the principle of ethnic proportions in social, welfare, and cultural affairs.

If ethnic proportions already exist in the province's administrative offices, the object is to make this principle also applicable to state bodies operating in the province, such as the post office and state railways. About 6,000 posts are involved, overwhelmingly filled by Italians. This situation originally occurred because of the Fascist government's policy of dismissing the South Tyrolese (on the grounds that they could not speak Italian) and continued *de facto* after the Second World War, since in competitions for posts few South Tyrolese applied, having to compete under equal conditions against candidates from all over Italy. The reluctance on the part of the South Tyrolese to compete was due to language problems, and their unwillingness to be transferred out of the province during the course of their career.

The final aim is to ensure ethnic proportions in employment not only in the organization involved as a whole, but in every single grade in the administrative hierarchy. On the other hand, there is no question of forced dismissal or transfer of officials already *en poste* to make room for South Tyrolese. The gradual replacement of Italians by South Tyrolese is to take place through the filling of vacancies as they occur naturally. The problem for the South Tyrolese has been to find out exactly the number of employees, in each grade, in each organization, so they can see how many South Tyrolese can be employed and where. They claim that the Italian government has been slow in providing the necessary information and that the organizations concerned are still recruiting Italians from outside the province, mainly young people, without regard to the principle of ethnic proportions, or their ability to speak German.

The South Tyrolese have therefore proposed that Italians recruited since 20 January 1972 should be transferable, and that for posts made vacant by death, retirement or voluntary transfer South Tyrolese should be admitted in larger than proportional numbers since only then would it be possible to have ethnic proportions in state offices before the end of the century. From the political point of view, ethnic proportions in offices of the state administration will adversely affect a bastion of the Italians in the province, since it is through the agencies of the state (bureaucratic or industrial) that the Italian State supports the Italian minority in the province. But this situation has come to be accepted as inevitable.

One area that the new autonomy statute has not regulated satisfactorily, however, is control of immigration and employment agencies. Immigration has always been a controversial subject in South Tyrol. Fascism attempted first to isolate and then to denationalize the South Tyrolese by encouraging mass immigration in the inter-war years. After the Second World War the South Tyrolese accused the Italian government of again encouraging immigration with the object of putting them into a minority in their own land – an accusation vigorously denied by the Italian government, which pointed out that under the constitution no one could be prevented from residing in whatever part of the country he or she wished. During all the negotiations between the South Tyrolese, the Italians and the Austrians, the first sought primary legislative control for the province over employment agencies, and this was consistently refused by the Italian government. And indeed, under the new autonomy statute the province has only a tertiary legislative power, that is, power merely to integrate the laws of the state already issued.

However, it has been pointed out that this situation offered no protection against immigration. It is true that under the new autonomy statute citizens resident in the province have the right to precedence in job placement in the province itself, but 'without discrimination on the basis of language group or length of residence'. But in order to take up residence it is only necessary to book a hotel room on entering the province, and next day register with the employment agencies and state the intention of residing in the province. According to a decree of the Ministry of the Interior, applicable all over Italy, officials in employment agencies cannot refuse to register such persons for employment.

The number of South Tyrolese serving in the forces is minimal, although some serve in the financial police, which acts as a customs and excise force, because South Tyrol is a frontier province. By gentleman's agreement South Tyrolese in the police or *carabinieri* serve in the province. Similarly, while all male Italian citizens are required by law to undertake a certain period of military service, South Tyrolese serve in the province.

The development of large-scale industries has always been viewed with suspicion by the South Tyrolese ever since the Fascists set up the Bolzano industrial zone, allegedly not for economic reasons but to encourage Italian immigration and thus denationalize the area. During the long negotiations between the South Tyrolese, the Austrians, and the Italians, the last refused consistently to have the fate of the zone's existing industries fall into the hands of the South Tyrolese, fearing that steps would be taken to run it down. Accordingly the negotiations centred on industrial development, and the province obtained secondary legislative powers in that respect. It was intended that a law should be passed that big nationalized industries would be allowed into the province only after the latter had been consulted.

On the other hand, if the South Tyrolese have been willing to see light industries established in the province so as to absorb the manpower coming off the poor mountain agricultural sector,[6] they have been unwilling to see Italian light industries establish themselves in the valleys, and have sought firms and financial assistance from Austria and West Germany instead. The agreement is that new industries financed wholly or to a large extent with foreign capital, can only be built after agreement with the state committee for economic planning and with the province. At present it is fair to say that the Bolzano industrial zone is not considered a threat to the South Tyrolese, and neither is the large influx of foreign capital from West Germany considered a threat to the Italian-speaking group.

With regard to schools in South Tyrol, each language group has its own nursery, primary, and secondary schools. Lessons are given in the pupils' mother tongue by teachers for whom that language is the mother tongue. South Tyrolese and Italians must learn the other language, and it is taught by teachers whose mother tongue is that second language. The South Tyrolese sought to have complete autonomy in educational questions, but this was not achieved. Whereas school administration comes under the authority of the province, the teaching staff remain under the authority of the state. However, a provincial educational council must be consulted – and gives binding opinions – on the creation and suppression of schools, on programmes and hours, and on curricula and the contents of courses. Pupils are enrolled in the appropriate language school at the request of the father or a person acting for him. In the case of a refusal to enrol a pupil, the father may appeal to the regional court of administrative justive. The province has primary legislative powers for school and nursery-school building, but the creation of new schools requires the consent of the ministry of public instruction, since the ministry has to provide the salaries of the teaching staff. Although the province has not obtained a complete school autonomy the present arrangements are considered adequate to secure a school administration which can meet the requirements of the linguistic minorities. The idea of separate schools is supported.

Conclusion

The population of the province of Bolzano according to the 1971 census amounted to some 414,000 persons, 63 per cent of whom are German-speaking, 33 per cent Italian, and 4 per cent Ladin. Although the bitterness of the years 1919–69 is well remembered, there is no doubt that relations between the two ethnic groups can be said to have very much improved. There is still a certain amount of wariness, perhaps born of habit, since enmity has been a consistent part of the daily lives of the province's political leaders.

Three factors have contributed to this healthier climate. The first is the economic health of the province, compared to other parts of Italy. All-the-year-round tourism, which has benefited not only the hotel trade but also the small farmer who rents rooms to tourists, the installation of light industry to absorb manpower coming off the land, and a serene climate of industrial relations, have all played their part. The second is the greatly improved state of education in the province, owing to the central government's school building programme begun in 1963. Previously, the mainly agrarian South Tyrolese rarely attended secondary and vocational schools since these were to be found only in the big towns and distances were great and lodgings expensive. This adversely affected the employment structure, and thus the economic and social flexibility of the group. The situation is now well on the way to being rectified, through a dwindling agricultural population, expansion in the handicrafts, tourism and light industry sectors, increased earning power and altogether better opportunities making for an economically better balanced and socially flexible ethnic group. The third reason is of course the general moral uplift that occurred when the South Tyrolese obtained almost all the reins for controlling their own destiny, while at the same time it was made clear that the Italian population would not suffer and that the security of the state would not be endangered.

The major credit for this situation must go to the South Tyrolese leader, Dr Silvius Magnago. His line of policy has been open and unswerving. He has consistently called for the province of Bolzano to obtain powers for the South Tyrolese minority to control their own destiny within the

Italian state. This led to his vilification as a traitor by the Italians, who thought that his demands would lead to the destruction of the Italian position in the province and then to secession to Austria. His outright condemnation of terrorism and his resistance to any treasonable activity by the SVP led to his vilification on both sides of the Brenner as a traitor to the South Tyrolese and the German people. For urging acceptance of the package deal he was labelled by some members of his party as the 'grave-digger of South Tyrol', and there are many who feel that it was his personality and prestige alone which not only swayed the SVP congress in 1969 into accepting the package by a narrow majority, but also enabled him to carry a majority of his party with him in a number of very tense political situations.

One important factor for the future is the explicit recognition that both groups have a particular role in South Tyrol, and for that, both groups must preserve their separate ethnic and cultural identities. There is no question of the creation of a separate and specific 'South Tyrolese' identity to be arrived at by an amalgamation of the two language groups. Some concern, indeed, was expressed that Italians living in the South-Tyrolese-dominated valleys might be culturally assimilated through natural processes in the course of time. Certainly the South Tyrolese would resist any assimilation as energetically as in the past, while for the Italians the problem is that there has not yet been raised a new generation of ethnic 'Italian' South Tyrolese. Most Italians have come from other provinces, still maintain their ties with their original provinces, and are inclined to keep together in groups related to their areas of origin.

What is recognized as being required, on the other hand, is the creation of a bi-lingual society, responsible behaviour by both language groups, and maintenance of the ethnic balance in an area that is an important crossroads in European culture and society and in the European economy. For this, the question of inter-group contact is important. Despite the progress of the last ten years, the South Tyrolese and the Italian man-in-the-street are still quite apart. Cooperation and contact takes place mostly in the commercial world, and in the big towns. On the other hand, even in the moments of greatest political tension there has been adequate political contact at provincial level. Even when the SVP withdrew from the regional government between 1959 and 1970 provincial government continued, as did personal relations, so that there were no doubts as to what each side was thinking. Certainly there has been no special mechanism established at provincial level for South Tyrolese to keep in touch with Italians and to monitor the veracity of statements made by one side or another. On the other hand, as part of the package deal, provision has been made for a permanent commission within the presidency of the Italian council of ministers to study the problems of the province of Bolzano, and formulate (non-binding) proposals and opinions. It is to consist of four South Tyrolese, two Italians, and one Ladin, all from the province of Bolzano.

One last point remains. The Austrian declaration that the package, as implemented, is a fulfilment of the De Gasperi–Gruber Agreement, and that therefore the South Tyrol question is closed, must be given within fifty days of the emission of the last executive measures, and is expected to be based on the judgement of the South Tyrolese. This declaration has not yet been given, and a lot of soul-searching is going on as regards the effect and value of such a declaration. The South Tyrolese may or may not advise Austria that the question can be declared closed. Austria may or may not give the desired declaration. But even if Austria does so, Italy's responsibilities for seeing that the South Tyrolese are protected economically and socially, legally and culturally, will not end. Society develops and creates new situations in the relationship between minorities and the majority, and if arrangements are not made to meet these developments and if the voice of the minority is not listened to, then the finest declarations, legal texts, and court decisions, will not stave off political discontent and will not prevent the minority appealing across the border.

Cyprus

The South Tyrol question was a struggle between the central government in Rome and the provincial government in Bolzano. The only foreign state involved, Austria, was a relatively weak power, which saw its role as acting at the behest of the South Tyrolese when Rome–Bolzano relations were blocked, but never thought in terms of annexation of the disputed territory. The situation is very different in Cyprus, where external rather than internal factors have dominated developments.

Cyprus is the third largest island in the Mediterranean, after Sicily and Sardinia, with a total area of 3,572 square miles. From the early classical period it was part of the Greco–Roman world. Because of its strategic significance and internal weakness, it changed hands often during the middle ages but the prevailing culture continued to be Greek Orthodox. In 1571 the island was captured by the Turks. The first half of the nineteenth century saw the vigorous flowering of nationalism – in Europe, Latin America and also the Middle East. In 1830 the Greek state was created following a decade of revolt against Turkish rule. The problem so far as the European great powers were concerned was how to reconcile the need to help the oppressed Christian nationalities of the Turkish Empire against their overlord with the need to maintain the balance of power by supporting the Turkish Empire against Russia.

Following the Congress of Berlin in 1878, the sultan of Turkey leased Cyprus to Britain. Britain wanted to use the island as a base to protect the Suez Canal and as an anti-Russian staging post, while the sultan wanted to pay off his debts to the British. However, Cyprus remained formally under Turkish sovereignty. In 1914 Britain, now in alliance with Russia, no longer sought the maintenance of the Turkish Empire but its dismemberment. Cyprus was formally annexed. During the five years following the end of the First World War Greek–Turkish relations were very bitter. By the 1920 Treaty of Sèvres, the Turkish Empire was dismembered, and reduced more or less to present-day central Anatolia. Greece obtained Smyrna and a large portion of western Anatolia. However, the convulsions of the preceding years led to a revival of Turkish nationalism. War broke out between Greece and Turkey. The Greek army was destroyed and the considerable Greek population in western Anatolia was decimated. The Treaty of Lausanne in July 1923 brought an end to the war. This treaty is important insofar as minority problems are concerned in that it consecrated the principle of population exchanges. Some 750,000 Greeks in Anatolia were deported to Greece; and in return some 450,000 Moslems, chiefly living in Macedonia, were deported to Turkey. Only about 100,000 Greeks remained in Turkey (mostly in Istanbul) and about 125,000 Turks remained in Greece. In addition, Turkey recognized British jurisdiction over Cyprus.

During the inter-war years the Greeks in Cyprus, who numbered some 75 to 80 per cent of the population, never gave up hope of *Enosis*, the principle of joining with their Greek motherland. In 1931 pro-*Enosis* riots were so severe that constitutional government was suspended. In 1946 the Greeks again sought *Enosis* from Britain, but this was rejected. The Greek government, heavily dependent on British aid in the civil war, was in no position to exert pressure. Later, the oil-producing areas of the Middle East became vital to the Western economy, and as nationalist pressure forced Britain to withdraw from Palestine and Egypt, and the British and Americans formed the Baghdad Pact to hem in the Soviet Union, so the strategic value of Cyprus to Britain was increased. From 1950 to 1954 Britain refused to discuss the future of Cyprus. Arguing that complete sovereignty over Cyprus was necessary for strategic reasons, Britain declared that the island would 'never' be independent. In 1954 Greece brought the Cyprus question before the UN but without success. In April 1955 the organization EOKA, lead by Archbishop Makarios and Colonel Grivas, began a campaign of terrorism designed to achieve *Enosis*.

The creation of the Cyprus republic
In 1960 the population of Cyprus was 577,165, of whom 448,857 were Greek (78 per cent), 104,350 were Turks (18 per cent) and 24,408 were British (4 per cent). By 1973 the population had increased by 10 per cent, but the relative proportions had changed little. There are six large towns: Nicosia, the capital, with 118,000 inhabitants in 1973; Limassol, 61,400; Famagusta, 44,000; Larnaca, 21,800; Paphos, 12,000; and Kyrenia, 5,000. There are also 617 villages, of which 393 are overwhelmingly Greek, 120 are overwhelmingly Turkish and 104 are mixed. However, the villages themselves are not usually to be found in clusters where one community or the other predominates. The more general pattern is for a mixture of Greek, Turkish and mixed villages. And although intermarriage has been rare, the religious difference being the main barrier, there seems to have been considerable intermingling, especially in employment and commerce. The pattern of settlement has been described as an 'ethnological fruitcake in which the Greek and the Turkish currants were mixed up in every town and village and often in every street'.[7] On the other hand, while intermingled, the two principal communities have remained in many respects distinct and separate. In particular, each has retained its own religion and educational system, and its own laws, customs and traditions.[8]

According to some Greek Cypriots, Turkish interests in Cyprus, allegedly renounced with the Treaty of Lausanne, were reawakened by the British, who called the Turkish Cypriots into the conflict to balance the Greek Cypriots, using them, for example, as policemen. This view is rejected by the Turkish government. As early as 1954 the Turkish government had informed the Greek government that as long as Cyprus was British, then the Cyprus problem was a British problem. But if there was to be a change in the status of the island (whether *Enosis* or independence), then Turkey would wish to have a say, and negotiations should be on a tripartite basis between Britain, Greece and Turkey. Certainly there could be no question of the unification of Cyprus with Greece. Apparently the Greek government of this time only took the question of the Turkish minority in Cyprus into account, and overlooked Turkish strategic interests, namely that the island should not fall into the hands of potential enemies (the Greeks).[9]

It may be as well to recall here that even if Greeks and Turks were together in NATO and are now seeking Common Market membership, the record of the last 450 years has made them traditional enemies. And the Turks have taken great pains to point out that Cyprus has never been, politically, a Greek island. In any case, the pressure for *Enosis* by Greek Cypriots 'led to an insistence that the Turkish Cypriot community had an equal right of union with Turkey, to be carried out by means of partitioning the country'.[10]

From 1955 to 1959 Cyprus was the scene of savage Greek Cypriot guerrilla warfare against the British, as well as of equally bitter communal strife between Greek and Turkish Cypriots. Numerous conferences were held, and draft constitutions drawn up, but without success. During the first three years the Greek government pressed at international level for the principle of self-determination for the island. Cyprus was cast as a 'colonial' question, and claims for *Enosis* were officially dropped since this implied outright annexation by Greece. Of course, the Greek government hoped that once self-determination had been achieved, Cyprus would then vote for *Enosis*. For its part, the Turkish government rejected any idea of *Enosis* and, aware of the ultimate aims of the Greek government, called for the partition of the island into separate Greek and Turkish areas (the principle of *Taksim*). The aim of the Turkish Cypriots and the Turkish government was to show that, as a result of the intercommunal killings, coexistence between Greek and Turkish Cypriots was impossible without partition.

But by late 1958 the pressures for a solution began to build up. Britain revised its defence requirements and saw that only a part of Cyprus was needed rather than the whole island. More important, a split occurred between Archbishop Makarios and Colonel Grivas. Whereas the latter still sought *Enosis* at all costs, Archbishop Makarios came round to the view that it might be better to have an undivided independent Cyprus. He and the Greek government began to be afraid that otherwise the British might lose patience and withdraw in such a way that the Greek Cypriots would have partition imposed on them. On the other hand, the Turks began to fear that Britain would withdraw and give Cyprus independence, and thus place the Turkish Cypriot minority at the mercy of the Greek Cypriots. In addition, neither the Greek nor the Turkish governments wanted a deterioration in their relations that might lead to ejection from NATO, loss of American economic or military aid, or even war.[11]

As a result the Turkish and Greek prime ministers and foreign ministers met in Zurich in February 1959 and drew up three documents. First there was the agreement entitled 'The Basic Structure of the Republic of Cyprus', which set out the constitutional framework of the proposed new state. Second, there was a treaty of guarantee between Cyprus, on the one hand, and Britain, Greece and Turkey on the other. Third, there was a treaty of alliance between Cyprus, Greece and Turkey. The foreign ministers then departed for London where the British government declared that it accepted the Zurich agreements as the foundation for the final settlement of the Cyprus problem.

The constitution of 1960
The most important single feature of the constitution and of the government administration of Cyprus was that it was based on a new concept – the equality of the Greek and Turkish Cypriot *communities* in setting up the new republic. In other words, what was required for the running of the state was joint agreement. This system was preferred to the alternative, seen in South Tyrol, of majority rule with protection of the minority built in through the creation of certain devices to enable the minority to take action should legislative or administrative acts deemed hostile to the minority be carried out.

Thus there did not exist in Cyprus a majority–minority relationship. The Turkish government and the Turkish Cypriots denied that the Turks were a 'minority' in Cyprus. They agreed that were Cyprus to be annexed to Greece they would be a 'minority', but in the republic of Cyprus, even though possessing only 20 per cent of the population, they were 'partners'. And indeed the first two articles of the constitution referred to the two 'communities', and not to any 'minority'. The second important feature – and one arising directly out of the concept of 'community partnership' – was that the principle of ethnic proportions was not applied on a strictly numerical basis. For although the ratio of Greek Cypriots to Turkish Cypriots is more or less four to one, the Turkish community had 30 per cent of the seats in the unicameral house of representatives, 30 per cent of the Council of Ministers, 30 per cent of the civil service and security forces, and 40 per cent of the army.

Executive power over all except communal affairs (see below) was vested in a president, a vice-president and a council of ministers. The president of Cyprus had to be a Greek Cypriot; the vice-president had to be a Turkish Cypriot. Of the ten members of the council of ministers three had to be Turks and one of the key portfolios of foreign affairs, defence or finance had to go to a Turk. Decisions in the council could be taken by majority vote but the president and the vice-president could veto any decisions relating to foreign affairs, defence and security. A number of decisions within the authority of the president and the vice-president required the agreement of both, including the promulgation of legislation and decisions of the council of ministers. The house of representatives could not modify the basic articles of the constitution, which referred to the rights of the Turkish Community. However, other articles might be modified by a two thirds majority on both sides.

In addition to the parliament there were also separately elected Greek and Turkish 'communal chambers' to deal with such matters as religious affairs, education and culture, marriage and divorce, and control of co-operative and credit societies. The chambers had the right to levy taxes on their own communities to supplement grants from parliament.

The five main towns on the island were to have separate Greek and Turkish municipalities, with their own elected councils. In each town there was to be a coordinating body of two Greeks and two Turks together with a chairman (to be agreed upon) to operate joint municipal services. There was, however, a provision that this situation should be re-examined by the president and the vice-president to see whether the system of separate municipalities should be continued.

In the court system, in cases involving Greek Cypriots only, the judges had to be Greek Cypriots. In cases involving Turkish Cypriots only, the judges had to be Turkish Cypriots. In cases involving both Greek and Turkish Cypriots, there had to be both Greek and Turkish Cypriot judges. The highest judicial organs, the supreme constitutional court and the high court of justice had to have neutral presidents – neither Greeks nor Turks – who, by virtue of their casting votes, held the balance between the Greek and Turkish Cypriot members of the courts.

The independent senior officers of state such as the attorney-general, the governor of the Bank of Cyprus, the auditor-general, and the heads of the army, police and *gendarmerie* could come from either community, but their deputies had to come from the other community. One of the heads of the army, police or *gendarmerie* had to be a Turkish Cypriot.

In addition to the constitution were the two treaties of guarantee and alliance that were an integral part of the complex political arrangement for Cyprus. Under the treaty of guarantee between Cyprus and Britain, Greece, and Turkey, the last two powers were given the right to station troops on the island.

To protect their security and rights, therefore, the Turkish community had no less than five guarantees – the presence of Turkish troops in Cyprus; the right of Turkey to intervene if the existing state of affairs should be changed; the Turkish vice-president's right of veto; the principle of separate voting majorities in the house of representatives; a guaranteed proportion of posts in the civil service, army and security forces over and above existing ethnic proportions.

As mentioned above, the arrangements were those agreed on by the Greek and Turkish governments. If the Greek Cypriots were kept informed of the Zurich and London negotiations, it cannot be said that they approved of them. Archbishop Makarios declared that he had been pressurized by the Greek government and felt he had to sign the package, since he feared that otherwise the Greek Cypriots would be abandoned and partition of the island would result. Furthermore, the treaties of guarantee and alliance, as part of the deal agreed upon in Zurich, were never presented for ratification by the Cyprus house of representatives.

It is not surprising that under these circumstances the Greek Cypriot population, barely consulted, has considered that the whole question was handled artificially and that the solution adopted was one designed to serve foreign ends rather than those of the great majority of the Cypriot people. Thus the republic was founded on agreements which did not emanate from the free will of the people, while the treaties of guarantee and alliance allowed interference in its domestic affairs.[12]

The general effect of the arrangements was to make most of the major affairs of state subject to the agreement of the representatives of both the Greek and Turkish communities either by joint decision or by renunciation of the right of veto. This invited deadlock on any question when the two communities had sharply differing views. Recourse to the supreme court did not necessarily provide a way out since the court could only resolve problems of interpretation, and not political differences.[13] The Greek Cypriots felt that satisfaction of Turkish demands was impossible without rendering the government impotent. Thus the Zurich constitution 'accentuated the separatism of the two communities at the very moment when close cooperation was needed to make it work'.[14]

The collapse of the Cyprus republic

The main cause of the collapse of the republic was suspicion. Both communities in Cyprus believed that the other regarded the Zurich and London agreements as transient: the Turkish side felt that the Greeks were preparing for *Enosis*, while the Greeks accused the Turks of exploiting the separatist constitutional provisions to promote communal interests at the expense of the island as a whole, with a view to securing partition.

To the Greek Cypriots the constitution was considered a separatists' charter, not a formula for harmonious integration. First, the fact that important bills in the house of representatives required separate majorities, and therefore eight Turkish votes could defeat a bill approved by forty-two out of fifty deputies, was seen as simply undemocratic. It could not be considered to have anything to do with protection against discrimination since any legislation considered discriminatory could be challenged before the constitutional court by the vice-president. Article 6 of the constitution laid down that no law or decision of the house of representatives should discriminate against either community or any citizen. Any and every citizen had the means to challenge any law.

Second, the separation of justice was a slur on the impartiality and integrity of judges. The very concept of justice defied separation. The system was detrimental to the cause of justice, since in cases involving Greeks and Turks judges would come to lose respect for each other and develop the mentality of an arbitrator appointed by one of the parties. Before 1960 justice had been administered by Greek and Turkish judges impartially and irrespective of community, and there had been no complaints.

Third, employment in the civil service, in every job and every grade, on the basis of seven to three was not working since there were not enough trained Turks to fill jobs in the higher grades. Fulfilling the letter of the law thus disrupted the civil service. In addition Greeks were being held back from promotion to jobs for which they were qualified in order to find jobs for unqualified Turks, and to a certain extent they suffered from discrimination, since although they formed 80 per cent of the population they could only fill 70 per cent of the posts. The Turks claimed that their candidates were being passed over. During the first three years some 2,000 civil service appointments were contested on communal grounds before the constitutional court.

Fourth, the Cypriot army never got off the ground. The Turks, taking into account the advice of military experts (both Greek and Turk) and believing that a mixed army would provide continued friction, called for separate Greek and Turkish units. The Greeks refused and their decision was vetoed. Archbishop Makarios then said it would be better to have no army since Cyprus was a non-aligned nation. The Turkish Cypriots accused the Greek Cypriots of manœuvring so that there should be no Cypriot army. The result was that both Greek and Turkish Cypriots began to train and equip their own armies in secret.

Fifth, the provision for separate municipalities in the five big towns was seen as 'separatist' and therefore a dangerous step to partition in that it gave the Turks administrative control of territory rather than functions.[15] Furthermore, the Turkish areas were poor and in bad condition and since municipal income would mainly have to come from Greek sources the Greeks would have to pay, and they felt the Turks would never be satisfied at the amount they received, so that there would be continual friction.

Two cases bear out the above points. First, the system of separate municipalities in the big towns was to be examined by the president and vice-president within six months of the coming into effect of the constitution. Until agreement on changes was reached, however, the system in force was to be renewed annually. The Greeks called for a unified municipal system with councillors elected on the basis of true ethnic proportions, and rejected a Turkish proposal to extend the old system for a second year. In January 1963 the council of ministers set up 'development boards' to run the towns, but while the Greek municipalities surrendered their powers to the boards, the Turkish municipalities did not. The dispute was taken to the constitutional court, which by the casting vote of its neutral president, declared the Greek 'development boards' invalid.[16] Second, there was the case of the duties and taxes bill. Under the constitution, the laws imposing duties and taxes which were in force before the constitution came into effect were allowed to continue in force until 31 December 1960, in order to give time for the preparation of new laws. But representatives of the two communities could not agree on a new scheme and the taxation laws expired. The government had no authority to collect customs duties and income tax, and government, both central and local, was paralysed. The Greek Cypriots alleged that the Turkish Cypriots had acted in the way they had not because the bill was discriminatory against their community but because they insisted that it ought to have been of a limited duration, so that they would gain another opportunity of exercising the right of separate majorities.[17]

Accordingly, towards the end of 1963 Archbishop Makarios proposed that the Constitution be amended by abandoning the presidential and vice-presidential veto, replacing the principle of separate majorities in the house of representatives by the principle of parliamentary majority, unifying the administration of justice and the municipalities in the big towns, and applying ethnic proportions of four to one in employment in the civil service and the armed and security forces. Furthermore, he proposed that the treaties of guarantee and alliance should be revoked.

He argued that the 1960 constitution 'created many difficulties in the smooth functioning of the state and the development and progress of the country; its many provisions conflicted with internationally accepted democratic principles and created sources of friction between Greek and Turkish Cypriots; and that its defects were causing the two communities to draw further apart rather than closer together'.[18]

In short, what the Greek Cypriots wanted was a completely independent, unitary, integral, sovereign state unfettered by any treaties, and with all the powers emanating from the people, *who would be entitled to decide the future on the basis of the internationally accepted principle of self-determination.*[19] The new constitution should be founded on the principle that the political majority at any election should govern and the political minority constitute the opposition. Elections would be by general suffrage on a common roll; all legislative power would be exercised by a unicameral elected parliament to which the executive power would be answerable; and the judicial power would be invested in an independent unified judiciary.

Human rights would be safeguarded for all persons and entrenched in the constitution. It appeared that what Makarios was contemplating was the guarantee of rights not less than those laid down in the European Convention for the Protection of Fundamental Freedoms and Human Rights of November 1950, to which Cyprus was a party. None the less, all communities and minorities would have complete autonomy in religious matters and certain aspects of personal status such as marriage and divorce and the administration of religious properties. In the realm of education and culture they would also be guaranteed certain rights, but the general responsibility for education would lie with the government. Finally, most amendments to the constitution would require a two thirds majority of the total membership of the parliament.[20]

The Turkish Cypriot attitude was that the whole structure of the Republic rested on the existence of two communities, and not of a 'majority' and a 'minority'. Since the amendments proposed 'were directed against those parts of the Constitution which recognized the existence of the Turkish community as such', the Turkish Cypriots refused to consider any of the amendments.[21]

Both sides had been arming for months, and following the Turkish Cypriot and Turkish government rejection of the Makarios proposals, bitter and bloody communal war broke out. As the Turkish Cypriots were driven into enclaves – the Turkish quarters of the big towns and the countryside between Nicosia and Kyrenia – by the superior numbers of the Greek Cypriots, they appealed to the Turkish government for help. The Greek government stated that if Turkey intervened, Greece would also. Both Greek and Turkish volunteers moved to the island in support of their ethnic brethren. Finally a United Nations peace-keeping force of 7,000 arrived and took up positions between the Turkish enclaves and the surrounding Greek Cypriot forces.

In the areas under their control the Greek Cypriots set up an administration which changed the taxation system, and established unified municipalities and a unified judiciary. Conscription was introduced and a national guard formed. An economic blockade of the Turkish areas was instituted. Archbishop Makarios stated that he was willing to talk with the Turkish Cypriots about majority and unitary rule, but not about partition or federation. In the view of Greek Cypriots the Turkish Cypriots were in a condition of rebellion having designs on the security of the state, and enjoying actual or potential military support from Turkey.

So far as the Turkish Cypriots were concerned, they felt that Greece and the Greek Cypriots would never give up seeking *Enosis*. They noted, for example, that the Greek Cypriots had never taken any steps against those who were trying to upset the constituted order by advocating *Enosis*. They therefore considered themselves to be under siege from the Greek Cypriots, and felt obliged to have recourse to arms to defend the political interests of a people 'who were not a mere minority but a distinct community in their own right'. Recent events had proved the various guarantees insufficient, and thus additional and more effective guarantees needed to be secured. 'These could best be obtained by providing a geographical basis for the state of affairs created by the Zurich and London agreements.... They wished to be physically separated from the Greek community ... through the concept of a federal state.'[22]

The Turkish Cypriots therefore proposed that Cyprus be divided into two communal areas, with themselves occupying some 38 per cent of the country in the northern and eastern part of the island. Some 10,000 Greek Cypriot families there would be exchanged for the same number of Turkish Cypriot families in the other parts of the island. Each of the two areas would enjoy self government for non-federal affairs and could have direct cultural and economic relations with Greece or Turkey as the case might be. To the federal authorities would be reserved foreign affairs, defence, the federal budget, customs, commerce, banking and criminal legislation and jurisdiction. Turkish Cypriots would fill 30 per cent of the posts in the civil service and seats in the house of representatives, 40 per cent in the army and police, and 50 per cent of the seats in a senate that would be established. There would be no *Enosis* and no partition.[23]

Not surprisingly, these proposals were rejected by the Greek Cypriots, who considered separation as a first step to partition, and argued that any compulsory transfer of populations was against the 1948 United Nations Declaration of Human Rights.

The deterioration in the situation caused others to propose solutions. The United States, fearing that Cyprus would become another Cuba, sent former Secretary of State Dean Acheson to mediate in 1964. Acheson proposed an *Enosis* solution, but that Turkey should have an area for a military base and one or two cantons with local autonomy. Greece would cede an island to Turkey in exchange. Greece and the Greek Cypriots rejected the plan on the grounds that it was a variant of partition; Turkey and the Turkish Cypriots rejected the plan because they wanted a much larger area so that the whole of the Turkish Cypriot community could take sanctuary there.

In 1965 the United Nations mediator, Mr Galo Plaza, called for a single Cypriot state with iron-clad guarantees for the Turkish community (including autonomy in religious, educational and personal matters, the contents of the European Convention on Fundamental Freedoms and Human Rights in the constitution, and representation of Turkish Cypriots in governmental institutions), and denounced the existing constitution and the treaties of guarantee and alliance. This plan was, of course, supported by the Greek government and the Greek Cypriots, and denounced by the Turkish government and the Turkish Cypriots.

Stalemate continued for some years, but as relations between the communities slowly improved talks began in 1968 on the establishment of a more equitable constitutional arrangement. But no agreement was reached: the Greek Cypriots continued to seek a unitary state, while the Turkish Cypriots continued to seek some form of federation. In 1971 General Grivas returned to Cyprus to begin another terrorist campaign for *Enosis* against Archbishop Makarios. In 1974 Grivas died and Archbishop Makarios ordered a purge of all EOKA sympathizers from the police and civil service, accusing the Greek government of subversion. The Greek Cypriot national guard, under the control of Greek officers, staged a *coup d'état* against the archbishop. At the invitation of the Turkish community a Turkish army of 40,000 landed in Cyprus to prevent the Greek Cypriot national guard from taking over the island. The Turkish army occupied the northern and eastern third of Cyprus, the main areas of economic strength in the country. This has enabled the Turkish Cypriots to establish a *de facto* government, which has begun to plan the development of an economically and politically independent sector, supported by Turkey. Two hundred thousand Greek Cypriots fled from the sector, and many still live in refugee camps in the other part of the island.

The subsequent negotiations between the two communities suggest that the solution desired by the Turkish Cypriots and brought about by the Turkish army will, in the end, become permanent, with the only issue still at stake being the size of the area under their control. Certainly it is impossible to envisage the Turkish Cypriots agreeing to return to their enclaves or even to their original homes. *De facto* population transfer has therefore won the day.

The single most important factor in the Cyprus question is the degree of external influence in the course of developments. It was the principle of union with Greece – *Enosis* – that guided the majority Greek Cypriot revolt against Britain. It was the non-consummation of this wish, at the behest of Greece and Turkey for their own reasons, that has caused *Enosis* to lie so close to the surface that Turkish Cypriots have felt the gravest concern whenever Greek Cypriots have talked of independence and the unitary majority state. It is this lack of faith that has driven Turkish Cypriots to seek security through separation in a federated state.

But to what extent do the Greek Cypriots, in fact, now wish for *Enosis*? There can be no doubt of the strength and sincerity of this wish before the founding of the republic in 1960. But did it decline thereafter? The Turkish Cypriot information office has provided a document replete with statements by Archbishop Makarios from 1960 to 1974 approving or promising *Enosis*.[24] And in 1965 the UN mediator wrote that the demands of the Greek Cypriot community for the right of self-determination required certain clarifications:

> Its leaders have indicated that the exercise of the right of self-determination should be taken in the sense that, once fully independent, it will be for the Cypriot people alone to decide their political status ... and it has been taken to mean a choice by the Cypriot people between continued independence and *Enosis*. But the leaders of the Greek Cypriot community have remained vague both as regards the timing of the referendum and the form of *Enosis*.[25]

Certainly after 1964 an ever increasing number of Greek Cypriots began to see independence as preferable. For one thing, the standard of living in Cyprus is higher than in either Greece or Turkey. For another, there had been increasing unease over political developments in Greece, and this was heightened after the overthrow of the Papandreou government by the Colonels' Junta in April 1967. Third, there were many who preferred the non-aligned status of Cyprus as opposed to joining a country then in NATO, but even now closely involved in cold-war politics. It has been stated on many sides that a majority of Greek Cypriots would today prefer independence to *Enosis*. And many believe that the 1974 *coup* was organized in order to break up what appeared to be the growing consolidation of the republic of Cyprus through the decrease in tension and the vastly improved standard of living, especially of the Turkish community. The Turks believe that Archbishop Makarios sought to break the existing structure of the Cyprus republic with his 1963 proposals, before it could take root. Then *Enosis* would have been easier and, at least at that time, would have probably been supported by the majority of the Greek Cypriot population.

Naturally Makarios had to tread warily. For even as within Cyprus itself the strength of the *Enosis* movement declined, Greek influence in the island (especially in the national guard) remained high, and *Enosis* is a factor in Greek domestic politics. The Zurich and London agreements of 1959 were signed by the prime minister of Greece, Mr C. Karamanlis, who returned to power after the overthrow of the Colonels in 1974. But from 1963 to 1967 the prime minister was Mr A. Papandreou, whose government was pledging *Enosis*. Matters did not go further at that time, ostensibly because Archbishop Makarios failed to make clear the terms under which he would accept *Enosis*. The real reason was simply that the international situation would not permit it. And Greece is not in a position to impose its will. If Greek Cypriots outnumber Turkish Cypriots by four to one on the island, the balance of power in the event of Greek intervention lies with Turkey. Cyprus is forty-five miles from Turkey, over 500 miles from Greece. The Turkish army numbers 400,000 men; Greece can only put 150,000 into the field.

However, the danger is that the Cyprus issue will always offer an easy field for hard-line foreign policy initiatives by a Greek government should it wish to increase its standing after failures on the home front. This the Greek Colonels' regime found to the cost of itself and the Greek Cypriots. For Turkey, matters are rather different. Since Cyprus is represented at the international level overwhelmingly by Greek Cypriots (and almost entirely so since 1964), Turkish Cypriots must rely on the Turkish government to air their grievances and obtain their rights. Thus close Turkish Cypriot–Turkish cooperation is mandatory in a way that Greek Cypriot–Greek cooperation is not.[26] But if the Turks will not tolerate *Enosis* and will insist on partition, *faute de mieux*, that does not mean to say that they want the destruction of the Cyprus republic. Partition would create yet another frontier with Greece. That is why it is preferred to have a federated state with two zones, in one of which the Turkish Cypriot population would be safely out of the reach of the Greek Cypriots and more easily supported by Turkey.

The province of Quebec

Canada is a federal state with a population, according to the 1971 census, of 21,568,310. Of these, 9,624,115 (nearly 45 per cent) are of British origin. Some 4,500,000 (21 per cent) are of migrant stock from Germany, Austria, Italy, Holland, Poland, the Baltic States, the Ukraine and Scandinavia, as well as Jews and native Eskimos and Indians who have almost all adopted English as their language in Canada. There are also 6,180,120 French-speaking Canadians (nearly 29 per cent). These, therefore, find themselves in a minority not only in Canada, but also in the English-language-dominated North American sub-continent with its 234 million inhabitants. Of these French Canadians 4,759,370 (77 per cent of the total) live in one of the ten provinces and two territories that make up the federal state of Canada – the province of Quebec. An additional 1,420,750 French Canadians live scattered throughout Canada, but mostly in the provinces bordering on Quebec (737,360 in the province of Ontario, where they form nearly 10 per cent of the population; 235,025 in the province of New Brunswick, where they form 37 per cent of the population). Within the province of Quebec, French-speaking Canadians form nearly 80 per cent of the population; English-speaking Canadians of British origin form some 10 per cent of the population, and the remaining 10 per cent come from migrant stock, with three out of five of the latter opting for the English language. The vast majority of the English-speaking population of the province live in the city of Montreal, where they form some 30 per cent of the population.

Like the Turkish population in Cyprus, the French Canadians do not consider themselves a minority but one of the two founding nations of Canada, alongside the British. The latter took over French Canada in 1760 during the Seven Years War against France, following the defeat of the French forces by General Wolfe outside Quebec city the previous year. However, it was not until more than a century later that Canada obtained the constitution which has guided the nation ever since. It was in 1867 that the British parliament passed the British North America Act (the BNA Act). This listed the separate powers of the federal and of the individual provincial parliaments. In some cases these powers overlap, and the exact division of competences has often been the subject of controversial interpretation. For example, under Article 91 (iii) the federal parliament is responsible for the raising of money by any mode or system of taxation. But under Article 92(ii) the province may impose direct taxation in order to raise revenue for provincial purposes.

Welfare was not a subject that preoccupied the founding fathers of the Canadian federation, but it became of increasing importance in the twentieth century. In 1940 the BNA Act was amended to give the federal parliament powers in regard to unemployment insurance. In 1951 a new article was adopted giving the federal parliament the right to legislate in regard to old-age pensions, provided that no such law should affect the operation of provincial laws in the matter. In 1964 this was extended to supplementary benefits, including survivors' and disability benefits. The provinces also received jurisdiction over property, civil rights, justice and education. The Act also guaranteed the use of the French and English language in Federal parliament and courts, and in the parliament and courts of Quebec. One feature of the Act was that it contained no amending clause, with the result that parts of the Act can only be amended by the passage of an ordinary act of the Westminster parliament. However, in 1949 the latter passed an act enabling the parliament of Canada to amend the BNA Act except as regards (among other things) provincial matters and subjects, and constitutional guarantees regarding education and the use of the French and English languages.

A second feature of the Act was that all powers not explicitly given to the provinces reside with the federal government. However, because of wide interpretations being given to Article 92(xiii) of the Act, the provinces have gained a considerable increase in powers at the expense of the federal government, especially as regards new fields that have recently been made available for action and control by governments, such as the regulation of intraprovincial production, trade, marketing, wages, hours of labour, industrial disputes, trade union legislation, health regulation and insurance legislation.[27]

From 1870 until 1930 the relative position of the French Canadians as an ethnic and cultural entity in Canada declined. First, there was the migration factor. The overwhelming mass of new immigrants that swarmed into Canada were either of British origin or adopted English rather than French as their language in Canada. The result was that as the rest of Canada became Anglicized, the small French-speaking minorities in the other provinces found it ever harder to resist cultural assimilation, and so the French Canadian element was driven in upon itself.[28] Second there was the French Canadian attitude to industry. There was a general cultural resistance in French Canada, led by the Roman Catholic clergy, to industrial and urban life, with the result that the industrial sector in Quebec became dominated by British and American firms, in which, of course, the English language was essential for success. Under the influence of the Catholic church, French Canadians came to regard agriculture and possession of the soil as the best means of conserving their ethnic identity. Industrial and city life was seen as Anglo-Saxon, secular and materialistic, whereas life on the land was considered more spiritual and Christian.[29] Unfortunately, in the second half of the nineteenth century the province of Quebec had the highest birth rate in the world, but the efficient arable lands had been largely occupied. The choice of emigration either to the melting-pots of the United States or to Anglophone Canadian cities imperilled the French Canadians as a cultural community.[30] Third, experience showed that when issues divided Canadians along linguistic lines (for example, the 1885 northwestern rebellion and conscription in the First World War) Anglophone Canadians were always in the majority and could control decisions in the federal capital, Ottawa.

In 1936 a political party with no federal affiliations – the Union Nationale – came to power in Quebec. Quebecois looked to it to defend *la survivance* – the survival of French Canadianism. French Canadians came to identify more than ever 'nation' and 'province'. With two short intermissions, the Union Nationale ruled the province for over thirty years. It was also a clerical, anti-labour party, but while resisting Anglophone Canada in the shape of the federal government at the front door by vigorously defending provincial rights, it opened the back door to 'foreign' (that is, American) capital. There were two results. On the one hand, because industrial and urban growth was being carried out by the investment of non-French Canadian capital, class lines and national lines tended to coincide. On the other, Quebec was behind hand in adopting the social welfare policies that make a modern industrial society acceptable to the mass of people who live in it without owning much of it.[31] At the cultural level there was an almost complete separation between French and English Canadians. Neither read each other's books or newspapers. Anglophone students took courses on British and American history but not on French Canadian history. Francophone students studied Canadian history largely in relation to the survival question.[32] In 1963 only 12 per cent of the Canadian population declared itself as bi-lingual. The proportion of inter-marriages in Quebec was low.

But by the mid-1960s a new French Canadian middle class was coming into being. Instead of entering the traditional Quebec professions of the law, medicine, and the church, young people were entering business, engineering and the social sciences. They discovered that they had to adopt the culture of the dominant Anglophone minority. It had originally been thought that if French Canadians controlled their own language (by being given powers in relation to education), had powers to issue their own laws, and could practise freely their own religion, then their survival would be guaranteed. Yet economically and socially, Quebec was becoming assimilated with the rest of north America. If this assimilation was to be resisted, then new weapons would be needed. This is the background that has caused almost all French Canadians to wish to control their own destiny, a wish that has come to imply an independent Quebec state or the establishment of a far looser association with the rest of Canada than that contained in the 1867 BNA Act.

Turning their backs on their nineteenth-century beliefs, the new generation of French Canadians has seen economic and industrial power and progress as the key to cultural survival. In order to bring this power and progress about, French Canadians believe that it is vital that the whole power of the state (the province of Quebec) be controlled by them and directed by them. And for this it is necessary to loosen the shackles they consider the BNA Act has cast round the province. For example, to expand economically, reform education, and extend welfare benefits, money was essential. But the Quebec government found that nearly every source of money was already being tapped by the federal government in Ottawa. It was Ottawa that had the initiative in the field of direct taxation under Article 91 of the BNA Act, and it was Ottawa that thus held the initiative in development policy. What French Canadians wanted, therefore, was such decentralization of powers, resources, and decision-making as to enable them to enjoy full unimpeded control over their own development and destiny. This, however, would mean changing the constitution, the BNA Act of 1867, not merely tinkering with its mechanism but revising it so completely as to raise the very question of the province of Quebec in the Canadian state. At stake, therefore, were three issues, all closely connected – the economic development of the French Canadians along lines chose by them; the cultural protection of their language; and above all, revision of the constitution.

Economic and linguistic reforms
It has been stated that the inadequate division of income between the federal government and the provincial governments is the biggest problem of Canadian federalism.[33] Usually there are both federal and provincial income, corporation and inheritance taxes, with both sides taking an agreed percentage. The province of Quebec is the only province to raise its own taxes. In general, the other provinces have been content to leave it to Ottawa to raise both the federal and provincial taxes and then to pay them back their share. In 1963 a new liberal government of Quebec, no less determined to defend the position of the French Canadians than its Union Nationale rival, demanded an increased percentage of tax revenues, rising to at least a quarter of all income and corporation taxes and all inheritance taxes. If Ottawa refused, then Quebec would take the necessary steps to procure the funds necessary for its own development. And at a provincial conference it was decided to raise the income tax percentage for the prov-

inces so that Quebec's demands were partially satisfied. Since then Quebec has made further gains, especially in the inheritance tax field, but there are many in Quebec who want the province to have complete control of all its sources of revenue.

Since 1957 the income obtained from federal taxes levied in the provinces has been unconditionally redistributed to the provinces in relation to their relative wealth. The three rich provinces of Ontario, British Columbia and Alberta receive nothing, but the province of Quebec has been in receipt of funds that amounted to $450,000,000 in 1972–3. However, the French Canadians claim that at least up to 1967–8 they merely got back from the federal government what they had paid to it.[34]

With respect to regional development, Quebec favours the promotion of suitable 'growth areas'. The province was divided up into ten sub-regions, and industries and services were directed to these with the intention of promoting sub-regional economic activity. Ottawa, on the other hand, tended to look at areas throughout Canada with high unemployment and low growth rates, with the object of giving financial and fiscal advantages to firms going to these 'designated areas' or expanding there. The province of Quebec considered that it was primarily responsible for the development of its own territory. It argued that it was already responsible for resource planning, municipal administration, and the provincial road system. In 1965 the province claimed that a policy of subsidies, the object of which was to create low-salary industries in outlying areas where further industrial development was unlikely, was economically unsound and irreconcilable with provincial objectives. A continual complaint was that the resources of the federal government allowed it to propose and apply practically any policy it wished while the province of Quebec, although considering it had the right ideas, had no money to put them into effect.[35]

In the field of welfare and employment the federal government took the initiative, almost by default, during the years of the Depression and the Second World War, and Quebec is now seeking to regain authority there. Thus, when in 1961 Ottawa sought to establish a coherent system of welfare assistance throughout Canada, with as much unity as possible, Quebec not only put forward its own programme (and had some of its ideas accepted by Ottawa), but claimed primary legislative power in the field of social policy. A cause for controversy was the wording of Article 94A of the BNA Act on old-age pensions and supplementary benefits. Quebec believed that the wording conferred primary legislative power on the provinces. However, the federal government argued that as long as the federal laws did not contradict provincial laws the federal government could legislate and operate even if there already existed a provincial pension and benefit scheme.[36]

One of the most controversial problems centres on cultural protection. On 31 July 1974 the Quebec parliament adopted its Official Language Bill.[37] This act stated bluntly that French was to be the only official language of the province. French was to be the official language of communication between the province of Quebec on the one hand and the federal government and the other Provincial governments on the other, as well as, within the province, between individual persons. However, the public could communicate with the administration in either language. French and English could be used equally in the courts, but judgements in English would have to be translated into French. Company names and labels, advertising, ordinary contracts, labour contracts, and official communications by employers to their personnel must be drawn up in French, with provision for accompaniment by an English translation if necessary.

The Official Language Act repealed a 1969 provincial law under which parents could choose whether their children would be educated in English or French. Immigrant children, speaking neither French nor English, would have to go to French-language schools. English-language schools could continue to operate, but pupils would be required to have a knowledge of spoken and written French. However, English would still continue to be taught in the French-language schools throughout the province. In addition, the province undertook to provide financial incentives to firms adopting programmes to make French their working language – that is, putting on courses in French; employing staff qualified in French; having a 'Francophone presence in management'; carrying on day-to-day dealings with customers and others in French; and having manuals, catalogues, terminology, and communications to the staff in French. English Canadians have noted that although English was a Canadian official language it has no guaranteed status as the language of instruction for English-speaking groups in the province. They claim that the law removes freedom of choice and infringes on basic civil rights.

At the federal level, Ottawa in July 1969 adopted its own Official Languages Act. It proclaimed English and French as the official languages of Canada, and stated that these should enjoy equal status, rights and privileges in every institution of the federal government and parliament. Thus within practical limits, members of the public may address any federal agency orally or in writing in either language and receive a reply in that language. Parliament also provided for a commissioner of official languages, who has the duty of ensuring that in the public service where persons are in contact with the public, hiring and promotion take account of the Act.

In addition, the federal government provides French language courses for Anglophone employees (and vice versa). In order to promote the use of French and employment of French-speakers at all levels within public offices, department and agencies of the federal government have set up French-language units within their own structures. The experiment has been considered very successful.

In Canada, in November 1974, it was estimated that there were some 280,000 federal jobs, 70 per cent of which lay outside the federal capital, Ottawa. For 53,000 of these posts (19 per cent) bi-lingualism was required; 60 per cent required only a knowledge of English; and 13 per cent required only a knowledge of French. It was estimated that bi-lingualism is required in 93 per cent of administrative-class posts, and in 45 per cent of the posts in the federal capital. Some 29 per cent of federal employees work in the province of Quebec, and 70 per cent of these are French-speaking. However, 90 per cent of the Quebec provincial administration is Francophone. It should be noted that nowhere in Canada, either at federal or provincial level, is there provision for the filling of posts according to the system of ethnic (or rather linguistic) proportions.

Finally, the province of New Brunswick has adopted both languages for provincial purposes. And in the (federal) Official Languages Act, in matters under federal jurisdiction, there is provision for the creation of bi-lingual districts anywhere in Canada where the proportion of either English- or French-speaking persons, though in a minority, is at least 10 per cent of the population.[38]

Constitutional revision?
As with Cypriots of Turkish extraction, ethnic preservation is seen by French Canadians in terms of separation, the only important question being the degree of that separation. French Canadians have always seen the Canadian nation as a federation of two cultures, and as with Turkish Cypriots, the concept of 'majority' and 'minority' is rejected.[39] The question French Canadians posed, therefore, was how could a numerical minority come to exercise a power equal to that of the majority?

Amendment of the constitution was not seen as the right answer. For one thing, there was the constitutional doctrine that confederation was founded on agreement between the provinces, and any change in the system would require their unanimous consent. The French Canadians were aware that the Anglophone provinces, especially in the west, were very uneasy over developments in Quebec that looked like breaking up the federation, and could be expected to be hostile to any further loosening of the ties that held the state together. The French Canadians therefore sought a system that would not depend on the good will of those applying it. The French Canadian answer has been to see Quebec not as one province out of ten but as the home of the French Canadian nation and, taking that as the point of departure, to call, in the words of a former Union Nationale prime minister of Quebec, for the transformation of the Canada of ten into the Canada of two. This is the origin of one of the two solutions currently being propounded in Quebec today – the two-nation state, or associated-state theory.

According to this theory, representation by population must be replaced by representation by peoples. Thus the English–French ratio would be two to one. Each 'nation' would be self-governing, with certain powers in foreign affairs, economic planning and natural resources. Both nations would establish a common central government, with general responsibility for foreign and defence policy, international trade, posts and telegraphs, monetary policy, and equalization payments from the rich to the poor sections of the confederation. Both nations should become unilingual. And, as in the case of Cyprus, both sides should have the right of veto. Like Greek Cypriots, English Canadians regard the associated-state theory as contrary to everything that they have been taught about democracy and the traditional belief in majority rule with minority safeguards. In particular, they point out that the right of veto imperils decision-making, especially in the economic field, since every issue would almost inevitably range Anglophone against Francophone Canadians.[40] A more extreme variety of the associated-state theory calls for the two nations to be completely self-governing. However, relations between Quebec and the rest of Canada would be on the basis of a monetary- and customs-union type of common market. Joint committees would decide such matters as external tariffs, freedom of movement for labour, and citizenship.

The second solution proposed is that the province of Quebec should be a completely independent state, deciding for itself the form of its relations with the rest of Canada. At the moment almost all French Canadians in Quebec support the associated-state solution as a minimum programme. The question arises, however, as to whether the partisans of complete separation are not in a majority. Ideologically, the latter may be on stronger ground among the population, but they do not have much parliamentary support; at the practical level the defenders of the associated-state solution are in a better position, and dominate the Quebec parliament.

Conclusion

By and large the South Tyrol question has had a happy outcome; the solution advocated for Cyprus ended in disaster; the situation in Quebec is still in the process of evolution. What have been the factors to note?

First, and without any doubt, the most important conclusion is that external influences must be sufficiently strong to ensure that the rights of the minority are respected and that an equitable solution is brought about and maintained, but that they should not be so strong as to upset the balance reached. There is a chicken-and-egg question in the problem of protection of minorities. It is to decide whether minorities are oppressed because they are potential traitors or whether they are potential traitors because they are oppressed. The spectre here is that of doubt, and the fear it provokes. It is on the removal of external fears that progress in internal majority–minority relations depends.

In the South Tyrol question the frontiers of Austria were laid down in the state treaty, which was signed and guaranteed by the great powers. This immediately put an end to any adventurism in Austrian foreign policy with the aim of annexing the province of Bolzano. It also removed annexation as a meaningful theme in Austrian domestic policy. The fact that the territorial destiny of the province of Bolzano could not be in doubt obliged the South Tyrolese in general to accept the situation, and this in turn powerfully aided the cause of moderation. It cut the ground from under extremists (including terrorist groups) within and outside the province who sought annexation; it made it easier for the South Tyrolese to bargain hard for the rights they considered necessary for their protection, since their negotiating position was rendered more credible; it made it easier for the Italian state to grant concessions; it made it easier for the ethnic groups in the province to concentrate on open cooperative relations.

In Cyprus external forces prevented the healthy development of majority–minority relations. A solution was imposed which did not take into account the wishes of the great majority of the population. In one of the countries imposing the solution there were strong forces that saw that solution as provisional. As a result, the forces for change remained strong, both in Cyprus and Greece. Since there were therefore doubts as to the territorial destiny of the island, the Turkish Cypriot minority concentrated on closed and defensive rather than cooperative relations with the Greek Cypriot majority. And these doubts were also responsible for breeding violence.

Second, and following from the preceding conclusion, the conditions under which a minority is to live in any given area (whether province, region or state) must be worked out by agreement between those who have to live with that agreement. And as much time as is necessary should be allowed to find a solution acceptable to all. The 1948 autonomy statute for the region Trentino–Alto Adige was more or less the brainchild of the Italian government in Rome. The 1960 Cyprus constitution was based on an agreement between the Greek and Turkish governments. The consultations with the South Tyrolese in 1947–8 fell very far short of what was required in such a delicate political, economic, and social situation. The Greek Cypriots could feel quite justifiably aggrieved at the decisions taken over their heads. It is significant that when proper negotiations took place between the South Tyrolese and the Italian government they lasted six years (1963–9). In contrast the Zurich and London agreements were a matter of six months (1958–9), and the 1948 Trentino–Alto Adige autonomy statute took one year to prepare.

No one should doubt that the process of negotiation may, in addition to being long, also be painful, and involve granting concessions that will be seen by extremists and exploited by the media as reversals of fundamental positions or humiliating climbdowns. However, it must be pointed out that it was by granting concessions that a peaceful solution was obtained in South Tyrol, while in Cyprus extreme rigidity played a large part in bringing the country to disaster in 1974. But again it must be stressed that the removal of doubts about the territorial destiny of the area in question is the single most powerful encouragement to the majority to give concessions to the minority in negotiations, as long as the majority is also aware that the loyalty of the minority is often the only card that the latter can bring into play.

Third, the system of checks and balances devised to protect the minority must not be one that can lead to a collapse of the system. The experiences of the three cases under review show how far minority groups wish to remain separate – even physically – from the majority, out of fear either of cultural assimilation through natural economic and social processes or even physical extermination. And it is to be noted that this fear would appear to be justified in the former case of cultural assimilation even when the group is a compact mass with an overwhelming majority on its own soil, as in the provinces of Bolzano and Quebec.

It is interesting that two models of relations between majority and minority have been put forward in the three case studies. In the South

Tyrol model the democratic principle of a parliamentary majority was given full rein, with constitutional guarantees for the German-speaking minority in the Italian state and the Italian-speaking minority in the province of Bolzano, against legislative and administrative acts deemed contrary to the interests of the minority. In South Tyrol this system encouraged a constructive dialogue between majority and minority, and imposed an obligation to understand respective positions and interests.

On the other hand, there is the Cyprus model of community partnership, also strongly supported in Quebec, which relies on the veto for protection. It is defensive in concept and, as the United Nations mediator in Cyprus noted, made the running of the system depend on the renunciation of that veto. But this requires an atmosphere of good faith and good will, which certainly did not exist in Cyprus – precisely because there were doubts concerning the territorial destiny of that island. Nevertheless, as the Cyprus case has shown, and as English Canadians have pointed out, the veto is a dangerous weapon. Psychologically it creates an atmosphere in which the obligation to understand and respect the position and interests of the other side loses its urgency. Practically the veto can be used for purposes which may not be relevant to the issue of minority protection. In either case the veto may well encourage the use of violence. And it must be pointed out in this connection that if French Canadians have seen separation and the veto as the alternative to bargaining because they believe that bargaining might take place in an atmosphere of ill-will, then it cannot be said that the example of its use in Cyprus improved the atmosphere of ill-will already there.

Fourth, it must be noted that power-sharing is, to a very large degree, the practice in all three models. It occurs in South Tyrol and it occurred in Cyprus. In Canada there are always French Canadians in the federal Cabinet. This is not because of the need for the province of Quebec, as such, to be represented, but simply because no political party with ambitions to form the federal government can ignore Francophone public opinion by not competing in Quebec or by not having Francophone representatives in its higher echelons. On the other hand, there have not always been Anglophone ministers in the Quebec government, mainly because few Anglophones have been members of the Union Nationale. Liberal governments, however, have usually had some Anglophone representatives. How the situation will develop in the future cannot be foreseen. The fact that power-sharing worked in South Tyrol but failed in Cyprus demonstrates that success or failure is not linked to that participation as such but rather to the conditions surrounding that participation. However, it must be repeated that representation in local or national government did not imply, either in South Tyrol or in Cyprus, commitment to a joint programme with the majority.

Fifth, the economic and social factor in minority protection must be considered just as important as legal guarantees. Minorities are living organisms. They fear cultural assimilation through the economic and social process. Yet they need to gain economic power both to promote and defend cultural characteristics, and to ensure that they are sufficiently balanced as a group in order to be able to compete with the majority during the continuous and often swift process of social development in the twentieth century. Existing economic and social relations between a majority and a minority must therefore be taken into account. In the South Tyrol question these relations were either not considered or were deliberately ignored at the time the 1948 autonomy statute was prepared. Greek Cypriot indifference to Turkish Cypriot poverty, as well as the Greek Cypriot wish to share development aid between the two communities on the basis of actual ethnic proportions rather than the proportions laid down for the civil service and parliament, have been mentioned as important factors contributing to the collapse of community relations.[41] And in the province of Quebec powers to control their own language and make their own laws were found by the French Canadians to be inadequate for resisting assimilation by the rest of Anglophone North America. It is not surprising therefore, to find that both in South Tyrol and in Quebec the attempt has been made to secure absolute control over the economy with the intention of directing it to defend cultural identity.

Sixth, a solution which accepts the principle of ethnic proportions in public employment yet does not respect the proportions themselves is unlikely to be a happy one. For more is involved in this principle than mere participation in the public service itself. Psychologically, the principle is important since, like power-sharing, it is the outward and visible sign that the minority is participating in and contributing to daily life and has not been left in isolation. Yet if the principle is not applied correctly it will cause at least concern if not downright distrust of the government apparatus. *De facto* it causes discrimination, as in Cyprus, against the majority, and may even lead to incompetence in the administration if posts come to be filled by unqualified persons. But employment in the public service is not only a psychological and administrative factor, it is also an economic and social factor in that jobs are usually well paid, permanent and pensionable. These are not unimportant points in predominantly agrarian and tourist-oriented societies such as South Tyrol and Cyprus. Reference has been made above to the need for minorities to be economically and socially well-balanced. To give minorities more than their fair share in public employment means not only that the majority in that sector will suffer, but also that the minority may come to be unbalanced in other sectors of employment vital to its development.

Finally, it must be said that minorities are very rarely entirely satisfied. In general they would much rather be with their own kind or even independent. Any government of the majority must realize that it can hardly ever hope to satisfy a minority all the time. If it has the legitimate right to demand loyalty from its citizens of the minority, it has the corresponding and necessary duty of responding to the legitimate demands of the minority, however weak or strong that minority may be. Only in this way will it ensure that dissatisfaction does not rise so high that the minority comes to feel that it can only find a response by threatening to withdraw that loyalty.

Notes

This chapter is a shortened version of a paper commissioned for the Northern Ireland
Constitutional Convention, 1975, by the Office of the Chairman.

1 The Ladins, a Romansch speaking group, number some 3 per cent of the province. However, they have always supported the German-speaking South Tyrolese group, and for that reason have been included with them in references to
  that group in the province's economic and political affairs.
2 Alto Adige – the Italian name for South Tyrol.
3 Enjoyment of primary legislative power meant that the regions and provinces
  could issue laws that only had to respect the constitution and international
  treaties. Secondary legislative power meant that the regions and provinces could
  issue laws that also had to respect state laws already in effect.
4 For the full details see A. E. Alcock, *History of the South Tyrol Question* (London,
  1970), pp. 448–9.
5 Including one Ladin member of the party.
6 The agricultural population (overwhelmingly South Tyrolese) numbered 43 per
  cent of the active population in 1951; 31 per cent in 1961, and 20 per cent in
  1971.
7 L. Clerides, *The Demands of the Turkish Cypriot Community since 1955* (Government of Cyprus Printing Office, 1975).
8 *Report by the UN Mediator on Cyprus (Mr Galo Plaza) to the Secretary General,*
  UN Doc. S/6253 of 26 March 1965, paras 17 and 18. (hereafter *Galo Plaza*).
9 S. G. Xydis, *Cyprus – Reluctant Republic* (Paros, Mouton 1973, pp. 43–4, note
  31.
10 *Galo Plaza*, para. 19.
11 R. Stephens, *Cyprus – A Place of Arms* (London, 1966), pp. 157–9.
12 *Galo Plaza*, paras 62, 65.
13 *ibid.* para. 30.
14 J. F. K. Gordon, 'The UN in Cyprus', *International Journal* XIX (1964), p. 331,
  cited in L. B. Miller, *Cyprus, the Law and Politics of Civil Strife* (Harvard
  Occasional Papers in International Affairs, 19, June 1968).
15 See Stephens, pp. 174–6; *Cyprus Past and Present*, pp. 161–3.
16 Stephens, pp. 176–8.
17 *Cyprus, Past and Present*, p. 158.
18 *Galo Plaza*, para. 39.
19 that is, leaving open *Enosis* as a future possibility.
20 *Galo Plaza*, paras 67–9, 63.
21 *ibid.* para. 44.
22 *ibid.* paras 70–72.
23 *ibid.* paras 73–6.
24 *Makarios on Enosis*, Turkish Cypriot Administration, Public Information Office,
  Nicosia, June 1974.
25 *Galo Plaza*, para. 95.
26 Miller, pp. 50–51.
27 R. M. Dawson, *The Government of Canada* (5th edn, Toronto), pp. 89–96.
28 For example, in 1912 the province of Ontario decided that French-speaking
  citizens could only receive education in French at primary level. Much of the
  hostility to French-language schools was due to hostility to Catholicism and
  to clerical influence in provincial affairs. R. Cook, *Canada and The French
  Canadian Question* (Toronto, 1966), p. 36.
29 'We do not want industry or money but to possess the earth, raise large families

and maintain the hearths of intellectual and spiritual life – that is our mission in America.' *ibid.* p. 86.

30 As Lord Durham had already written as early as 1839: 'If French Canadians attempt to better their condition by extending themselves over the neighbouring country they will get more and more mingled with the English population: if they remain stationary the greater part of them must be labourers in the employ of English capitalists. In either case it would appear that the great mass of French Canadians are doomed ... to occupy an inferior position and to be dependent upon the English for employment.' *ibid.* p. 82.

31 *ibid.* p. 11.

32 *ibid.* p. 145.

33 C. Morin, *Le Pouvoir Québecois en négociation* (Quebec, 1972), p. 51.

34 *ibid.* pp. 53, 65–6.

35 *ibid.* pp. 120–22.

36 *ibid.* pp. 118, 144, 151–2.

37 Bill 22, National Assembly of Quebec, 2nd Session, 30th Legislature.

38 Dawson, pp. 38–9.

39 'If force of numbers alone rules the relations between an ethnic majority and an ethnic minority then a common life becomes impossible and only separatism remains.' Cook, p. 52.

40 *ibid.* pp. 51–76.

41 Stephens, p. 173.

13

A reappraisal of existing theory and practice in the
protection of minorities

A. E. Alcock

As with most subjects, there have been times when the study of protection
of minorities has been fashionable, and other times when the topic has
been almost universally ignored. An examination of bibliographies shows
that there was a great interest in the topic – for obvious reasons – in the
first ten years of the League of Nations. Then, with the exception of one
or two works,[1] there followed a silence. At the end of the Second World
War, and for a few years after that, interest picked up again but by 1955
had died away. However, since 1968, activity in the field has again become
intense.

The reason for this development is to be found in the very different
circumstances in which minorities are engaging in their dialogue with
majorities today as compared with twenty-five years ago. Reference has
already been made in chapter 1 to the classic definition of minorities
formulated in 1950 by the United Nations Sub-Committee on the Prevention of Discrimination and the Protection of Minorities, with its guiding
principle that the wish by minorities to preserve their special characteristics should be the basis for protection, since if that wish did not exist
there would be no need for any special measures of protection, and non-
discriminatory treatment for the individual as a citizen of the state would
suffice.[2] But this definition contains an implication that does not appear
to have been fully understood, let alone accepted universally by majorities
– the implication that the wish to preserve these special characteristic is
something on-going, that it continues to take place over time. In other
words, the concept of protection of a minority's special characteristics is
not a static but a dynamic one, involving adaptation to the changes that
take place in the economic, social and political environment in which that
minority lives and moves and has its being. Just what this means can be seen
by an examination of the changes that have taken place in the three areas in
which the majority–minority dialogue has traditionally been engaged.

First, there has been a change in the quality of that protection. Before
the First World War, international instruments such as the Treaty of Paris
(1856), the Treaty of Berlin (1878) and the Treaty of Constantinople (1881)
were concerned that there should be no civil or political discrimination
against citizens on religious grounds in countries or areas in eastern Europe
gaining independence, territory, or autonomy. But between the wars there

was an advance. Under the so-called minorities treaties between the principal allied and associated powers and Poland, Czechoslovakia, Yugoslavia and Rumania (1919), Greece (1920), Turkey (1923), as well as under declarations made by Finland and Albania (1921), Lithuania (1922), Latvia and Estonia (1923) and Iraq (1932) upon becoming members of the League of Nations, certain minorities were granted so-called 'negative' and 'positive' rights in the cultural field. The former were rights similar to those enjoyed by all citizens, such as the right of the minority to use its language in private commerce, press, meeting and religion, and to establish private schools, while the latter referred to special rights granted to the individual members of the minority with the object of helping them maintain and develop their special characteristics. These included the right to use their language on certain public (as opposed to private) occasions, such as in the courts; the right to receive instruction in their own language in state primary schools in those towns and districts where members of the minority formed a considerable proportion of the population; and the right to an equitable share in public funds for educational, religious, or charitable purposes.

However, as a result of the widely held view that the exploitation of the privileged position of German cultural minorities by National Socialism had been an important cause of the Second World War, there was a general reluctance after 1945 to provide minorities with any special 'positive' rights and instead it was considered that all countries should maintain a universal standard of human rights which would provide individual members of a minority with protection against discrimination, and that it should be up to the state concerned to decide whether or not to grant its minorities any special 'positive' rights. Thus the peace treaties with the Axis powers included a general article providing that the country concerned would take all necessary measures to ensure that everyone within its jurisdiction, without distinction as to race, sex, language or religion, enjoyed fundamental human freedoms, including freedom of thought, press, publication, culture, opinion, and meeting. The best known examples of states granting special rights to minorities through national constitutions are the cases of Italy (with respect to the French-speaking population of Val d'Aosta), Cyprus, and Lebanon. Some states have extended special rights to their minorities on the basis of bilateral agreements. For example, the 1921 agreement between Sweden and Finland regarding the Aaland Islands, signed at the same time as the Finnish declaration upon entering the League of Nations, is still in force. More recently the status of Danish-speaking West German citizens in Land Schleswig-Holstein and the status of German-speaking Danish citizens in the province of North Schleswig has been regulated by the Bonn declaration of 29 March 1955. The reversion to the concept of 'negative' rights for protecting minorities was based on the view that a government that violated the basic human rights of its ordinary citizens would in any case be unlikely to respect special rights for its minorities.[3] And indeed on only four occasions did the great powers intervene to see that states provided special rights for minorities.[4]

Second, there has been a change with regard to what minorities have been seeking in the nature of minority protection. From the prohibition of discrimination on religious grounds before the First World War, to the granting of 'negative' and 'positive' rights in the cultural field between the wars, cultural protection has come now to be accepted, by and large, by most host states, particularly in western Europe. This is certainly the case where the minorities concerned have kin states, and an important additional contributing factor has undoubtedly been the rise of national interdependence in the West, as exemplified by the mutual acceptance of high standards with respect to human rights and cultural values through adherence to such instruments as the Council of Europe's Convention on Human Rights and Fundamental Freedoms of 1950.

This encouragement to settle disputes juridically has greatly reduced the likelihood that minorities will be able to engineer political trouble between states on grounds of cultural discrimination by the host state. The problem has changed today in that minorities are seeking protection for their cultural values less against deliberately hostile actions by the majority in the field of schools and language than against the effects on their culture of natural economic and social developments.

Similarly, even where cultural minorities have no kin state, as is the case with minorities in France, Spain and Britain, and where the struggle is concentrated on gaining the same degree of cultural freedom as has been achieved elsewhere in western Europe, there is the same concern with the effects on their efforts of the natural process of economic and social development.

Third, there has been a change in the locus of protection. Originally it had been the desire of the international community, as expressed by the great powers, to prevent international conflict breaking out because of the transfer of groups of people from the authority of one state to that of another, that had been the departure point for the protection of minorities. Thus, before the First World War it was the great powers that required that the host state should not discriminate against religious minorities as a condition either of its recognition or of acceptance of an increase in its territory. The opportunity was provided for individual great power intervention in case of a breach of obligations by the host state. Then between the wars it was the great powers again that required certain host states to provide their minorities with 'positive' and 'negative' cultural rights either as a condition of their entry into the League of Nations, or as Clemenceau stated in his famous letter to Paderewski, because it was owing to the efforts of the great powers on the allied side that these states owed their existence or increased their territory, and the great powers felt that since the chief burden for the maintenance of peace lay with them it was not unreasonable for them to see that possible reasons for the disturbance of world peace should be removed.[5] The great powers accordingly erected machinery under the aegis of the League of Nations both to deal with petitions from minorities regarding their treatment and to settle disputes between the host and kin states arising out of that treatment.

However, after the Second World War, because of the widespread feeling that minorities should not receive any special rights, that all countries should maintain a universal standard of human rights, and that it should be up to the state concerned to grant its minorities any special rights; and because of the return to the principles of state equality and sovereignty, as expressed by Article 2(vii) of the United Nations Charter, the great powers neither continued the League of Nations' machinery to supervise protection of minorities, nor revised it. Instead, they sought to have the international machinery of the United Nations used to see that individual members of a minority were not subject to discrimination, even though the extent of that organization's capacity to intervene in cases of discrimination by a host state clearly rested with that state itself.[6]

The result of these three changing circumstances is that the degree and form of protection of minorities have come to depend overwhelmingly upon the state just at a time when this form of organization is finding it increasingly difficult to grapple with the complexities of modern life.

By 1955 the period of reconstruction after the Second World War could be said to be over, and since then the world has embarked on a period characterized, in the first instance, by an increasing rate of interdependence of societies. One example of this is the new relationship between suppliers and users of raw materials that has developed with the revolution of rising expectations and the end of colonialism. But this interdependence has been accompanied by rising populations, with the corollary that more jobs, food, housing and energy sources have to be found. As technology has been put to solving the problems involved, so has society become increasingly technologically oriented. This has led to premiums being put on education, to concentrations of human beings in soulless urban concrete conglomerates, and to a great mobility of people, money and skills, as individuals scurry frenetically, frequently changing jobs and homes in order to maximize the advantages of the consumer society. States have responded to these developments, by and large, in two ways.

First, they have tended to gather ever more power into their own hands and to take on ever more responsibilities. This has led to sharp increases in government expenditure, a massive increase in legislation, and a corresponding increase in the number of civil servants to administer it.[7] The end result has been not only an ever increasing government control over all the elements that affect daily life, but also an increase in the number of sectors of life affected by government behaviour.

Second, they have tended to seek the answers to their problems by adopting, as far as possible, simplified and uniform approaches, based on the view that their citizens have the same economic and social aspirations, and that they should therefore be treated on the basis of formal equality. As Patricia Mayo has so eloquently written, for the bureaucrat a uniform society simplified administration, while for too may others – and here she specifically mentioned those on the left of the political spectrum – it was synonymous with social justice.[8]

What has been the attitude of minorities to these developments? Perhaps it might be as well to speak at this moment about those involved. In general about forty million persons in the western industrial world are concerned.

Some eleven million live in four states that acknowledge the multicultural principle as the basis of their political existence – Belgium, Canada, Cyprus and Switzerland. The rest can be divided into three groups – those that have a recognized place and status and enjoy harmonious relations with the cultural majority, such as the Aaland Islanders; those that have a recognized place and status but are only in the process of achieving a satisfactory relationship with the cultural majority, such as the South Tyrolese; and those so-called 'forbidden nationalities', such as Bretons, Basques, and Catalans, who are struggling to keep their heads above the waters of cultural centralism and uniformity.

What has caused the crisis in so many majority–minority relations is that minorities are rejecting the above-mentioned behaviour of states and the principles upon which it is based. From their point of view, they do not wish to be sucked into this government–industrial vortex if there is any possibility of losing their separate characteristics. There is a widespread tendency to think that the existence of different cultures within a nation and the existence of systems to separate these different cultures are divisions which in themselves are a source of conflict, and that cultural assimilation is either desirable or inevitable. But in fact the exact opposite is true. The point about culturally divided societies is that they wish to remain culturally divided. Each group draws the essence of its being, its group consciousness, from the fact that it *is* different and that it *wishes to remain different*. Those who see division as a source of conflict overlook the fact that conflict arises because of threats to the factors which make for that division – threats to the separate identity, characteristics or even existence of the group. These threats may be active (such as physical or cultural genocide or discriminatory legislation), or passive (such as non-recognition of the group, or benign neglect by the majority of the effects on the minority of economic, social or technological change or pressure).[9]

Given the above, these minorities first reject the view that they have the same social and economic problems and aspirations as the cultural majority. Second, they reject the view that they should be treated on a basis of formal equality. And third, they resent the remoteness of modern government, its grasping and all-pervasive nature, and the suffocating bureaucracy that seems to be its inevitable accompaniment.

In the first case, it is clear that the over-riding aim of cultural minorities is to preserve and develop their culture. This is not a primary aim of the majority, whose main concerns are with the politics and economics of the nation as a whole. It is doubtful whether the majority even thinks about the preservation and development of its culture, since it is unlikely to be under attack, and if it were, the majority would have at its disposal all the means to defend it. Furthermore, there is almost always a difference in the economic and social situation of minorities vis-à-vis majorities. Usually minorities are poorer, earning lower *per capita* incomes, with large proportions of their active population coming from declining economic sectors, usually agriculture, such as has been or still is the case with South Tyrolese, Val d'Aostans, Bretons, Basques, French Canadians and, some will say, Scots, Welsh, and Catholics in Northern Ireland. Yet there is an example of a minority – the Catalans – who are better off than the rest of the country. The object of those in the poorer group is to pull themselves up to parity with the majority and to see that their relatively backward economic and social position does not have adverse effects on the attempt to preserve and develop their cultural distinctiveness. On the other hand, the Catalans are complaining that their richer area is being plundered in order to help prop up the rest of Spain. It is important to realize that the two issues – preservation of culture and economic and social capacity – are related to a degree that majorities have not really understood or taken much care to examine.

The fact of the matter is that it is upon a minority's cultural power that its ability to express and maintain an identity distinct from that of the majority depends. But what is the source of cultural power? And is it right to talk in terms of 'power' at all? There are many – particularly from the cultural majority – who will argue that it is quite wrong to talk of 'power' when referring to the culture of minorities and that separate cultural identity can be quite adequately assured by the building of the appropriate programmes to foster cultural difference – with teaching in the mother tongue, publication of newspapers, books and journals as well as broadcasting and television in the language of the minority, the restoration and maintenance of objects of historical and archival interest, and the promotion of folkloristic activities (usually for the benefit of tourists). The corollary is that it is immaterial whether these facilities are controlled by the majority or the minority.

According to this view all that is needed is toleration of the minority culture: the institution of the appropriate cultural instruments will do the rest. Only a little thought is needed for one to realize that this cannot by itself be sufficient. If it is true that the culture of a minority is the outward expression of a community or group of individuals which is conscious of having an identity different from that of the majority group in the state, it is equally true that the will to retain such a separate identity – the fount from which all minority protection flows – implies that the aspirations of the majority and minority will also be different. They may share – or have been forced to share – the same political framework, but this does not mean that they share a common destiny – an assumption all too blithely accepted by the majority. On the contrary, it is precisely the feeling of members of the minority that they have a different destiny that is the mainspring of the will to retain their separate identity. Thus the destiny of a minority is not linked solely to its ability to speak its language but also to its ability to maintain itself as a group – and that means politically, economically, and socially – vis-à-vis the host state. The two factors are complementary, and cultural minorities, like the French Canadians and the German-speaking South Tyrolese discussed in the previous chapter, are only too aware that failure to maintain themselves politically, economically and socially can lead to erosion of cultural identity.[10] Cultural power may therefore be expressed as the ability of a culture to maintain itself in a world of rapid social and technological change. This means that a cultural minority must be able to develop itself at least so as to keep pace and compete with the host state majority at the economic and social level, and this in turn means that when one talks of 'protection' of minorities it is not merely a question of introducing measures that would 'preserve' minorities, like flies in amber, but of ensuring that their ability to develop their cultural characteristics as they wish in response to the changing environment is an inherent parts of the 'protection' process.

Second, cultural minorities are rejecting the idea of formal equality with the majority. Here a distinction must be made between equality in law and equality in fact. As the Permanent Court of International Justice declared in its advisory opinion in 1935 in the case of the minority schools in Albania:

> For minorities to live on equal terms with the majority it would be necessary for them to have the juridical, social, economic, and cultural institutions to allow them to cultivate and develop their own language and culture under the same conditions as the majority. . . .
> Equality in *law* precludes discrimination of any kind, whereas equality in *fact* may involve the necessity of different treatment in order to attain a result which establishes an equilibrium between different situations.[11]

In the case in question, the Albanian government had closed down all private schools in the country and argued that since this applied to the private schools of the Albanian majority and the Greek minority alike, no discrimination was involved. In its opinion, which was adopted by eight votes to three, the court held that the Albanian government's action was incompatible with Article 5 of the declaration of the Albanian government on entering the League of Nations, that Albanian nationals belonging to racial, religious, or linguistic minorities should 'enjoy the same treatment and security in law and in fact as other Albanian nationals'. The three dissenting judges argued that were the Greek minority to have the right to keep their private schools open, which was unconditional and independent of that enjoyed by others, it could not be described as equal. Was the intention of the declaration therefore to grant to the minority an *unconditional* right to maintain, and establish these schools? The court, in its opinion, answered this question in the affirmative. The reason is easy to find. Whereas the Albanian government was quite free to decide on the measures necessary for the maintenance of the majority culture, the Greek minority did not have that same freedom. Therefore the cultivation and development of their language and culture could not 'take place under the same conditions as the majority', and different treatment would be needed to bring those same conditions about.

After the Second World War the same problem of the meaning of equality arose in South Tyrol. In their memorandum to the Italian government in April 1954, the South Tyrolese leaders stated that for the protection of minorities one needed equality, but this equality must be more than formal. It must also be effective, and this meant that the minority should have the faculty and possibility of satisfying its own interests, and spiritual, cultural, economic, administrative and political needs with means as effective as those used by the majority.

The memorandum continued with these immortal words:

> There is no greater inequality than to treat equally unequal things. Therefore special laws to protect a minority are not privileges but measures to create this material equality between majority and minority.

The South Tyrolese pointed out that the Italian constitution provided in Article 6 for the protection of minorities through special measures. Furthermore certain general constitutional rights, such as free private property and the movement of the citizen in the territory of the republic, could be limited when a higher interest demanded it.[12]

Third, there is the resentment of distant government, so often unresponsive to local needs, and resentment of the bureaucracy that seems to stand between government and people, applying policies, plans and laws of little relevance to the local community. Since so many minorities come from the poorer regions of host states, two causes, economic and social protection of minorities to strengthen their cultural characteristics, and economic and social development of backward regions so as to improve living standards and GNP of the nation as a whole, come to be linked. However, all too rarely does the central government's approach take into account the danger of the latter to the former and seek to reconcile the two. All too often the government's approach is based on equalitarianism and uniformism in the interest of equality of standards. In Britain, for example, central government is reluctant to permit autonomy at regional level in case it should lead to geographic variations in social and economic standards and the provision of public services.[13]

Thus Scottish and Welsh nationalists have criticized Westminster's uniform management of the economy on the grounds that when the southeast of the United Kingdom was fully employed economic expansion had to stop, although there was still considerable unemployment in Scotland and Wales. They therefore called for revenue-raising and expenditure powers to stimulate the economy at the regional level and thus help iron out regional disparities, but it was argued that although this idea was attractive to many economists, 'there are thought to be political difficulties in increasing further ... disparities in public expenditure *per capita*, and it also thought that it would be unacceptable to the majority of people if taxes are to be charged at different rates in different parts of the United Kingdom'.[14]

Nevertheless, discussion of such points as the role of economic and social factors in cultural viability, the need to be able to compete against the majority, and the need not for non-discrimination, but rather for positive discrimination in the treatment of minorities, raises further questions. For example what is the source of that cultural power upon which the ability to compete successfully against the majority depends? What evidence is there that formal equality in the treatment of minorities is not enough? And if minorities are resentful at developments, what is their answer?

The time has come to tie up these loose ends and answer these questions through examination of something which has tended to be overlooked in the consideration of minority problems, namely, the land upon which the minority dwells – its homeland. The chief importance of the homeland is that it is directly related in two ways to the minority's economic power, and it is upon economic power that the minority's cultural power depends.

First, most old-established cultural minorities in Europe, with the exception of Jews and gypsies, have a homeland. They may be a majority in that homeland or even a minority there, but in either case that area is the land upon which they and their ancestors have lived for centuries. That land, and the natural resources contained therein, is their economic heritage. Agricultural, industrial, touristic, or a combination of these, it is, for better or worse, for richer or poorer, the motor for their cultural power and the motor upon which will depend their ability to keep pace with the majority, resist the latter's economic and social pressures and survive the challenges of natural economic and social development.

But if power is expressed by the combination and mobilization of resources, and it is the cultural majority that controls resources, then the cultural majority also controls the life chances of the minority, especially the terms on which the minority has access to resources, jobs, education and wealth. In that the minority will thus be dependent on the majority for the rate at which it develops, the direction in which it develops, and the level of development it attains, it can be said that the relationship between majority and minority will be like a colonial one.[15]

If the natural resources contained in the land upon which the minority dwells are also of significance to the nation as a whole, then the likelihood is that there will be competition between the majority, representing the state and the national interest, and the minority, for those resources. This has created problems, for example, in Canada, where separatism is casting its shadow over the province of Quebec, which is particularly rich in natural resources, thus making it vital not only to the Canadian but also to the international, and in particular North American, economy. The issue of Scottish claims to the oil lying off its shores, under the North Sea, needs no further elaboration here. Brittany and South Tyrol have sources of hydro-electric power that are important to national industrial development and have been issues in disputes with Paris and Rome respectively. In addition to large coal deposits, Wales exports 440 million gallons of water daily to the Midlands of Britain, but this water is controlled by the (national) Severn–Trent authority. And if geographical features can be considered important natural resources in that they provide the basis for tourism, an increasingly important source of national income, then South Tyrol, Val d'Aosta, Brittany, Scotland, Wales, and Quebec all have additional significance.

This in turn raises the question of the ability of the minority to defend its land, and brings us to the second way in which this is related to the minority's economic power – namely the technical ability to make use of that power, its social composition. For in order both to exploit the resources of the homeland and to keep pace and compete with the majority, the minority must be sufficiently flexible in its social composition. That is to say, it must be balanced in order to meet the demands of the local economy, and this point should be taken in connection with one made earlier, namely that all too often cultural minorities come from the poorer regions of the state, those suffering from sectoral decline, usually in agriculture. The issues, in this kind of situation, are two: how are those leaving the one sector to be absorbed into other sectors so as to avoid emigration by members of the minority? And how can immigration by members of the majority to take up employment in those sectors where the minority is unrepresented be avoided?

These issues will be referred to later on, but in the meantime, since one of the pillars of minority protection is that the minority in question must have the will to preserve itself in order to benefit from protection, it is not surprising that this will can be translated as a determination not to be involved in a colonial situation, not to rely on the majority for the rate, direction, and level of its development, but rather to take charge of its destiny and control these factors itself. Consequently if the sources of a minority's cultural and economic power, namely its homeland and social composition, begin to be eroded, then tensions between the minority and the host state will become acute. But what has so far been underestimated is the degree to which the principle of equality of human rights and non-discrimination, particularly in the economic field, contributes to the process of erosion.

Two examples, both in the field of employment, spring to mind. The first of these is liberty of movement, and freedom to choose one's place of residence. Not only is this right enshrined in most national constitutions, it is also contained in Article 13 of the (non-binding) Universal Declaration of Human Rights; Article 12 of the United Nations Covenant on Civil and Political Rights; and Protocol 4 of the European Convention on Human Rights. Liberty of movement and residence in order to take up work anywhere in the Common Market is laid down in Article 48 of the Treaty of Rome. This means that in most states, and in any country ratifying the above-mentioned binding instruments, members of the cultural majority will have the right to go and live and seek work in the homeland of a cultural minority.

The reason for such immigration may be entirely honourable – to participate in the expansion of a sector of the economy in the area, or to participate in the development of an entirely new sector, such as the exploitation of newly discovered raw materials. But as previously mentioned, if the minority does not have the manpower, skilled or otherwise, or the finance, to participate in that development, then the vacuum will be filled by members of the majority. This highlights the importance of vocational education and technical skill and the need for social flexibility, since the danger that members of the majority swarming into the minority's homeland will upset its ethnic and cultural nature is very real and has ample precedent – the encouragement of German immigration into mainly Danish Schleswig-Holstein and the Polish duchy of Posen in the 1860s, and the Italian immigration into the Istrian peninsula, South Tyrol and Val d'Aosta, encouraged for denationalization purposes between the wars.

On the other hand, a minority that has no control over the economic forces in its land nor social flexibility may see itself weakened by emigration, especially if facilities for retraining those leaving declining sectors are not adequate. Whether through immigration of members of the majority or emigration of members of the minority, it will be increasingly difficult to defend the homeland, and the danger – particularly applicable to areas of mixed population – is that the population of the minority will decline to such an extent that its position in terms of local politics and government will be adversely affected. Indeed, there is little that a minority views with greater concern than being turned into a minority even in its own homeland.

The second example of equality of human rights eroding the minority culture in the homeland occurs in the public administration. In almost all national constitutions, in the Universal Declaration of Human Rights and in the United Nations Covenant on Civil and Political Rights, the principle is established of equality in access to employment in the public administration, although, interestingly, this principle is not mentioned in the European Convention on Human Rights. Public administration of a minority's homeland is, of course, more than a question of mere administration. It has cultural, economic and social significance. Culturally, members of the minority wish to see their own kind administering their land. They wish to be able to use their own language in speech and in writing when communicating with the public authorities and when receiving replies. Economically, employment in the public service is important since it provides jobs – relatively well paid, secure and pensionable jobs. This is crucial if the minority as a whole is economically worse off than the majority. Socially, in that the public service provides jobs, it is an important element in providing the employment balance the minority needs in order to obtain the necessary flexibility.

For all these reasons minorities prefer to see the principle of proportional representation used in the public service, and that this should apply not only to the local government of the homeland but also to jobs in those branches of the central or federal government that have their offices in the homeland. The problem is that the principle of proportional representation is difficult to equate with that of equality of rights, and offends against the principle of merit when it comes to recruitment and promotion. The resentment and political difficulties this has caused in, for example, Cyprus, have already been referred to.[16] On the other hand, it will be difficult for members of cultural minorities to get jobs at all, particularly at higher career levels, if, with their often very small percentage of the total national population, their candidates have to compete on terms of equality against candidates from the whole country. They argue therefore that the only way to ensure that their candidates obtain places would be to reserve a certain percentage for them.

Another aspect of this problem is that civil servants are often transferred during the course of their career to other parts of the country, especially the national capital. Minorities are therefore keen to see that members of their group employed in the civil service, with the obvious exceptions of the ministries of external affairs and defence, are kept *en poste* in the homeland. This particularly applies to the police. However, the fact remains that the principle of proportional representation in the public administration is hardly accepted anywhere, although it is applied in some areas, notably in South Tyrol and Val d'Aosta, with respect to local government. At present efforts are being made in South Tyrol to get it accepted with respect to national administrations with offices in the South Tyrolese homeland, the province of Bolzano, such as the state railways and the post and telegraph service, but the difficulties involved have not been negligible.[17]

The vulnerability of minorities to these kinds of situation has not really been helped by a line of defence based on the ideas that minorities have a right to their homeland (*Recht auf die Heimat* or *droit au sol ou foyer natal*); that minority groups should be protected as such, rather than as previously, through rights being granted to the individuals that make up the group; and that their existence in their homeland should be 'untroubled'. Behind this last word lies the issue of 'self-determination'. The reason why this defence is not effective is that the attempt is being made to give these ideas a legal basis. The advocates are mainly German and Austrian jurists – for reasons which will become apparent later. But the arguments deployed have not been generally accepted, and the results have been confusing and unsatisfactory. The point of departure is that the homeland is seen as the area where the individual is rooted from birth, the country of his ancestors, where he lives in a cultural community, sharing the same spiritual patrimony. And it is argued that this homeland would have no legal importance if it were not recognized as the basis for rights of residence on the ancestral land, with the citizenship that flows from it. And here the right of residence is considered as the individual right of domicile. This question should now be examined from the individual and group point of view.

According to the same Article 13(ii) of the non-binding Universal Declaration of Human Rights referred to earlier, the individual's right of emigrating and returning to his or her country by domicile is postulated. This principle has been reinforced by the Fourth Protocol to the European Convention on Human Rights and Fundamental Freedoms, adopted in 1963, in which it is laid down that no one should be expelled from or prevented from entering the territory of a state of which he or she is a national, and that anyone lawfully on the territory of a state has the right to move freely and choose his or her place of residence. This then fixes the right of the individual to go and live on his ancestral soil. On the other hand, it has been argued that ethnic groups are the only groups that can speak of an inherited homeland, because they are the only ones to be able to base their claim on natural factors, and independent of the will of the individual. The fear here is that with expulsion or dispersion of the ancestral inherited community, the cultural or religious community is destroyed, and *vice versa*: the destruction of the cultural or religious community leads to the destruction of the ancestral, inherited community.

However, does the group as a whole have a legal right to its homeland? One answer is that the right can be made through the collective individual claims to residence rights of the members of the group. Nevertheless it has not yet been accepted in international law that groups, as opposed to individuals, have legal personality, although there is a slow movement in this direction. The point at issue, however, is not so much the right of minorities to go and live in their homeland, but the effect on these minorities when members of the majority go and live there too.

The next stage in the argument is that the right to live in one's homeland is only one aspect of that right, and that in order to be effective this residence must be 'untroubled'. This has been interpreted to mean more than just the existence of a state of non-discrimination against the individual and the group, and respect for international agreements, conventions and declarations on human rights in the cultural field in the homeland, but also that the subject should be protected in law and fact against any discriminatory measures in the fields of education, employment, professional activity, housing and information. But, it must again be said, danger now arises from the fact that minorities may be placed at a disadvantage not from discrimination but from non-discrimination.

The difficulties and contradictions involved in this line of argument become even more apparent when one proceeds to the third and final stage – the claim that the right of ethnic groups to their homeland will only be assured if they are in a position to give themselves a social and political status. In other words, the right of these groups to their homeland is the basis of their right of self-determination. And here it is particularly emphasized that the right of self-determination is the right that all peoples possess to decide upon all statutory measures necessary for the maintenance of their ethnic character and their cultural and economic development. It is equally firmly denied that the right of self-determination is *ipso facto* a right to separation, although it is a call for that degree of autonomy – full or partial, legislative or administrative – necessary to ensure the task in hand, and depending on the degree of culture and civilization of the group in question.

It has also been made quite clear that when one refers to the self-determination of 'peoples' this includes ethnic groups. For example, it has been held – with specific reference to the Potsdam decisions of 2 August 1945 to deport the German-speaking communities of Poland and Czechoslovakia – that the right of any state or government to deport whole peoples resident on their territory without a plebiscite contradicts the right of self-determination of peoples, and of course the right to the homeland. Deportation of the Crimean Tartars is another case that may be mentioned.[18]

Two difficulties immediately spring to mind in considering these arguments. The first is the contradiction that has formed the subject of this chapter, between 'non-discrimination' and the claim that ethnic groups should have the right to decide upon all statutory measures necessary for the maintenance of their ethnic character and their cultural and economic development. The second concerns the fact that up to now only whole peoples, and not fractions of peoples or ethnic groups, have been recognized as having the right to self-determination. As has been stated elsewhere, if the principle of self-determination of peoples is laid down in Article 55 of the United Nations Charter, in order to speak of a right there has to be a legal definition of that right, and such a definition is contained neither in the Charter nor in any official United Nations document.[19]

On the other hand the most recent argument in favour of granting rights of self-determination to ethnic groups adopts the line that if one accepts the concept of nation as an ethnic rather than a statal or political entity, one can see that there is no difference between the ethnic nation and the ethnic group of the same nation except in regard to numbers and the political territories on which the two live apart. Therefore if the right of self-determination is granted to the ethnic nation as a whole, the same right should be extended to the various groups that are members of that nation.[20]

In conclusion, it can be said that a leading cause of tension between majorities and minorities is the rejection of the idea that minorities have a right to their homeland because neither the personality of the group nor the link binding ethnic groups to past and future generations is recognized. Minorities are much afraid of the view expressed, for example, by Italian jurists that the protection of minorities cannot constitute an absolute value because it would conflict with other aims set out in the national constitution, such as protection of the right to work, and of the need to carry out the economic and social development of depressed areas. Indeed the view of the Italian school is that protection of minorities is not an absolute value but only one among many that needs to be examined and compared in the search for a generally acceptable solution, and that therefore the possibility should not be excluded that cultural and linguistic values might have to give way to others. Furthermore, even if a cultural minority obtained an autonomy, the fact that the territory of the autonomous area corresponded to that inhabited by the minority should not imply any recognition of rights on the territory in favour of the minority.[21]

A second cause of tension stems from the problems involved in trying to find legal solutions to economic and social problems, especially when the arguments deployed are neither firmly anchored nor generally accepted. Of course, it can be said that a start must be made somewhere if, one day, these arguments are to be accepted, but the problem is that when the legal approach is adopted, there is a temptation to believe that any juridical decision reached is final. Thus, for example, in the South Tyrol question the Italians were convinced that they had a cast-iron legal case for the way they handled the problem – a conviction strengthened by Austrian reluctance to submit some of the differences in interpretation of the international agreements involved to the International Court. Indeed this reluctance, and the fact that the dispute seemed to continue interminably, appeared to be proof that instead of doing the honourable thing and withdrawing, the other side was bent on political mischief with the object of bringing about secession of South Tyrol from Italy. But even if the case had been submitted to the International Court, and even if Austria had lost, none of the fine legal victories of the Italian government would have solved any of the problems involved in the efforts by a cultural minority to attain the degree of economic and social power and flexibility that would enable it to compete against the majority, and preserve its special characteristics in the face of economic and social development and technological progress.

At heart, therefore, the problem of protection of minorities is not one minorities accept as being related to cultural matters only, but concerns also their right to develop along their chosen path. They see that right as including the right to the degree of political power needed to see that this process evolves effectively. But even behind the issue of political power stands another far more fundamental question, which may guide politicians and administrators and businessmen in their dealings with minorities: and that is the question whether these minorities are not merely citizens but also co-founders of the nation in which they dwell with the majority, and whether the development of that nation should not be considered, therefore, a joint endeavour.

Notes

1 Notably C. A. Macartney, *National States and National Minorities* (London, 1934).
2 See above, p. 2.
3 I. L. Claude, *National Minorities* (New York, 1955), pp. 56 ff.
4 These four were the Austro–Italian agreement of 5 September 1946 on South Tyrol, annexed to the peace treaty with Italy, 10 February 1947; the London agreement of 5 October 1954 on the Free Territory of Trieste, and the status of Italians in the zone under Yugoslav control and of Yugoslavs in the zone under Italian control; the Austrian state treaty of 15 May 1955, and in particular Article 7 on the Slovene and Croat minorities; and the London and Zurich agreements of 1959 on the constitution of the Republic of Cyprus.
5 Partial text of the letter in P. de Azcaraté, *League of Nations and National Minorities* (Nendeln, 1972), pp. 166–7.
6 Cf. texts of the UN Convention on Civil and Political Rights, and the Optional Protocol to the Convention, December 1966.
7 The share of total general government expenditure has increased in all EEC member states from 25–36 per cent of GDP in 1959 to 40–55 per cent in 1975. *European Community*, London 1977, no. 2, p. 10.
8 P. Mayo, *The Roots of Identity* (London, 1974), pp. 1–2.
9 A. E. Alcock, 'A New Look at Protection of Minorities and the Principle of Equality of Human Rights', *Community Development Journal* XII (1977), pp. 85–95.
10 See, also, with particular reference to French Canada, the Report of the Royal Commission on Bi-lingualism and Bi-culturalism, 1, para. 49, p. xxxv (Ottawa, 1976).
11 Advisory Opinion of 6 April 1935, PCIJ series A/B n. 64.
12 A. E. Alcock, *The History of the South Tyrol Question* (London, 1970), pp. 238–9.
13 D. L. Coombes, 'Regionalism and Devolution in a European Perspective', Rowntree Devolution Conference Papers, Sunningdale, May 1976, p. 10 (hereafter *Sunningdale Papers*).
14 C. Smallwood, 'Economic Aspects of Devolution', in *Sunningdale Papers*, p. 37.

15 Cf. A. G. and R. J. Dworkin, *The Minority Report* (New York, 1976), p. 20.

16 See above, pp. 208 and 223.

17 See above, p. 198.

18 For a fuller discussion of the position of the German school see T. Veiter, 'Le droit des peuples a disposer d'eux-mêmes et a leur foyer natal' in *Studi in onore di Manlio Udina* (Milan, 1975), pp. 828–58.

19 J. L. Kunz, 'The Principle of Self-Determination of Peoples, particularly in the Practice of the United Nations' in *Studien und Gespräche über Selbstbestimmung und Selbstbestimmungsrecht* (Munich, 1964).

20 Veiter, p. 852.

21 A. Pizzorusso, *Il pluralismo linguistico tra Stato Nazionale e autonomie regionali* (Pisa, 1975), p. 9, note 2 and p. 144.

Index

norma